MW01088498

Los Adaes

THE FIRST CAPITAL OF SPANISH TEXAS

Summerfield G. Roberts Texas History Series

Los Adaes

THE FIRST CAPITAL OF SPANISH TEXAS

Francis X. Galán

Texas A&M University Press
College Station

This paper meets the requirements of ANSI/NISO Z39.48-1992 (Permanence of Paper).
Binding materials have been chosen for durability.
Manufactured in the United States of America
♾ ❀

Library of Congress Cataloging-in-Publication Data

Names: Galán, Francis X., author.
Title: Los Adaes, the first capital of Spanish Texas / Francis X. Galán.
Other titles: Summerfield G. Roberts Texas history series.
Description: First edition. | College Station: Texas A&M University Press, [2020] |
    Series: Summerfield G. Roberts Texas history series | Includes bibliographical
    references and index.
Identifiers: LCCN 2020005304 (print) | LCCN 2020005305 (ebook) |
    ISBN 9781623498788 (hardback) | ISBN 9781623498795 (ebook)
Subjects: LCSH: Texas—History—To 1846. | Los Adaes State Commemorative
    Area (La.)—History. | Presidio de Nuestra Señora del Pilar de Los Adaes
    Site (La.)—History. | Texas—Capital and capitol. | New Spain—Boundaries. |
    New Spain—Colonies—America.
Classification: LCC F389 .G235 2020 (print) | LCC F389 (ebook) | DDC 976.4/01—dc23
LC record available at https://lccn.loc.gov/2020005304
LC ebook record available at https://lccn.loc.gov/2020005305

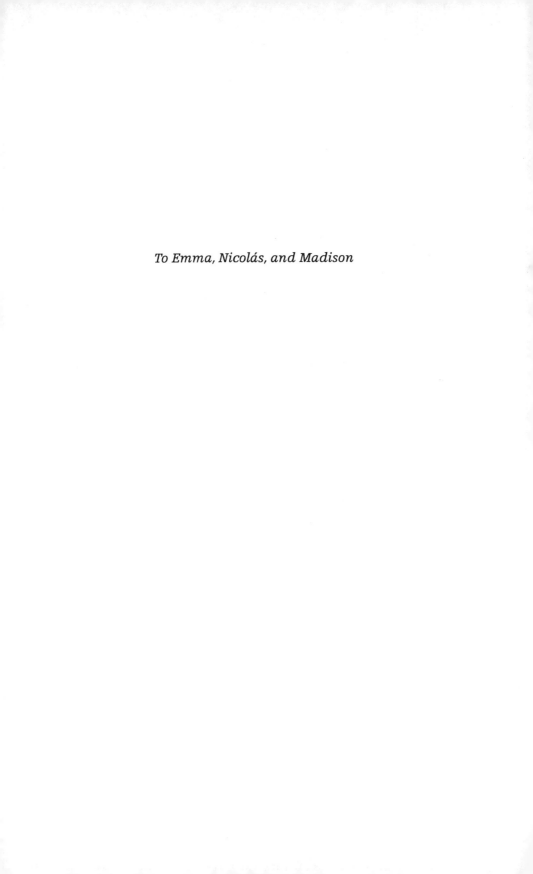

To Emma, Nicolás, and Madison

Contents

Maps and Figures

Acknowledgments

There are many individuals I wish to acknowledge for their help at different stages of this book. First, my history colleagues at Texas A&M University–San Antonio (A&M-SA) provided tremendous encouragement and support, including Amy M. Porter, who gave crucial feedback on an early draft of the manuscript; William Bush, our program chair for many years; and Edward Westermann and William Kiser, who contributed to many thoughtful discussions. Philis Barragán Goetz, April Najjaj, Dolph Briscoe IV, Sandra Lara, Carla Mendiola, and former colleague Thomas Greene, all in their own way, have also made for a great work environment. The administration at A&M-SA, including President Cynthia Teniente-Matson and Provost Michael O'Brien, made a faculty summer research grant possible, while multiple students in my classes and History Club have been equally motivating for the completion of this work.

Next, I wish to thank former classmates and friends from the PhD history program at Southern Methodist University (SMU), including Jimmy Bryan, Matthew Babcock, Alicia Dewey, David Rex Galindo, and George Díaz, to name a few, who have proven to be sources of strength, inspiration, and perseverance at various times over the years. The same applies to a number of past history fellows at SMU, including Omar Valerio-Jiménez and Joaquín Rivaya Martínez. Professors of mine at SMU, especially the late David Weber, John Chávez, and Edward Countryman, served on my dissertation committee, together with Frank de la Teja from Texas State University, and all challenged me to think more critically beyond the research. The Clements Center for Southwest Studies at SMU provided a research grant in 2001 that helped launch this project, so thanks to its faculty and staff, past and present.

I would also like to thank individuals from various archival collections and libraries who facilitated my research. They include Susan Eason (former director) and Eric Hartmann of the Catholic Archives of Texas in Austin; the late Adán Benavides Jr. from the Benson Latin American Collection at the University of Texas at Austin; the late Sister Maria Eva Flores, CDP, who directed the Center for Mexican American Historical Research that houses the Old Spanish Mission Records at Our Lady of the Lake University in San Antonio, Texas; George Avery, former station archeologist at the Los Adaes State Historic Site in northwestern Louisiana and currently with the Cultural Heritage Center at Stephen F. Austin State University in Nacogdoches, Texas; Alfred Broden (former director) of the Mission Dolores Visitors' Center and Museum in San Augustine, Texas; Leslie Stapleton, archives/collections manager at A&M-SA and former director of the DRT Library at the Alamo; Alfred Rodriguez (former director) and David Carlson, director of the Bexar County Spanish Archives; Sheila Richmond at the Creole Heritage Center of Northwestern State University (NSU) in Natchitoches, Louisiana; Rachel Galan (formerly) at the Special Collections of the Ralph W. Steen Library at Stephen F. Austin State University in Nacogdoches; Jonathan Gerland, director of the History Center in Diboll, Texas; and many other wonderful people at the Watson Memorial Library at NSU, Dolph Briscoe Center for American History at the University of Texas at Austin, and the John Peace Library at the University of Texas at San Antonio. Also, James Schneider who facilitated my research at UTSA while doing a teaching practicum arranged through Thomas Knock of SMU.

A special thank you belongs to descendants of Los Adaes for sharing some of their family history, kinship connections, and photos. Among them are Mary Lucille (Betty) Rivers, Lydia Arriola Jasso, Troy DeSoto, Dionne Procell, Dan Flores, Juan Castille, Yolanda Garcia Kirkpatrick, and Carmen Ramos Ferrer. I also got to meet and learn from members of the Adai Caddo Nation, including Chief Rufus Davis; the Choctaw-Apache Indian Nation, including Robert Caldwell and former chairman Tommy Bolton; and Rhonda Gauthier at Fort St. Jean Baptiste State Historic Site in Natchitoches, Louisiana. Inspiration also derived from the American Indians of Texas at the Spanish Colonial Missions in San Antonio and the Tap Pilam Coahuiltecan Nation, including their executive director, Ramon J. Vasquez; the Tehuan Band of Mission San José, especially Epifanio

Hernandez; and Vincent Huizar of the Pedro Huisar Descendants at Mission San José. Additional folks from various Hispanic history-interest organizations of San Antonio have also shared insights, such as Los Bexareños, Canary Islands Descendants Association, Order of Granaderos y Damas de Gálvez, and El Patronato Hispanoamericana, as well as fellow members of the Bexar County Historical Commission, including Chairman Félix D. Almaráz Jr. Fellow historians from the East Texas Historical Association (ETHA) meetings in Nacogdoches provided great camaraderie and perspectives over the years, including Mark Barringer, Scott Sosebee (executive director, ETHA), Charles Grear, Kenneth Howell, Alexander Mendoza, and Gene Preuss. Also, thanks to David Montejano, Andrés Tijerina, and Donald Chipman for much-needed encouragement while I was still in graduate school, as well as F. Todd Smith, H. Sophie Burton, Richard White, and Pekka Hämäläinen following graduate school. There are simply too many old friends to thank, but I would especially like to mention the late Martin Gomez III, from whom I did not learn until after college that he was a descendant from Mission San José and the Canary Islanders.

Lastly, I want to thank my own immediate family, including my parents (the late Enríque Manuel Galán Dobal and María del Pilar Martínez-Galán), brothers (Henry, Joseph, John, and Mark) and their spouses, father-in-law and mother-in-law, sister-in-law (Marina) and her spouse (Rafael de la Garza), brother-in-law (Fidencio) and his spouse, and many cousins, nieces, and nephews—in addition to my tío Rafael Gomez of Madrid, Spain; late tío Nilo Messer of Miami, Florida; and tío Roberto Galán of Córdoba, Veracruz, Mexico—for their wisdom. I thank my beautiful spouse, Dr. Emma L. Mata-Galán, whose work for veterans at the VA Hospital of San Antonio is truly inspirational, for her patience, and our children, Nicolás and Madison—may they come to appreciate the value of history in their own lives.

Los Adaes

THE FIRST CAPITAL OF SPANISH TEXAS

Introduction

Broken Border

I n March 1804, less than a year after the Louisiana Purchase, Charles Pinckney, US minister to Spain, wrote William Lee, US agent for commercial affairs in Bordeaux, noting how King Carlos IV opposed "the sale of Louisiana by France to us."[1] Duped by Napoleon Bonaparte, who broke his agreement with Spain in 1800 not to transfer Louisiana to a third party, the Spanish tried to recover their former colony at the same time the United States claimed that the western limits of the Louisiana Territory extended to the Rio Grande and included Texas.[2] Tensions mounted when President Thomas Jefferson deployed US troops to the Texas-Louisiana borderlands under the command of Gen. James Wilkinson while Lt. Col. Simón de Herrera, commandant at Nacogdoches, led Spanish forces to halt the American westward march. Wilkinson and Herrera, however, averted war in the fall of 1806 when each agreed to a demilitarized zone between the Sabine River and the Arroyo Hondo, the latter a tributary creek of the lower Red River that Spain claimed as the Texas-Louisiana border between its former settlement of Los Adaes and the French post in Natchitoches, Louisiana.[3] To reinforce its claim, the Spanish revealed shortly after the agreement between Wilkinson and Herrera that the mixed community of Bayou Pierre consisted of ranches "belonging to these same citizens of Los Adaes; they owned them when the place was inhabited and, at the time of the removal [in 1773] to Béxar [San Antonio], they remained on them."[4] The following book is a history of Los Adaes and argues that the colonial border between Texas and Louisiana at the Arroyo Hondo had been broken from the start as its settlers crossed boundaries for survival in accommodation with neighbors through commerce, faith, and kinship rather than Spanish conquest.

Over the course of the eighteenth century, Los Adaes became dependent on French and Caddo neighbors for relief and trade in present-day East Texas and northwestern Louisiana as Spain became increasingly anxious over British movements east of the Mississippi, in the Caribbean, and along the Pacific Coast. By the early 1730s, the establishment of the Georgia colony and *comercio ilícito* (smuggling) centered on the island of Jamaica—combined with indigenous rebellions, African slave revolts, and pirate attacks—gravely threatened the silver mines in New Spain (colonial Mexico) and Peru, if not the overthrow of Spanish rule in the Americas. In response to this series of events and the potential coordination of each under another powerful rival, the Spanish entered into a so-called Family Compact with the French Bourbon dynasty, the first of several over the middle decades of the eighteenth century, since the king of Spain was the grandson of King Louis XIV of France and provided some reassurance for both monarchs should war break out with England.[5] At the local level, the Spanish did not wait for any formalities in Europe as eighteen soldiers from Los Adaes arrived at French Natchitoches in joint defense against the Natchez revolt, one in a long series of indigenous rebellions after British traders increasingly sought Indian alliances to counterpunch French and Spanish possessions in Louisiana and Florida.[6] If Los Adaes did not hold the line on the Texas-Louisiana border, the penetration of New Spain and capture of the silver trade by rivals might lead to a domino effect from east to west by land and sea and the possibility of similar movements into New Spain from north to south via New Mexico and California.

The Spanish goal of policing the border with Louisiana, however, had much to do with preventing guns and ammunition from falling into the hands of Southern Plains Indians intent on raiding or trading with vulnerable Spanish settlements exposed on the northern frontier of New Spain, especially the provinces of New Mexico, Chihuahua, Nuevo León, Coahuila, Nuevo Santander, and Texas. During the summer of 1736, when Lt. Joseph Gonzalez wrote Gov. Manuel Sandoval about problems at Los Adaes, which was designated the capital of Spanish Texas in 1729, more urgent matters demanded the governor's attention in San Antonio—namely, incessant warfare against Lipan Apaches, diseases, disputes with missionaries over control of Indian labor, and legal wrangling about land with river access for families recently arrived from the Canary Islands.[7] Lieutenant Gonzalez's concerns had to wait, as Governor Sandoval could not be at opposite ends of Texas simultaneously.

Many questions arise about Los Adaes that this book seeks to answer: What problems did Los Adaes struggle with that required equal if not greater attention than the troubles at San Antonio? How did Spain's goals on the border with Louisiana affect problems elsewhere on the frontier of New Spain? How exactly did a border appear in the first place? Did such a border really even exist? If so, what meaning did it have for local peoples? Who were the people of Los Adaes? Were there any mission Indians? Did slavery exist at Los Adaes? Why did Spain abandon Los Adaes in 1773 and then reassert its claim decades later after the Louisiana Purchase of 1803? What was the legacy of Los Adaes? Were there any Spanish land grants in East Texas and northwestern Louisiana as there were in South Texas? What communities emerged in the aftermath and remain to this day? Lastly, what are some of the lessons that may be drawn from Los Adaes in subsequent eras with the expansionism and security of national borders? A US National Historic Landmark marker placed at the Los Adaes archeological site in 1984, amid heightened concerns from illegal immigration and civil wars in Mexico and Central America, simply states it "possesses national significance in commemorating the history of the United States of America." This book ultimately seeks to recover a lost history that helps with understanding how borders can serve to unite and divide people and nations across time and place.

Fortunately, there are many hidden stories found within Spanish archives that resurrect Los Adaes from the ash heap of history and reveal how, despite its isolation from the interior of New Spain and dire circumstances in Texas, opportunities existed along the border with Louisiana that challenged the authorities and forced adaptation to the environment. Specifically, Lieutenant Gonzalez informed Governor Sandoval about the likelihood of mass desertion from the Spanish *presidio* (fort) of Nuestra Señora del Pilar de los Adaes (Los Adaes) to French Natchitoches if he did not return soon from San Antonio. Gonzalez explained how fellow officer Lt. Pedro de Sierra delivered the governor's warning to the commandant at Natchitoches, Louis Juchereau de St. Denis, to cease the relocation of his fort on the west bank of the lower Red River in territory the Marqués de Aguayo claimed for King Philip V of Spain in 1721. St. Denis allegedly encouraged officer de Sierra and Spanish troops to flee "the tyranny of your governor who has kept your soldiers in such misery and nakedness that only their patience, goodness, and docility prevents them from making demands for relief from so much wretchedness." Apparently, the only supplies received lately included a few bundles of wheat and gunpowder from Saltillo, a town in the neighboring province of Coahuila, located 750 miles southwest along the Camino Real (Royal Road) in northern New Spain. To make matters worse, the troops from Los Adaes were not paid their wages under Governor Sandoval, who doubled as the fort's commandant. Gonzalez also noted how several French soldiers "daringly whisked away my daughter, Victoria," so she could marry Jean Baptiste Derbanne, a French officer at Natchitoches, where a Jesuit priest allegedly orchestrated the plot.[8] The *frontera* (border) that Lieutenant Gonzalez ostensibly guarded had been broken as the Adaeseños (Hispanic / American Indian community at Los Adaes) forged ties with the French and Caddos that compromised objectives of imperial Spain and its mercantile economy in the conquest of Texas.

Collectively, these stories impacted regional and global concerns and vice versa, but Los Adaes has been overshadowed between the triumph and tragedy of Spanish-Indian relations in the Southwest borderlands and the rise of plantation slavery in the lower Mississippi valley of the Atlantic world.[9] These regions formed part of Spain's imagined frontier in North America, which included Florida, Louisiana (after 1762), Texas, New Mexico, Arizona, and California, comprising the southern third of the present United States from coast to coast. The late historian David Weber explained that the problem of understanding the Spanish borderlands in North America intellectually has been their location, which, "poised on the margins of American and Latin American history, do[es] not fit squarely into the core of either area."[10] The same applies to Los Adaes, which appears as an anomaly in the histories of both Texas and Louisiana, buried beneath the Alamo or antebellum South as part of some "lost world" with no lasting significance to the formation of the United States and Mexico.[11]

Historians Gerald Poyo and Gilberto Hinojosa stress the need for scholars to examine regional links that connected Texas with Louisiana and
Coahuila along the Camino Real. In this manner, "continuities across
sovereignties" can be identified by examining the origins of transnational
"commercial ties, migration patterns, class structures, racial attitudes,
economic pursuits, and cross-cultural relationships" that are important
themes into the modern era. Historian Jesús F. de la Teja adds the other
provinces of New Mexico, Nuevo León, Nuevo Santander, and Coahuila in
order to fully comprehend Texas under Spain from a regional perspective.[12]
Los Adaes contributes not only to the complexity of European, Indian, and
African relations in early North American history but also to the diversity
of the Hispanic population in the United States today, who are otherwise
viewed largely as recent immigrants in barrios or ethnic enclaves cut off
from deep roots in the land and isolated from other groups in society.[13]
Paradoxically, Los Adaes and the Adaeseños are akin to the Caddos, whom
historian Juliana Barr argues present a "scholarly conundrum" because
"they do not fit; they diverged; they were distinct" on the western edge of
the Mississippian world.[14] In essence, the Adaeseños are another forgotten
people, in some sense like the Adai Caddo, Choctaw-Apache, and Creoles in
northwestern Louisiana today who do not fit neatly into the narratives of
either Texas or the lower Mississippi valley and remain in-between groups
on the margins in blended communities of the Louisiana backcountry.[15]

This book is based heavily on original research drawn from the Spanish archives to shed light on the Adaeseños who sought to make a living
and a new home in Texas and Louisiana. Translations are modernized, and
any errors remain my own, but the original Spanish appears in the notes.
Borrowing from historian Elizabeth Jameson, the term *border* in this
study refers simply to a line that separates or divides, while *borderlands*
are "zones—sometimes around borders—where diverse peoples come
together or mingle."[16] While Turner's frontier thesis remains hotly debated
for the American West, the Spanish translation of "frontier" is *frontera*, a
term commonly applied in present Mexico to its "border" with the United
States following the Treaty of Guadalupe Hidalgo (1848), which formally
concluded the Mexican-American War and carries a whole other national
debate and bone of contention.[17] *Frontera*, however, also connotes a much

older border in Spain during the Reconquista (Christian Reconquest) of the Iberian Peninsula against the *moros* (Arabs) and Roman-era warfare against *bárbaros* (barbarians) long before, notions the Spanish carried into the New World. As historians Donna Guy and Thomas Sheridan note, from a comparative perspective of the northern and southern edges of the Spanish Empire in the Americas, frontiers are "zones of constant conflict and negotiation over power—economic, political, and cultural."[18] For the Adaeseños on the Texas-Louisiana borderlands, at least while the Caddos and French remained in the region, negotiation, trade, and general friendships trumped conflict while much anger and frustration was leveled against their own government.

Whether as frontiers, borderlands, or middle, divided, or contested ground, the Adaeseños entered the "Kingdom of the Tejas" in East Texas, where the Hasinai Confederacy policed their own "borders and interiors." They kept watch over the Spanish in addition to the emergent powers of Apaches and Comanches riding onto the Southern Plains. The Kadohadacho Confederacy, located in the corners of present-day Arkansas, Oklahoma, and Louisiana (and considered the Caddo Nation proper of Oklahoma), equally kept guard against Osage expansion from the north.[19] All frontiers were contested, yet somewhere along a pendulum appeared "mutual interdependence" among different groups in the face of external threats from European and indigenous rivals that resulted in "ambivalent common ground."[20] Historians Pekka Hämäläinen and Samuel Truett note that borderlands "are ambiguous and often-unstable realms where boundaries are also crossroads, peripheries are also central places, homelands are also passing-through places, and the end points of empire are also forks in the road."[21] Los Adaes became one such place, as did many other communities on the Texas-Louisiana borderlands that challenge master narratives.

The term *community* itself, though, requires explanation, as Los Adaes has escaped scholarly attention. In his classic work on Spanish presidios, historian Max Moorhead argues that the "presidio evolved from a simple garrisoned fort with a purely military mission into the nucleus of a civilian town, a market for the produce of neighboring farms and ranches, and an agency for an Indian reservation." By this standard, Los Adaes fell short as a community because the Spanish eventually abandoned the fort and could never forcibly gather Caddos into the missions and convert them to Christianity. The governors never had any interest in developing Los Adaes into a town but rather maintained it and the Spanish missions of East Texas as part of their personal fiefdoms. Meanwhile, Natchitoches, as historians H. Sophie Burton and F. Todd Smith describe, became "a regional trade center" located just across the border.[22] Natchitoches served as the French counterpart to Saltillo at the far eastern end of the Camino Real, without which Los Adaes could not have survived from the start or for as long as it did in Caddo country.[23] For the French, the Camino Real ended with Natchitoches even though it officially stopped at Los Adaes, which they viewed as another potential market for French tobacco, clothing, and other goods.

On the other hand, Weber noted that presidio communities "took on the characteristics of small villages as soldiers, their families, and nonmilitary personnel settled around them" and later became municipalities. Los Adaes was a "military" community abandoned by 1773 under the Bourbon Reforms, which sought to modernize Spain's economy and armed forces. After Spain acquired Louisiana from France in 1762, the Spanish no longer saw a need for a border with Texas, since New Spain expanded farther east to the Mississippi such that Louisiana became the new buffer against the British American colonies. Forgotten Spanish presidial communities such as San Fernando (present Memphis, Tennessee) and Nogales (present Vicksburg, Mississippi) functioned the same as Los Adaes after the Louisiana transfer, as did St. Augustine and Pensacola in Florida or San Diego and San Francisco in California.[24] The bulk of the Adaeseño families, including a small number who remained in the region, still felt attachments to East Texas and returned soon after its abandonment by royal order and established a temporary settlement, Bucareli, on the lower Trinity River. This was followed by the founding of the present town of Nacogdoches in 1779 on the site of a former mission of the same name under the leadership of Capt. Antonio Gil Ybarbo, a criollo who was born at Los Adaes and joined the military like his father did from Spain.

According to de la Teja, the term *community* usually implies a settlement or town but can also refer to a place that exerts "a powerful force on an individual's and a group's sense of identity."[25] In essence, the Adaeseños became attached to the eastern woodlands environment and to "other" peoples on the Texas-Louisiana borderlands, which encompasses the Piney Woods region in northwestern Louisiana from Natchitoches, on the lower Red River, across the Sabine River state line through Nacogdoches, to the Trinity River in East Texas, and from the Gulf Coastal lowlands in south-western Louisiana to the lower Brazos River near Houston, Texas. Although Los Adaes appeared to be an "artificial" town because of its military, not civilian, function, the saga of Lieutenant Gonzalez and many more stories that follow in this book provide flesh and blood to a people who came to Texas long ago and whose descendants became pioneers in many small towns across the American landscape. Just as historian Light T. Cummins describes the "enduring community" of Anglo-American settlers that emerged from British West Florida between Baton Rouge and Natchez along the Mississippi north of New Orleans, some of whom came to Texas, the same applies to the mixed communities of Hispanic, American Indian, French, African, Anglo-American, and other early immigrants of the Texas-Louisiana borderlands before the arrival of Stephen F. Austin.[26] The purpose of this book is not just to present a local history but also to point out the enduring presence and perseverance of diverse groups of peoples regardless of changing borders and flags, whose loyalty and identity are defined more by their immediate community than their region or nation.[27]

Historians Kevin Terraciano and Lisa Sousa note, "We have reached a point, ironically, where we know as much, if not more, about indigenous society as we know about Spaniards, other Europeans, and creoles in New Spain."[28] What began as research into slavery in colonial Texas and Louisiana under the Spanish and French Bourbon monarchies brought me to Los Adaes by way of serendipity. Like Alfred Young's desire "to get a handle on ordinary people" of the American Revolution and Fred Anderson's "a people's army," this story of Los Adaes emerged from my interest in the soldiers, civilians, and their families who are overlooked in the Spanish conquest of the Americas with its focus on conquistadors and missionaries. Several generations of Adaeseños increasingly identified with a region and environment that were much different from other Spanish communities in northern New Spain, such as Saltillo, Santa Fe, and San Antonio.[29] This book thus seeks a deeper understanding of the peoples on the Texas-Louisiana borderlands with a focus on Los Adaes and the Adaeseños, whose significance in history is greater than meets the eye.

Although the Spanish conquest of East Texas and northwestern Louisiana began with much pomp and circumstance, chapter 1 reminds us that the French had already forged bonds of trade and kinship with Caddos, who considered the region their homeland for millennia, and this is where the Spanish and French became caught up in the "currents of Native history."[30] This chapter seeks to answer the following questions: How did the Spanish presidio-mission system of colonization move from one of conquest to accommodation in a relatively short amount of time from 1690 to the 1730s in spite of Spain's attempt to enforce the easternmost border of New Spain with Louisiana? What factors led to the transformation of this frontier into one of many borderlands in North America? Scholarly attention to the saga of René Robert Cavelier, Sieur de La Salle's ill-fated colonization in Texas obscures the fact that St. Denis succeeded in establishing a French settlement at Natchitoches with a claim to Texas for France all the way to the Rio Grande, near present Eagle Pass, where the Spanish fort of San Juan Bautista was founded around 1700 along with a mission.[31] St. Denis helped the Spanish reestablish their presence in East Texas by 1716 as their guide, along with a Caddo female guide, after his marriage to Manuela Sanchez Navarro of the local commandant's family at San Juan Baustista. Meanwhile, Antonio Margil, a Franciscan friar, celebrated mass for the French at Natchitoches and reinforced a shared Catholic faith among the Spanish and French. Against this backdrop, Spanish soldiers and families, such as Lieutenant Gonzalez and his wife, Gerturdis de la Cerda, established Los Adaes. Unable to harvest maize or receive timely supplies for a variety of reasons, the Spanish became dependent on neighbors before, during, and after distant officials delineated any borderline. Fortunately for the Adaeseños, commercial, religious, and kinship networks among the French and Caddos proved to be beneficial models for relationships on the Texas-Louisiana borderlands rather than bloody wars of conquest and rebellions.

Meanwhile, the French needed sustenance of the soul even if the Caddos did not. As chapter 2 reveals, Spanish friars from the missions in East Texas played a critical role in bridging cultures of the Texas-Louisiana borderlands in the spirit of Father Margil, who died in 1726, with the administration of the holy sacraments to the French at Natchitoches, where a Jesuit priest did not regularly reside until the 1730s. Franciscans continued to make their presence known there for several more decades. While the Caddos refused to congregate at Spanish missions, the friars did not sit idly counting rosary beads. Without Spain's authorization to use military force, Franciscans moved beyond the mission, crossed many boundaries, and engaged in commerce and ranching while preaching patience and prayers to the bitter end, should the Indians change their minds and convert to Christianity. As historian David Rex Galindo notes, among the accomplishments of the missionaries was "their evangelical ministry to the Catholics"—and not just missions in the "business of salvation." The Spanish at Los Adaes were just as likely to forge trade as incite military or religious conquests, depending on the circumstances.[32]

Chapter 3 shows how the border communities of Los Adaes and Natchitoches shared kinship in both real and fictive bonds of marriage, reflecting the Bourbon ties among their respective crowns in Spain and France. Unlike the Catholic versus Protestant religious divide of the St. Lawrence River between colonial New England and Canada or other borderlands in colonial Latin America, such as the Yucatan-Belize frontier in Mesoamerica, the Spanish and French communities on the Texas-Louisiana borderlands were both Catholic. Certainly, the Caddos recognized this similarity and played the Spanish against the French, watching with delight as these Bourbon cousins bickered over boundaries and commerce. Yet Caddos hedged their bets and witnessed, if not participated in, rituals of kinship at both Los Adaes and Natchitoches, introducing these rituals into the Caddo world along with broader meanings of brothers and sisters, fathers and mothers, whom Church sacraments recognized as *padrinos* (godparents)—*compadres* (godfathers) and *comadres* (godmothers). Caddos could worship ecumenically at chapels in the Spanish or French posts without taking communion and, in turn, accept non-Indians who fit into their own world, affording an intimacy that was otherwise unimaginable on other frontiers in North America. Such participation potentially provided another means of "border control" for Caddos beyond surveillance and trade with the Spanish.[33] In gathering to *convivir* (coexist peacefully), women played a key role in the survival of Los Adaes. Women such as Manuela Sanchez Navarro de St. Denis and Gertrudis de la Cerda Gonzalez became role models on the frontier. Historian Andrés Reséndez describes Spanish women as "inter-ethnic brokers par excellence." Historian Amy Porter also shows how women on the borderlands wielded power informally within an otherwise patriarchal society.[34] There might have been more to the story of Victoria's "elopement" than Lieutenant Gonzalez actually shared with Governor Sandoval. Gertrudis perhaps had been the real mover and shaker with the arrangement of their daughter's marriage, quite possibly through her counterpart Manuela, despite their husbands' positions as commandants at opposing forts. Victoria married the son of François Derbanne, another prominent family's patriarch and business partner of St. Denis, a union that mirrored French-Caddo trade and kinship patterns at Natchitoches.

The Caddos possibly took pity on the Adaeseños, who gradually became known as a different "tribe" than the Hispanic communities to the south at San Antonio and La Bahía (present Goliad). Chapter 4 unveils a dark side of the Spanish military on the frontier with the abuses the soldiers suffered. Some of the governor-commandants used the soldiers at Los Adaes as personal laborers, siphoned the soldiers' wages into their own smuggling networks throughout the region, and became *caudillos* (regional strongmen), often at the troops' expense. Historian Eric Van Young explains that in the Guadalajara region of late colonial Mexico, there appeared many "estate laborers (*gañanes*, *indios*, *laborios*, *peones*, etc.) who were at least nominally free, worked for wages, rations, and in some cases perquisites, and owed credit advances" to the *tienda de raya* (company store) of the haciendas or to merchants.[35] In a similar vein, we see the rise of debt peonage among the Adaeseños, some of whom also sought wages as *vaqueros* (cowboys) on landed estates in Louisiana and/or as muleteers in the contraband trade of a regional economy based on tobacco production and livestock raising, which the French increasingly dominated. Among Lieutenant Gonzalez's other important responsibilities was the management of the company store at Los Adaes, which the governors often considered as their own private storehouse and held as leverage over soldiers who lacked basic necessities and sometimes starved to death.[36]

Trade thus emerged at two different levels, from small to large scale and more frequently illicit, as impoverished soldiers, Indians, and African Creoles engaged in an underground or subaltern market economy on the Texas-Louisiana borderlands. Chapter 5 shows how the governors, their officers, and sometimes the Franciscans collaborated to expand smuggling operations that undercut the Spanish mercantile system instead of keeping out foreign traders and illicit goods. Meanwhile, rank-and-file soldiers deserted across the border just as African slaves from French Natchitoches took advantage of their proximity to trade in contraband goods at Los Adaes, which may be considered what historian George Díaz calls "petty smuggling," meaning "contraband trade for personal consumption" as compared to "trafficking" (professional smuggling for profit). Government oversight and legal challenges could only slightly modify injustices but not completely stamp out serious problems that the drawing of a "border" invited. Spanish troops from Los Adaes spent much of their time deployed to other presidios in dangerous territory fighting Indians, traveling as far as Saltillo and New Orleans in search of supplies, or patrolling for smugglers, fugitives, and deserters (see map 1.1). The Texas-Louisiana borderlands, with their forests and smuggling, appear to have been drawn straight out of the Pyrenees region in northern Spain and southern France. Historian Peter Sahlins argues that in the latter, "contraband trade was not just an activity, it was a morality," and for most locals who participated in smuggling, this activity "was less a way to make a fortune than to survive."[37] At Los Adaes, small-scale or petty smuggling offered that relief and could be tolerated, but not the larger variety, especially as it corrupted high-ranking governor-commandants and involved the "trafficking" of guns, tobacco, captives, hides, and alcohol.[38] Smuggling impacted trade everywhere; historian Andrew Konove shows the intersection of the "shadow economy" and legitimate trade in late colonial Mexico City that linked "most elite traders in New Spain to some of the lowliest through a far-reaching credit network."[39] In this sense, Los Adaes fell deeper into debt with creditors at Natchitoches, where legal trade in foodstuffs, religious rituals, and kinship provided avenues into legitimate markets beyond the smuggling frontier. Ultimately, Bourbon reformers became fixated on closing down the fort at Los Adaes and removing the Adaeseños to San

Antonio, which became the new official capital of Texas in 1773, with the idea of keeping Spanish subjects from temptations to trade in Louisiana.

Chapter 6 reveals that Texas under Spain became a "society with slaves," while Louisiana developed into a "slave society," descriptions historian Ira Berlin applies to early North America but does not take Indian slavery into account.[40] Los Adaes particularly lagged behind Natchitoches, which grew dependent on African slave labor for the production of tobacco despite the legality of Indian slavery in French Louisiana. This distinction between Los Adaes and Natchitoches mattered because soldier-settlers from the former glimpsed life on the other side of the border in Louisiana, or Caddo country, and took opportunities that were perhaps not so readily attainable to the Spanish elsewhere in northern New Spain. Although some Indian captives appeared at Los Adaes, especially Apaches, they were the property of the governors, while most were sold into slavery in Louisiana. Meanwhile, Indian captives and African slaves reinforced notions of hierarchy, coercion, and lack of freedom in Spanish society even in the remotest of locations on the frontier, where greater fluidity of race and ethnicity did not necessarily translate into equality.[41] Los Adaes became an extension of slavery and servitude that existed in northern New Spain, but on a much smaller scale.[42] Although the Spanish imagined the potential of plantation agriculture in Texas, as did their Louisiana counterparts, the labor involved required the subjection of the Indians or the importation of African slaves. Instead, ranching, subsistence agriculture, and smuggling predominated on the Texas-Louisiana borderlands, where cattle were traded for African slaves and Indian captives, whose interactions with impoverished soldier-settlers made the Spanish anxious about the potential for rebellion.

Chapter 7 shows that the abandonment of Los Adaes created a "trail of sorrows" for the Adaeseños under the king's order, most of whom marched southwestwardly along the Camino Real, a trek that resulted in the loss of life, including children, and great resentment against Spanish rule. Lt. Joseph Gonzalez himself, after serving at Los Adaes for many decades, dutifully carried out the royal decree and rounded up his own people, then died en route to San Antonio, as did many other fellow residents. Ironically, Los Adaes had stabilized by the mid-eighteenth century despite the many challenges to its existence just as Spain ushered in the Bourbon Reforms, which were designed to professionalize the army and curb the smuggling that drained Spanish frontiers in the Americas. What military inspectors reported at Los Adaes were more akin to fiestas and undisciplined troops, most of whom belonged to an inferior caste beneath *español* (Spanish). Instead of conquest, the soldiers and their families from Los Adaes welcomed outsiders and became very much interconnected with other communities on the Texas-Louisiana borderlands—similar to "regional neighborhoods" that historian Anne Hyde describes as multiethnic communities in the early American West that were based on family and trade connections.[43] The Adaeseños appeared as a displaced group of migrants disillusioned with the government after its closure of Los Adaes and their tragic journey to San Antonio amid the heat, sickness, and death along the road.

As legal scholar Tamar Herzog explains, *fronterizos* (frontier settlers) did not care whether "borders were linear or zonal, internal or external, artificial or natural. Instead, they mostly cared about the extension and nature of their usage rights."[44] For Adaeseños, salvation came as many returned to East Texas and established a permanent *pueblo* or *villa* (town) at Nacogdoches while others obtained *suertes* (twenty-six-acre lots) in San Antonio on secularized Mission San Antonio de Valero lands, where they helped forge a Tejano homeland far from the centers of any European power and closer to indigenous ones. The Adaeseños continued crossing boundaries in Texas and Louisiana for the sake of survival and adapted. Meanwhile, the cultural identity of the Adaeseños in East Texas and San Antonio changed over time through trade, religion, and kinship yet never fully disappeared amid many other immigrants and the continued growth of ranching- and plantation-based economies in Texas and Louisiana. The border with Louisiana remained fluid despite Spanish attempts at enforcement, whereupon local communities defied Spain and traded with enemies.[45] The spirit, resiliency, and faith of the Adaeseños endured throughout the trials and tribulations of the Texas frontier regardless of borders.

The Adaeseños settled and resettled in between different worlds that overlapped with the crossing of the smuggling frontier and transatlantic commerce in a region that historians describe as the "nexus of empire" in North America.[46] The border between Texas and Louisiana that Spain defined as the Arroyo Hondo in the 1730s and again in the early 1800s during a global contest of empires is merely a creek today but serves as a reminder of the importance Los Adaes held for the people in the region. The Adaeseños repeatedly found themselves called to duty despite the bitter memory from Spain's abandonment of the fort and frequent non-payment of wages. They served imperial interests that did not necessarily match their own throughout the conflicts and accommodations in Texas and Louisiana.[47] In so many ways, local stories from the Texas-Louisiana borderlands, both tragic and hopeful, resonate today. Los Adaes reflected both the old Spanish Empire and a young American republic that was coming to grips with its own fears and dreams within and across borders, where indigenous peoples remained the dominant force.

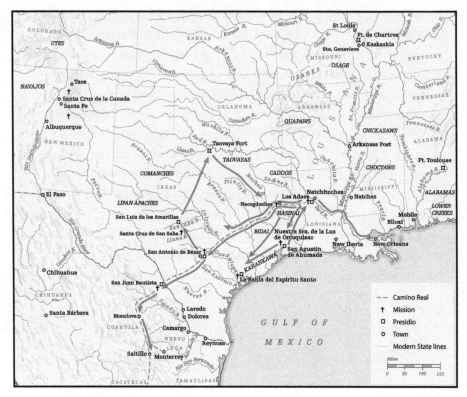

Map I.I: Spanish troop movements from Los Adaes, 1730s–70s. Source: *Béxar Archives*; David J. Weber, *The Spanish Frontier in North America* (New Haven, CT: Yale University Press, 1992), 185.

CHAPTER ONE

Forged in Blood

The mid-1730s certainly appeared to be the nadir of Los Adaes and its total collapse when Lt. Joseph Gonzalez wrote Gov. Manuel Sandoval about the dire circumstances on the border with Louisiana. Gonzalez explained to the governor that "too much rain here [Los Adaes] did not allow us time for reasonable planting upon the land." In addition, "the soldiers you dispatched lost your livestock on the road [Camino Real] because of the rigorous weather; only Juan de Mora arrived without losing any of his cattle," while other troops appeared with just one, two, or three cows.[1] Los Adaes lacked adequate natural drainage such that flooding meant the potential loss of life and property without any government relief in a region that was seemingly isolated from New Spain and even San Antonio.[2] The vicissitudes of the natural environment in the Piney Woods, with its lush forests, rolling hills, many rivers and creeks, and abundant wildlife, made this region different than the Chihuahuan or Sonoran Deserts and the semi-arid mountainous frontier of northern New Spain. Instead, it appeared more like the temperate lowland areas of southern Mexico and Central America, with greater opportunities to diversify the economy beyond livestock ranching and to challenge mercantilism through smuggling in the "Kingdom of the Tejas" and Louisiana.[3] Natural disasters, problems with the cultivation of maize, and great distances from the interior of New Spain led the Adaeseños to seek material support and sustenance across realms into the economic, political, military, and cultural spheres of the Caddos and French. For sake of survival, the Adaeseños effectively extended the farthest branch of the Camino Real from the interior of

New Spain along Indian pathways through East Texas, which, in the minds of distant Spanish officials, was supposed to end at Los Adaes and not Natchitoches.

<hr/>

The founding of Los Adaes in 1721 on the northern fringe of the Spanish Empire in the Americas marked the culmination of a decades'-long imperial struggle to contain the spread of French westward expansion into New Spain. Located at the end of the Camino Real, which stretched from Mexico City to Louisiana, Los Adaes represented Spain's third attempt to block the French following La Salle's provocative but disastrous efforts to establish an outpost at the mouth of the Mississippi River in the mid-1680s, a particularly harrowing time after the Spanish were kicked out of neighboring New Mexico following the Pueblo Revolt. The Spanish, first under the Hapsburg and subsequent Bourbon monarchies, imagined Texas as a defensive perimeter that would prevent "unlicensed" European traders and Indian raiders from penetrating silver-mining communities in northern New Spain. The initial attempts of Spanish conquest in East Texas, however, failed miserably by 1693, and Spain did not return again until 1716 and 1721 after a series of imperial wars in Europe. By the late 1720s, the Spanish overreached in East Texas and attempted to reform Spain's military in the wake of its reconquest of New Mexico. The latter province shifted to military defense rather than expansion of missions and conversion, with less strain on a royal treasury still trying to recover from a century of stagnation in the silver economy. The Spanish could not contain trade, kinship, and religious ties that Los Adaes, Natchitoches, and Caddo communities forged in blood, which in turn compromised any boundary imagined between Texas and Louisiana. The emerging transatlantic market in New Orleans, established in 1718, connected Natchitoches via the Mississippi to its Red River tributary and pushed Los Adaes in East Texas away from the core of Hispanic civilization in New Spain and deeper into the French and Indian orbit.

Against the backdrop of imperial rivalries, Spanish-Indian violence, trade, and missions, one must consider the vastly contrasting environments of the Texas-Louisiana frontier and northern New Spain, especially the neighboring province of Coahuila, where the Camino Real extended to the San Juan Bautista presidio-mission complex on the Lower Rio Grande. It is hard to fathom that the towns of Saltillo, from where many Adaeseño soldiers derived, and Parras, which produced the Alamo Company that gained fame against Santa Anna, were founded in 1577 and 1598, respectively, in the province of Nueva Vizcaya (later part of Coahuila) at a time when no permanent French or English settlements existed in the New World. Mexican scholars lay out five major themes that characterized this region of northern New Spain: (1) a vast territory, mostly desert with irregular terrain, brush, and scarce water sources; (2) chronic shortage of settlers and isolation; (3) a permanent state of war beginning in the mid-1500s—with resistance from independent Indians against Spanish conquest and the expansion of silver mining north from Mexico City—until 1880, in the aftermath of civil wars, foreign occupation, and the beginnings of industrialization; (4) diverse peoples and towns characterized by autonomous social organization; and (5) border experiences of settlers in distinct frontiers of colonization, war, civilization, politics, and culture. One modern theme refers to a dynamic industrial and urban base centered on Monterrey, a town originally founded in the 1590s in the border province of Nuevo León on the eve of don Juan de Oñate's crossing at El Paso del Norte in 1598.[4] Each of these themes fanned out to include Texas at different times and places.

With its archaeological site in present northwestern Louisiana, Los Adaes stood in the woodlands region of eastern North America, where independent Mississippi-based cultures also fended off Spaniards when remnants of Hernando de Soto's troops first arrived in East Texas from Florida in the early 1540s. For nearly 150 years, after conquistadors Cabeza de Vaca and Francisco Coronado meandered through Texas in search of gold and other treasures, the Spanish largely ignored Texas and paid greater attention to the developing mission field in New Mexico. La Salle's appearance in 1685, however, ignited Spain's desire to make Texas a defensive barrier in the absence of minerals. Meanwhile, Native Americans held strategic positions as farmers and traders from the Jumanos in West Texas to the Caddos in East Texas, each with connections to semi-sedentary Indians on the Southern Plains and coastal peoples in between both regions. Little could indigenous peoples of Texas have known how different worlds would rush in and affect their own respective environments, ways of life, and beliefs.

First and foremost, the Spanish claimed a monopoly over any lands west of the line the pope drew between Spain and Portugal in 1493, then ratified in the Treaty of Tordesillas the following year. For Coahuila and the rest of colonial Latin America, including Spanish Texas, the king's dominions included forests, rivers, and mountains, which meant no settler or company could profit from the natural environment without the Crown's permission and payment of the *quinto* (royal tax). Monarchies effectively imposed an unintended conservation of lands and trees with the regulation of virtually every economic activity in the Americas, such as silver mining and producing sugar, tobacco, and timber. Through its mercantile system of trade, Spain monitored production from its overseas colonies for the sole benefit of the Crown and not its predominately rural Spanish subjects.[5]

Historian Susan Socolow notes that throughout the colonial era, as much as 75 to 90 percent of the total population of Spanish and Portuguese America lived in the countryside and that societies were "far from uniform through space and time" across two important complimentary systems. First, the large *haciendas* (landed estates) of central and northern Mexico and highland Peru, where mining proved most productive, and second, lowland plantations of the Caribbean, Brazil, and southern coastal regions of Mexico, where sugar and tobacco production were most successful. Elsewhere, small- to medium-scale farming predominated, with individual owners, renters, cash tenants, sharecroppers, or squatters for subsistence agriculture, and supplied local town or city markets with excess products. More remote regions, such as northern New Spain, became involved with cattle ranching and raising sheep as well as supplying Indian captives for labor in the mines. Much of the rural history of colonial Latin America, Socolow adds, was greatly influenced by pre-Columbian population patterns unevenly spread out from highly organized agricultural-based societies to hunter-gatherer tribes.[6] The land in Coahuila ultimately fell under the control of a handful of powerful Spanish families, including the Sánchez Navarro, Ramón, and Aguayo clans, whose vast semifeudal estates made the present King Ranch of South Texas (the size of Rhode Island) look small by comparison and impeded economic development as well as the growth of towns and cities.[7]

Against this background in colonial Coahuila, multiple empires began what historian F. Todd Smith calls a convergence on Caddo country in East Texas and northwestern Louisiana.[8] In 1684, the shallow beaches and tempests in the Gulf of Mexico that discouraged Spanish colonization of Texas by sea, following Cabeza de Vaca the preceding century, forced La Salle's ship to make landfall near Matagorda Bay between present Houston and Corpus Christi, Texas. Thinking he arrived near the mouth of the Mississippi River, La Salle established a post farther inland and staked a claim to Texas for France. The Spanish launched successive military expeditions from northern New Spain under Capt. Alonso De León in search of La Salle's rumored colony. Shortly after confirming the demise of the French and La Salle's death at the hands of his own men, the Spanish determined to make Texas a buffer province against French encroachment from the Mississippi.[9] La Salle's colonization schemes backfired, never with the full support of King Louis XIV of France, who held less interest in settlers than establishing a harbor on the Gulf of Mexico to facilitate raids on Mexico and grab its precious minerals.[10]

By then, Franciscans became the primary agents for colonization. They emerged from missionary colleges in colonial Mexico, since Spanish law prohibited the entry into new lands under military leadership without evangelization.[11] Misinterpreting the friendship of the Caddos as a desire for Christianity, Spain founded missions on the Texas-Louisiana frontier in 1690 under the guidance of the friars. With a Spanish military escort, they established several missions among the Tejas, a settled agricultural society along the Neches and Angelina Rivers in East Texas. By 1693, the Spanish wore out their welcome. The Tejas formed part of the largest and westernmost Caddo confederacy known as the Hasinai, who resisted conversion to Christianity and threatened to kill the newcomers. Far from Mexico City, without indigenous allies or Spanish female companions, low on supplies, and with only a handful of undisciplined troops, the Franciscan friars abandoned the missions and returned to New Spain.[12]

II

By the early 1700s, an astute Franciscan missionary named Francisco Hidalgo still held out hope for converting the Caddos and ironically renewed French designs on capturing Mexico's silver trade. Father Hidalgo grew tired of bureaucratic delays on his government's part and secretly rekindled the second Spanish attempt to colonize Texas following the War of the Spanish Succession, 1700–1713, known as Queen Anne's War in England. During this imperial conflict in Europe, which began when King Louis XIV of France established his grandson Philip V as the first Bourbon monarch of Spain, French officials in the fledgling colony of Louisiana became frustrated in their attempts to open legal trade with New Spain through the port of Veracruz on the southern Gulf of Mexico. Coincidentally, in 1713, a letter Father Hidalgo had drafted two years earlier reached the governor of Louisiana, Antoine De La Mothe Cadillac, requesting the governor's assistance with reestablishing Spanish missions in Texas. Governor Cadillac jumped at this opportunity to introduce French merchandise overland into northern New Spain. As historian Donald Chipman describes, the appointment of Louis Juchereau de St. Denis, a Canadian-born adventurer, as the leader of a French trading party from Louisiana across the Sabine River into the land of the Tejas Indians "would change the course of Texas history."[13] A successful St. Denis would bode well for his government's preference for commercial expansion in North America over territorial conquest, since the War of the Spanish Succession had drained the French treasury. After Spain blocked legal trade between France and Mexico by sea, St. Denis could pioneer an overland contraband trail through Texas, far beyond Veracruz, with the missions as cover.[14]

Commercial trade between St. Denis and the Tejas commenced in the fall of 1713, perhaps even earlier, and endeared him to the French Crown, though he became a person of interest to Spanish officials in New Spain.

After visiting with the Tejas, St. Denis pushed toward northern New Spain in the company of twenty-five Tejas men with some of their horses. Traversing the dangerous southern range of Lipan Apaches, St. Denis arrived safely in 1714 at Presidio San Juan Bautista, situated on the lower Rio Grande River across the present US-Mexico border near Eagle Pass, Texas (just north from Laredo). The commander of this Spanish fort, don Diego Ramón, placed St. Denis under house arrest in the commandant's own home and confiscated his goods. Transferred to Mexico City the following year for interrogation, St. Denis left San Juan Bautista after having "romanced" Commandant Ramón's step-granddaughter, Manuela Sánchez y Navarro, which likely saved his life and improved prospects for trade.[15]

In 1715, anxious Spanish officials launched the reoccupation of Texas under the command of Domingo Ramón, son of don Diego, from San Juan Bautista, which the historian Robert Weddle characterizes as the "gateway to Spanish Texas" after having been founded on the border of Coahuila in 1700 as a fort and mission complex. St. Denis swayed Mexico City officials to appoint him as a commissary officer and guide of the Ramón expedition with his professed intentions of marrying Manuela and becoming a Spanish subject. The commercial and social exploits of St. Denis, combined with the missionary zeal of Father Hidalgo, ultimately convinced Spanish Bourbon officials to counter the French threat to Spain's mercantile system in Mexico. By 1716–17, the missions in East Texas were reestablished, with additional ones deeper into the Piney Woods at Mission Dolores near present San Augustine, Texas, and Mission Los Adaes across the present Sabine River state line in Louisiana near Natchitoches, the French post St. Denis established in 1714 before his arrival at San Juan Bautista. The missions were placed under the protection of a Spanish fort in East Texas, called San Francisco de los Dolores, under Commandant Domingo Ramón, which the abandoned missions from the early 1690s did not have for defense. Franciscans reported that a Caddo woman named Angelina, who was "Hispanicized" at Mission San Juan Bautista del Rio Grande, also acted as a guide and interpreter for the Ramón expedition to East Texas.[16]

Once again, the missionaries failed to congregate the Tejas and convert them to Christianity, except this time, the Spanish placed blame squarely on the French, who traded guns and ammunition with the Indians in exchange for hides obtained from hunting buffalo, deer, and other wild animals that supplemented the Caddoan economy.[17] Although the Tejas accepted Spanish gifts of clothes, tobacco, and other items, they returned to their settlements and traditional culture once the soldiers left the missions. Beyond the mission grounds, however, Father Antonio Margil from Mission Los Adaes established an important precedent in 1717 when he administered the Catholic Church sacraments to the residents at French Natchitoches.[18] Assuming the role of chaplains in the absence of Jesuit priests, the Franciscan missionaries bartered religious services originally intended for the Caddos in order to obtain French goods (see chapters 2 and 3), which complicated the purpose of the missions from the outset.

Based on a mutual Bourbon dynasty, French officials revisited the establishment of formal trade relations with New Spain. In 1716, St. Denis formed a commercial company with several other French Canadians under the direction of Antoine Crozat, to whom Louis XIV had granted a trade monopoly in 1712 over the undetermined limits of the Louisiana colony. Among St. Denis's business partners were François Derbanne, a relative of Governor Cadillac's wife and keeper of the warehouse on Dauphin Island at the mouth of the Mississippi River, an important port prior to the establishment of New Orleans. The purpose of this merchant company was to search for mines and initiate commercial ventures in Bourbon Mexico.[19]

The Spanish, however, remained suspicious of French motives and again confiscated St. Denis's goods on his return trip to San Juan Bautista. Spanish suspicions were well founded, as St. Denis capitalized on his friendship with the Tejas in East Texas and his kinship with Capt. Diego Ramón on the lower Rio Grande. St. Denis smuggled French merchandise into northern New Spain in the provinces of Coahuila and Nuevo León. Captain Ramón protected his own reputation with Mexico City officials by confiscating some contraband items from St. Denis, consisting mostly of textile products, including red and blue woolen hose, thread, laces, Brittany and Rouen linen, and some heavy satin. But St. Denis left other boxes of trade goods behind among the Tejas on the Rio Grande that Captain Ramón did not confiscate. He reported to Mexico City officials that raiding Apaches had stolen the rest. Whether Captain Ramón told the whole truth only made Spanish government investigators question what else might have been smuggled and whether there were any more accomplices. Indeed, François Derbanne stayed behind on the Rio Grande while St. Denis sought a commission from the government in Mexico City, believing that his influence among the Indians on the frontier could be leveraged to trade legally. Upon learning of St. Denis's arrest, Derbanne and their other French companions returned to Louisiana. Spanish officials, including don Martín de Alarcón, the governor of Coahuila and Tejas y Nueva Filipinas—the latter in honor of King Philip V with designs for Texas like the Old Philippines in East Asia—became convinced that Capt. Diego Ramón was in league with the French, making the entire country north of Saltillo full of "Ramonistas," like a modern-day equivalent of a drug cartel in Mexico. Governor Alarcón correctly believed that they had formed a large commercial enterprise "in such a manner that all this country is full of contraband goods."[20]

The viceroy's two principal advisors in Mexico City, the *oidor* (attorney general) and *fiscal* (treasurer), however, held conflicting views toward St. Denis. The former remained sympathetic while the other considered the French Canadian's presence on the frontier dangerous to Spanish interests. Learning of his imminent arrest for having failed to obtain a proper bond in his prior release from prison, St. Denis fled Mexico City in the fall of 1718 for Louisiana and arrived at Natchitoches before continuing to Mobile in early 1719.[21]

Upon hearing of St. Denis's predicament in New Spain, French officials indicated that their Spanish counterparts should have understood, and remained thankful, that French Louisiana became a barrier against English settlements east of the Mississippi. Besides, France held plenty of territory in Louisiana and did not wish to "invade" Mexico.[22] Nonetheless, St. Denis's trade in northern New Spain, legal or not, legitimized any potential claims of France to the Rio Grande as the western limit of Louisiana. In addition, the Spanish lacked native allies and sufficient military forces in East Texas to forcibly congregate the Caddos, without whom Spain could not effectively counter French influence over the region.

The escape of St. Denis from Mexico City added to the anxieties of the Spanish, especially after war broke out in Europe between France and Spain in 1719. The central imperial conflict in North America occurred over Pensacola and Mobile Bay, but in June, a tiny force of seven soldiers from French Natchitoches seized Mission Los Adaes, guarded by just one Spanish soldier who apparently did not know their respective nations were at war. The French troops allegedly stole supplies and chickens from Mission Los Adaes, hence the infamous "Chicken War" that scholars describe. Fearful of a combined French-Caddo alliance, the Spanish soldiers and Franciscan friars abandoned the six missions and Presidio San Francisco in East Texas, having fled to San Antonio, a Spanish fort and mission complex established the previous year as a halfway station between the settlements in East Texas and San Juan Bautista on the Rio Grande.[23]

St. Denis's commercial ties with the Tejas, kinship at San Juan Bautista, "illicit" trade with Spanish settlers, and legal troubles with Mexico City officials together with Franciscan service rendered at Natchitoches established a pattern of Spanish-Franco-Caddo relations and, in the process, foreshadowed the transformation of the Texas-Louisiana region from frontier to borderlands over the next several decades. In its grand imperial scheme, the primary interest of Bourbon France in the Americas remained access to Mexico's silver economy while the fur trade and Indian alliances made this dream a possibility. During the previous century, French military officials and colonists in Canada had ascribed a new understanding to Native Americans as "able traders" in a commerce that reaped great profits for investors. French merchants recognized that Indians had their own "self-interest" in response to temporal and physical needs—beyond the spiritual—which trade helped satisfy.[24] This philosophy carried south along the Mississippi and into the West as St. Denis fortified trade alliances through marital and fictive ties with Indians *and* Spaniards to establish what one scholar has called "frontier trade cartels."[25] He and his wife, Manuela Sánchez Navarro, had two of their eldest children born at San Juan Bautista on the lower Rio Grande and another five children born at French Natchitoches on the lower Red River. Based on military, commercial, religious, and kinship networks, St. Denis and Manuela also became "godparents" to French, Spanish, Caddo, and African Creoles, drawing diverse communities closer together than ever imagined in the North American wilderness.[26]

The Adaeseños left Coahuila behind in the quest for their own lands and greater opportunities—perhaps with the expecation of extending Spanish conquest, if not their own self-interest. Following the "Chicken War" of 1719, Spain sought to occupy East Texas for the third time, except with another fort and mission farther east on the "border" with French Natchitoches. St. Denis contemplated the destruction of San Antonio in retaliation for his previous incarceration and had the broad support of Jean Baptiste LeMoyne, Sieur de Bienville, as the governor of Louisiana and the Duke of Orleans in France, who favored continuing an aggressive foreign policy. French officials in Paris, however, believed this to be counterproductive to future commerce in the Americas, as they instead leaned toward the development of agriculture in Louisiana with the beginning of the African slave trade after the establishment of New Orleans in 1718. The latter view prevailed and became the new French Bourbon policy toward Spanish territory west of Louisiana.[27] Spanish officials, on the other hand, mistook French commercial advances as territorial gain and maintained the belief that the Tejas and other Indians wanted to become Christians. For settlers at Los Adaes, however, the French appeared not as a threat but as saviors, with much-needed provisions. This difference of opinion at the local level only served to compromise any advantages a fort might offer the Spanish on the border with Louisiana.

Furthermore, by May 1720, a French soldier-trader named Bérnard de la Harpe informed the directors of the French Company of the West that he had been on the verge of establishing trade with the Spanish at New Mexico and Nuevo León before the "Chicken War" disrupted his plans. De la Harpe had commanded the recently established French posts among Caddo Indians from the Kadohadacho Confederacy on the upper Red River in present southwestern Arkansas. He emphasized the importance of Spanish settlement "near our posts because of the trade and of the cattle that we could draw from them." De la Harpe ended his account by informing the directors that five hundred Spanish troops were on their way to the Hasinai Confederacy of East Texas.[28] Hence the French did not initially oppose this third Spanish *entrada* (expedition) from establishing themselves near Louisiana despite a still-seething St. Denis.

Whereas the French looked forward to expanding trade opportunities in New Spain, the Spanish sought territorial and spiritual conquest like the previous De León and Ramón expeditions. With the symbols of God and king by their side, the Spanish entrada fell under the leadership of the Marqués de San Miguel de Aguayo, an *adelantado* (entrepreneur) who hailed from a prestigious military family in Spain and acquired his noble title through a propitious marriage. The Marqués de Aguayo became the natural choice in 1719 as governor and captain general of the provinces of Coahuila and Texas after he provided livestock for the previous failed reoccupation of East Texas under Captain Ramón and maintained troops at his own expense against Indian raiders in Coahuila.[29]

The Marqués de Aguayo chose don Fernando Pérez de Almazán as his lieutenant governor and captain general, who then succeeded Aguayo as the governor of Spanish Texas in 1722. The five-hundred-man army to whom de la Harpe referred were not professional troops from Spain; rather, they were recruited throughout New Spain, including the silver mining center at Zacatecas, north of Mexico City, and Celaya, a military outpost founded shortly before 1570 to protect the Camino Real leading to rich mining districts in the north. A majority of the recruits were *castas* (mixed-bloods), poor, single, illiterate workers off vast haciendas, many of whom were also indebted, in support of mining with food and clothing from livestock operations. Some of the recruits were Indians—in fact, Tlascalans, possibly from the town of San Esteban de Nueva Tlaxcala near Saltillo.[30] Thirty-one of the one hundred soldiers originally garrisoned at Presidio Los Adaes in 1721 arrived with their families, unlike the first all-male expedition into East Texas, and with more women than were brought along with the second venture. The Marqués de Aguayo divided his troops into eight companies, with one battalion of mounted infantry he called "San Miguel de Aragón."[31] The leading standard of the sanctioned expedition bore images of Our Lady of Pillar, San Miguel, and San Rafael, with the motto *Pugnate pro Fide et Rege* (fight for your faith and king). On the second standard appeared Our Lady of Guadalupe (Mexico's patroness) along with San Miguel and San Francisco Xavier. The third and final standard pictured the Lord with St. James, after whom the cathedral at Compostela in the province of Galicia, Spain, is named. This image was also symbolic of the Reconquest against the Moors.[32]

The Aguayo expedition arrived at San Antonio from Coahuila on April 4, 1721, having crossed the Rio Grande at the aptly named Paso de Francia (French Pass), near San Juan Bautista, along the Camino Real. Franciscan friars from the Zacatecan and Queretaran missionary colleges, including Father Margil, joined the expedition, and they all left the following month for East Texas. In July, they finally came upon a large group of Tejas near the Trinity River led by Chief Juan Rodríguez, who served as a guide and informed the Spanish that the French had given their flag and guns to other Indians. By August 1721, Aguayo's expedition came upon another Hasinai group, the Neches, and reestablished Franciscan missions with a fort called Presidio Tejas near present Nacogdoches, Texas.[33]

Crossing the Sabine River past hills, ravines, pine forests, pecans, oaks, and clearings, Governor Aguayo's expedition camped overnight near present-day Ft. Jesup Historic Site in Many, Louisiana. The following day, August 29, 1721, they arrived at the abandoned Mission Los Adaes. Governor Aguayo disliked this location for his troops because the low elevation subjected them to flooding, and there was no fresh running water in the nearby creek. The scouts he dispatched into the surrounding area discovered a spring that flowed into a large plain that Aguayo selected as their campsite between present Robeline and Shamrock in northwestern Louisiana. This spot, conveniently located along the Camino Real, was just seven leagues (fifteen miles) west from French Natchitoches.[34]

They planned on the construction of Presidio Los Adaes but were delayed, as they did not "find a single Indian at Los Adays" to provide labor. Surrounded by greater numbers of Caddo Indians who had French allies nearby, and with regulations against the enslavement of Indians, the Spanish could not simply impose their will on the natives. On August 30, 1721, Governor Aguayo dispersed troops into the forest, and on the following day, they "found Rancherias [Indian settlements] nearby." As instructed, the soldiers informed the Indians about the arrival of Aguayo's expedition. Reportedly, the "Indians were extremely happy, and their captain-general said he would immediately gather his people and come to see His

Lordship."[35] These Indians were the Adaes, a small agricultural community consisting of approximately four hundred men, women, and children who were associated with the Caddos. The Adaes lands were located farther north in the Red River valley, which was rich in wildlife—including bears, deer, and many varieties of ducks and fish—as well as pecans and medlar trees. The Spanish learned that the Adaes stored much food for winter, especially "bear lard, which is very delicious." In addition, they practiced agriculture with staples of maize and beans, plus tobacco production, in the tradition of their ancestors. The many rivers and trails facilitated economic exchange with other Indians over great distances.[36] For Aguayo and his troops, this remote region appeared a vastly different environment than the semidesert mountain stretches of northern New Spain (see map 1.2).

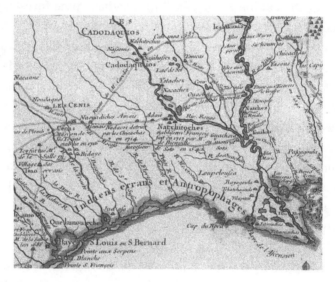

Map I.2: Guillaume Delisle, *Carte de la Louisiane et du cours du Mississipi Dressee sur un grand nombre de Memoires entrau,* 1718. This map is perhaps the first to depict an Adais (Adaie) settlement, shown to the west of a cluster of Natchitoches villages where the French established a fort and trading post on the Red River. This map is said to have remained the primary cartographic reference for the Mississippi valley until the late 1700s. Source: Courtesy of Texas beyond History, https://www.texasbeyondhistory.net/adaes/images/delisle-1718-crop2.html.

The French at nearby Natchitoches soon became alarmed that the Spanish had moved so close to their post and become potentially a more disruptive neighbor than de La Harpe had envisioned. On September 1, 1721, a Frenchman immediately brought word from the acting commandant at Natchitoches that the Spanish had no authorization to settle at Los Adaes and should remove themselves until the return of Captain St. Denis. After convoking a war council, Governor Aguayo sent Lieutenant General Almazán and Capt. don Gabriel Costales to Natchitoches with instructions to observe the approaches from the island in the Red River where the French had built their post. Almazán and Costales were also told to study its fortifications. Almazán informed the French commandant that the Spanish military objective was to occupy the "land of the Adays." He said that Governor Aguayo intended to reestablish Mission Los Adaes and construct a presidio. The French commander in charge responded that he had no "specific orders to agree to this or to prevent it," but he also knew of the "truce which existed in Europe between the two crowns and that he would uphold it in America if His Lordship agreed to it." For Governor Aguayo, resistance to Spanish occupation appeared less likely now that both sides were at peace, though he reaffirmed that "all which the Arms of His Catholic Majesty had possessed in that Province would be returned to the rule of Our Lord the King (may God protect him)."[37]

The Adaes chief and many of his people also appeared at the Spanish campsite on September 1 and purportedly expressed great joy as Governor Aguayo embraced them and distributed gifts of clothing to their captains. According to Aguayo's diarist, Juan Antonio de la Peña, the chief said they were happy to be under Spanish protection "because the French and the Natchitoches Indians displayed hostility towards them after invading Mission San Miguel de los Adays and the Adaes having lamented the retreat of the Spaniards. [The French and the Natchitoches] took some captives including men, women, and children at the time of the [Spanish] retreat. For this reason they had been forced to abandon the country and move to more distant and harsh land from which they had come to see the Governor."[38] After gifting the Indians, Governor Aguayo assured the Adaes of his Lord's protection, for which reason a fort with one hundred soldiers would be placed near the reestablished Mission Los Adaes. The Adaes then promised to congregate at the mission.[39] Having reached a modus vivendi with the Adaes, Tejas, and French, the Spanish soldier-settlers turned to internal affairs.

By autumn 1721, Spanish soldiers began construction of the fort at Los Adaes, which became the foundation of a more enduring Hispanic presence in East Texas and northwestern Louisiana. Governor Aguayo liked his campsite's location in an open field surrounded by dense forest at the terminus of the Camino Real from Mexico City. Plentiful land with a natural spring on a rise near the site appeared promising for cultivation. Governor Aguayo and his troops set about the task of building a hexagonal post based on seventeenth-century French fortifications (see figure 1.1). Unlike the presidio and missions at San Antonio, built from limestone from nearby quarries and adobe utilizing Indian labor, the Spanish could not count on mission labor in the lower Red River valley, where there were stones just east of present Robeline. The Adaeseños applied their own labor, cutting down trees for construction of small wooden structures and outlying ranches while burning timber for local fuel consumption (figure 1.1).[40]

Spanish governors and observers often complained, however, about great distances and environmental conditions as impediments to communication and transportation of vital news and supplies. The Texas province was located about 1,500 miles from the viceregal capital in Mexico City and 400 miles from Los Adaes and San Antonio in Texas across difficult terrain.[41] Mail delivery became a more hazardous occupation. For example, in 1724, one soldier drowned on the lower Colorado River trying to deliver letters from Governor Almazán regarding a royal declaration abolishing the *quites* (unauthorized payroll deductions), keeping news from reaching Presidio Texas or Presidio Los Adaes.[42] In July 1726, Governor Almazán wrote to the viceroy how February rains were so abundant that high waters delayed a convoy from San Antonio to Presidios Texas and Los Adaes for four long months. The governor expressed anguish about leaving with a convoy of livestock and supplies from San Antonio to these eastern presidios, explaining he would leave once "the rains have calmed and the rivers can be crossed," adding that "this trip will be painful for me because of my broken health and it being the season of scathing heat."[43]

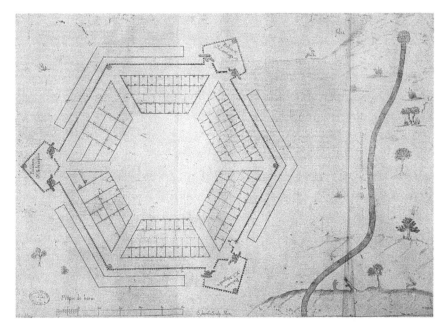

Figure I.I: *Plan de Presidio de Nuestra Señora del Pilar de los Adays en la frontera de los Texas, Nuevo Reyno de Philipinas*, whose fortification was marked and executed by Marqués San Miguel de Aguayo, November I, I72I. Source: Courtesy of *Archivo General de Indias—Sevilla*, Spain, digital copy.

The Spanish often cited flooding as the main reason for crop failures, not infertility of the land or laziness, which forced the residents of Los Adaes to look for outside sources of food. In the early 1730s, Spanish officials discussed the possibility of moving Presidio Los Adaes to a more favorable location, but to no avail. The spot Gen. don Pedro Marqués de Rivera recommended for Presidio Los Adaes during his military inspection tour (1727–28) was inundated with the waters of the lower Red River. The Spanish raised concerns about inadequate drinking water as livestock meandered "some distance away" to Natchitoches, where "everything is abundant because that settlement is in the middle of the Caudachos [Red] River, and provisions are easily found that our soldiers lack." In late 1731, after searching fifteen days for a better place to plant corn and vegetables, Gov. Juan Antonio Bustillo Zevallos ultimately determined that no better spot existed than where Presidio Los Adaes already stood.[44]

The Spanish community at Los Adaes faced harsh conditions in East Texas and northwestern Louisiana, where contraband trade became critical for survival. Following the completion of Presidio Los Adaes on October 12, 1721, the feast day of Our Lady of the Pillar, a cargo of maize and flour arrived from Nuevo León along with the Marqués de Aguayo's livestock, numbering three hundred cows and four hundred sheep. Historian Robert Weddle notes that these caravans became "the forerunner of the cattle drives which were to play such an important role in the later history of Texas."[45] The soldier-settlers' joy at the arrival of this cargo was short lived, however, as problems with maize cultivation and irregular transit overland from northern New Spain made them look to provisions from French Natchitoches—less than a day's journey from Los Adaes and with safer passage.[46]

The initial French trade with the Spanish at Los Adaes logically followed commerce that St. Denis pioneered with Caddos *and* Southern Plains Indians. To the consternation of Lieutenant General Almazán, who governed Texas from 1722 to 1727, the Apaches traded with the French from Natchitoches, obtaining guns, knives, and ammunition.[47] The settlements at San Antonio took precedence for the Spanish as they intermittingly waged battles against Lipan Apaches, whom Spaniards called *indios bárbaros* (savages), who thrived on bison ecology as they fought to remain independent and expand their own territory.[48] The same violence attended the Spanish settlements at La Bahía, where the Karankawas repeatedly resisted European incursions along the Gulf Coastal Plain. Meanwhile, the soldier-settlers at Los Adaes enjoyed comparative peace thanks in large measure to commercial and social ties developed with the French and Tejas.

In contrast to the Apaches and Karankawas, the Caddos remained largely sedentary agriculturalists with substantial housing in an environment that had sustained their culture for centuries. By the early 1700s, in response to the devastation wrought by European diseases, invasion, and Indian warfare, the Caddos regrouped: the Hasinai of East Texas or the westernmost Caddo; the Kadohadacho, settled near the present state borders of Arkansas, Texas, and Oklahoma; and the Natchitoches in northwestern Louisiana, among whom the French established their post with the same name. The Adaes and Ais Indians were small, independent, Caddo-related groups, the former situated east of the Sabine River near the Natchitoches Indians and the latter west of the river near present San Augustine in Tejas country. Although warfare was not central to their culture, the Caddos united against their traditional enemies: the Osage to the north; the Natchez, Choctaw, and Chickasaw to the east; and Apaches to the west, all of whom took captives.[49]

For the Spanish, the Tejas became part-time allies to check Apache (and subsequent Comanche) encroachment in the woodlands region of East Texas. Meanwhile, problems arose for the Franciscan friars at nearby Mission Los Adaes—indeed, with all the East Texas missions that kept the Spanish from utilizing Indian labor. In 1728, Friar Miguel Sevillano de Paredes, the guardian of the Missionary College of Santa Cruz de Queré-taro, explained the impossibility of the missions in Texas "to settle Indians into towns who live scattered in those parts, nor has there been anyone to the present to find a most fitting place necessary for their way of life in order to catechize and instruct them in the mysteries of the faith."[50] General Rivera agreed with Paredes's assessment. In the New Regulations of 1729, based largely on his report, Rivera cited not a single Indian in the East Texas missions. He suggested that the soldiers from Los Adaes be sent on expeditions to look for the Indians dispersed in their *rancherías* (settlements).[51] He also noted that the French could have easily conquered this land, which not even one hundred Spanish troops could oppose.[52] The lack of Indian converts posed difficulties, as the missionaries had to rely mainly on coerced labor of Spanish soldiers if not Indian captives.

Unbeknownst to General Rivera, the French would benefit from having Spanish troops located nearby in times of trouble. In 1731, the French at Natchitoches requested assistance from Governor Bustillo of Texas to resist an attack from the Natchez Indians, who rose in rebellion against the French on the lower Mississippi River. In this conflict, eighteen soldiers from Los Adaes fought alongside French and Caddo allies in the successful defense of the Natchitoches post. A French official stated that without this prompt military support, the French post would have been destroyed.[53] In addition, the French became more apprehensive about the growing English threat in North America and looked to Spain for backing.[54] Following the end of the War of the Quadruple Alliance (1719–21), Franco-Spanish relations softened while Anglo-Spanish clashes increased in northern Florida, especially as Georgia became an English colony. The Bourbon monarchs of France and Spain sealed formal alliances (Family Compact) beginning in 1733 as a counterbalance to the growing English presence east of the Mississippi.[55] Amid both internal and external threats between the Southern Plains and Mississippi valley regions, the Adaeseños looked across the border to Caddo country and French Louisiana for survival.

V

Commerce at the local and regional levels reinforced interdependence despite the attempts of distant Spanish officials to define the border between Texas and Louisiana. The smuggling of weapons, ammunition, and other foreign goods from Louisiana into Texas created high anxiety in Mexico City and Madrid, where officials imagined the worst scenarios should their own subjects, like the Adaeseños, become involved in such trade and upset the commercial mining enterprises of New Spain. For Spain, the stakes heightened in the eighteenth century with competing British and French interests in North America—all while the Spanish feared another great Pueblo-like revolt. In virtually all the *residencias* (administrative reviews) of Texas governors, the question of "illicit commerce" arose in the interrogatories in addition to questions about Indian captives in East Texas. Soldiers ventured southwest as far as Saltillo in northern New Spain, exchanging hides for horses, saddles, and corn, and eastward down the Red and Mississippi Rivers to New Orleans, trading saddles for clothes and other goods. In doing so, they compromised New Spain's eastern boundary with Louisiana and gradually pulled Texas into the frontier exchange economy of the lower Mississippi valley and New Orleans. With scarce quantities of specie available, hides and tobacco became accepted currency in the predominantly barter-exchange economy of the Texas-Louisiana border-lands.[56] The smuggling of tobacco, along with guns and alcohol, became problematic for Spanish officials, as the regulation and interdiction of such trade proved virtually impossible to stop during the course of the eighteenth century. The commercial, political, and military links Los Adaes forged with their French and Caddo neighbors helped maintain relative harmony while the Bourbon monarchs of Spain and France grew closer together in alliance against the English.

Social ties also promoted trade relations in a spirit of accommodation between Spanish Los Adaes and French Natchitoches, where many different ethnic groups came together in worship and celebration. Just as kinship played a pivotal role among various intertribal groups and French traders, public rituals of baptism, marriage, and burial reinforced *relaciones parentescas* (family ties) through *compadrazco* (coparenthood) among Spaniards, French, Caddos, and African Creoles.[57] With few Adaes Indians, if any, at Mission Los Adaes, the Franciscans went beyond their missionary duties and served an important secular role with the administration of the sacraments to settlers at Los Adaes and Natchitoches. Meanwhile, the baptism, marriage, and burial of Adaeseños at French Natchitoches, which began as early as 1734, emerged from the de facto secular work Franciscans continued throughout the remainder of the century, suggesting a more collaborative, if not accommodative, relationship bridging local communities.[58]

Spanish and French officials disputed the limits of the Texas-Louisiana boundary but could not break emerging business and familial networks at the local level. The most serious border disagreement arose over St. Denis's decision in 1735 to move the Natchitoches post to the west bank of the Red River, which the Spanish viewed as encroachment into their territory. In effect, St. Denis and his soldiers had already maintained dwellings on the west bank for three years before making his permanent residency on that side of the Red River. St. Denis had a stockade, church, and fourteen houses built for his garrison and the settlers. The Adaeseños themselves were not so concerned. When Governor Sandoval ceased communication with Natchitoches in protest, the Adaeseños were dismayed because they depended on the French for grain supplies. Still, the viceroy ordered an investigation into Governor Sandoval for permitting St. Denis to expand the Natchitoches post into Texas while he was in office. Sandoval, however, was absolved after the boundary between Los Adaes and Natchitoches was recognized as the Arroyo Hondo, a tributary creek to the Red River, which had always been the de facto border, located about two and a half leagues (seven miles) west of the lower Red River.[59] The viceroy later issued a decree to block French advances without the ability to enforce such a law and against the wishes of locals.

VI

By the 1730s, the soldiers and residents at Los Adaes had formed a small community of approximately 250 settlers, gradually transforming themselves into ranchers and farmers who confronted isolation and poverty as Spanish officials sought to control the border. Historian Max Moorhead notes that the Spanish frontier was ultimately defended "by colonists who were part-time soldiers and part-time settlers" under the command of presidial captains doubling as merchants, ranchers, or mine owners and wished "to secure or extend their private enterprises." In practice, a presidial captain "was as much a *patrón* (political boss) or *comandante* who looked upon his troops, often his social and ethnic 'inferiors,' as personal vassals."[60] Such was the case for the inhabitants of Los Adaes, especially without the presence of mission Indians. The Adaeseños fell into a premodern form of debt peonage, a term historian William Kiser has identified in northern New Spain, and likely tried to escape by joining the Caddo or French communities.[61] Historian Norwood Andrews explains that presidial service as "convict labor" had deep roots with the Spanish conquest in North Africa at the beginning of the sixteenth century and how two types of *reos* (inmates) emerged by the eighteenth century: *desterrados* (exiled to military service) and *presidiarios* (those condemned to hard labor at presidios).[62] At least some of the troops at Los Adaes fell into one of these two categories and were apparently "recruited" from prison in New Spain for debts incurred on haciendas or perhaps recalcitrance against their masters, but the line between military service and involuntary servitude was blurred.

General Rivera's military review sought the improvement of troop morale through better pay and an end to the abusive practices of presidial captains who used soldiers as personal laborers on their ranches, farms, or mines in northern New Spain. Commandants paid soldiers in commodities instead of their salary and then made unauthorized service charges from the presidial payroll.[63] In particular, General Rivera saw many areas that needed attention at Los Adaes. He did not think it even deserved the title of presidio because all he saw were only a "few huts made of sticks and grass, and very poorly constructed ones at that." Among the abuses were the governor's appointment of more officers than were necessary, inflated prices charged for basic goods, and soldiers utilized for illegal assignments—and all the while, the governor's own pay was too high. Most importantly, General Rivera believed that the one hundred soldiers at Los Adaes should be reduced to sixty. He reassured his superiors that the surrounding Caddo Indians, including the Adaes, "are docile and peace-loving," negating any need for guards or sentinels. He noted that even though the French supplied the Caddos with guns, these Indians showed respect and submission toward "mounted and armed soldiers." Moreover, the Indians did not even live in the East Texas missions, which could be protected with no more than two soldiers assigned to each mission.[64]

General Rivera ceded the Louisiana-Texas frontier to French control even though Spain had a larger force at Los Adaes than the French maintained at Natchitoches. Many of the Spanish troops often dispersed on assignments elsewhere in Texas, provided escort service for pack trains and guard duty at missions, or stationed at other presidios to battle Southern Plains Indians. The French had the ability to draw on a formal army under experienced officers from the Mobile or Illinois regions. They also were more accustomed to warfare, with more accurate long-range firearms. However, rather than express alarm over the apparent French hegemony in this area, Rivera noted that the French and Spanish crowns were at peace. Because of this reality and the fact that the captain and soldiers were "not doing the jobs of military men," Rivera felt "the presidio should be eliminated." At a minimum, he recommended the presidio remain with fifty-seven soldiers paid at 420 pesos, a lieutenant at 450 pesos, an *alférez* (lieutenant) at 440 pesos, and a sergeant at 435 pesos.[65] Rivera's reforms were implemented half-heartedly, and life for soldiers and their families at Los Adaes essentially remained the same.[66]

The frontier had changed greatly, on the other hand, since the late seventeenth century, when the worlds of the Spanish, French, and Caddos initially collided in Texas. Caddos likely felt that their position as the primary gatekeepers of trade between southeastern and southwestern Indians was increasingly challenged by Europeans and the "Columbian Exchange," historian Alfred Crosby's term for the exchange of diseases, goods, and ideas. Meanwhile, the Hapsburg monarchy faded from Spain as the new Bourbon crown rearranged relationships with France and became ever more watchful of foreign traders who pushed the limits of transatlantic commerce into northern New Spain. At the local and regional levels, no one could have predicted that by the third decade of the eighteenth century, the Spanish, French, and Caddos would meet each other's needs with trade at the heart of their relationship, which was buttressed by a myriad of environmental, military, political, commercial, and kinship connections. Distant Spanish officials exhibited frustration, unable to extend exclusive control and pacification of Texas. The transformation of the Texas-Louisiana frontier into a borderlands compromised imperial designs at defining and enforcing New Spain's weakest boundaries. However, these officials likely never suspected that Franciscan friars would undermine border enforcement, but it was precisely those "conquistadors of the spirit" who never gave up on the "salvation of all souls—pagan and Christian."[67]

CHAPTER TWO

Food for the Soul

Shortly after the founding of Los Adaes in 1721, a Spanish priest from the mission of San Miguel de los Adaes (Mission Los Adaes) performed mass on Sundays at Natchitoches, picking up where Father Margil left off several years earlier.[1] In 1724, Gov. Fernando Perez de Almazán, residing at San Antonio, informed Mexico City officials that Presidio Los Adaes received critical food supplies from Natchitoches after Spanish missionaries "took the initiative to administer the Holy Sacraments and celebrate mass on feast days, a comfort the French greatly appreciate for not having ecclesiastical ministers themselves." Governor Almazán stressed the importance of maintaining open lines of communication with the French through trade and religion.[2] That same year, François Derbanne, St. Denis's business associate and would-be father-in-law of Victoria Gonzalez, reported that the French sold maize to the Spanish at Los Adaes because the latter could not cultivate their own basic foods. Derbanne said here that the French "made their biggest trade—because they [Spaniards] were starving to death."[3] Despite frustration over the lack of progress at conversion of the Caddos, the Franciscans began ranching operations at the six missions of East Texas, including Mission Los Adaes in northwestern Louisiana, which required less labor than intensive agricultural enterprises elsewhere in New Spain, in addition to attempts at maize cultivation. The friars in East Texas also avoided strained relations with the governor over the control of Indian labor, which had contributed to recent troubles at San Antonio and La Bahía.[4] In effect, Franciscan missionaries bridged the communities at Los Adaes and Natchitoches and, in the process, reinforced local ties through worship that served as cover for trade in foodstuffs and other goods despite Spanish efforts to create a border between New Spain and Louisiana in order to regulate commerce.

Franciscan missionaries lamented the lack of Caddo Indians congregated inside mission walls, citing isolation from New Spain and the environment as initial obstacles. In 1727, during an inspection of Mission Los Adaes, less than a mile south from Presidio Los Adaes, friar Pedro Muñoz stated that while "visiting the pagans of this mission, none presently acknowledge the [mission] bell because they live far off on their lands with huts spaced far in between and located about eight to fifteen leagues [twenty to thirty-seven miles] from the mission." This distance between the mission and Indian settlements, according to Muñoz, caused "the missionaries to work extremely hard just to see them, which also makes perfecting their language impossible." He added that the Indians "invoked the temporary advantages of their own residence, which they would not have any if they gathered into one place because the land [of the mission] is not suitable."[5] The dense forest and swelled rivers made passage to and from remote Caddo communities difficult for missionaries on foot or horseback.[6] Without adequate equipment or manpower to help them clear and work the land, the Franciscan task of congregating these Indians made evangelization difficult from the start, as the environment remained largely wilderness and remote.

The East Texas missions were humble wooden establishments, unlike other Spanish missions in northern New Spain constructed of stone and adobe by Indian laborers. The East Texas missions were built of timber on a much smaller scale with manpower derived mostly from Spanish soldiers at Los Adaes. Father Muñoz visited the church and sacristy at Mission Adaes, which he described as having "two altars that are poor and curiously adorned with ornaments of all colors" and "a house currently under construction."[7] There were no ornate church structures, living quarters, or lookout towers, and they were not painted in vivid colors like the San Antonio missions. The Indians remained in their rancherías while Franciscan missionaries learned about local native customs and adjusted to Caddo country.

The missionaries could not sway the minds or hearts of Caddos into turning away from their own religion. These Indians, said Father Muñoz, basically ignore the Franciscan priests and "insist on maintaining themselves as is because they have their own rituals and shamans" even though some of their spiritual leaders "are lying elders, even sorcerers, who persuade the ignorant that only what they say is what they should know," and "even if they suspect something is untrue, they do not want to disgrace the elders, which is due to their peaceful and cowardly nature." Still, the Franciscans persisted with evangelization. Father Muñoz reported that the zealous missionaries "do not cease being diligent, wishing God our Lord to enlighten all these poor pagans who inhabit the environs of this country and hope to gather in this mission [Adaes], those known in their language as the Adaes, Pachinais and Catanacha." This aspect of Caddo resistance to Christianity appeared virtually everywhere in colonial Latin America.[8]

Perhaps most telling for peaceful coexistence is that Spanish officials did not allow the use of military force against the Indians on the Texas-Louisiana borderlands. In 1728, Friar Miguel Sevillano de Paredes petitioned the king to allow soldiers from the presidios at Los Adaes and Tejas, the latter reestablished under Aguayo in 1721 just west from present Nacogdoches, to gather these Indians into a pueblo where missions were located or at other more convenient locations. Paredes argued that "experience has clearly shown it is not feasible to congregate [the Indians] only through the missionaries' own efforts" in order to achieve "the primary goal of reducing Paganism."[9] The viceroy, Marqués de Casafuerte, eventually published a royal *cédula* (law) on July 31, 1733, which denied Paredes's request for such military force out of fear of provoking French and Caddo rebellion. Viceroy Casafuerte, who cited General Rivera's recent military report about Spanish Texas, concluded that such action was unnecessary, besides "the burden that it would be to my royal treasury."[10] Following General Rivera's recommendations, the viceroy reiterated his prior order to the governor of Texas about providing Franciscan missionaries no more than two or three soldiers for escort duty to the Indian settlements, which subsequent viceroys reiterated.[11]

This predicament contrasted sharply with the San Antonio missions at Mission San Antonio de Valero and Mission San José, where the governors of Texas repeatedly allowed the military to reduce more mobile hunter-gatherer nations, collectively referred to as Coahuiltecans, to mission life as revealed through the residencia of a governor's tenure in office. For example, in 1738, when asked if Governor Sandoval increased the population of Texas and gathered Indians to live peaceably at the San Antonio missions, Mateo Antonio Ybarbo, along with other troops from Los Adaes sent to reinforce San Antonio, testified in the affirmative. Ybarbo added that "if some Indians fled to the wilds, the governor had them brought back to the missions, admonished them that here was where they should be, and never permitted their use of barbarous dances or disorderly gatherings."[12] Despite Los Adaes's designation as the capital of Spanish Texas under the New Military Regulations of 1729, following General Rivera's inspection, Governor Sandoval resided in San Antonio to deal directly with the external threat from raiding Lipan Apaches and internal challenges to his power from missionaries as well as Canary Islanders who arrived at San Antonio in 1731 and established the Villa de San Fernando with a *cabildo* (city council). Many subsequent governors also resided at San Antonio rather than Los Adaes.[13]

The Adaeseños were fully aware of the danger at San Antonio, where they also likely availed themselves with *Bexareños* (Hispanic residents of San Antonio) in the taking of Indian captives or their adoption, a source of servant labor not so readily available for the Spanish in East Texas and northwestern Louisiana. On July 6, 1728, Mateo Ybarbo, a Spanish immigrant from the province of Andalucía in southern Spain, and his wife, Juana Luzgardea Hérnandez, celebrated the baptism of their "legitimate" daughter, Juana Antonia, together with her Spanish godparents, Lt. Mateo Perez and his spouse, Maria de San Juan, at Mission San Antonio de Valero.[14] Ybarbo also became a godfather at Mission Valero later that summer of an eighteen-day-old baby, named Juana Rosa, described as "a Payalla Indian of Gentile Parents," an indication that the infant's parents had perished under assault from the Apaches, and the child was "rescued" or taken from Spanish raids in search of Indians from the wilderness and deposited at the missions.[15] Baptismal records of the San Antonio missions also reveal the adoption of Apaches, mostly children, into Spanish military families.[16] By comparison, historian Brian DeLay notes that there were many "captive baptisms" of Apaches and Comanches in New Mexico throughout the course of the eighteenth century.[17] Such captive baptisms occurred at the Spanish missions in San Antonio and La Bahía but were noticeably absent from East Texas, where missionaries remained without the authorization to use any military force against the Indians. Spanish-Caddo relations on the Texas-Louisiana borderlands differed drastically from South Texas and New Mexico, but this did not necessarily mean that the Adaeseños had no access to Indian labor.

The main reason for the viceroys not mobilizing the Spanish military to facilitate congregation of the Indians in the East Texas missions was more than a lack of resources; rather, they were dissuaded by the French presence across the border at Natchitoches and their Indian allies in the Red River valley and beyond to the Mississippi. Mexico City officials could not send enough troops to match the French-Indian alliance and feared that utilizing Spanish forces at Los Adaes to round up Indians would spark a revolt they could not put down. Other Spanish settlements in northern New Spain, such as San Antonio and Santa Fe, required more resources and troops on volatile borders with the Southern Plains than East Texas, which sat on a relatively peaceful border with French Louisiana and Caddo country. The Franciscans in East Texas, meanwhile, complained about the lack of military personnel made available to them. The friars estimated that even twenty-five Spanish soldiers were insufficient for Mission Nacogdoches. They cited fifty-eight Indian nations altogether from "New Louisiana" and East Texas that could completely overwhelm the missions. The powerful tribes included the Choctaw, Mobilien, Thunica, Natchez, Nachitos (Natchitoches), Caudachos, Nacoudoches, Tejas, and Bidais, in addition to weaker ones like the Ais and Adaes. The governor at Los Adaes gave a total estimate of eighteen thousand Indians living west of the Mississippi, and there were no assurances that friendly nations could be won over from trade with French settlements.[18]

The specter of another Pueblo-like revolt from equally settled, agricultural societies in the southeastern woodlands loomed large in the Spanish imagination, whereas pockets of mobile Apache fighters could be contained. In such an event, Franciscans from the East Texas missions would be forced into seeking safety at Presidio Los Adaes without defense from mission Indians or other allies. By contrast, the French governor in New Orleans mobilized seven hundred soldiers and two thousand Indian allies, mostly Choctaws, against the Natchez in 1730–31. At Natchitoches, the French called on Caddo allies in addition to Spanish troops from Los Adaes. As historians H. Sophie Burton and F. Todd Smith explain, during the 1720s, officials from the Company of the Indies, which governed Louisiana as a private venture, permitted larger numbers of French settlers to establish tobacco plantations with their African slaves near Natchez villages along the Mississippi. By early October 1731, a band of several hundred Natchez refugees had fled the violence and attacked French Natchitoches. Among the defenders of Natchitoches were 350 Hasinais and Kadohadacho (Caddo) warriors, twenty-two French soldiers, and Adaeseño soldiers from Los Adaes who forced the Natchez into retreat. Because of the Natchez War, King Louis XIV of France dissolved the company's charter in late 1731, and Louisiana became a royal colony.[19] One Adaeseño soldier died, whose death symbolized the cross-border ties among the French and Caddos. French and Indian allies indeed could have wiped out Spanish neighbors entirely, but at what cost? French imperial defenses in North America were increasingly geared toward the east against the growing English threat with their own set of powerful Indian allies, most notably the Chicases (Chickasaws).[20]

Some of the distinctive Caddo nations in East Texas—particularly the Tejas, Nazones, Nacogdoches, and Adaes—avoided joining any Franco-Indian alliances during the Natchez revolt, having recently battled the Choctaw. Perhaps they were concerned about the reduced numbers of their own warriors. On his way to the rancherías of the Adaes during the Natchez uprising, Friar Paredes reported, "I found no one at Mission Nacogdoches, and proceeded to Mission Ais, which had its wooden cell doors in pieces and the Church door yanked off hinges, everything stolen by the Indians."[21] Several years earlier, Father Muñoz had reported at

Mission San Francisco that the Neches Caddo "only visit this mission when they know the missionary will give them powder, candles, clothes, and other things."[22] The Natchez War likely presented the Caddos with an opportunity to exploit the dangers of not providing them with material gifts, and they expressed their displeasure whenever Spanish officials attempted to disrupt trade. Perhaps the Caddos were also cautious about draining their own resources and preferred to keep their options open without committing to the Spanish, whom they still distrusted despite kinship and worship with French Natchitoches.

Normally, only one or two Franciscan friars were assigned to each mission during the 1720s, but by 1730, the East Texas missions were reduced in number from six to three following General Rivera's recommendations in addition to the closure of Presidio Tejas. The three missions that belonged to the College of Santa Cruz de Querétaro—Concepción, San Francisco, and San José—were transferred to San Antonio, which left the College of Zacatecas as the only missionary school with any missions in East Texas: Nacogdoches, Ais, and Adaes. Presidio Tejas was eliminated entirely, leaving Los Adaes as the only remaining Spanish fort in East Texas.[23] The military force at Los Adaes, despite its reduction to sixty soldiers from the original one hundred troops under Governor Aguayo in 1721, continued to be diverted to other missions and presidios across the province of Texas. The use of Spanish soldiers from Los Adaes to coerce Caddo Indians into the East Texas missions would not be allowed for the rest of its existence as long as there were powerful French-Indian alliances and the potential for rebellion from across the border in Texas.

II

Spanish missionaries faced another major obstacle to Indian conversion in the East Texas missions with competition from French trade among the Caddos. The Caddos increasingly depended on French arms and goods to help ward off the Apache threat. In 1744, Gov. Felipe Winthuysen mentioned that Apaches did not penetrate beyond the Brazos River because it marked an ecological boundary separating the Southern Plains from the Woodlands, the latter home to the Bidais, Yadoces, and Tejas. In order to defend themselves against Apaches, the governor remarked that the Caddos were "very skillful in the use of the arrow, and even better with guns, which they and their partners get from the French colony." Governor Winthuysen also described Caddo traders as "experts at hunting bear and deer, making the latter into chamois, and from the former removing the lard for commerce with the French and Spanish."[24] He added that "the Tejas Indians are the most industrious of these three nations, preparing their fields, planting their vegetables and storing them, but they are all irreducible to political and mission submission, having frustrated many efforts toward this end."[25] Besides, the Caddo slash-and-burn method of agriculture discouraged large gatherings of Indians into one place despite abundant rainfall for irrigation.[26] The Caddos had no incentives to resettle their communities at the Spanish missions like Coahuiltecan Indians at San Antonio, who faced greater exposure to the Apache threat. The Caddoan ability to defend themselves in their native forests, aptitude for commerce and farming, strong religious beliefs, and sense of independence convinced Franciscan missionaries to shift their strategy away from a reliance on Spanish military force; instead, the missionaries would trade with the Caddos directly as a means of luring them into the missions in case their fortunes changed and they sought conversion.

This meant focusing on the development of the mission ranching economy as much as possible despite the lack of Indian converts. The East Texas missions experienced greater success with ranching operations than farming by relying mostly on labor provided from Spanish soldiers and residents at Los Adaes. The Caddos assisted the Franciscans perhaps "voluntarily" at various times with fieldwork because the friars could not count on the Spanish military to round up and coerce a dependable supply of laborers. The Caddos also likely hedged their bets and preferred trade with the Spanish. Before the transfer to San Antonio of the three Santa Cruz missions, all six of the East Texas missions engaged in small farming and ranching (see appendix A). According to Friar Muñoz, Mission Los Adaes had "farm tools consisting of hatchets, large curved hoes, etc., for fieldwork and regularly plant (sow) three *almudes* [twenty-one dry quarts] of corn. Sometimes there is a harvest, sometimes not. It has livestock, 26 cattle both small and large guarded with care by the soldiers, and also has some saddled horses, which the friars use to visit the Indians in their ranches and move from one mission to another. There is also a pack train used to transport the alms [gift offerings] with the brother procurator in charge."[27]

The soldiers included the Adaeseños from Presidio Los Adaes and possibly the smaller contingent from Presidio Tejas before its abandonment. Muñoz did not specify who worked the fields and ranches at the other five missions—just that no Indians were congregated. All of the original six East Texas missions had various equipment and livestock for farming and ranching, which provided a foundation on which ranching operations began in Spanish Texas together with mission ranches of San Antonio and La Bahía.

The East Texas missions apparently relied on similar irrigation methods as the San Antonio missions, where water was diverted from the San Antonio River to the *labores* (fields) through an elaborate *acequia* (canal) system, but perhaps with different goals for distinctive Indians in contrasting environments, with rainfall amounts greater in East Texas making for dry irrigation possible.[28] Historian Félix Almaráz explains how, in theory, the missions were a "transitory medium" of about twenty years, or a generation. The development of the institution "involved five steps: 1. *misíon*, commitment to establish an objective; 2. *reducción*, congregation of Indians in a suitable location; 3. *conversión*, formal religious instruction; 4. *doctrina*, acceptance and observance of Spanish Christianity; and 5. *parroquia* and *pueblo*, political designation of parish and civil status, secularization." The last phase involved the transfer from the missionaries of various regular orders "to the diocesan clergy" and the "emergence of a civil community of resident landowners (*vecinos*) and parishioners" that consisted of Hispanicized Indians.[29] The Caddos likely sought trade with the East Texas missions and presidios, but not the conversion experience or coercion process associated with the mission-presidio complex elsewhere in northern New Spain. The major problems at the East Texas missions had more to do with either too much rain or drought and an unstable labor source than with Indian raids.

The issue of labor was partially solved with soldiers from Los Adaes who likely served missionaries as part-time field laborers and also provided guard and transportation duty. By contrast, after soldiers at San Antonio assisted the missionaries with a formal *acto de posesión* (requisite act of sovereignty) of the missions, fort, and town, the Franciscans relied mostly on mission Indians to work the farms and livestock.[30] Despite the lack of Indian labor, Mission Concepción in East Texas, prior to its transfer to San Antonio, appeared to succeed economically with over a hundred livestock and greater amounts of corn harvested than the other East Texas missions. It also yielded some wheat, a crop conspicuously absent or not yet harvested at the other East Texas missions. The expansion of farming required far more intensive labor in East Texas than even the soldiers could provide, such that mission ranching became the basis of the frontier economy beyond subsistence farming and contraband trade.

Most interesting is that various Caddo settlements did eventually cluster around the East Texas missions and remained agriculturally based societies, occasionally lending farm skills to the missionaries. Friar Muñoz, upon the conclusion of his inspection of the missions in 1727, stated, "the nations found in the district of these six missions are called the Hasinai, more commonly, the Tejas, each composed of around 200 people, but there is no way to know exactly their numerical strength because they are so widely scattered. In sum, there may be 1,300 to 1,400 persons more or less in the missions. These [Indians] plant fields of corn, beans, and pumpkin on their own ranches, spend part of their time hunting or at war, which most of them are very dedicated."[31] Perhaps by *war* Muñoz meant "Apache troubles," but at least the Caddos intended to maintain their way of life despite Spanish and microbial invasions. Bérnard La Harpe, the French soldier-trader from Natchitoches, remarked just prior to the return of the Spanish that the Adaes Indians harvested potato and persimmon fruit from which they made bread, but he made no reference to European farm implements or animals just yet.[32] After the Spanish reestablished the missions, the Caddos likely incorporated European tools into their own traditional farming methods, and it was the Spanish who drew upon them and the French for sources of food to make up for shortfalls in harvests from the missions. Whether the Caddos might have congregated eventually at the three more successful Santa Cruz missions had these not been abandoned in 1731 is possible but unlikely if done through force because they would have rebelled.

Regardless, the Caddos who assisted the East Texas missions evidently did so with detrimental results and remained wary of farm labor at those sites. In 1740, Father Ildefonso Joseph Marmolejo mentioned Indians working the farms and ranches at Mission Ais, where the "Indians were used as laborers until that ranchería was depopulated by 1728 and again, until the year 1732, when the demand for Apostolic labor reduced not just this one, but also nine or ten rancherías that today are maintained at most a league and a half away." He added that Mission Ais was "assisted by twelve poor Indians without any grain and relied upon hunting." Who were these Indians? Were these Caddoan seasonal laborers mentioned earlier? Might they have been Apache war captives sent to supply the East Texas missions with labor? Apparently, Mission Ais had one ranchería of Indians in 1717 before its abandonment two years later due to the Spanish-Franco "Chicken War," but then the number of Indian rancherías that Mission Ais administered increased during the 1720s before experiencing a decline by the 1730s.[33] According to Father Marmolejo, Mission Ais did function well despite diseases having reduced the number of any Indians helping missionaries raise crops over time, which correlates with the greater frequency of baptisms *en articulo mortis* (at or near death). The Ais Indians' concern over declining numbers and preference for independence, however, likely led them to abandon their ranchería in the mission's vicinity, and they carried the European diseases with them deeper into the forests. The Adaes Indians reportedly did not provide labor at Mission Adaes but were still struck by disease. Spanish soldiers and residents from Los Adaes likely assisted the Franciscans at the mission in exchange for religious services that Franciscans performed at the presidio's chapel. The Ais and Adaes Indian communities in turn perhaps consolidated with each other over time in response to declining numbers.

Meanwhile, internal administrative problems also affected evangelization efforts in the East Texas missions, including missionary college finances, lack of priests on the frontier, and illness. In 1727, six years after Mission Adaes was reestablished, Father Muñoz recorded 8 individuals in the administrative books, both adults and children, baptized en articulo mortis. He recorded a similar number of baptisms at Mission Ais, another 109 at Mission Nacogdoches, 115 at Mission Concepción de los Neches, 26 at Mission San Francisco de los Neches, and 20 at Mission San José de los Nasones.[34] The following year, Father Paredes noted that some adults were also baptized when they were in extreme need of this sacrament and near death but returned to their "barbarism" when the danger passed.[35] Epidemics occurred often—measles, smallpox, or even colds—which kept missionaries traveling on the roads for as much as three weeks from one ranchería to another administering to sick Indians.[36] Apparently, the Adaes and Ais visited the East Texas missions, received baptism, and returned to their communities after contact with the Spanish and possibly spread sickness and forced missionaries into venturing deeper in the Piney Woods.

The lack of Caddos residing within the missions made it theoretically impossible to incorporate independent Indians into the Hispanic community as occurred elsewhere in northern New Spain. For example, the Jesuit Pimería Alta in southern Arizona had eight missions with four thousand to five thousand resident Indians guarded by a presidio. Mission Tumacácori and Presidio Tubac, near present Tucson, Arizona, became one community with civilian settlers clustered around the presidio. Many of the Spanish settlers at Tucson were *padrinos* (godparents) of Indian children, relationships created from the sacramental rite of baptism.[37] At the San Antonio missions, Apache children as young as three years old were baptized with their godparents listed as soldiers and residents from the presidio at San Antonio. Adult Indians were also baptized in the San Antonio missions while their godparents derived from the presidio as well.[38] The same incorporation process applied at Mission Refugio de la Bahía, where Karankawa children were baptized with soldiers and residents from

Presidio La Bahía named as their godparents.[39] Likely more common are the documented baptisms of Apache captives, Caddos, and African slaves at Natchitoches through Catholic rituals where the Adaeseños became godparents and witnesses. The incorporation, if not the acculturation, of multiethnic peoples into French frontier society at Natchitoches remained strong throughout the eighteenth century, and a Creole cultural identity remains in the region today, just as Indians and *castas* (mixed-bloods) at the San Antonio Missions became culturally Hispanic or Tejano.

Incorporation into a Spanish orbit at Los Adaes proved more difficult, since Caddo Indians did not "congregate" at the East Texas missions—except perhaps for seasonal work—and were baptized only at or near death before returning to their rancherías if they recovered. The baptisms en articulo mortis established little more than a tentative link by comparison with the stronger commercial and religious ties between the Caddos and French at the Natchitoches post, where the latter had similar bonds with African slaves.[40] The Caddos who did engage the East Texas missions and Presidio Los Adaes likely did so voluntarily and traveled freely between Spanish and French settlements in search of trade or work. The Adaes and other small Caddo-related nations had not yet disappeared from the written records during the eighteenth century despite the onslaught of disease, dislocation, and possibly refugees from other frontiers. The Franciscans had fewer options for the congregation and conversion of Caddos but kept the East Texas missions functioning without a permanent source of Indian labor.

IV

Small-scale ranching also formed the basis of the local economy for Presidio Los Adaes. The combination of royal mercantilist policies, the governors' control over local commerce, and labor problems discouraged both the growth of an independent merchant class and the production of a cash crop such as tobacco like Natchitoches. While the tradition of slash-and-burn agriculture among the Caddos remained even when European tools and animals were introduced, ranching in East Texas became sustainable in the Piney Woods. Ranching required labor for felling trees; clearing pasturage; rounding up stranded, lost, or stolen livestock; and driving cattle to market. At the same time, small ranching—as opposed to large haciendas of northern New Spain, especially Coahuila—presented a more egalitarian form of social organization and required labor that women could be expected to perform should their husbands be sent far away for duty.[41] Ranches at the presidio and the missions became nodal points of contact with Caddos that familiarized the Adaeseños with preexisting Indian trails and granted them access to trade. The transportation of livestock and goods, not the plow, provided a more stable niche for the Adaeseños on the Texas-Louisiana borderlands.

Demographically, the Hispanic population at Los Adaes fluctuated during times of war, epidemic, and natural disaster. In 1721, the Adaeseños numbered around 210 residents, while French Natchitoches had just 52 (24 free whites, 20 African slaves, and 8 Indian slaves).[42] Los Adaes's initial figure included 100 troops, a third of whom brought spouses and had children, like Lieutenant Gonzalez and his wife, Gertrudis. The number of billets (quarters) was reduced to sixty in 1729 following General Rivera's inspection, which drew away from the overall population. French troop strength at Natchitoches, however, reached no greater than 45 soldiers, perhaps an indication of the reliance on the Caddos for protection on the frontier without the expense of additional resources.[43] By comparison, San Antonio's population had around 200 residents in the mid-1720s, including 54 troops and 4 civilians, but received a boost with the addition of fifteen families from the Canary Islands in 1731.[44] The slow population growth at Los Adaes without migration, mission Indians, and unfree laborers underscored difficult early development and a motive for cross-border relations.

The Caddos, on the other hand, maintained a considerably larger population than either the Spanish or the French. Around the year 1700, after permanent French occupation of the lower Mississippi valley commenced at Mobile, the Caddo population numbered approximately 8,500 to 10,000 people, a figure that is drastically less than the estimated 200,000 around 1500 prior to the DeSoto-Moscoso expedition of 1539–42 in the present southeastern United States, including East Texas. By the early 1700s, the three Caddo confederacies of the region each experienced downward population shifts: (1) the Hasinai (or Tejas) of East Texas had 5,000 people; (2) the Kadohadacho, located near the borders of present Arkansas, Texas, and Oklahoma, numbered 3,500 inhabitants; and (3) the Natchitoches of northwestern Louisiana, near the French post, comprised 2,000. The "urbanized" Caddo communities in the densely populated areas of the Arkansas, Ouachita, and Red River valleys particularly experienced great depopulation, while decline was more gradual among Caddo communities in the Neches, Angelina, and Sabine River valleys in East Texas.[45] Diseases and warfare contributed to the rapid decline of Indians everywhere and continued over the course of the eighteenth century.

The Adaes Indian community, located in the Caddo backcountry near the Sabine River between the Hasinai and Natchitoches confederacies, numbered roughly 400 people in the year 1721. Their population declined to 100 persons (or fourteen families) by the 1760s as disease evidently impacted them while others migrated into other nations. The Ais Indians, another remote community located farther west across the Sabine River from their Adaes cousins, increased slightly from 180 to 300 persons (or twenty families) over the same time frame, which suggests that some Adaes or other Indians might have contributed to the slight growth among Ais society. The neighboring Natchitoches Caddo declined in population from 450 men (perhaps a couple thousand if counting women and children) in 1721 to roughly 80 adult males over the same period after a portion of their nation merged with the Kadohadacho Confederacy.[46] Collectively, the Caddos outnumbered the residents of Los Adaes and French Natchitoches on the Texas-Louisiana frontier, which gave more reason for the Spanish to follow the example of their Bourbon cousins in local and regional trade with the Caddos rather than risk additional warfare in Texas, especially along the border with Louisiana.

In 1724, Governor Almazán reported to the viceroy about the need for trade at Los Adaes because of the lack of supplies and requested permission to send soldiers from there to San Antonio in order to help fight the Lipan Apaches. The governor also wanted Adaeseño troops in San Antonio to provide labor due to a shortage of mission Indian workers.[47] Presidio La Bahía likewise had its own Indian troubles with the Karankawa uprising that kept the Spanish governor from establishing a trade route to Los Adaes.[48] These other two presidios of Spanish Texas also suffered from a lack of supplies and struggled despite closer to sources of provisions in Saltillo than Los Adaes.[49] Close proximity to Louisiana proved more attractive for the Adaeseños than dangerous passage through Apachería. Perhaps the governor realized he could ill afford to stop the flow of trade with the French and maintained amicable relations with the Caddos, unlike Spanish-Indian relations in South Texas.

The weather and illness again made life more problematic as the lack of supplies at Los Adaes became so desperate that Spanish officials considered opening trade with French Natchitoches. Governor Almazán proposed to the viceroy that he allow "licit commerce" with the French because the soldiers and residents at Los Adaes were unable to grow sufficient amounts of food for basic survival two consecutive summers after its founding in 1721 due to illness and great difficulties in the transportation of goods, with "so many impassable rivers and creeks, which delayed the movement of 100 loads of wheat and a herd of cattle for seven months last year, the majority having died in transit, despite placing canoes in the swollen rivers." The governor included the dire warning that "until this presidio [Los Adaes] can achieve harvests, it appears more convenient not to close all points of communication with Natchitoches where missionaries took the initiative to administer the Holy Sacraments, and celebrated mass on feast days which the French greatly appreciate for lack of a religious minister."[50] The governors apparently did not mind such interactions in local trade and worship, hoping their superiors agreed.[51] These important intercultural exchanges of the 1720s established a pattern of commercial and kinship networks between Los Adaes and Natchitoches while bonds forged from interdependence increased contraband trade across the border.

The relative tranquility of the Texas-Louisiana frontier enabled soldiers and residents from Los Adaes to settle beyond the presidio's walls, since Caddos did not threaten Spanish families. Los Adaes had direct access to the French, who might act as intermediaries should conflict or misunderstandings arise between individuals or settlements, whereas this recourse to a third party was unavailable for Spanish-Apache relations at San Antonio.[52] With more assurances for their own safety, the Adaeseños cleared land, built log houses, raised livestock, planted corn, and tended gardens. Small ranchers relied on family labor for subsistence ranching and farming with less opportunity or need for Indian captives or servants. Single soldiers resided inside the fort at Los Adaes, while those who were married and raised children generally settled outside its palisade. Initially, the families of soldiers at Los Adaes would have selected the most suitable lands around the fort that did not belong to the missions, hoping to obtain Spanish title to the land.[53]

Hispanic women at Los Adaes, however, did not enjoy any more power or freedom than their counterparts elsewhere in New Spain. Spanish settlements such as Saltillo and Santa Fe were considerably older, larger, and more diverse with greater opportunities for the accumulation of wealth, lending or borrowing money, and managing dowries.[54] As noted earlier, Los Adaes residents starved to death on their own without help from neighbors, and husbands were often not paid their salaries or were away on duty, which made the labor of women vital to the ranching economy. Women tended to cattle, gardens, and children, in addition to cooking, sewing, and bartering with the Caddos in a "frontier exchange economy," as historian Daniel Usner describes for the lower Mississippi valley, defined as "more regional in scope, networks of cross-cultural interaction through which native and colonial groups circulated goods and services." This economic interaction entailed "small-scale production, face-to-face marketing, and prosaic features of livelihood" that allowed local communities to share in each other's worlds, and women played critical roles beyond the formal channels of power.[55] Susan Socolow notes that for rural Latin America, economic advantages and social prestige went to those fortunate enough to own large tracts of land (the haciendas) and control Indian labor on that land.[56] This was not the case for Texas—at least not yet—but especially not for Los Adaes, where poverty prevailed. Few, if any, Adaeseñas (Hispanic women at Los Adaes) other than the spouses of governors and high-ranking officers likely brought dowries into marriage or acquired much property. The women of Los Adaes evidently did not leave behind any wills during the fort's existence despite the fact that women did so in other frontier communities of northern New Spain and held certain rights under Spanish law.[57]

Women such as Gertrudis de la Cerda Gonzalez, however, noticed differences between the Los Adaes community and French Natchitoches from social interactions in church and trade at each other's posts. The French settlers at Natchitoches were given free tracts of land, around 170 acres, and almost every free white owned more than one slave, while local elites each possessed more than fifteen African slaves. The Adaeseños were more like tenants dependent on the Spanish governor to distribute seeds, farm equipment, weapons, gunpowder, and other basic goods like soap, sugar, and clothing. If they were fortunate, the Adaeseños supplied French Natchitoches with surplus meat in exchange for goods they lacked or were hired out to French merchants.[58] While the Spanish at San Antonio and La Bahía circled the wagons against Indian raids, the Adaeseños' worst fears were not hostile Indians but rather their own hunger, nakedness, and embarrassment vis-à-vis increasingly prosperous French neighbors.

Although ranching provided a more sustainable livelihood than farming, it did not prevent poverty. Like the provisions required from the governors for farming, the Adaeseños needed horses in order to perform multiple tasks besides ranching, such as escorting convoys, transporting goods, policing the border, and fighting Indians when they were assigned to other presidios. Soldiers had in their possession anywhere from one to eight horses (three to four on average).[59] While stored grain supplies often spoiled, smoked or cured meats were the preferred daily food, which residents supplemented with corn and possibly beans or tamales. In April 1731, Governor Bustillo arrived at Los Adaes from La Bahía with more than 90 loads of wheat, weapons, clothes, and other items, plus 200 horses, 250 cattle, and 500 head of sheep. At Los Adaes, the Spanish governor witnessed deteriorating watering holes and became anxious that only a few Adaeseños plowed the land.[60]

The arrival of French traders from Natchitoches at Los Adaes became a welcome relief, and such visits retroactively gained limited approval from Spanish officials, including lodging for visitors. French traders bartered vegetable products from Spanish soldiers in exchange for chocolate, sugar, and soap, while Governor Bustillo granted a license to one Frenchmen that permitted his passage through Spanish Texas for trade possibly as far as Saltillo.[61] By 1733, after occasional supplies from other parts of

Texas and Coahuila provided insufficient relief, the viceroy recognized the extreme hardships along the border with Louisiana and finally permitted Los Adaes to buy corn and beans from French Natchitoches, but nothing else.[62] This "legal" trade helped solidify cross-border ties and became a more dependable pattern of relief for the Adaeseños.

General Rivera's inspection of Los Adaes also revealed that Governor Almazán had inflated the prices of goods he sold to the soldiers. Almazán used troops on "illegal" assignments, mostly farming, which took away from "soldiering" on the border. Presidio Tejas, near Mission Nacogdoches, experienced similar problems as Los Adaes, but no charges were filed against the governor-captain. Instead, General Rivera imposed *tasas* (regulations) on the cost of goods and equipment that the governor distributed among the troops.[63] He also recommended the closure of Presidio Tejas while Los Adaes survived and ironically was named the capital of Texas despite its rather tenuous early existence. General Rivera's military inspection of presidios across northern New Spain indeed brought to light the dire circumstances of frontier soldier-settlers and their families, but he nevertheless prohibited French and Indian trade out of growing fear of smuggling.

According to archaeologist Timothy Perttula, the grain shipments between Los Adaes and Natchitoches indeed became "one of the covers used for contraband trading" among the Spanish, French, and Caddos.[64] A local market developed in Los Adaes, which attracted Indian and French traders. The convergence of multiethnic trade on the Texas-Louisiana frontier arose during the 1720s–30s from the misery of living conditions the Adaeseños confronted as well as commercial interests of the French Company of the Indies. The latter sent great quantities of goods in 1727 to the Natchitoches post and ordered Commandant St. Denis to "open" trade with Spanish Texas.[65] The company stores at Natchitoches and Los Adaes each served as the equivalent of a backcountry store or tavern of the Piedmont region in the British Carolinas, a distribution point for the movement of goods along the frontier. For the French, trade with Los Adaes marked the first step toward opening lines of communication and credit and ultimately obtaining direct access to the silver mining communities of New Spain.[66]

Ironically, Franciscans contributed to the development of trade shortly after the reestablishment of the East Texas missions and Los Adaes in 1721 through a secular role of administering to the French at Natchitoches just like Father Margil. Bérnard de la Harpe commented that a Father Manuel from Mission Adaes said mass at Natchitoches on March 1, 1719, just prior to the "Chicken War."[67] During Governor Almazán's rule (1722–27), the governor realized the Franciscans could spy on the intentions of the French in Louisiana while administering the sacraments in exchange for supplies as well as keeping an eye on Adaeseño behavior. In 1727, Fray Pedro Muñoz reported that Spanish missionaries from Mission Adaes continued celebrating mass and the sacraments among the soldiers at Los Adaes, service that was originally intended for mission Indians.[68] The Franciscans became de facto government agents in the secular realm on the Texas-Louisiana borderlands.

The failure of the East Texas missions to convert the Caddos into Christians must be weighed against the success Franciscans managed to have with bridging border communities from the beginning. Small-scale ranching at the missions and Presidio Los Adaes, trade, and worship became a foundation on which to strengthen bonds between the Spanish and their neighbors. Franciscans never discounted the possibility that changing circumstances or authorization to use the military might someday force the Caddos into seeking conversion at the missions and sacrificing their way of life. Nor did Spanish women, like Gertrudis, keep from planning the arranged marriages of daughters to suitable French partners even if their husbands or the state disagreed.

CHAPTER THREE

Bourbon Kinship

The marriage between Victoria Gonzalez and Jean Baptiste Derbanne in the spring of 1736 at French Natchitoches reinforced local and regional ties in much the same way that the union of Manuela Sanchez Navarro and St. Denis signaled the reestablishment of the Spanish presence in East Texas.[1] Lt. Joseph Gonzalez reportedly opposed this union with Victoria's French partner, with whom she allegedly eloped under the cover of darkness in the Piney Woods following mass at the chapel of Presidio Los Adaes.[2] The Gonzalez-Derbanne marriage marked the first of a dozen Spanish-Franco weddings at Natchitoches, together with many interethnic baptisms and burials, which emerged from commercial and religious barter that ensured the survival of Los Adaes.[3] While the governors expected their officers to keep watch over the border, they relied on missionaries for social control beyond the administration of the sacraments. Missionaries ventured outside mission walls into the French and Caddo communities. They accompanied the governors' troops on expeditions, trade, and social functions, but they were not permitted to interfere with the governors' rule, and they could only charge the scheduled fees for performing religious services.[4] Beneath the veneer of imperial competition between Spain and France for the allegiance of Caddo nations stood an emerging Franciscan-Jesuit contest for the loyalty of subjects at Los Adaes and Natchitoches to their respective crowns—at least until the Jesuits were expelled from all Spanish dominions in the New World. Bourbon kinship on the Texas-Louisiana borderlands crossed lines in ways that distant officials did not anticipate. Lieutenant Gonzalez;

his wife, Gerturdis; and their daughter Victoria seemingly became pawns in the king's forest as they sought their own opportunities for survival.

Much more surfaced during the mid-1730s, however, when Lt. Gen. don Fermín de Ybiricu, the second-highest ranking officer at Los Adaes, got into legal trouble for his questionable business dealings at Natchitoches, which involved Lieutenant Gonzalez's son-in-law, Jean Baptiste Derbanne. Ybiricu, who testified in the residencia of Governor Sandoval's tenure in power, declared that various French settlers at Natchitoches specifically requested *partidas* (certificates) from Spanish missionaries whose services remained to be paid by Governor Sandoval.[5] In effect, the Franciscan friars were more than missionaries for the Indians in East Texas; they became cultural brokers in the conquest of souls everywhere. While some missionaries, such as Eusebio Kino, the Jesuit priest in Arizona, and Junípero Sierra, a Franciscan in California, have been either celebrated or vilified, the friars of East Texas remain largely in their shadows.[6] The multifaceted roles of Franciscans in East Texas, who followed in the footsteps of Friars Francisco Hidalgo and Antonio Margil, need more scholarly attention, as researchers have done elsewhere in northern New Spain.[7] The Franciscans on the Texas-Louisiana borderlands kept watch over the Spanish and French flocks—as did their Jesuit counterparts—through church sacraments, lest the temptations of illicit commerce mixed with sex, alcohol, tobacco, and chocolate undermine the legitimacy of conquest in the eyes of God and king.

Significantly, Franciscans kept alive Spain's claim to East Texas at Los Adaes while being confronted with daunting challenges of legitimacy in addition to poverty and desertion. Historian Ann Twinam states that the three most important documents of a Spanish colonist's life were the birth certificate, the marriage certificate, and the will, which recorded for posterity the personal lives of previous generations and whether someone was "legitimate." Such accounting was crucial for preserving the honor of elite families in society. A great portion of this honor was racial and religious, which evolved with the concept of *limpieza de sangre* (purity of blood) from medieval Spain. This notion originated in response to the presence of Moors, Jews, and heretics on the Iberian Peninsula and was carried overseas to the Spanish colonies, where it excluded Indians, Africans, and Asians. But honor also was found in a family history of "proper action" that signified generations of legitimate births and sanctified marriages.[8] Mired in poverty and with little to no property, the Adaeseños looked to French Natchitoches for relief while some also likely sought more suitable marriage partners across the border, as many officials believed the Spanish troops were inferior with too many mixed-bloods. The sacraments became important instruments for community formation at Los Adaes especially in the absence of wills and relative wealth.[9] Franciscans signaled for mass through the church bell, just as they tried to attract Caddos, lest the flock get too dispersed in the wilderness.

Proper behavior from colonial subjects was paramount even on this remote frontier of northern New Spain, where a variety of means existed to check everyone. Masses, baptisms, marriages, and even burial services at Los Adaes and French Natchitoches brought everyone together for worship, song, and remembrance, including the governor-commandants (when they were not at San Antonio), soldiers, merchants, women, families, children, servants, and slaves. These religious occasions were followed with fiestas that provided opportunities for the Adaeseños to share in joyful celebrations amid the poverty of frontier life through interethnic relations with their Caddo, French, and African neighbors.

The Franciscans likely called the Adaeseño community together rather frequently through worship at the chapel in celebration of the sacraments and on special feast days. As historian Father Charles O'Neil explains about regular mass in Louisiana, it was "part of the ordinary rhythm of life."[10] The same applied to Los Adaes, where the goal of maintaining a "Spanish" community became increasingly confounded with the French, Caddo, and African presence on the frontier. Although the regulation against illicit sex and commerce in the Piney Woods of Texas and Louisiana was virtually impossible to enforce, the Franciscans helped the Spanish crown legitimize its claim to East Texas with a settlement of "Spanish" subjects and social control through the sacraments. Ultimately, the loyalty of the Adaeseños mattered most to Spanish officials, not just their race or caste, whereas officers and their spouses begged to differ concerning their own standing vis-à-vis French Creole society across the border and particularly when visitors attended mass at the chapel of Los Adaes.

Interestingly, Lieutenant Gonzalez insinuated that the Jesuit priest at Natchitoches was a troublemaker. Gonzalez informed Governor Sandoval that this Jesuit was "the author and principal motivator of all inquietude," as the Jesuit wanted the father president from Mission Los Adaes to interpose his authority and ask Gonzalez's permission for his daughter to be married in Derbanne's name. But the Franciscan president disagreed with this marriage because "of the inequality of the newlyweds" and the absence of the governor.[11] Gonzalez added that the Jesuit priest from Natchitoches convinced Derbanne to come to his home and personally request permission for his daughter's hand in marriage. But Gonzalez told Governor Sandoval that he also declined because of the governor's absence from Los Adaes and that even if Derbanne was a "gentleman and the highest French nobility, I would refuse to have my blood mix with his." After Sunday mass on April 8, Lieutenant Gonzalez wrote that while conversing with Fray Ignacio Laba in the friar's home, the Frenchmen committed their thievery and took his daughter across the lake in a canoe. They arrived at Natchitoches by midnight and were immediately wed by the Jesuit priest. Gonzalez believed that the foster brother of his wife (Gertrudis) with the same surname (de la Cerda) acted as a liaison for Jean Baptiste and Victoria, as proved by de la Cerda's own desertion from Los Adaes. Gonzalez also claimed that another Adaeseño, Juan de Mora, was responsible for their escape, for which he was imprisoned to await the governor's arrival for sentencing. Gonzalez remained noticeably angry over the stealth departure and even claimed to disown his daughter.[12] More than likely, however, the marriage of Lieutenant Gonzalez's daughter had been prearranged with or without his consent through his wife, who was working behind the scenes to broker such kinship. The role of Gertrudis speaks to the informal power historian Amy Porter ascribes to women on the borderlands and the subversion of patriarchy. Lieutenant Gonzalez likely protected his own personal honor as the interim commandant as well as his family from possible prosecution for desertion through his letters to Governor Sandoval about the state of affairs at Los Adaes in 1736.

The institution of marriage provided a semblance of control and order to Spanish colonial society amid many political, economic, and social challenges in New Spain. Building on the laws of the *Siete Partidas* (Seven Books) from late medieval Spain, which placed great weight on betrothal or mutual consent and made matrimony a public contract, the Roman Catholic Church through the Council of Trent in 1563 definitively established marriage as a ritual by requiring witnesses to attend the ceremony and the celebration by a priest. Because illegitimacy was pervasive in colonial cities during the seventeenth and eighteenth centuries, baptismal and matrimonial records used euphemisms, while canon law offered legitimization for those couples engaged in sinful behavior so as to protect a family's honor. By the eighteenth century, the church began favoring greater parental say in the marriage of their children to help ensure the preservation of social status and the general hierarchy of society through marriage between equals. Historian Patricia Seed explains that the demands for equality of marriage partners emerged by the 1740s and that interracial marriage in colonial Mexico became interwoven into a broader crisis of the aristocracy over status.[13]

At the Texas-Louisiana border, however, Lieutenant Gonzalez could not ignore the importance of French trade for the survival of the fort despite his apparent embarrassment that his daughter "eloped" under his watch at Presidio Los Adaes. The fact that his grandchild later served under him at Los Adaes and that the Adaeseños continued to rely on commerce across the border suggests that the lieutenant might have overcome his initial misgivings. Los Adaes's dependence on French Natchitoches belied the balancing act that local officials maintained between obeying higher commands and navigating the hardships of life on the frontier with the infamous *obedezco pero no cumplo* (I obey but do not comply) doctrine in New Spain. The Derbanne-Gonzalez marriage controversy holds intriguing comparisons with the fictive example of Shakespeare's Romeo and Juliet and lesser-known real marriage controversies from Mexico City centered on conflicts between young couples and their families. While the Derbanne-Gonzalez families were from "border towns" separated by

Spanish and French imperial jealousy, in all cases, people sympathetic to the couples acted as intermediaries, with a Catholic priest willing to marry the couples without the knowledge of at least one of the parents. In Victoria Gonzalez's case, there was no murder or tragedy but rather a happy outcome even though she likely drove her father's anxiety higher than it needed to be guarding the border as interim commandant at Los Adaes.[14]

Equally intriguing, Lieutenant Gonzalez avoided informing the governor that another wedding occurred at Natchitoches between a young Spanish daughter from Los Adaes and a Frenchman from a wealthy family just three months following his own daughter's marriage. In July 1736, Juana Victoria García, the thirteen-year-old daughter of soldier Pedro García and Marie Joseph Condee, married a French soldier named Francois LeMoine, aged forty, whose father was another founding member of the Natchitoches post along with St. Denis and François Derbanne. The LeMoines were the most prominent family of French Louisiana. St. Denis originally arrived in Louisiana from Canada in January 1700 with Pierre LeMoyne de Iberville, whose brother, Jean Baptiste LeMoyne de Bienville, became the governor of Louisiana in 1716. Unlike Lieutenant Gonzalez's daughter, this other Spanish maiden already lived at French Natchitoches for two years prior to her marriage. Juana was two years younger than Victoria Gonzalez and mostly likely under an arranged marriage due to the vastly greater age difference between bride and groom. Juana and François LeMoine were wed "after publication of bans" in the event that anyone objected to their marriage.[15]

Ironically, Juana García's father was a rancher in the Los Adaes vicinity and not of equal social status with the prominent LeMoine family. The two "lovers" also eloped supposedly, but at some point, a procession traveled from Natchitoches to celebrate mass at Mission Los Adaes.[16] An elopement was possible if a mass similar to the one described in the Derbanne-Gonzalez case was celebrated and the couple later fled into the woods for Natchitoches. The age difference, however, likely raised more eyebrows in objection, since François LeMoine was three times Juana's age. The question arises, What advantage could have accrued to each side from such a union? Such marriages reinforced an emerging Spanish-Franco trade network that developed across the border, linking a ranching economy from Los Adaes with a plantation system in Louisiana much like herding ecologies and slave systems on other borderlands in the Atlantic world.[17]

Additional issues are raised by the role marriage played in Spanish-Franco relations. What was Juana García doing for two years at French Natchitoches before her wedding? Was she a servant within LeMoine's household? Was she an Indian, maybe an Apache captive, from Los Adaes? Did her father, Pedro García, desert to Natchitoches? If so, his whereabouts went unrecorded. Did he already have commercial relations with the LeMoine family and they wanted more livestock? What role, if any, did Lieutenant Gonzalez play as the interim commandant at Presidio Los Adaes? Gonzalez described his own actions to Governor Sandoval as having dutifully guarded against French encroachment, but he might have allowed for the Adaeseños to spread out farther from Los Adaes to begin their own *ranchitos* (small ranch). Regardless of how the events unfolded, Spanish girls from Los Adaes married into French Creole families around the age of fifteen, while the French grooms were considerably older than their brides. More than anything, Juana García's prearranged marriage likely served the same ends as did Manuela Sanchez Navarro de St. Denis's and Victoria Gonzalez Derbanne's.

French merchants used such marriages to strengthen commercial ties with the Adaeseños, who in turn took advantage of opportunities to relieve their own poverty by participating in markets beyond the control of the Spanish governor. In particular, the Prudhomme family of the Natchitoches post aligned their interests with the Flores and Ybarbo families from Los Adaes, while the Derbannes partnered with the Chirino and Mora families.[18] Spanish-Franco weddings, though relatively few overall, in combination with the celebration of mass and baptisms, drew both border communities into greater Atlantic trade and social networks, as the French did with the Caddos. The late historian James McCorkle noted that events like the Derbanne-Gonzalez marriage suggest the extent "to which even barriers of nationality succumbed to the potency of frontier romance."[19] Regardless of whether it was romance or arranged, certainly marriage as a historical contingency played a mediating role on the Texas-Louisiana frontier.

Other weddings at the French Natchitoches post that involved Adae-seños also might have created tensions yet reveal intimacy across the border with the Spanish fort and mission of Los Adaes that was not so readily available in northern New Spain. In July 1737, after the publication of three bans at both Natchitoches and Los Adaes, Francisco de Torres, a twenty-five-year-old Spanish soldier from Los Adaes, married Señorita Flores, the seventeen-year-old widow of Joseph de Alvarado who resided at Natchitoches. Francisco's parents migrated from the province of Nuevo León in northern New Spain, while the bride's parents came from San Luís de Potosí farther south in Mexico. Her godfather was none other than Lt. Pedro de Sierra from Los Adaes.[20] In 1738, after the publication of bans at Natchitoches and Mission Los Adaes, Antonio Rodríguez, a mulatto, married Marie Marcelle, an Indian slave of a Frenchwoman named Lucretia. The witnesses included Derbanne, [Jacques?] de la Chaise, and two other Frenchmen.[21] Why were notices given at Mission Los Adaes in advance of this wedding? Was Antonio a servant, runaway slave, or deserter from Presidio Los Adaes? Interestingly, Brother Juan Gregorio de la Campa, from Mission Adaes, had served as a witness for the marriage of a Frenchman named Jacob de la Chaise with a daughter of St. Denis in 1733, which Father Francisco Vallejo recorded in Latin at Mission Los Adaes in 1744, the same year St. Denis passed away.[22] More questions are raised about the interaction

Figure 3.1: Ancestors of historian Dan L. Flores, ca. late 1800s, whose family was from Los Adaes and Natchitoches. Source: Dan L. Flores, with permission.

of residents at Mission Adaes with the Caddos and French. A number of folks from different walks of life have shared some of their family photos including historian Dan Flores. It appears that more happenings occurred than historians may ever actually realize (see figures 3.1 and 3.2).

Figure 3.2: Ancestors of Louisiana resident Juan Castille, ca. late 1800s, from the Ramos and Rodrigues families at Los Adaes and Natchitoches. Source: Juan Castille, with permission.

The location of the Adaeseño community on the Texas-Louisiana border-lands with sparsely settled ranches clustered loosely around Presidio Los Adaes and Mission Los Adaes near Caddo and French neighbors disrupted political, economic, and social boundaries. The Spanish governors and missionaries exerted as much control as possible over every aspect of frontier life from baptism to burial practices, including racial and ethnic designations, to maintain a patriarchal and hierarchal Spanish society in the wilderness. The Adaeseños married for the most part within their own class, defined predominantly by such factors as illiteracy, few material possessions, and poor housing and labeled with a Spanish, mestizo (mixed Spanish-Indian), mulatto (mixed Spanish-African), or other racial/ethnic designations in the *sistema de castas* (caste system) of New Spain. While some Adaeseños already held the *español* (Spanish) label upon their arrival at Los Adaes, especially the officers, others attained this highest category, which also signified whiteness. A few also earned the distinction of *don* (title of respect) as a prefix to their names, which denoted nobility, but this was normally reserved for the governor, officers, and a few other literate residents. Although Presidio Los Adaes began with a three-to-one ratio of single to married soldiers and remained a majority-male population, local Spanish society stabilized as more families settled with children, who in turn eventually married if they survived past childhood. The Adaeseño community experienced further migration over time from New Spain, which created greater demand for ranches as well as trade in the region beyond the immediate environs of the fort and mission.

According to Patricia Seed, Spanish colonial society that followed the conquest of Tenochtitlán broadly consisted of Spaniards, Indians, and Africans, which resembled the division of Spain into nobles, plebeians, and slaves. As Spanish colonization continued northward from Mexico City, the *mestizaje* (intermixture) of all three major groups increased over the course of two centuries, plus Asians who arrived via the Spanish port of Manila, Philippines, largely as slaves or servants. All these movements resulted in racially and ethnically mixed subjects whom Spanish officials designated in the caste system to distinguish them as intermediate groups between Spaniards and Indians. Interracial sexual unions, Seed says, occurred "only occasionally in marriage and largely outside it," but this was due more to social prejudice than laws that prohibited intermarriage. By the late seventeenth century, the mixed population of New Spain had grown significantly such that the state increasingly recognized the legitimate participation of castas in marriage. By the mid-eighteenth century, mestizos and mulattos formed the majority of Hispanic society throughout New Spain as part of the *república de españoles* (Republic of Spaniards), which included Africans, under governance of the king, while a segregated *república de indios* (Republic of Indians) referred to Indians ruled under the Crown but governed by their own *caciques* (chiefs).[23] The Adaeseños generally reflected the same racial/ethnic characteristics as other Hispanic communities in northern New Spain, with some Indian and African residents.

The caste labels symbolized social inequality and fluidity on the frontier rather than a literal definition, such as white-black ancestry for the term *mulatto*. Historian Cheryl Martin explains that for colonial Chihuahua—a mining town in northern New Spain located about three hundred miles due south of present El Paso, Texas, where few Spaniards of titled nobility traveled—*mulatto* referred to a combination of European, African, and Indian, not just white and black. The caste label *coyote* was also used derogatorily for a person of black-Indian, mulatto-Indian, or even mestizo-Indian background, though the modern-day meaning refers to a smuggler along the present US-Mexico border. According to Martin, race provided a "convenient initial screening device" to determine who merited local elite status. The classification of racial origins for anyone of mixed ancestry was left to the whims of state and church authorities. Mexico City officials were more concerned about distinguishing between Spaniards and non-Spaniards from among so many "barbarous" Indians, while caste labels created further separation in the minds of Spanish authorities. A person's *calidad* (character) could also include a particular caste label that specified a person's rank or place in colonial Spanish society. Calidad along with caste emerged from the legal distinctions among Spaniards, Indians, and Africans that dated from the sixteenth century. These notions carried over from the centuries' old Reconquest of Spain from the Moors; those who proved their Christian faith and valor on the battlefield achieved noble status and claimed bloodlines that were untainted by the Muslim and Jewish presence in Spain. Those who fought for the Christian king and queen of Spain but lacked formal titles of nobility could earn the coveted distinctions of purity of blood and hidalgo status. In northern New Spain, a person could alter one's calidad through such characteristics as birthplace, wealth, occupation, acculturation, legitimacy, and proper behavior.[24] Sacrifices in frontier warfare against the Apaches and Comanches, for example, brought ultimate honor to oneself and one's family with an even greater likelihood of changing one's classification to Spanish—if not having *don* affixed to one's name.

The Adaeseño soldiers acquired the honor of being called "Spanish" more often than having *don* placed before their names despite lacking certificates proving the purity of blood in the family or hidalgo status from Spain. Obtaining these distinctions through war, however, was more problematic for the Adaeseños unless they also served at the presidios of San Antonio, San Sabá, or La Bahía, where Spanish troops waged intermittent warfare against the Apaches, Comanches, Norteños, and Karankawas. The Caddo Nation on the Texas-Louisiana borderlands was more interested in trade than raiding Spanish settlements, though some allied with Indians from the Southern Plains. Meanwhile, the attainment of wealth at Los Adaes through commerce with the French and Caddos or through marriage into prominent French families at Natchitoches became increasingly attractive as alternatives to war for attaining higher status in Spanish society. Fluidity of race and ethnicity existed, but movement into a higher class was limited at Los Adaes. Becoming a wealthy merchant or slave owner proved beyond the means of virtually all the Adaeseños, while exhibiting valor and exalting one's status also remained difficult to achieve in military service at Los Adaes on the relatively tranquil Texas-Louisiana borderlands.

The hierarchy of the Adaeseño community appeared roughly diamond shaped with little social mobility. The governor and a handful of officers remained at the top, while rank-and-file troops and other residents became ranchers and farmers who composed a broad middle group. This category also included muleteers, foremen, and ranch hands on lands that belonged to the governor, missionaries, and Adaeseño officers. There were no artisans at Los Adaes that developed like at Santa Fe or even San Antonio to a lesser degree. Many women at Los Adaes (*Adaeseñas*), like frontier women elsewhere in New Spain, traditionally worked as seamstresses, cooks, washerwomen, and *curanderas* (folk healers), or they peddled trinkets while they were also expected to become mothers, raise children, and tend to the elderly, infirm, and family gardens. As mentioned previously, however, women often supervised the ranch when their husbands, fathers, uncles, and sons were absent. Widows usually remarried after a relatively brief period of bereavement. Evidently, at the bottom of Adaeseño society lived a much smaller number of Apache captives and African slaves, while men and women from various castes also filled the ranks of domestic servants mainly under the governor and his officers or missionaries.[25]

Few Adaeseños actually entered the governor's inner circle, which was reserved naturally for the officers with whom he placed his trust on the border. Only a handful married into wealthy families at French Natchitoches. Unlike the two extremes of society, the occupations of the middle group were not exclusively defined by specific racial or ethnic categories. Although a person's calidad was arbitrarily designated, Adaeseño society remained rather rigidly divided into Spaniards, mixed-bloods, Indian servants, and *negro* (black) or mulatto slaves.[26] Whether one passed as "Spaniard" within his or her community, those Adaeseños who claimed legitimacy at birth behaved properly, attended church, and remained loyal to the Spanish crown could still earn individual or family honor.[27] Social mobility at Los Adaes, like calidad, depended greatly on the whims of Spanish governors and their officers or possibly the missionaries, who had a monopoly on trade.

The growth of the Adaeseño border community was not dependent on Spanish-Caddo marital unions. Spanish officials and Franciscans had learned that wives and families best accompany Spanish soldiers in order to live peaceably among the Caddos. The governors at Los Adaes became more interested in illicit trade than congregating Caddos into Spanish missions and could not always prevent casual relations or sex among

Adaeseños and their neighbors.[28] Although Los Adaes remained a closed society under the watchful eyes of subordinates like Lieutenant Gonzalez or the friars, the Adaeseños in reality welcomed visitors, especially independent Caddo and French traders. Despite the lack of sacramental records from the chapel at Los Adaes, which have virtually disappeared from the archives, the possibility remains that some Adaeseños might have taken up residence with Caddo women as concubines or mistresses.

By contrast, marriage patterns for French Natchitoches did not preclude illicit unions with the Spanish, Caddos, or Africans. French Creole society incorporated the Caddos more than their Spanish counterparts likely could have done under the watch of Franciscan missionaries. The French and Caddos strategically sought linkages with each other as military allies and economic trade partners based on both real and fictive kinship. Intermarriage was commonly practiced among people from the French posts and Caddo settlements to solidify political alliances. French Natchitoches initially lacked female colonists, which made the settlers more dependent on outsiders for reproduction, whether through marriage with the Caddos and then Spaniards or through sexual unions with Apache captives and African slaves. Having Caddo wives and concubines also gave Frenchmen access to the Indian trade and gift giving beyond formal diplomacy among nations.[29]

Governor Cadillac of Louisiana from the beginning felt that marriage between Frenchmen and Indian women was an effective means of assimilating natives into a French-oriented society, creating a bond of fidelity between them. When the French superior council of Louisiana outlawed such interethnic marriages in 1728, priests ignored the prohibition, believing, as one official reported to Versailles, that "there was no difference between a Christian Indian and a white person."[30] Although Spanish-Franco marriages were fewer than Franco-Indian unions, the former involved elite French families at Natchitoches that drew the Adaeseños, intentionally or not, into the military, economic, and cultural orbit with the Caddos and Africans. The French acted as cultural brokers just like Franciscans and Jesuits did for Spaniards, Caddos, and Africans through fictive kinship as godparents based on baptism and as witnesses to other sacramental rites. This extensive kinship and religious network, combined with economic opportunities, made Creolization, as historians F. Todd Smith and H. Sophie Burton argue, the dominant pattern among the free people of Natchitoches on the frontier based on French norms.[31]

Elites controlled both Spanish-Franco border communities under different political structures. Mexico City officials appointed the Spanish governors in Texas, who arrived for duty largely as outsiders and not part of local elite families like the French commandants at Natchitoches. The Spanish governor-commandants exerted power as *caudillos* (regional strongmen) atop the Adaeseño community. The few officers among the Adaeseños—for example, Lt. Joseph Gonzalez and Lt. Pedro de Sierra—became local elites who managed the presidio in the absence of the governor, yet they and their fellow Adaeseños fell under the absolute rule, if not tyranny, of governors. Commandants at French Natchitoches, on the other hand, tended to share power and influence among family clans at the top of society. St. Denis ensured his leadership and increased his power and influence through extensive commercial and kinship networks. Local Adaeseño elites came from the officer ranks but certainly could not expect to become governors or generals someday regardless of kinship and trade attained with the French.

Cross-cultural marriages also raised friction, distrust, and unrest within the Adaeseño community, exemplified best by the Spanish-Franco marriage in 1754 at the Natchitoches post between Manuel Antonio de Soto Bermúdez and Marie des Nieges de St. Denis, a daughter of St. Denis and Manuela Sanchez Navarro.[32] Manuel de Soto was a Spaniard from the coastal province of Galicia in northwestern Spain who immigrated to Mexico in search of his father but discovered "love" and fortune along the way. He might have been at French Natchitoches before his marriage, but he was definitely engaged in business transactions there by 1755, when a rather boisterous Adaeseño soldier, named Andrés Chirino, became indebted to de Soto. Manuel de Soto's knowledge of Caddo-French trade networks, which he acquired as a secretary under former Gov. Pedro del Barrio, combined with his connections to the Adaeseños, made him valuable to St. Denis's family interests. Gov. Jacinto de Barrios y Jáuregui had labeled de Soto a deserter from Los Adaes after he allegedly encouraged the Adaeseños to rebel against the governor's rule. Mexico City officials also wanted to question de Soto, whose marriage conjured up fears that the French intended to conquer northern New Spain through trade, as St. Denis had threatened long before.

The greatest issue perhaps was whether Manuel de Soto's marriage to a Frenchwoman affected his loyalty to Spain. His emergent power and recognition of growing discontent among the Adaeseños made him public enemy number one for Governor Barrios. De Soto likely preferred fewer trade restrictions and better government at Los Adaes. Maybe he wished to be like St. Denis, who provided the Adaeseños with a different role model than the infamous Spanish conquistadors. Did de Soto's fallout with the governor and his desertion indicate greater freedom of movement at French Natchitoches than Los Adaes? Manuel de Soto evidently stayed at Natchitoches longer than the Spanish governor allowed. In May 1754, Commandant César de Blanc granted a license to de Soto so he could cross the border from Los Adaes to Natchitoches and marry St. Denis's daughter. Governor Barrios subsequently tried him for desertion along with Andrés Chirino and two other Adaeseños with the surnames Losoya and Esparza.[33] De Soto availed himself of opportunities at Natchitoches that were unavailable at Los Adaes and perhaps wanted to follow in the footsteps of wealthy French merchants-slaveholders and possibly undermine the governor's rule from Los Adaes.

Apparently, Manuel de Soto led other Adaeseños into desertion from Los Adaes to French Natchitoches, including the aforementioned Chirino, Losoya, and Esparza. De Soto was considered the principal actor behind unrest at Los Adaes, having obtained the signatures of residents on a petition against Governor Barrios, though supposedly they did not know what they had signed. The Marqués de Aranda and Domingo Valcarel, each advisors to the viceroy in Mexico City, suggested that the governor should deter the other Adaeseño residents from signing such petitions, and the government concurred on February 21, 1756.[34] The viceroy, Marqués de Amarillas, did not waste any time before writing Governor Barrios. He ordered the governor "to capture said Soto and transfer him to the prison in Mexico City, and severely admonish Chirinos and Esparza to abstain from creating unrest among the residents [of Los Adaes] . . . forewarning all these citizens not to be induced into such occurrences."[35] Spanish officials were concerned about rebellion within the king's dominions, including the Texas-Louisiana borderlands, so close to the French and so far from Mexico City. De Soto somehow eluded Spanish authorities, and over the course of a decade, he and his wife, Marie St. Denis, raised their five children and extended their family network in Natchitoches.

In 1763, de Soto appeared before Gov. Angel de Martos y Navarrete, successor to Barrios Jáuregui, after he learned of a royal clemency and pardon for Spanish deserters published at Los Adaes on February 28, 1763. In his petition to the governor the following month, de Soto humbly asked for reinstatement to his post "in the ignorance of having become delinquent."[36] Governor Martos Navarrete responded, "He cannot act upon this because [de Soto] made his home in a foreign kingdom, and because of the pending case against his predecessor, Barrios Jauregui."[37] The heart of the controversy was not simply de Soto's marriage to St. Denis's daughter but de Soto's conflict with former governor Barrios Jáuregui over the monopoly on trade with the Caddos. Marcos Losoya, an Adaeseño resident—presumably the same Losoya who was in league with de Soto, Chirino, and Esparza—testified before Governor Martos Navarrete about how after a dispute over some cattle, the residents of Los Adaes became "upset that don Jacinto [Barrios Jáuregui] prevented them from travel for commerce with the Indians because he wanted the gifts of hides and other bartered goods from the Indians only for himself, and they [Adaeseños] were presented a petition, which said don Manuel [de Soto] induced them to sign without them having read it until hearing it now."[38] Spanish officials relented and granted de Soto's request for restitution to Texas.[39] His desertion for marriage implied an aspiration for greater economic opportunities that were unavailable at Los Adaes under autocratic rule and Spanish mercantilism.

A few other Spanish marriages celebrated at Natchitoches also brought borderland communities together for better or for worse. In April 1755, less than a year after de Soto's wedding, Antonio Gil Ybarbo's own brother, Manuel, married Manuella Seyena from Los Adaes, and de Soto happened to be a witness for this wedding.[40] Whether Manuel Ybarbo's appearance in Natchitoches had Governor Barrios Jáuregui's blessing remains uncertain, but de Soto's attendance raised doubts and further questions. The Ybarbo brothers, like de Soto, took advantage of business opportunities at Natchitoches, but whether they engaged in business without the governor's knowledge remains unknown, though possible. Previously, in 1750, as an assistant to former governor del Barrio, de Soto served as a witness in Commandant de Blanc's marriage at Natchitoches to another daughter of St. Denis and Manuela, while a French officer and a Father Eustache, likely a Jesuit, served as witnesses for the bride. Father Pedro de Ramírez de Arellano from Mission Los Adaes officiated.[41] Many border crossings occurred—whether legal or not—as people celebrated Catholic rituals, and trade multiplied.

Social control could also be achieved with the avoidance of illegitimacy through the sacrament of marriage, but scandalous behavior outside formal channels potentially threatened Spanish rule. The most notorious controversy involved (once again) Lt. Gen. Fermín de Ybiricu, who was the highest-ranking officer at Presidio Los Adaes while Governor Sandoval resided at San Antonio. Ybiricu not only conducted the governor's business at the Natchitoches post; he had earned a reputation for undue intimacy with the French and was later charged with keeping Frenchwomen at Los Adaes. The sources do not explicitly state whether prostitution occurred, but Ybiricu's indiscretions likely added to the anxiety Lt. Joseph Gonzalez felt while in temporary command at Presidio Los Adaes during the mid-1730s.[42]

Throughout colonial Mexico and Latin America, both the state and church held overlapping concerns about the need to preserve social order. The state focused primarily on the legal issues surrounding sexual behavior and the institution of marriage, especially the legitimacy of the marital union for the purpose of inheritance and the division of benefits among spouses and children. The church's goal was to establish a sacramental bond between the material and spiritual that geared all actions, including sexuality, toward the salvation of the soul. According to historian Asunción Lavrin, the reality of Spanish conquest in the Americas and the lax sexual mores of the conquerors over time forced the church "to bend and accommodate its theoretical norms to the social reality." This meant that there was a high degree of social tolerance, Lavrin says, for the "incidence of consensual unions, the numerous illegitimate children, and the variety of ethnic mixtures."[43] The Adaeseño community was not immune from infidelity or racial/ethnic mixing on the Texas-Louisiana borderlands. Illicit sexual unions invariably emerged from commercial and social interaction that the governors and Franciscan missionaries sought to control during celebrations of mass, the sacraments, and fiestas.

Historian Patricia Seed states that during the eighteenth century, romance and sexual desire became dangerous passions that needed to be "controlled, disciplined, and subjected to other more rational forces." The state and church recognized that there was a greater respect for the motive of self-interest in the form of self-aggrandizement and gain. This recognition was directly related to the increasing involvement of New Spain's merchants, miners, and bureaucrats in a world market that awakened attitudes toward money and interest that were new to Hispanic culture. Spanish writers of the eighteenth century increasingly challenged the traditional prejudice against commerce. Such worthy praises of profit, however, did not sit well among the clergy, who still viewed trade, greed, avarice, and covetousness as moral offenses related to sex.[44] For the Franciscan friars on the Texas-Louisiana borderlands, the need to control the sexual behavior of inhabitants and a dislike for the Spanish governors' avarice, including his officers, had to be reconciled with French and Caddo commerce, which remained vital to the survival of the missions and provided relief for the Adaeseños.

The subjection of sexual desires and regulation of marriage partners at Los Adaes and Natchitoches also reflected the increasing influence of contraband trade. Over the course of the eighteenth century, many Spanish subjects in New Spain had direct experience with the new economic reality of the world market. British exporters based in Florida, Louisiana, and the Caribbean sold goods to Spanish merchants, which Seed argues was done through "an elaborate but stable contraband network." The mercantilist renaissance expanded through the Bourbon Reforms and a closer association with the world market, but the former was based on the social organization and values of families in the New World. Honor as status had become increasingly more important than honor as virtue, meaning that it was harder to cross social and economic barriers.[45] The same did not apply evenly to marriage patterns on the Texas-Louisiana borderlands, where elite status coalesced around the interests of wealthy French families and Spanish governors. Although the majority of impoverished Adaeseños did not have this opportunity of intercultural marriage at Natchitoches and instead were restricted mostly to partners within their own community or migrants from New Spain, the possibility arose of illegitimately marrying with independent Caddos in search of trade and survival.

III

The symbolic act of baptism into the Christian faith proved to be another important religious sacrament with political and economic significance along the Texas-Louisiana border. Lt. Joseph Gonzalez, who testified in the Spanish government's attempt to determine the boundary between Texas and Louisiana, declared that the Red River divided Louisiana from Texas even though the French already had three small houses on the river's west bank when Presidio Los Adaes was established in 1721. Gonzalez added that around the year 1729, Friar Francisco Vallejo, president of the East Texas missions, left for French Natchitoches at the urgent plea of its commandant, St. Denis, to baptize his child. The local French priest initially gave permission for the Franciscan to perform the sacrament and then changed his mind for no apparent reason. His refusal angered St. Denis, who then asked Father Vallejo to cross the river with him so the child could be baptized on lands belonging to the Catholic king of Spain. According to Lieutenant Gonzalez, however, the baptism did not actually take place.[46] Nonetheless, Mexico City officials viewed this baptismal controversy as an attempt on the part of the French to encroach upon Spanish Texas.[47] Evidently, baptism on one side of the border or the other mattered a great deal, as it helped determine the king's sovereignty over his subjects.

Meanwhile, Spanish officials appeared less concerned that Franciscan missionaries performed baptisms at French Natchitoches and served as witnesses to them. Perhaps they condoned Franciscans who brokered such religious occasions to obtain food and supplies from the French in collaboration with Spanish officers from Los Adaes. The first known recorded baptism at Natchitoches officiated by a missionary from Los Adaes occurred in 1730 for a French child. Franciscan friars performed or witnessed a total of thirty-two baptisms at the Natchitoches post until 1765. Additional baptisms occurred at Natchitoches of children from Spanish-Franco unions where Adaeseños became godparents or served as witnesses for French residents.[48]

Entry into elite circles at French Natchitoches came through kinship for some Adaeseños, which provided an avenue out of poverty at Los Adaes, especially after desertion. Although each began under difficult circumstances, Natchitoches grew wealthier than Los Adaes through free trade and an increasingly African slave–based system of plantation agriculture, primarily tobacco and indigo. A year after marrying the French soldier Jean Baptiste Derbanne in Natchitoches, Victoria Gonzalez became godmother to a French girl for her new sister-in-law, Jeanne Derbanne. In June 1744, Victoria also became godmother to a black child, named Louis Francois, son of Nanette, who was a slave of the widowed Manuela Sánchez Navarro after St. Denis passed away earlier that year.[49] A few years after marrying a Frenchman in 1736, as Victoria Gonzalez did, Jeanne Victoria García, originally from Presidio Los Adaes, baptized her infant son at Natchitoches with French residents named as godparents. Jeanne García also had two daughters baptized in subsequent years.[50] For Lt. Joseph Gonzalez, the Spanish governors, and Adaeseños who became connected with French families and other residents from Natchitoches, children became potential assets through marriage if not servitude.

The St. Denis, Derbanne, and LeMoine families set a precedent for French settlers at Natchitoches as godparents not only to Adaeseños but also to Indians and Africans, drawing multiethnic communities together into a larger kinship network. Such fictive relationships fostered political and commercial relationships at the top of French society while securing a tighter grasp on Indian and African slaves at the bottom. Elite French families literally became godparents of the Texas-Louisiana borderlands through the sheer number of recorded baptisms at Natchitoches. In May 1729, the year of the earliest recorded baptisms, a baby with the name of Louis Pierre was described as a *négrillon* (black child) and the property of Commandant Louis de St. Denis. Jeanne Derbanne and Pierre Duplessis were named the child's godparents. In July of that year, a child named Marie, baptized two days after birth and the daughter of African parents, was also the slave of Commandant St. Denis. Another slave child named Marguerite, born in May 1729 to black parents, was baptized with the sister of St. Denis shown as her godmother. Interestingly, the godfathers for both of these slave children were listed as members of the bourgeois class in Natchitoches, as was Jeanne Derbanne, the daughter of François Derbanne. Derbanne's paternal grandfather helped colonize Canada, having arrived there with St. Denis's ancestors, and both likely continued French customs of interethnic kinship ties in addition to commercial ones. French merchants, in turn, became slaveholders at the top of Natchitoches society.[51] Also, in 1729, the black children named Pierre and Louise, born four days apart to parents enslaved under François Derbanne, had been baptized with Jeanne Derbanne listed as their godmother.[52] The extended family networks appeared without end and reveal the beginnings of the African Creole community at Natchitoches.

There were many other such baptisms at French Natchitoches that widened family ties on the Texas-Louisiana borderlands. In May 1729, an Osage Indian, likely a captive taken in war and baptized as Marie Louise, was the twenty-year-old slave of Francois Viard, a bourgeois member of Natchitoches society. Marie Louise's godparents were St. Denis's sister, Jeanne, and her husband, Duplessis. In 1735, an Indian slave girl named Marguerite was four years old at her baptism and the property of Commandant St. Denis, whose wife, Manuela, and a French officer were named the child's godparents. Marguerite was listed as *endoyée*, which meant she was initially baptized by a layperson because she was near death and had to be formally baptized later if she survived.[53] In 1740, Juan Flores from Presidio Los Adaes and a Frenchwoman named Marie Therese Fleur became godparents to Marie Therese, a *canneci* (or Lipan Apache) child who was the slave of Commandant St. Denis. Neither Flores nor Fleur knew how to sign their names, so the symbol *X* appeared next to their names.[54] The young Apache captive was likely baptized with Fleur's first name, whose ethnic identity was hidden, suggesting that she too might have been a former captive and possibly a concubine or spouse. Whether Flores was a deserter and became Fleur's husband also remains unclear, but his illiteracy and presence in Natchitoches as a godfather to one of St. Denis's many slaves suggests that Adaeseños from comparably less affluent backgrounds became tied into elite French circles of kinship.

African slaves were baptized as required under the French Code Noir for Louisiana in 1724. This code basically reiterated the laws of 1685 for the French Caribbean islands, where sugar plantations eventually flourished. Black slaves were also baptized following Louisiana's transfer to Spain, as Gov. Alejandro O'Reilly declared in 1769 that the Code Noir of 1724 be "observed with exactitude."[55] Chapter 6 examines some of the differences between captivity and slavery on the Texas-Louisiana borderlands beyond baptism, through which communities were linked regardless of race and ethnicity.

IV

Another significant rite linking these border communities involved the burial of individuals at Los Adaes and Natchitoches with services from Franciscan missionaries and Jesuit priests, reflecting a common bond in death and dying on the Texas-Louisiana borderlands. Whenever someone passed away at Los Adaes, a missionary said mass privately for the family or at a public funeral attended by the community. Burial at Los Adaes occurred on the grounds adjacent to the presidio chapel or mission or on outlying ranches, possibly in a private family cemetery. Death was a common experience, and the loss of children proved especially heartbreaking for frontier communities frequently affected by disease, natural disaster, and warfare. Historian Amy Porter notes the spiritual nature of women's last wills and testaments on the borderlands, and while no wills are known to exist for Los Adaes, the Adaeseñas likely took spirituality, last rites, and burial just as seriously as their counterparts elsewhere in northern New Spain. Historian Martina Will de Chaparro notes that not all parishioners in New Mexico, for example, received last rites for a variety of reasons. Those who were perceived to be insane or mentally disabled as well as those who committed suicide did not receive the traditional rites, but repentance did offer the possibility of a solemn burial. She also explains that Indians living in or near Spanish towns received last rites as often as did Spaniards.[56] Whether this pattern was followed in East Texas remains unclear, but surely devotion to religion helped inhabitants through difficult periods in spite of frontier challenges. Burials brought diverse communities together in sorrow across the Texas-Louisiana border.

Franciscan missionaries played a key role in bridging multiethnic communities by celebrating mass and administering the sacraments. The anointing of the sick, another frequently requested sacramental service, became crucial, as all residents were susceptible to premature death. French Natchitoches society, however, increasingly relied on the town doctor, who arrived sometime in the late 1730s, though they and African slaves also sought traditional folk cures. The Adaeseños in particular looked to *curanderos* (folk healers), while the Caddos maintained their own shamans. Despite cultural differences, Indians and Africans could also turn to Franciscans or Jesuits and syncretized indigenous, European, and African religious practices with Catholic rituals. The administration of the Eucharist, symbolic of Christ's body, that missionaries consecrated at mass for any occasion gathered border peoples into a celebration of life and death, as did smoking tobacco in Native American ceremonies.

Meanwhile, the Adaeseños and other Spaniards were also buried at French Natchitoches. For example, Xavier Cortinas, a twenty-five-year-old Spanish soldier from Presidio Los Adaes, was buried in 1737 at Natchitoches.[57] Franciscan missionaries performed or witnessed burials for the French, Caddo, and African residents at Natchitoches, just as they did baptisms and weddings. A funeral that historians often cite was for the pioneer commandant of French Natchitoches, Louis de St. Denis, which the Spanish governor from Presidio Los Adaes and Father Francisco Vallejo from Mission Los Adaes attended. Gov. Boneo Morales reportedly told the viceroy that "Saint Denis is dead, thank God; now we can breathe easier." While Spanish officials appeared less fearful of foreign invasion as a result of St. Denis's death, most Adaeseños and Indians on both sides of the Texas-Louisiana border likely mourned his loss.[58]

The image of the Virgin Mary also played a significant intermediary role by joining together various ethnic communities. When Franciscan missionaries first arrived to East Texas in 1690, the Hasinai Caddos knew about the legend of the "Lady in Blue," an apparition of María de Jesús de Agreda, who was a Franciscan nun living in Spain who appeared among Jumano Indians in present West Texas. She was the first Spanish missionary to the Indians of Texas in a spiritual sense, which spread across Indian trade channels as a symbolic association of peace with the Spaniards. The Caddos bestowed such meaning upon the arrival of the Spaniards in East Texas. Although their first encounters with Spanish missionaries and soldiers ended miserably, the Hasinai celebrated the return of Franciscan friars in 1716. Following the abandonment of the East Texas missions in 1719, the Adaes in particular welcomed the missionaries back to East Texas in 1721.

The image of the Virgin Mary remained prominent, especially Our Lady of the Pillar, the patroness of Spain, along with Spanish female settlers, which made a difference to the Caddos. According to Fray Juan Antonio de la Peña, the Spaniards dedicated Presidio Los Adaes and its church on October 12, the feast day of Our Lady of the Pillar. Father Antonio Margil extolled devotion to Nuestra Señora del Pilar with his sermon followed by fiestas with drinking, dancing, plays, and masquerades. The Caddos continued to witness regular performances of daily masses, processions, and celebrations all in honor of the Virgin Mary manifested variously as Our Lady of the Pillar, Guadalupe, Refugio, and all the saints.[59] Such public displays became avenues into the Spanish world for the Caddos in addition to diplomacy and trade.

The Caddos did not necessarily associate the Virgin Mary with French society in the Louisiana colony, where commerce usurped conversion as the primary object of French imperial policy.[60] The French presence at Natchitoches, its commercial and religious exchanges with Presidio Los Adaes, and the settlement of Adaeseño soldiers with families helped restore the peaceful image that the Caddos had associated with the Virgin Mary in the previous century. The caveat was that the Caddos played the Spanish against the French, as neither imperial government could be entirely trusted, the Virgin Mary notwithstanding.

Various artists in New Spain in the seventeenth and eighteenth centuries expanded on the sacred image of the Virgin Mary to include an emphasis on St. Anne and Joachim, Jesus' maternal grandparents, a cultural adaptation that evolved independently in colonial Latin America. Renditions of the Holy Family took indigenous forms with the depiction of people of color and the important status of women. By 1746, the Virgin of Guadalupe was elevated to the status of copatroness in Mexico.[61] Ten years later, a Spanish official in Madrid wrote Governor Barrios of Texas requesting the establishment of a shrine and sanctuary for Our Lady of Guadalupe.[62] The Adaeseño devotion to the Virgin Mary and the presence of Hispanic families on the Texas-Louisiana borderlands—together with the secular work of missionaries beyond the missions—fostered military, political, and social ties in the region.

V

By the mid-1730s and 1740s, a snapshot of the Adaeseño community became apparent. Who were the first soldier-settlers at Presidio Los Adaes beneath the glory that often went to the Spanish governor-commandants? Where did they come from? Many Adaeseños were fathers and sons who served together at Los Adaes after the first generation arrived from central and northern New Spain, either single or married, and raised native-born children in Spanish Texas. Antonio Gil Ybarbo, born at the fort of Los Adaes in 1729, became an infamous frontiersman and the founder of Nacogdoches in 1779. His father, Mateo Ybarbo, emigrated from Spain to Mexico before joining de Aguayo's expedition to East Texas in 1721, then served at San Antonio and passed away at Los Adaes in 1744. Brothers and cousins served together at Los Adaes as well as the presidios at San Antonio, La Bahía, San Agustín, San Xavier, and San Sabá. The "Chirino boys" were among the most numerous band of brothers, including Domingo, Manuel, Andrés, Juan, Luís, and Cristóbal, who established reputations as either "good" or "rebellious" soldiers. In their early twenties, brothers Domingo and Manuel, originally from Saltillo, became the first Chirino recruits for duty at Presidio Los Adaes in 1735. The small town of Chireno, Texas, located between Nacogdoches and San Augustine near the present Texas-Louisiana state line, was named after one of their descendants.[63]

The Adaeseño soldiers came from diverse backgrounds. The Spanish labels most frequently applied to them were Spanish, mestizo, and mulatto. These were not chiseled in stone, since an individual listed as a mulatto one year later "passed" as an español.[64] The only known military roster of names designating caste labels for each soldier was recorded in 1731 (see appendix B). The majority of troops at Los Adaes for this year were not labeled Spanish. Twenty-seven soldiers in particular were designated as español, including the officers, 2nd Lt. Joseph Gonzalez, Sgt. Manuel Antonio de Losoya, and rank-and-file troops like Mateo Ybarbo and Phelipe Bermúdez. Governor-commandant don Juan Antonio de Bustillo y Ceballos and his first lieutenant, don Joseph Cayetano de Bergara, were not classified, but the governor was from Spain, while Lieutenant Bergara was already classified as español before his arrival at Los Adaes.[65] Of the remaining thirty-two Adaeseño soldiers, there were fourteen mestizos, nine mulattos, seven coyotes, one *lobo*, and one other soldier, Joseph de Alvarado, designated as an *indio*, possibly a Tlaxcalan Indian from Coahuila. The New Military Regulations of 1729 required that the governor-captains designate the caste status of their troops, but for some reason this was done only once for Presidio Los Adaes, as there were no census records taken during its existence.[66]

An officer's position, or plaza, normally became available when that person became too sick or died. Lt. Joseph Gonzalez was promoted to second lieutenant in 1731 after the person he replaced fell chronically ill.[67] There were few job opportunities available other than military service, ranching, and farming. With such limited means for Adaeseño soldiers and residents to climb out of poverty and challenge the governors, the temptations of the Texas-Louisiana borderlands seduced many into venturing beyond any boundaries under threat of punishment.

Meanwhile, the archaeological evidence suggests that a material culture flourished at Los Adaes that ironically reflected both hierarchy and intercultural trade on the Texas-Louisiana borderlands. The structures excavated at the fort, principally the governor's house and several *jacales* (thatched roof huts) adjacent to the presidio, reveal sharp distinctions in status and ethnicity. Ceramics, such as Chinese porcelain, German stoneware, and decorated Caddoan pottery, were concentrated around the governor's house and thus indicated higher status. The archaeological assemblage includes roughly equal amounts of tin-enameled wares from France and Puebla, Mexico. Fragments of French wine bottles are abundant at the site, while most of the lead cloth seals are also French. British- and French-manufactured guns and knives appear less frequently. British goods, including tin-enameled shards, salt-glazed ceramics, and pipe-stem fragments, also appeared in small amounts, as did German (stoneware) and Asian (porcelain) products.[68]

Hispanic-oriented traditions are represented at the Los Adaes archaeological site. Basalt, or volcanic tuff; *metates* and *manos* (hand tools) for the grinding of corn; *higas* (amulets) to repel the *mal de ojo* (evil eye); Spanish horse gear; weaponry; religious medals; and a cloth seal from the port of Cádiz have been found. Faunal remains comprise the greatest number in the Los Adaes samples, mostly from domesticated cattle, pigs, and horses. Floral remains included maize, beans, and assortments of hardwoods and pine along with peach tree and watermelon. Significantly, archaeologists Hiram "Pete" Gregory and George Avery conclude from the material culture and extant historical accounts that intercultural relationships were defined more by accommodation and mutual support than by perpetual conflict or warfare.[69]

Just as Caddos incorporated European clothes, tools, and other items into their world, so did the Spanish and French at Los Adaes and Natchitoches adjust on native ground. Archaeologist Diana DiPaolo Loren refers to the Creolization of the Texas-Louisiana frontier, where a culturally mixed identity was important for survival.[70] Historian Richard Slatta explains through a comparison of the northern and southern edges of the Spanish Empire in the Americas how the "porous membrane of the frontier permitted cultural transmission in both directions." The Spanish did not reject all of Indian culture, as they learned to "appreciate the utility of buffalo hides" beyond profits, while deerskin clothing afforded at minimum to cover their nakedness and allowed them to move about more comfortably in Indian country.[71]

Transnationalism, or the movement across borders, manifested as material cultural transmissions and accommodation through trade and kinship networks, which helped offset the underlying causes of poverty at Los Adaes from the nonpayment of wages in the Adaeseño community (chapter 4) to the governor and his officers' smuggling operations (chapter 5). The governor's authoritarian rule involved a monopoly on commerce with the French and Caddos while Franciscans negotiated the sacraments that revealed hierarchy and conformism on the fringes of New Spain. The Adaeseños, in turn, needed French and Caddo trade for the outright survival of their own largely impoverished community and wanted relief, if not greater autonomy, from Spanish mercantilism and corruption.

Blood Debt

Among his litany of complaints to Governor Sandoval in 1736, Lt. Joseph Gonzalez stressed his own "exhaustion to overcome and convince all of the company to give their power of attorney," which the soldiers resisted "until you settle their accounts and pay them."[1] Governor Sandoval risked mutiny in East Texas by staying at San Antonio to direct military campaigns against the Lipan Apaches despite the New Regulations of 1729, which designated Presidio Los Adaes the capital of Spanish Texas. Lieutenant Gonzalez and the Franciscan missionaries informed Governor Sandoval of happenings on the Texas-Louisiana frontier, particularly the difficulties with farming and ranching, passport issues with Natchitoches, and French troubles from southeastern Indians. Friar Francisco Vallejo, president of the East Texas missions residing at Mission Adaes, anticipated Gonzalez's troubles when he wrote the governor about the Frenchmen's hesitancy to sell corn at Presidio Los Adaes, fearing the penalties levied against transgressors of the Spanish Crown. Father Vallejo complained that he could only get two barrels of maize delivered to the fort at one peso each.[2] While the sustainability of the remaining three Spanish missions, the planting of crops, and trade hung in the balance, serious problems arose over the quality of the troops, payroll, and military supplies that threatened the very existence of Los Adaes. These issues, the Spanish feared, might push the Adaeseños over the edge into French Louisiana and Caddo country for relief from, if not mutiny against, Spanish rule.

In his report, General Rivera recognized that properly equipping and transporting quality soldiers became an expensive task because of the distance from Presidio Los Adaes to recruiting centers in New Spain. In 1731, he initially suggested to the viceroy that soldiers with a higher social status be sent to Gov. Juan Bustillo Cevallos of Texas for replacement of those castes *de color quebrado* ("of broken color," or mixed blood), which was a derogatory reference that implied African and Indian blood.[3] In practice, Spanish military forces were mostly irregular militias recruited from large haciendas and mining towns in New Spain, as described in chapter 1.[4] General Rivera advised the viceroy to give Governor Bustillo what he needed so he could pay troop salaries. In this manner, the governor could "end the abuse introduced of advanced payment in supplies to all the soldiers" rather than wages. Meanwhile, he said the creditors of the previous governor, don Melchor de Mediavilla y Ascona, should be paid in the amount of 6,853 pesos. Otherwise, Rivera believed no soldiers would be willing to serve his majesty without proper support.[5] Indeed, Spanish governors often funded expeditions into new lands as *adelantados* (entrepreneurs) at their own personal expense. Since Texas still lacked government *situados* (subsidy), this also perpetuated corruption and abuse without any other oversight. In effect, the labor situation at Los Adaes amounted to soldiers held in a premodern form of debt peonage or sharecropping, especially without a reliable stream of migrants, captives, or slaves.[6] Unless the Crown could send Spanish troops overseas directly from Spain, frontier outposts like Los Adaes in northern New Spain continued to attract socially inferior recruits who had been peasants.

The governor continued to receive dismal reports from Presidio Los Adaes and the East Texas missions. Lieutenant Gonzalez informed Governor Sandoval about his efforts to bring corn from Natchitoches, but the French commandant, St. Denis, and some of his soldiers prevented the transport of supplies. Gonzalez also sent the governor a bill of expenses for the soldiers from San Antonio transferred from Los Adaes and the seven-soldier escort provided to one missionary. There was no other activity with the company cavalry and nothing to report either at *el rancho* (ranch) of the Los Adaes company. By late 1735, however, Lieutenant Gonzalez reported the lack of maize, much sickness, residents dying, and repairs needed on the fort. Supplies were distributed when the Adaeseños' attempts to plant corn failed, while they also worried over the lack of soap. The lieutenant added that he distributed forty-six horses to the soldiers and assigned a billet that had been empty. Gonzalez also requested that the governor send a blacksmith to Presidio Los Adaes. By early December, Father Ignacio Antonio Ciprian, from Mission Ais, informed the governor that a squadron of six Adaeseños had gone hunting. Father Ciprian could not blame them for their temporary absence from mission duty considering the Adaeseño community's suffering at Los Adaes and the fort's dilapidated barracks and walls.[7]

By 1736, poverty overshadowed the Los Adaes community like never before, and the Adaeseños became angry. In April, Lieutenant Gonzalez, apart from dealing with his daughter's elopement, reported that the soldiers were all dressed in deerskins and that their women and children went about naked, making them ashamed of attending church. He urged the governor to come to Presidio Los Adaes and quiet those residents who wished to tarnish his credibility and nobility. He was anxious about the expected relief of four hundred bushels of corn and concerned over the lack of mules and harnesses for transporting supplies to the missions, which he hoped would be remedied soon. Presidio Los Adaes's dependence on trade with French Natchitoches became more evident when Lieutenant Gonzalez had to "forewarn [the governor] of the debts" that have been contracted with the French for necessary supplies. He again encouraged Governor Sandoval to return to Los Adaes and "satisfy the creditors, who are owed almost 400 pesos."[8] During this time, the Spanish tried regulating the price of seeds and gave preference to presidial captains at San Antonio, La Bahía, and Los Adaes in the sale of garden products.[9] The Adaeseño community grew only more indebted, as their governor-commandant did not see the urgency of local matters on the Texas border with Louisiana as compared to San Antonio's own plight.

Lieutenant Gonzalez also reported on the state of ranching at Los Adaes, which revealed a working relationship between the governor and the missionaries as well as the importance of the Caddo salt trade for curing meats. The lieutenant informed Governor Sandoval that Father Ciprian offered the presidio some young bulls, but he did not know whether these animals should remain at the mission or if he should occasionally slaughter some cows that the governor kept at Mission Ais. Gonzalez added that one female calf was lost, which an Indian "of these *Salineros* [salt people]" killed, but he seemed unconcerned. He then noted an increase of fifty-nine male and female *chiqueros* (pigs), which he sold to the troops, who had clamored for them. Finally, Lieutenant Gonzalez advised the governor that he was sending him as many *gamuzas* (chamois or deerskins) as he could gather with 1st Lt. Joseph Cayetano Vergara but that other deerskins he "considered necessary to give to some soldiers by which means to cover their nakedness."[10]

Meanwhile, the specter of Indian rebellions threatened Louisiana once again and perhaps concerned Lieutenant Gonzalez more than anything. In 1735, the Tunica revolted against the French, as did the Natchez five years earlier, followed by the Chickasaw allies of the English in 1736. The French reaffirmed their Indian alliances with the Caddo, Illinois, and Arkansas.[11] The French needed the Spanish as allies mainly to ensure tranquility not only along the Texas-Louisiana border but also on the Florida-Louisiana borderlands, where Pensacola, founded around 1700 with soldiers dispatched from the Port of Veracruz in southern Mexico, stood across from the French post at Mobile on the lower Mississippi River. The friction created over St. Denis's relocation of the Natchitoches post to the west bank of the Red River in 1735, which the Spanish considered encroachment into New Spain, paled in comparison to the increasingly ominous presence of the English with their Indian allies east of the Mississippi.

Scarcity of supplies and indebtedness at Los Adaes also affected military readiness at San Antonio, where the Adaeseños faced similar problems yet still expected to fight the Apaches, whereas the Spanish were at peace with the Caddos in East Texas. While Lieutenant Vergara and five of his fellow troops from Los Adaes were garrisoned at San Antonio, they petitioned the governor for an order instructing its captain, Joseph Urrutia, to give them their supplies and other necessary goods.[12] The governor agreed and ordered the provisioning of tobacco, paper, soap, corn, and meat for the duration of their duty at San Antonio. Despite barely having enough to supply his own company, Captain Urrutia gave what he could "as done before by verbal order of [the previous governor] don Carlos de Franquis, despite not having any equipment to give them." Evidently, the lack of necessary supplies followed each successive governor at presidios elsewhere in northern New Spain.[13]

The soldiers' accounts reveal that most of the Adaeseños remained indebted to the governor-commandant at Los Adaes. In order to receive their salary, the soldiers first had to settle their accounts, attach their signature, and grant power of attorney to an agent from Mexico City, normally a merchant or official with the Royal Treasury Office. Most of the Adaeseño troops, however, were illiterate and did not know how to sign their names, so the governor or one of his subordinate officers signed on their behalf. *Testigos* (witnesses) signed documents along with the governor and the parties involved in contracts or legal proceedings, especially since paper stamped with the official seal of the Crown proved scarce, as did public notaries. This permitted greater manipulation by the governors or officers. Pesos were exchanged at Los Adaes whenever soldiers were fortunate enough to receive a portion of their salaries or when the governor had a bill of sale for the purchases of livestock and slaves. The Adaeseños more than likely turned to the frontier exchange economy of the Texas-Louisiana borderlands for relief as they ventured deeper into the Piney Woods.[14]

The governors at Los Adaes also purposely withheld payment from the troops and coerced them into informal labor arrangements in exchange for supplies. The earliest known record of such indebtedness came from a list of accounts for a group of Adaeseños at the end of April 1731 under Gov. Melchor de Mediavilla y Ascona. Of the fifty-seven troops listed, only three (two of these officers) were paid a third of their salaries through April 30, 1731. Eleven soldiers were owed parts of their salary, displayed on the left-hand column of the document with the designation of *alcanse* (due), while forty-four soldiers owed various amounts, shown on the right-hand side as *deviendo* (indebted). The credits of the soldiers totaled 291 pesos, four reales, and three-fourths *quartillas* (cents), and the indebtedness equaled 6,853 pesos, three reales, and three-fourths quartillas.[15]

The governors perpetuated the practice whereby soldiers collectively owed more than what they were paid, which carried over into the books of the new governor's administration. While General Rivera's inspection recognized this problem at many presidios in northern New Spain, the New Regulations of 1729 that followed did not reform payroll problems to the satisfaction of the soldiers.[16] The location of Los Adaes on the border with French Louisiana contributed to the abuse of troop salaries, as Franco-Caddo trade tempted the governors into diverting resources for their own pleasure, as described in chapter 5.

Account books from the late 1730s through the early 1770s specify goods the soldiers received from their governor-commandants and charged to their accounts. The number and variety of items that the Adaeseños either purchased or credited to their names increased over time, an indication of their increased reliance on non-Hispanic markets for survival. A sampling of the goods shows that in addition to their dependence on basic comestibles, such as corn and beans, the Adaeseños desired lots of chocolate and sugar. The account books also reveal a great demand for soap, cotton, cowboy hats, saddles, shoes, knives, gunpowder, and *balas* (ammunition). Many of the soldiers bought *zapatos para mujeres* (women's shoes) and stockings for their spouses and perhaps daughters. Some Adaeseños enjoyed the occasional luxury items, especially silk shirts, handkerchiefs, and linens, or imported china and other goods from central Mexico, France, and England.[17] Such goods indicate the mixing of *comercio lícito* (legal trade) under Spanish mercantilism with *comercio ilícito* (illicit commerce or smuggling) of contraband in the broader transatlantic commerce that crossed the Texas-Louisiana border.

The Adaeseños overstepped commercial boundaries and, likely unaware that the power of attorney they gave to the governor and his agents from Mexico City, added to their account problems. A power of attorney was required to obtain salaries and gunpowder allotments for troops on the frontier, which began for Los Adaes in the mid-1720s and formed part of irregular accounting practices for years to come. The Adaeseños, most of whom remained illiterate, settled their accounts with the governor even if they expressed doubts. On January 24, 1738, Gov. Prudencio de Orobio Bazterra, residing at San Antonio, described the power of attorney that the

Adaeseños gave to him "first and secondly to *don* Domingo de Gomendio Urrutia, resident from the Commerce Department in Mexico City," for the collection of their salaries. Governor Orobio, in turn, gave agent Gomendio Urrutia "my power in whose right is necessary" to bring the pesos from the viceregal capital.[18] The officers and soldiers from Los Adaes had annulled their power of attorney to former Governor Sandoval and transferred it to interim Gov. Carlos Franquis de Lugo, who oversaw the residencia of Governor Sandoval. The Adaeseños subsequently granted power of attorney to Governor Orobio, while Gomendio Urrutia remained the agent in Mexico City (see figure 1.4).[19]

The Adaeseños were owed salaries for the years 1733, 1734, 1735, 1736, and 1737, which coincided with intense Apache troubles at San Antonio and meant that problems at Los Adaes played second fiddle to warfare elsewhere. The illiterate soldiers had several witnesses—including Lt. Juan Antonio de Amorín, 2nd Lt. Felipe Muñoz de Mora, and Juan de Armijo, all residents from Los Adaes—sign *a ruego de* (in behalf of) those Adaeseños who did not know how to sign their own names. Unfortunately, Governors Lugo and Orobio did not bring immediate relief to the soldiers and residents at Los Adaes. Under Governor Lugo's brief (seventeen-month) tenure, the Adaeseños only sparingly received corn, cattle, and horses, which were charged to their families. The troops were left with a bitter taste for war while they hoped for better administration from the next governor-commandant.[20]

While the governors of Spanish Texas changed command rather frequently from the beginning, the Mexico City agents with power of attorney for the Adaeseños remained in service for many years. If a governor was corrupt or abusive, the Adaeseños expected legal redress through a residencia proceeding. There were no similar procedures, however, for the removal of a financial agent who might have diverted funds meant for troops on the frontier into bribes of royal officials and the *baratillo* (marketplace) of the viceregal capital. Historian Andrew Konove notes that the emergence of a shadow economy in Mexico City was not simply an "informal economy" because much of it mixed with the legal, which appeared to be the case on the Texas-Louisiana border. British linen and silver plates, for example, were goods that should have been under the exclusive control of the *consulado* (merchant guild), which Konove says was "the sole legal importer of overseas goods into Mexico from incorporation in 1592 until 1778." Secondhand items or fakes could be purchased in the baratillo to imitate the rich while the agents perhaps also engaged in a premodern form of money laundering. In addition to the residencias, which apparently began in Spanish Texas after General Rivera's inspection, two other government investigations were the *pequisa* (inquiry), a secret examination with interrogations, and the *visita* (inspection or review) by an outside official, into the activities of local officials and merchants to ensure their adherence to regulations. In reality, investigations of any kind appeared to exclude the agents who likely lined the pockets of royal officials in Mexico City.[21]

Los Adaes did not have sufficient supplies and equipment in its early years to stock both its troops and gift Indian allies, which compounded payroll and logistical issues. This forced governors to supply their own forts and haggle with bureaucratic officials in Mexico City for the return of equipment from other presidios. There was little in the arsenal at Los Adaes when Sandoval became the governor of Texas in 1734 (appendix C). Horses were also purchased for the troops, with an average of three per soldier. The inventory included military equipment too cumbersome for transport over such long distances through rough terrain and proved obsolete for guerrilla-type warfare on the Southern Plains. The heavy cannons displayed the king's power but had no tactical advantages against highly mobile and well-armed Indians—not to mention, there were no cannonballs to fire. The six pairs of shackles likely restrained captive Indians if not slaves or miscreant servants and soldiers, while the one small pair of shackles perhaps meant the captivity of children. The six pounds of rope likely secured goods in transport or was used for additional captives, if not for hangings. Governor Bustillo, who commanded Los Adaes at the time of this inventory near the end of his tenure, had petitioned his successor (Sandoval) for a certificate showing that he brought two of his own small iron cannons as well as more than thirty iron balls for the said cannons.[22]

The expense of managing frontier presidios went beyond the capacity of royal coffers to sustain. The account books of the Royal Treasury in Mexico City included, among war-related expenses, the salaries of governors, officers, and soldiers at Los Adaes. The New Regulations of 1729 reduced the amounts expended annually for wages at Los Adaes from 43,850 pesos "of common gold" in 1725 to 27,265 pesos in 1730. The salaries of the governors and first lieutenants in Texas remained the same at 2,000 and 450 pesos, respectively, while officer and soldier pay was reduced from 450 pesos in 1725 to 440 pesos for second lieutenants, 435 pesos for sergeants, and 420 pesos for each soldier.[23] The account book also refers to the power of attorney given to Lt. Col. Francisco de Ugarte, resident of Mexico City, for the collection of salaries for the governor and soldiers from 1725 to 1728, whose responsibility passed to Fernando de Ugarte, also from Mexico City, for the years 1729 to 1733 before Domingo Gomendio received power of attorney in 1734.[24] The New Regulations of 1729 curtailed expenses for salaries by reducing the number of plazas at Los Adaes from the original one hundred troops to sixty and by abandoning Presidio Tejas near Mission Ais.

There were many other related expenses paid from the Royal Treasury that received higher priority than Los Adaes. The payment for services to the agents came from the royal treasury and listed another agent, Diego Giraud, who received 282 pesos for his power of attorney on behalf of another governor of Texas. An additional sum of 368 pesos was paid to Col. Joseph de Escandón, 167 pesos went to Justo Boneo y Morales, and more similar payments were sent to other individuals and presidios throughout New Spain, Florida, and the Caribbean. Los Adaes received the fewest funds of any other Spanish fort. For all the anxiety the border between Texas and Louisiana ostensibly created, Los Adaes received nowhere near the official resources necessary, and this was likely symptomatic of greater problems elsewhere on the Spanish frontier.[25]

||

From the perspective of Los Adaes, the most notorious governor of Spanish Texas was Manuel Sandoval during his rather brief rule from 1734 to 1736. In April 1738, Cristóbal de Santiago, Felipe de Sierra, and Domingo del Río, soldiers from Presidio Los Adaes sent on assignment to San Antonio, filed a petition and appeared before the residency judge, Juan Joseph Briseño Zúñiga. They complained that former governor Sandoval never liquidated their accounts and did not pay them their salaries before the books were taken to Mexico City. Judge Briseño promptly ordered that their request be satisfied. Sandoval's notary, however, declared that the accounts were taken over by Lt. Joseph Gonzalez and Lt. Gen. Fermín Ybiricu, who "governed" Los Adaes while Sandoval resided in San Antonio. However, it appeared that Ybiricu spent more time across the border at Natchitoches and left his lieutenant officers in charge at Los Adaes. The notary said that Gonzalez and Ybiricu should have satisfied the complainants' requests. The amounts still owed the soldiers were from May 3, 1734, when Sandoval became governor and took possession of the books but paid only a portion of their salaries.[26]

Governor Sandoval had twenty soldiers from Los Adaes assigned to him at San Antonio, many of whom ultimately testified against him. Domingo Chirino, a new recruit from Saltillo for Los Adaes in December 1735, was assigned to San Antonio the following year and appeared before the residency judge because he was owed his remaining salary for 1736 and 1737 in the total amount of 190 pesos. Chirino was the second generation of his family to serve in East Texas, as did his father, Lazaro Chirino, who accompanied the Ramón expedition nearly twenty years earlier. Another soldier from Los Adaes, Salvador Esparza, stated that he was still owed 543 pesos. Although Lieutenant Gonzalez had been left in charge of the books, he accumulated debts himself in the amount of 378 pesos. By May 1738, all the soldiers from Los Adaes had appeared before Judge Briseño and complained that Governor Sandoval never supplied them equipment except for very little flour and many costly horses at 50 pesos each. He also charged their salaries for shoes and *pilonsillos* (sugar cones) at higher prices. By this time, the new governor, Franquis de Lugo, arrived and had the soldiers escort Sandoval to Los Adaes from San Antonio. Governor Lugo promulgated an order that Sandoval be "punished with placement into the stocks or whipped." The soldiers requested that Sandoval appear before the residency judge with the books from Lieutenant Gonzalez so they could be paid.[27]

Rank-and-file soldiers and residents from Los Adaes, including women, appeared at Sandoval's residency to protest the cruelties he and his officers had committed. An Adaeseño soldier named Juan Sánchez Továr stated that he had not been paid in three years and that Sandoval took away "his male and female horse and, being afraid, I did not show outrage, as I am poor with a family and should be quiet." When Továr arrived for duty at San Antonio, Sandoval seized his horse because it looked beautiful and said it "belonged to the Criollos." Apparently, Továr's social status was beneath those who, like Sandoval, had been born in Mexico and whose parents had immigrated from Spain. Agustín Morrillo, a resident of Los Adaes, sought justice because his brother, Encarnasio, also a soldier, had died. Encarnasio's estate consisted of "ten domesticated horses, a black chamois [deerskin] with silver buttons, a new bullfighter's cape with sleeves, and two pairs of silk socks," which passed into Lieutenant Gonzalez's possession as the officer in charge of the warehouse and the fort during Sandoval's absence. Juan Francisco, a resident from Los Adaes and the company barber, was supposed to be paid in *libranza* (bill of exchange) from the presidio's store. Instead, he received a *valeto* (pay slip) from Lieutenant Ybiricu, who adjusted his account balance for the amount of thirty-six pesos. He said Továr would be paid the next day, but the latter never received payment.[28]

More Adaeseños testified against Sandoval before Judge Briseño. Fernando Santiago de la Cerda, a soldier, informed the residency judge that Lieutenant Vergara recruited him from Saltillo. Apparently, he was a sibling of Lieutenant Gonzalez's wife, Gerturdis. When de la Cerda arrived at San Antonio, Governor Sandoval said he would pay him when they reached Los Adaes, but he never did. Lastly, Juana del Toro, the widow of Pascual de Leyva, stated that "she was a poor old woman without any more shelter or protection after God in His Divine Majesty took away her husband." Juana's husband was a soldier from Los Adaes who served two years and five months into Governor Sandoval's term when he died. Sandoval did not provide her with any relief or supplies.[29]

By late May 1738, former governor Sandoval came forward with his own petition before the residency judge and denied as false the claims of the Adaeseños. He said that with regard to the soldiers' salaries, he merely did the same as his predecessor, Bustillos Cevallos, and that he satisfied whatever accounts remained and distributed equipment and supplies at the regulated prices. He considered the lawsuit frivolous as far as the soldiers were concerned, but he did say that he would satisfy the amount owed the barber, Juan Francisco, and that the widow, Juana del Toro, would be paid something too. Sandoval's pleas notwithstanding, the residency judge ordered that all the soldiers be paid what they were owed.[30]

These petitions were an extension of another legal battle against former governor Sandoval for extortion of the troops. In May 1737, after interim governor Lugo arrived at Los Adaes, the soldiers requested his help to have Sandoval and Ybiricu pay their salaries. The troops stated they "endured 2,000 acts of violence such as verbal threats and abuse by said Ybiricu . . . wrongs done with the goal of obligating us to settle our accounts and sign." Specifically, soldier Joseph Trejo declared that both Ybiricu and Sandoval took away his plaza and wished to punish him for not settling and signing his accounts. Another soldier, Julian Flores, said his superiors wanted to *abaquetiar* (whip) him for the same thing. Domingo del Río declared that he and his family were threatened with forced exile. Ygnacio, the Parraleño (from the town of Parral in Coahuila), said that Sandoval and Ybiricu "took away his plaza" because he refused to retrieve their cattle.[31]

The testimony revealed a convoluted mix of violent threats to extort salaries, barter of food and equipment, and price gouging. Ygnacio added that many injuries and insults were committed against the Adaeseños in order to get them to sign their accounts. He declared that Sandoval "took away our blood that is the salary the King gives us to support our wives and children." Ygnacio noted that Sandoval "had us naked during the time he was governor with our bodies covered only in deerskin and our women maintained such in the flesh." Sandoval allegedly sold horses at fifty pesos each, *piloncillos* at four reales each, and a pound of sugar at six reales, and he distributed "rotten, foul smelling wheat, due to suspension of corn rations, that we took as ordered." Sandoval finally ordered Lt. Joseph Gonzalez to suspend any soap, piloncillo, and corn and only distribute such goods if the troops bartered with him the horses they had for duty. Ygnacio stated, "We needed the corn for our nourishment, the soap so our wives could clean, and the piloncillo since it was our only chocolate, or to drink a little bit of *attole* instead." The soldiers bartered their horses with Gonzalez for these other items, which were sold back at higher prices of sixteen, thirty, and fifty pesos.[32] The Adaeseño soldiers also requested Lugo to order Lieutenant Gonzalez to testify to the accuracy of their testimony. Interestingly, they wanted their salaries to be "the same as our fellow companions at the Royal Presidio of San Antonio." Those Adaeseños who did not know how to sign their own names, like Pedro de Sierra, Domingo Chirino, and his brother Manuel Chirino, had fellow soldiers who were literate, such Mateo Ybarbo and Joseph Antonio Lascano, sign for them.[33]

In his own defense, Lieutenant Gonzalez testified that he only carried out his duty. "Although repulsed by Sandoval's tyranny," Gonzalez stated, "the force of obedience obligated me to blindly follow his orders." He added that because of the bad treatment they received, the soldiers became "so desperate that they intended to cross over to France [Louisiana] and leave presidio Los Adaes abandoned."[34] Since Lieutenant Gonzalez's own daughter, Victoria, left Los Adaes to marry a French soldier at Natchitoches, he likely felt added pressure to follow orders and protect his honor. According to the testimony of Manuel Ramírez de la Piscina, the *criado* (servant) of Sandoval and his personal *amanuensis* (scribe), the temptation for Sandoval and Ybiricu to charge interest and remove a third of the soldiers' salary proved overwhelming.[35] Piscina did not mention whether Gonzalez profited from the corruption, though he apparently regained the respect of his fellow soldiers in sympathy with his daughter's desertion from Los Adaes.

The chronic shortages and extortion at Los Adaes contributed to contraband trade. Joseph Antonio Rodríguez, formerly a resident at San Antonio and then Los Adaes, followed Piscina's testimony and declared that "with the motive of trying to make a living for the maintenance of his wife and children, he went to Presidio Los Adaes with some trinkets his spouse made, and distributed them to various soldiers of this company." Rodríguez requested payment of 105 pesos from Sandoval and Ybiricu that the company owed him after having seen the fixed amounts in its account book. He was instructed to make a *libranza* with the soldier Juan Sánchez Továr, who later offered to pay Rodríguez the 105 pesos "in mules, horses, and deerskins." Továr wished to indemnify Rodríguez's request quickly so he could have a plaza at Los Adaes. As for Rodríguez, "this was the means he had for recovering from his poverty, neither did Sandoval wish to pay said amount nor was any justice possible with said Ybiricu."[36] Both Rodríguez and Továr agreed to the barter and went to the home of Ybiricu, who gave them their bill of exchange and the 105 pesos paid in mules or deerskins.[37]

The residencia proceeding also revealed the problem of gambling that concerned Franciscan missionaries over the behavior of their secular flock, including the governor. Sandoval allegedly forced the troops to gamble away their wages through *rifas* (raffles), cards, and dice, which only worsened their situation. He named Bacilio Ximénez as the *testafero* (or acting representative) for the soldiers from Los Adaes and gave him silver pesos. Ximénez then placed sixteen pesos on a table as the price for a cow. Sandoval told the fifteen to twenty starving soldiers who participated that they had to place their bets verbally before he could pay them. The soldiers supposedly did not have the liberty to decline participation in the game. They bet verbally and matched the amount Ximénez placed on the table, and as one soldier explained, "in this manner he destroyed us" such that "Sandoval stayed with all of our salaries" after the governor authorized Ybiricu to charge the accounts twenty-five pesos for every five pesos and fifty pesos for every ten pesos handed over to him. The scheme was so crooked that it "motivated the Reverend Friars of Mission Los Adaes to reprimand Sandoval from the pulpit for leaving us with no money."[38] Franciscans, who frequently celebrated mass for the Adaeseños at the chapel of Los Adaes, occasionally came to the residents' defense, evidently with an eye toward social control of the entire community. Historian Amy Bushnell notes that friars in Spanish Florida viewed themselves as defenders of the people against "autocracy." Perhaps the same applied at Los Adaes, but the record is largely silent other than to suggest that the Franciscans and governors at Los Adaes generally enjoyed good working relationships, notwithstanding Sandoval.[39]

The Adaeseños testified that they were handed goods at higher prices than allowed under the New Regulations of 1729, which affected their own ability to perform duties and threatened their livelihoods. For example, they apparently purchased socks for women and children at five or six pesos a pair when the regulations set the price at three. The soldiers stated that Sandoval "never gave us a grain of gunpowder from the six pounds that the King at least allows for us." This particular equipment was not on the *arancel* (regulated price list), which allowed the governor to set his own price. Sandoval also gave them cows with calves at twenty-five pesos, though the fixed cost was sixteen pesos. All the officers from Los Adaes signed the petition for justice, including Lt. Joseph Cayetano Vergara, Lt. Joseph Gonzalez, Manuel Antonio Losoya, Felipe Bermudes, Marcos Ruíz, Juan Mora, Andrés Sánchez, Francisco Antonio Nápoles, Joseph Acosta, Juan Antonio Luna, and Joseph Castro.[40] To take advantage of the rank-and-file soldiers was one thing, but mistreating the officer corps proved intolerable.

In the meantime, the crooked raffles commonly practiced under Sandoval swindled the Adaeseños together with cards and dice games. In June 1737, Lieutenant Cayetano Vergara testified before Governor Lugo: "There were many raffles with the soldiers of the Los Adaes Company and that the person who invented them was Bacilio Ximénez, a soldier from Presidio San Antonio who became a resident of this one [Los Adaes]." As for the "games, there was also excess dice and playing cards . . . and that the soldiers came out indebted so much so that they could not even purchase a shirt from the [company] store." The goods Sandoval actually gave the Adaeseños were also *podrido* (rotten).[41] The officers at Los Adaes perhaps became most concerned about the governor's business through his most senior officer, Ybiricu, at Natchitoches.

Lieutenant General Ybiricu's own testimony thickened the plot with his revelation that he and Sandoval had commercial relations with their French neighbors at Natchitoches. Asked to explain how Sandoval could have allowed such disorderly raffles to occur and force soldiers to participate, Ybiricu responded that he was in Natchitoches when Sandoval began these raffles. After receiving notice of such excesses, Ybiricu stopped the raffles once he returned to Los Adaes. Perhaps Lt. Joseph Gonzalez sent word to Ybiricu separately from his appeal to Sandoval, urging him to return to Los Adaes from San Antonio and settle the accounts for fear of mutiny by the troops. In response to another gambling-related question, Ybiricu declared that he "received 50 silver pesos from Sandoval in order to place them in the possession of *doña* Manuela [Sánchez Navarro], the wife of Commandant *don* Luis de San Denis" from nearby French Natchitoches. Sandoval evidently used the soldiers' wages to purchase goods from French merchants in Natchitoches with Ybiricu acting as his liaison.[42]

Did Governor Sandoval engage in smuggling beyond the Crown's allowance for trade in foodstuffs with Natchitoches? Perhaps he turned a blind eye, with not just Spain's honor but family interests at stake on the border. Maybe the governor figured that trade with Natchitoches could alleviate the difficulty of bringing supplies from markets so far away in Saltillo or even San Antonio, but the Adaeseños saw things differently. Ybiricu ultimately blamed Sandoval for all the trouble and admitted that soldiers lost their wages, but he asserted that he could not intervene with settling their accounts. Ybiricu also confessed to the wrongs against the Adaeseños, who had received rotten goods at higher prices, but was basically powerless to stop the swindling, since Sandoval had established the notes, points, and rules of the games only he understood.[43]

The lawsuit the Adaeseños brought against former governor Sandoval for back pay stood in stark contrast to testimony in the interrogatory of his *residencia* proceeding conducted by Judge Briseño at San Antonio. While these witnesses contradicted the malicious behavior cited in the Adaeseño lawsuit, the *residencia* might have been nothing more than a whitewash of the governor's behavior. In response to the question of whether Sandoval carefully distributed soldiers' salaries, provided them and their families with supplies, and distributed guns, horses, and gunpowder, Mathias de Montes de Oca, a young, unmarried soldier from Mexico City, formerly resident at Los Adaes and then San Antonio, testified that the soldiers were "never mistreated, officers and soldiers spent their own salaries, well equipped with arms and horses, while their families assisted with all things because nothing was denied in the governor's store, and everything he gave was at the regulated price, threatening punishment to any of those who spent their salaries badly." Montes de Oca added that "no one plays games under any pretext nor any raffles done because the governor prohibited it, which he also heard said about the other presidios."[44] Mateo Ybarbo, a Spanish soldier from Los Adaes, stated that Sandoval was careful about the officers and soldiers being decently clad, well equipped, and supplied. According to Ybarbo, the governor "said that otherwise they could cause harm in service to the King and pays them so punctually without denying anything they requested." Whoever spent their wages unwisely or played games was punished. Ybarbo added that the governor "never permitted games among the soldiers of the presidios, nor raffles or anything like it whatsoever."[45] The other witnesses also testified in Sandoval's favor during his previous residencia hearing.

Both types of proceedings reveal the mixture of commerce and social ties that crossed the Texas-Louisiana border. Whether or not Sandoval prevented commerce with the French—except of goods permitted by law—and punished violators, Montes de Oca stated that Sandoval prevented soldiers and citizens at Los Adaes from trading with the French and did not allow anyone to go to Natchitoches, permitting only commerce in food but nothing else. Mateo Ybarbo reiterated that after the French entered Los Adaes, Sandoval ordered his officers to sell vegetables such as *camotes* (sweet potatoes) and did not allow the Adaeseños to purchase anything else from them. He also did not "permit the French to enter their homes but instead to sell goods publicly in the Plaza de Armas" of the fort. Ybarbo added that on another occasion, Sandoval "grabbed a soldier, named Pedro Becerra, who had some French white linen and took it from him, then watched as a soldier publicly burned his goods in the Plaza." Becerra received a warning against clandestine purchases; if it happened again, he would be severely punished.[46] In response to whether Sandoval tolerated any feasts and dances with the French that gave rise to disorderly conduct, Montes de Oca stated that the former governor only went once to French Natchitoches in order to visit the priests and Commandant St. Denis, but without any scandal. Ybarbo testified further that Sandoval often went to Los Adaes and "cordially visited with French officials and a priest of the company who administered sacraments to them." These visits were "celebrated with food and *fiestas* without going beyond the limits of modesty or any disorder in the soirées."[47]

Mateo Ybarbo's testimony and Lt. Joseph Gonzalez's letters offer contrasting narratives about Governor Sandoval's predicament during a volatile period for the Spanish on the Texas-Louisiana border and their counterparts at San Antonio. Did Gonzalez overly dramatize conditions at Los Adaes? Perhaps he simply wished to see his daughter at Natchitoches but was too afraid to desert his own post as the interim commandant. Quite possibly he and other Adaeseños sensed opportunities for economic development and growth that were being stifled by Spanish mercantilism and corruption; hence they expressed frustrations. Life appeared better on the other side of the border, as St. Denis allegedly tempted Lt. Pedro de Sierra into desertion along with his fellow troops from Los Adaes. Many Adaeseños were made aware of difficult times in Spanish Texas through military service at San Antonio on the border of Apachería and likely preferred to take their chances in Louisiana, where life appeared safer even in the face of poverty. Adaeseños at least took away some satisfaction with Sandoval's punishment and public humiliation at Los Adaes following their lawsuit even though his residencia proceeding at San Antonio essentially cleansed his record. Meanwhile, Lieutenant General Ybiricu had been transported from the prison at Los Adaes to the presidio at La Bahía.[48]

III

The governors of Spanish Texas who avoided legal problems during the 1730s and 1740s also cruised through their residencia proceedings. Those Adaeseños who testified revealed nothing negative about their administrations. These governors genuinely concerned themselves with the condition of Los Adaes and the soldiers and their families. In 1730, for example, Governor Mediavilla Ascona remarked that he did not have his full contingent of troops at Presidio Los Adaes because twelve soldiers were garrisoned at the East Texas missions, four escorted the postal courier, and fifteen cavalry were on patrol, presumably guarding livestock in harsh terrain that delayed them at least a week. A great many of the horses and some cattle intended for the troops at Los Adaes had been lost. Mediavilla Ascona noted that the price of clothing and food at Los Adaes did not exceed the regulated amounts that General Rivera instructed.[49] The residencia proceeding of his successor, Governor Bustillo, conducted at San Antonio, also occurred without any legal wrangling. All the witnesses were soldiers from the presidio at San Antonio or residents of Villa de San Fernando, while some Indians from the San Antonio missions also testified, but none offered incriminating evidence.[50]

The residencia of Gov. Tomás Felipe Winthuysen in the mid-1740s was also straightforward, with no Adaeseño complaints lodged against him. Felipe Muñoz de Mora, from Los Adaes, testified that Governor Winthuysen, who ruled from 1741 to 1743, equipped the soldiers with weapons, horses, and gunpowder and distributed their salaries. Mora declared that no illicit commerce took place under Winthuysen's administration—only the legal trade with the French for corn and beans—and that the governor did not allow anyone to travel to Natchitoches without permission or legitimate purpose.[51] Interestingly, the plazas of soldiers were traded among themselves like any other good. Bernando Leal *permutó* (bartered) his plaza with Cristobal del Río on June 1, 1741. On the same day, Andrés Chirino entered service at Presidio Los Adaes, having bartered with Ygnacio Gomes for his plaza.[52] The swapping of one's place in the fort was apparently common but gave no indication of duress or trouble—at least under Governor Winthuysen.

Checks and balances against the governor-commandants at Los Adaes, however, were nonexistent, and their absence was a source of the problems that arose occasionally. The governor had sole authority over the company's account books as the highest-ranking official in Texas. By comparison, in Spanish Florida, a province founded primarily for defensive purposes like Texas, governors also had a military role as captain general and were supposed to work closely with other officials residing in St. Augustine, Florida, on purchases for the troops. These officials had been entrusted with keeping the personnel records of the presidio and account for the goods stored in the warehouse and arsenal. St. Augustine, like San Antonio, had an active cabildo so that governors contended with various officials looking over their shoulders, yet even Florida officials mixed the treasury books with their own personal accounts, while audits rarely occurred.[53] The governors at Los Adaes ruled supremely with the temptations, personal motives, and unusual opportunities for rampant corruption due to their location so close to French Natchitoches. Governors who stayed above the fray, like Winthuysen, actually preferred to see Los Adaes shut down and the capital moved to San Antonio.

Conflicts over soldier indebtedness and the lack of a permanent source of labor contributed to the Adaeseños' growing resentment toward the governors. In 1744, during an investigation into the abuses committed in Texas, one official in Mexico City commented that the soldiers "always live in debt, often without necessary weapons and horses for duty, and made mere servants of the commanders."[54] He found that the price of goods were *arancelados* (at fixed prices) under the Regulations of 1729 but that the "governors and captains take these duties out, while the troops report increased profits for their superiors." Soldiers remained indebted often without weapons, horses, and other supplies.[55] In 1746, Friar Velasco from San Fernando College in Mexico City wrote about the problems at Los Adaes. He stated that the soldiers "have practiced planting corn in the following manner: the governor provides them equipment, including oxen, seeds, plowshares, large-curved hoes, mules, sacks for transport, and other necessary provisions, while the soldiers personally attend to plowing, planting, harvesting, storing, and gathering corn, and then place it in the governor's house." The governor kept half of the harvest and distributed the rest to the individuals of the company, but because of the "large and profound waste of the product, the governor charges their accounts five pesos per fanega which is the fixed price of the regulations." The soldiers were allowed to plant separately for themselves, which they often tried.[56] Father Velasco added that the "poor soldiers are prisoners of the governors in that barren land of Texas" and referred to the governors as "sovereigns to whom the settlers are supposed to give tribute, like Old France practiced with the inhabitants of the New Louisiana."[57] While distant government and church officials in Mexico City discussed these issues, they could not entirely punish governors of Texas who turned soldiers from Los Adaes into de facto field laborers, which served Spain's desire for settlement on the border of New Spain and Louisiana.

Meanwhile, the Adaeseños bartered whatever they managed to grow with Caddo and French visitors, but governors often disapproved of the practice and intervened. Friar Velasco mentioned the injustice and violence of the governor retaining the corn in his power with title of buyer. This "tyrannical injustice," he described, was "gravely detrimental to the soldiers by depriving them of what they can barter in exchange with the Indians for furs, buffalo skins, bear grease, which are the most common items said Indians exchange and the most highly regarded not only in the Presidio, but in the lands beyond." Rather than mistreat the troops, Velasco urged the Spanish governor to "look upon the soldiers as his own children for their advancement."[58] Spanish mercantilism restricted the manufacture of certain goods to Spain and discouraged free trade in its overseas possessions everywhere. The greatest obstacles to the development of the Adaeseño community were those governors who monopolized local and regional trade and kept soldier-settlers like indentured servants.

Despite the hardships under military rule, the soldiers and residents from Los Adaes became the first Hispanic ranchers and farmers to settle permanently on the Texas-Louisiana border. Adaeseño troops were supposed to receive their salaries from the governors for their plazas but often took side jobs as well. Amy Bushnell explains that in Spanish Florida, the "soldier's plaza was not his sole source of income"; he also had a secondary trade in that "every family man was also a part-time farmer."[59] This appeared to be the situation at Los Adaes, except the key to survival remained bartering with the French and Caddos due to location, blood ties, and scarcity of supplies as well as the uncertainty of living under despotic rule.

Spanish observers particularly noted the problem of governors and captains defrauding their soldiers by paying them on credit in overpriced food, supplies, and equipment. For example, the governor charged the soldiers' accounts sixty pesos for a leather coat of armor when the regulated rate was thirty pesos. According to Friar Velasco, supplies were "so miserly" distributed that the troops "went about barefooted, barelegged, poorly dressed, malnourished, and equipped" with daily rations of "parched tortillas without chili, which was scarce." Yet despite the soldiers' poor financial straits, their "bosses" (governor-captains) remitted the accounts to Mexico City as if the soldiers were all well paid and equipped, and they censored any desertions.[60]

The Regulations of 1729 set prices theoretically in favor of the soldiers against "avaricious governors, who recognized no rule of law, enriched themselves with a desire of *engrassar* [grease or fuel] their own fortune."[61]

The governors and captains at presidios in northern New Spain commonly practiced such extortion from their troops with or without regulations.[62]

The governors at Los Adaes monopolized the company's store and finances, which concerned royal officials in Mexico City. Friar Velasco suggested a solution to the problem of administering meat by instructing the governors to sell it according to reason and good conscience, with lower prices in the soldiers' favor during bad times. He also suggested that soldiers be allowed to buy corn elsewhere for two pesos or less rather than the five pesos the governor charged. The governors also should not charge excessive prices for beans and lard, which were considered the vital sustenance of life and more nutritious than corn. Velasco likened the price gouging to a "monopoly similar to a merchant having his ship seized by the English lacking such goods, and sells the stock back to the merchant at higher prices without making amends with that unhappy merchant." The governor's exclusive right to the corn was called into question as well as the soldiers' obligation to buy only from him.[63] Spanish mercantilism could no longer sustain the king's troops on the frontier, who needed more liberal trade policies.

The governors, on the other hand, defended charging interest on the goods they sold to the soldiers for a variety of reasons. Their main argument was that money had to be transported from the governor's account in Mexico City to purchase horses for the company and for beans and lard from the French. A governor ran the risk of pesos getting lost in transit along the Camino Real, and such losses came from his own pocket and not the soldiers'. In consideration of such risks, a two-peso increase of the premium above the eight pesos for late-arriving goods in one year became a 25 percent charge that seemed reasonable. According to the governors, the royal merchants in Mexico City charged 7 percent for lending money to the bosses of the presidios, which had to be recovered.[64] There were additional costs, such as the governor's use of an agent and power of attorney from Mexico City to make purchases for the protocol of requisitioning supplies and payment of salaries to the troops.

By the late 1740s, the viceroy, Juan Francisco Güemes Horcasitas, considered the legal complaints the Adaeseños made against Gov. Francisco García Larios at Los Adaes. Among the list of charges were the following:

soldiers lacked money to buy seeds from settler families because the governor paid their salaries only in goods (charge 4); gunpowder left over from the soldiers was used by the governor for trade with the Tejas Indians in exchange for deerskins, seeds, and other goods that he sold at higher prices (charge 5); and the governor sold corn, horses, and hides at higher prices to soldiers despite the first two items being set at a fixed price under the Regulations of 1729 (charge 6). Since these items became more abundant over time, they should have cost less, but the governor profited from the higher prices. Another one (charge 7) referred to soap that the governor purchased from Saltillo at one peso apiece and then sold for two pesos at Presidio Los Adaes.[65] Additional charges related to the improper use of the soldiers as personal laborers for farming and ranching, as former governor Sandoval had done the previous decade. Perhaps the Adaeseños remained hopeful in light of their successful litigation against Sandoval and improved governance under Orobio Basterra (1737–41), Winthuysen (1741–43), and Boneo Morales (1743–44).

The viceroy, however, noted "the difficulty and near impossibility" of the current investigation into Governor García and instead arrested the complainants. Specifically, four soldiers from Los Adaes—Andres Sánchez, Joseph Arias, Joseph Villarreal, and Marcos Losoya—were charged with arriving in Mexico City "without license and abandoning the presidio and cavalry." Apparently, they did not receive the proper passports from the governor.[66] That they bothered to travel along the Camino Real from the Texas-Louisiana border to the capital of New Spain, a distance of nearly 1,500 miles, reveals great desperation at Los Adaes or perhaps the extent of illicit trade on behalf of the governor or even French creditors at Natchitoches.

The viceroy deliberated the case and exonerated Governor García from all the charges. Regarding the charge that the Adaeseños lacked money to buy goods, the viceroy declared that "with so many settlements around them [the Adaeseños], the French colonies and various peaceful Indian settlements, it is doubtful the gravity of this charge." He added that since the prices were fixed by the new regulations and approved by the king, there was no justification specifically to this charge. As for the governor not providing adequate gunpowder and selling it to the Tejas

Indians, the viceroy consulted former governor of Texas Bustillo, who was Sandoval's immediate predecessor. The viceroy reasoned that with the many rivers and great distance from Mexico City to Presidio Los Adaes, it was possible that the governor lost gunpowder, but even if he had some, he could sell it to whomever he pleased. The viceroy merely said that governors should sell this equipment at just prices in order to avoid wrongs.[67] Ironically, the viceroy himself acknowledged the importance of the Adaeseños' dependence on their French and Indian neighbors as one solution to their problems of supply.

The viceroy likewise absolved the governor of two other charges. To the accusation that the governor sold goods at higher prices than the established costs under the law, his defense was, "It is well known that prices have increased since the *arancel* of 1729 some one-hundred percent for the goods in cotton, wheat, and china, which are the most expensive, yet the soldiers do not complain, and they even confess this." The viceroy found Governor García not guilty of this charge but said it was something that could arise later in his residencia proceeding. As for the last allegation about soap, the viceroy simply said the governor was not culpable in this complaint.[68] The Adaeseños were left with the impression that Spanish law was not always in their favor despite the custom of military *fueros* (rights and privileges) and their early success against Sandoval.

The Adaeseño soldiers who had traveled to Mexico City were released from jail but denied the justice they originally sought. Months later at Los Adaes, Governor García made all the soldiers of the company appear before him and obey the viceroy's order.[69] In this case, the viceroy's judgment in favor of Governor García also showed that there was not much the Mexico City official could do to ameliorate the conditions on the Texas-Louisiana frontier other than to reassign a bad governor and consider the possibility of expanding legal trade with the French to include clothing and equipment. After all, the viceroy could not ignore the likelihood of mass desertion in northern New Spain, especially for those Adaeseños on the border with Louisiana. Perhaps the arrest and release of Sánchez, Arias, Villarreal, and Losoya served as a reminder of their own duty to police the border and to question any persons suspected of disloyalty to the Crown or the governor.

Desertion became another form of resistance against corrupt governors, and the practice came up in the residencia of Governor Sandoval. An Adaeseño soldier named Juan Paulino deserted to French Natchitoches in July 1734 shortly after Sandoval became governor.[70] Juan Villarreal deserted a year later.[71] Sometimes the viceroy banished individuals to other forts before they stirred up trouble.[72] On December 9, 1735, Diego Villa Franca, Agustín Avila, and Juan Armijo were vacated from their plazas.[73] There were so many empty positions that Sandoval's residency judge, Governor Lugo, became alarmed.[74] Some of the twenty Adaeseño troops at San Antonio who served directly under the governor evidently fled to Los Adaes.

Soldiers still deserted whether governors were good or bad, so other motivations such as poverty might have pulled individual Adaeseños in either direction along the Camino Real into Louisiana or northern New Spain. On October 22, 1740, during the residency of Gov. Orobio Bazserra, the "deserter Felipe Sanchez sought shelter in French Natchitoches on the frontier of Louisiana, and his place was filled by Rafael del Trejo on December 20, 1740."[75] Under Governor Winthuysen, a soldier named Juan Antonio Luna "deserted to the city of Monterrey [Nuevo León] on September 4, 1742, arriving with a horse on escort duty from this presidio [Los Adaes], and in his place Joseph Antonio Peña entered service on January 1, 1743." The records do not reveal precisely why soldiers deserted, but whenever a soldier abandoned his plaza, his account was turned over to the Royal Treasury Office.[76]

The most wanted fugitive in Texas was don Manuel Antonio de Soto Bermúdez, as mentioned in the previous chapter. His immigration from Spain in search of his father he never knew led him eventually to Los Adaes, where he was a soldier. Manuel de Soto became a trusted advisor to Governor del Barrio in 1748. In 1754, de Soto fell from the good graces of the subsequent governor, Barrios Jáuregui, after having deserted Presidio Los Adaes for French Natchitoches. The Spanish governor considered de Soto's abandonment of his royal service an insult to the king's honor and his own.[77]

In the meantime, the work of missionaries among the soldiers and residents at Los Adaes and Natchitoches continued to fill spiritual needs and served as a means to keep governors informed of any movements across the border. Governor Winthuysen reported that Franciscans from Mission Adaes continued to perform the "duties of parish priests for the presidial soldiers and settlers by administering the sacraments and giving them spiritual nourishment."[78] In 1751, friar Pedro Ramírez Arellano from Mission Adaes certified that he went to Natchitoches "from time to time, when I found myself alone after the death of my companion, for the purpose of having frequent recourse to the holy sacraments." He also stated that many French troops and families had arrived from Europe at New Orleans, which Governor Barrios Jáuregui included in his own report to the viceroy.[79] Missionaries served as witnesses to legal documents and thereby possibly as eyewitnesses for the governors about any illicit behaviors. The presidial chapel at Los Adaes became a message board; laws and public announcements were posted on its doors.[80] The majority of the Adaeseños were illiterate, so they might have heard the governor, his officers, or friars read decrees aloud as part of weekly announcements near the end of church services. While the missionaries rarely castigated the governor's conduct in office from the pulpit, they offered hope to the Adaeseños through parables illustrating that salvation could be found in heaven if not on earth. The Franciscans, in turn, helped governors negotiate trade and peace with the Indians and eased tensions while they kept watch over the border.

Spanish officials juggled logistical support at Los Adaes in their preoccupation with guarding the border as the Crown sought to expand settlements in Texas due to additional threats from the Comanches on the Southern Plains and pirates in the Gulf of Mexico. In the early 1750s, Governor Barrios Jáuregui wanted his seventeen soldiers returned to Los Adaes from Presidio San Xavier, which was established in Central Texas with missions for the Tonkawa Indians. A *consulta* (council of advisors) held before the viceroy in Mexico City favored restitution of the Adaeseño troops to Los Adaes. Their presence on the border with French Louisiana maintained "the honor of the King's arms on its frontiers" should Spain and France turn against each other, especially considering "the deplorable state of one Presidio [Los Adaes] which on occasion does not even have three soldiers present and the disadvantage of being so far away that no other troops can sustain it."[81] The viceroy added that a French-Indian alliance could easily overtake Los Adaes because of its "defenseless condition" and, worse yet, could "cause us insult as well as loss of credibility in the King's forces and, by consequence, my own." The viceroy at last ordered the restitution of the seventeen soldiers to Los Adaes perhaps just in case of danger from across the border.[82]

Governor Barrios received good news about the return of his troops and desired to project an image of strength on the Texas-Louisiana border amid increased militarization in North America. In reality, Spanish forces remained no match for the combined French and Indian allies, but the governor likely had ulterior motives with trade or a future residencia in mind. He asserted "the grave necessity" for having these soldiers at "Presidio Los Adaes, the capital of this province on the frontier, which serves as a wall against the enemy to contain whatever hostility that its dominant pride intends." He added the Spanish justifiably could be more suspicious and afraid than ever.[83] The governor's comments reflected his concerns about the arrival of French ships in New Orleans to strengthen forces and settlements in Louisiana. The governor noted that the recent peace with the Lipan Apaches at San Antonio in 1749 further supported the return of his soldiers to Los Adaes, though perhaps he was unaware or unconcerned about greater threats elsewhere. After all, the French had grown more concerned with British American colonies east of the Mississippi than with Louisiana's border with Spanish Texas. The Spanish remained zealous about guarding New Spain's border with Louisiana against contraband trade, and movements by the French worried the commandant at Presidio Santa Rosa (Pensacola) in Spanish Florida.[84] The French and their Caddo allies could wipe out Los Adaes at any given moment, but each had their own reasons for keeping this Spanish fort in existence.

The concerns of Governor Barrios Jáuregui at Los Adaes included shoring up Indian alliances through gifting that mixed with contraband trade—perhaps more for his own material benefit than that of a remote king. He believed that commerce between the Spanish and Indians could divert the Indians' loyalty away from the French and toward Spain. In 1755, the governor sent Sgt. Domingo del Río and four other soldiers from Los Adaes—Cristóbal Cordova, Pedro Granados, Joseph Castro, and the sergeant's brother, Cristóbal del Río—for trade with the Bidais of East Texas on the San Pedro River (present lower Trinity River).[85] Sergeant del Río testified that he tried gaining a *patente* (alliance) with a Bidai Indian named Mateo by offering him a "braided sombrero, dress coat, shirt, and a rod"; he offered the same to another Indian named Tomás. In addition, he supplied them with "thirteen *arrobas* [325 pounds] of powder, fourteen arrobas [350 pounds] of ammo, three dozen *belduques* (long knives), five and half pounds of vermilion, twenty-five pounds of tobacco, twenty-one *sacatrapos* (wad hooks or corkscrews), and twenty-four combs."[86] This diplomacy raises questions about the diversion of resources intended for Spanish troops to the Indians of Texas as well as illicit trade.

Sergeant del Río testified later that Captain Mateo of the Bidai nation told him about a French ship on the lower Brazos River that left for New Orleans and the arrival of four Frenchmen with horses for commerce with the coastal Orcoquiza Indians. The Frenchmen told these Indians that they could trade with the French because France and Spain were friends.[87] The sergeant's brother, Cristóbal, added that the Orcoquizas also requested a Spanish mission for their people.[88] Another soldier, Granados, testified that the captains of the Bidai—Mateo and Tomás—returned with the Adaeseños to Presidio Los Adaes and met with Governor Barrios Jáuregui, "sat down at his table and were given meat, corn, salt, lard, and beans in abundance, and that upon returning to their rancherías distributed more powder, ammo, combs, vermilion, beans, and maize." Captain Mateo had asked Father José de Calahorra from Mission Nacogdoches if he could establish a mission for the Orcoquizas.[89] The gift giving to the Indians directly from Los Adaes explains in part why equipment and supplies for the Adaeseño troops were often in short supply. Just how long this gifting took place is unknown, though likely based on diplomacy and precedent, Aguayo established in 1721. Evidently, guarding the Louisiana border evolved into gaining the confidence of coastal Indians as well as the Caddos through gift giving.

The fact that there were few forwarding agents from Mexico City for Los Adaes over the course if its existence from 1721 to 1773 only served to strengthen the monopoly the governors had on goods and their distribution. During this period, there were fifteen governors with an average tenure of three to four years but only six agents. The longest-serving agent was Diego Antonio Giraud from the Royal Trade Office in Mexico City, like his predecessor Domingo Gomendio. The power of attorney that Gomendio received from the Adaeseños endured for nine years and four governors. Giraud became the new collecting agent in June 1741 during Governor Winthuysen's first year as governor-commandant.[90] Giraud held power of attorney for twenty years, minus the intervening years of Governor del Barrio Junco Espriella (1748–51), who actually utilized the services of former governor Bustillo as power of attorney for the soldiers at Los Adaes.[91] Giraud regained power of attorney by 1751 during Governor del Barrio's last year in power and stayed in this role until 1761, when another agent from Mexico City, Manuel de Cozuela, replaced him.[92] Cozuela held power of attorney until the end of the 1760s.[93] Diego Giraud simultaneously held power of attorney for Spanish troops at Presidio San Agustín de Ahumada from 1759 to 1760, where the garrison included Adaeseños.[94]

The power of attorney documents for the collection of salaries and equipment for soldiers were essentially legitimate tools for the diversion of resources into gift giving and trade with Indians and the French. The Adaeseño soldiers were owed around 25,275 pesos and 360 pounds of gunpowder annually.[95] By 1761, Governor Martos Navarrete certified to the king of Spain, his viceroy, and senior judges in Mexico City that the officers and soldiers at Presidio Los Adaes "have served their plazas and are on hand, trained for royal service without lacking in any obligation."[96] He repeated this certification over the next four years.[97] Governor Martos Navarrete added that in 1763, just two years after assuming command, he provided gunpowder to Caddo Indians, including the Tejas, Adaes, Ais, and Nacogdoches, plus Bidais, Tehuacanas, and Yscanis.[98] Such certifications did not appear under previous administrations in Spanish Texas, especially governors' reports on Indian gifts, which became increasingly common during the eighteenth century. The impoverishment and treatment of Adaeseño troops made desertion and smuggling very tempting alternatives for survival on the Texas-Louisiana border.

Evidently, the appearance of Los Adaes and the Adaeseños became disconcerting when the French visited for church, trade, and festive celebrations. Manuela Alcázar Barrios, wife of Governor Barrios Jáuregui, remarked in 1758 that she felt ashamed of the presidio's feeble conditions and the tattered clothing of the Adaeseño troops. When Governor Martos Navarrete reported for duty at Los Adaes in 1760, the hexagonal shape of the fort was formed by a flimsy wooden structure with a half-rotten stockade. The governor's wife felt that it was a matter of pride to improve the presidio, especially when she compared it to the French Natchitoches post.[99] Her husband, however, seemed more consumed with trade than the condition of the fort or troops at Los Adaes. Indeed, if the soldier-settlers from Los Adaes faced such dire poverty and corrupt officials that spiritual nourishment could not alleviate, then why bother sticking around when legal remedies were not guaranteed and the "border" with French Louisiana was so close? The opportunity for contraband trade with their Caddo, French, and African neighbors tempted the Adaeseños deeper into the forests of East Texas and Louisiana as they came into greater contact with foreign traders and merchants across a vast border region despite the Spanish officials' occasional attempts to prosecute smugglers.

Smugglers' Paradise

The French and Caddos lodged complaints against Spanish governors for disrupting trade on the Texas-Louisiana frontier, which coincided with Lieutenant Gonzalez's assertion that St. Denis encouraged the Adaeseños to desert across the border to Natchitoches. In May 1737, a Frenchman named Jean Baptiste Legros protested the unjust manner in which Sergeant Manuel Antonio de Losoya and five other soldiers from Los Adaes took him prisoner after his own commandant at Natchitoches sent him on April 12 to the Cadodacho Indians. Legros claimed they falsely accused him of introducing commerce into the Spanish nation, and he requested justice from Governor Lugo through the restitution of goods the Adaeseño troops confiscated from him, including 150 pounds of ammunition, 63 pounds of gunpowder, three guns, two dozen swords, nine hatchets, three horses, French clothing, a sombrero, farm tools, a kettle, and eight pounds of beads. He added that Lieutenant General Ybiricu, the highest-ranking officer from Los Adaes, issued him a license in early February granting him permission to pass through Texas and visit the Indians.[1] In his own defense, Ybiricu stated he owed money to a number of Frenchmen at Natchitoches, including Jean Baptiste Derbanne, from whom he obtained a gun, fine shirts, blue cloth, and other more conspicuous items, such as liquor and a deck of Spanish cards, from another French resident—all debts former governor Sandoval was responsible for.[2] Apparently, Ybiricu also smuggled Frenchwomen for prostitution at Los Adaes and was charged with excessive intimacy at Natchitoches.[3] The remoteness of Los Adaes from legal ports of entry in New Spain made the region a smugglers' paradise where governors monopolized commerce and Spanish officials could not entirely stop burgeoning contraband trade.

Indeed, Spain's empire became a sieve for contraband and corruption wherever its subjects came into contact with foreigners. During the eighteenth century, France sought to eliminate the commercial privileges that Spain had granted England at the conclusion of the War of the Spanish Succession in 1713. The English held legitimate rights to introduce goods and slaves at Havana (Cuba), Veracruz (Mexico), Cartagena (Venezuela), and Buenos Aires (Argentina), which became the sources of contraband on an unprecedented scale in colonial Latin America. Spanish Bourbon reformers, who remained divided over how best to protect its fledgling national economy and increase the flow of goods from Spain to its colonial ports, received a boost with the ascension of Carlos III to the Spanish throne in 1759. The English occupation of Havana and Manila in 1762 near the end of the Seven Years' War also prompted calls for Spanish reform of the military and economy. While the upsurge in mercantile trade and mineral production increased Spanish government revenues from customs duties, sales taxes, and tobacco and mercury monopolies, reformers also sought to restructure colonial administration to reduce complicity in contraband from more lucrative and dynamic transatlantic economies.[4] Historian Marcy Norton explains how contraband trade in tobacco, for example, had long been the greatest impediment to the Spanish Crown's ability to maximize profits, with huge gaps between market prices from Virginia or ports in France and the Netherlands compared to monopolized prices from Cuba. Contraband also arose internally from fraud and corruption that took hold over workers and contractors.[5] Any notions of "free trade," on the other hand, remained potentially devastating for Spain's control over its own subjects, much less Indians, Europeans, and Africans on its frontiers in Latin America.

Those fears became real at the local and regional levels in Texas, where some governors manipulated the account books of soldiers and controlled the company's store yet entered into illicit trade in deerskins and buffalo hides. Like their counterparts elsewhere in northern New Spain, the governors of Spanish Texas dominated this "shadow" economy that left no opportunity for the development of a merchant or middle class.[6] Deerskins and tobacco were frequently exchanged for desirable French products and Spanish livestock, which became effective currency on the Texas-Louisiana borderlands, similar to other backcountry regions in North America.[7] Such a setting was akin to the eastern Caribbean, which Norton describes as a "colonial backwater" that long had been a "place where unlikely alliances formed between autonomous native American communities, English and Dutch privateers, Portuguese merchants, and desperate Spanish settlers."[8] Historian H. Sophie Burton describes something similar in the formation of vagabond communities on the Louisiana-Texas frontier among castoffs or deserters from French, Indian, Spanish, and African Creole societies. Bayou Pierre—located north of the boundary between Los Adaes and Natchitoches at the Arroyo Hondo—became one such mixed community and was problematic for Spanish and French control. The Yatasi at Bayou Pierre had been one of three Indian villages through which French traders initially entered illegally into Spanish Texas for trade with the Hasinai and Tonakawa between the Trinity and Guadalupe Rivers. These traders would also acquire stolen horses and cattle from ranches of San Antonio and La Bahía.[9]

To be sure, the governors at Los Adaes occasionally enforced Spanish prohibition against foreign trade by arresting French merchants from Louisiana and attempted to win over the loyalty of the Caddos at the center of contraband activity with the Spaniards and French.[10] Although contraband overseas from Louisiana's harbors proved more lucrative for Spanish ships, the reach of illicit trade goods extended well into the interior of North America.[11] The lure of smuggling in New Spain remained attractive enough for French traders, especially during the early development of plantation agriculture in Louisiana and the dependency of Indians, settlers, and slaves on a frontier exchange economy.[12] Adventurous French traders kept crossing into Spanish Texas and beyond as long as markets existed. The blending of the smuggling frontier with mercantilism ran deeper into the Texas wilderness despite any attempts of the Spanish governors to prevent the illicit flow of goods and people across the border with Louisiana.

The Texas-Louisiana borderlands remained fluid into the middle decades of the eighteenth century and compromised not only the purpose of Los Adaes (to halt the flow of illicit commerce) but also the goal of the missions (to convert the Indians). Friar Joseph Ortes de Velasco wrote that Gov. Francisco García Larios engaged in illicit commerce with the Indians while "removing the liberty that everyone has by natural right to buy and sell to whomever they please." The governor, Velasco argued, "prevented the infidel Indians, with whom most trade in *chamois* and buffalo skins, from gathering around and becoming intimate with the Spaniards and people of reason from the presidio [Los Adaes]," as had occurred in the neighboring provinces of Nuevo León and Coahuila in northern New Spain. This upset the Indians and the French from Louisiana. Friar Velasco also blamed the governor's control of commerce for delaying the Caddos' reduction to mission life. He said the Indians had "come to regard all the Spaniards as greedy and miserly, like the governors, since they take in all the skins and furs for the increased interest they gain."[13]

Governor García acquired gamuzas from the Indians and, in turn, sold the same deerskins to his soldiers at higher rates for his own profit. Father Velasco reported that the governor "bartered" gunpowder and ammunition in exchange for hides from the Indians. The governor justified such transactions as beneficial to his troops because they could sell these furs in Saltillo at two hundred pesos each, or ten reales in silver, and purchase necessary goods there at prices cheaper than at Presidio Los Adaes. The governor also claimed that "if it is legal to profit from [selling] buckskin armor to the troops at sixteen pesos and reales, then it is also licit to profit from the fur trade."[14] Even if the distant officials knew about the Spanish governors' private dealings in the growing fur trade of French Louisiana, there was little they could do about the commercial monopoly or corruption of the governors at Los Adaes other than to abandon the fort altogether, as Governor Winthuysen had suggested earlier.

Father Velasco offered solutions to Governor García's questionable fur trade with the Indians. He suggested regulating the gunpowder and ammunition the governor bartered for the furs by having it purchased first from the royal government's *estanco* (monopoly store) in Mexico City "even though all the [freight] costs would be added until arrival at [Presidio] Los Adaes." Expenses could be curtailed with the purchase of gunpowder and ammunition from the French nearby in Louisiana instead of Mexico City. This gun trade already occurred illicitly under Governor García, to which he alluded in his own *consulta* (conference) with Spanish officials, so why not legalize such weapons sales? Father Velasco also expressed the concern that the Adaeseño soldiers were employed more for the governor's own benefit than for the Spanish Crown. He believed the governor charged exorbitant interest for the skins, in excess of eighty to one hundred pesos, which soldiers were forced to purchase. To buy furs from the governor, Father Velasco lamented, "deprived the soldiers of their liberty; current theology and jurisprudence would annul all such contracts as illicit and sinful." He compared Governor García to a *contrabandista* (smuggler) who sold products at greater costs than licensed traders and merchants.[15] Father Velasco believed the governor's trade monopoly had to be addressed.

Spanish governors who engaged in contraband trade on the Texas-Louisiana borderlands in fact also urged the relaxation of mercantilist policies, but to no avail. In 1753, Gov. Jacinto de Barrios Jáuregui requested permission from the viceroy for Spaniards to trade freely with the Indians in the same items that the French bartered with the Caddos, especially gunpowder, ammunition, muskets, cloth, blankets, razors, and knives. The governor argued that these goods could "be obtained without expenditure of money since the French want deerskins more than gold or silver and this trade affords them a huge profit." By paying in skins, the Spanish avoided having to barter equipment, such as saddles and horses, which were needed for royal service to the king.[16]

Governor Barrios Jáuregui offered to send the viceroy samples of the goods the Indians traded with the French, against whom the Spanish could not compete directly unless Spain permitted its own subjects to participate freely in frontier commerce. Besides the guns and ammunition from the

French, the governor specifically referred to red and blue breechclouts; a blanket; red, white, and blue glass beads; a mirror; and a shirt. All these items were of better quality than what the Spanish produced, and it was less costly to transport these goods from French Louisiana than to receive supplies from the interior of New Spain. This increased the French advantages in their gift giving with Indians, especially with an emphasis on commerce over religious conversion.[17] Should officials in Mexico City or Madrid still refuse to allow open trade with the French and Caddos, the governor of Texas was prepared to carve out his own little kingdom in Los Adaes through an underground market.

The governor apparently took the prerogative to trade with French Louisiana without the approval of distant officials. As governor-commandant of Los Adaes during the 1750s, he monopolized the Spanish trade with the French and Indians, particularly at the lower Trinity River, with the establishment of Presidio San Agustín in 1755, which was meant to guard against European encroachment into Southeast Texas along the coast. The governor used Adaeseño soldiers—Lt. Marcos Ruíz, Domingo del Río, Juan Antonio Maldonado, and Jacinto de León—as his agents to smuggle goods from French Natchitoches to extend illicit commerce with the Bidai and Orcoquiza Indians, whom French traders visited on the lower Trinity and Brazos Rivers. The Adaeseños bartered the French merchandise for Indian corn, hides, and horses. The Caddos acquired horses through trade with Southern Plains Indians, who raided Spanish settlements and ranches elsewhere in northern New Spain.[18]

Governor Barrios Jáuregui profited most handsomely during imperial warfare, though he was likely not the first governor to take advantage of trade opportunities wherever possible. He also avoided the legal troubles and investigations into smuggling that faced other governors, especially during border disputes with French officials over the Texas-Louisiana boundary. His term as governor totaled eight years, from 1751 to 1759, more than any tenure of his predecessors. He apparently benefited from increased trade on account of the French and Indian War, which broke out in the Ohio River valley in 1754. Spanish concerns about French intentions in Louisiana heightened following the War of Austrian Succession (1744–48), during which Spain and France allied against Britain. The ensuing peace ironically allowed King Ferdinand VI of Spain to shift his attention to colonies overseas, particularly French claims to Texas.[19] The French, however, remained concerned about their increasingly bloody competition with the English over the fur trade in North America and reinforced French settlement in reaction to population growth in British American colonies. France did not need distractions on Louisiana's border with Texas and encouraged trade into the west.

Meanwhile, the Spanish became concerned about the lack of subjects in Texas on the periphery of the imperial rivalry between France and England in North America. By 1750, the English had over a million settlers in its thirteen colonies along the Atlantic coast, while France had around sixty thousand settlers scattered beyond the Appalachian Mountains, northwest of the British colonies, from the Saint Lawrence River to the Great Lakes and southward along the Mississippi River to New Orleans. When the French and Indian War erupted, there were four large Indian confederacies strategically situated between the French and English colonies in North America that held the balance of power throughout much of the war. These great Indian nations included the Iroquois in the Great Lakes region and the Cherokees, Creeks, and Choctaws on the southeastern frontier of North America, all of whom ably played the French and English against each other. While the French relied mostly on alliances with Indians to fight the imperial struggle, the British eventually pumped massive economic and military assistance into its North American colonies in addition to their alliance with the Iroquois in the northern borderlands and the Chickasaw in the southern borderlands.[20] Meanwhile, approximately 5,000 Caddos surrounded the Spanish and French on the Texas-Louisiana borderlands without the seemingly endemic violence on other frontiers. Overall, Spanish Texas had around 2,500 subjects by the mid-eighteenth century, so the small band of settlers at Los Adaes continued to rely on friendly commerce with the Caddos and French Natchitoches as Spain considered proposals for expansion of defensive settlements in Texas to protect against an invasion from the Gulf of Mexico.

The Spanish grew more alarmed, however, over French movements in Louisiana on the eve of the French and Indian War. In 1752, the viceroy convened the Royal Council of War and Estates in Mexico City to investigate the latest French threat to Spanish Texas and delineate a firm border between their respective colonies. Among the many issues debated was whether a Spanish force should be placed on the San Pedro River (lower Trinity River) to monitor the French more closely along the coast, which eventually led to the establishment of Presidio San Agustín and Mission Orcoquiza several years later. They also considered sending an engineer to survey the border with Louisiana. The council debated sending instructions to the French to pull back from the west bank of the Red River before they became fortified. In the meantime, the Spanish could reinforce Los Adaes, as they did with Veracruz in the southern Gulf of Mexico, to defend Texas against the French and Indians. The council equally desired to determine if the Texas-Louisiana border was the Colorado River (present Red River) or the Mississippi in order "to avoid any danger and oppose whatever trade there might be between the two crowns." Members of the royal council believed that border problems at Los Adaes began under Governor Sandoval's rule precisely when St. Denis had moved a portion of his post across the Red River. Without the resources to build a line of forts along the Texas-Louisiana border, the Spanish continued to investigate the matter.[21]

The viceroy in Mexico City ordered the governor at Los Adaes to take testimony from the Adaeseños about French activities along the border just as France began to shore up its Louisiana settlements. The interrogatory consisted of just four questions. First, where precisely was the border between Spain and France along the Texas-Louisiana frontier? Second, what year did the French trespass into Spanish dominions, particularly Texas? Third, what amount of territory did the French actually take from Spain? Lastly, what posts, settlements, and forts did the French construct in Spanish territory? By early 1753, Governor Barrios obeyed the viceroy's command and questioned twelve Adaeseños.[22] The first witness who appeared before the governor was Juan Antonio Amorín, one of the original soldier-settlers in Aguayo's expedition that established Los Adaes. According to Amorín, the border between Spanish Texas and French Louisiana was the Colorado (Red) River. He stated that the French trespassed into Spanish territory in 1735 during Governor Sandoval's administration even though there were already three French houses on the west side of the Red River when Governor Aguayo arrived in East Texas. The amount of Spanish territory France "usurped was probably a rock's throw in distance." In response to the last question, Amorín said he did not know if the French had constructed more posts.[23]

The other witnesses provided testimony similar to Amorín's. Lt. Joseph Gonzalez, another original settler at Los Adaes, said the border also was the Colorado River, which the French called "Rus." He said the French trespassed in 1735 or 1736 but that "some residents had passed much earlier and permanently to this side of the river where there were three houses that the Sir Marquis [Aguayo] found." Gonzalez described the distance as "a musket shot away" but said that the French did not construct any more fortifications in Spanish territory. Another witness, Joseph Antonio Rosales, stated that the border between both crowns was the Gran Montaña (Great Mountain), or Arroyo Hondo, but that it should have been the Red River.[24] All twelve Adaeseño witnesses appeared undisturbed, however, about minor French encroachment from Natchitoches across the Red River.[25] Governor Barrios also seemed unconcerned with the French presence nearby in Louisiana. He stated that he could not determine the border between Texas and Louisiana, so he asked the viceroy for advice in the matter.[26] Meanwhile, the governor continued to trade with the French and Caddos, which truly mattered most to him regardless of any border.

The viceregal officials in Mexico City, apparently determined about defending New Spain's border with Louisiana, could only send additional recruits, as they remained distrustful of the French building forts in New France and shoring up Indian alliances. During its questioning of Governor Barrios Jáuregui, the Council of War and Estates remained adamant that former governor Sandoval did absolutely nothing to prevent the French from trespassing into Texas other than having protested in writing. Advisors to the viceroy, on the other hand, noted that even if Sandoval had resisted encroachment from Louisiana, "he could not have done so considering his few forces compared to the French together with the Indians." The advisors made reference to the many treaties St. Denis and his son held with the Indians, among whom he distributed many items "the Indians craved."[27] The council fretted over the fact the French entered into agreements with Indians from Texas, such as the Tejas, Nacogdoches, Nazones, and Nadotes, and provided them with "muskets, gunpowder, ammunition, shirts, blankets, loincloth, beads, vermillion, and other appreciable goods."[28] The Spanish remained unsatisfied with the testimony from the Adaeseños and the failure to intercept illicit French commerce in Spanish territory. Clear demarcation of an international boundary between Texas and Louisiana remained elusive for Spain for the remainder of the eighteenth century.[29]

While Mexico City officials perceived this potential threat from Louisiana between 1735 and 1754, they worried about the complicity of governors in Texas who monopolized trade with the French and Indians at the expense of the Adaeseño community. However, it proved difficult to indict Spanish governors. For example, the residencia of Gov. Orobio Bazterra in 1741 revealed that he only permitted "licit" trade in corn between French traders and Spaniards at Los Adaes and took precaution against the introduction of "contraband" goods, such as gunpowder and ammunition. He forbade any Adaeseño from "trading or entering into agreements with anyone from Natchitoches."[30] The residencia of Governor García in 1748 revealed that he too forbade the Adaeseños from trade with the French. García stated that he "did not tolerate, but rather burned and scattered the few shirts, bottles of liquor, and some gunpowder" trafficked at Presidio Los Adaes.[31] One French trader arrived at Los Adaes "with a license to sell sweet potatoes and peaches, but also brought gunpowder in his basket, not realizing that the guard of the company's registry discovered it, which the governor ordered to be burned, and then admonished the Frenchmen that if it happened again he would be punished."[32] Governor Winthuysen's recommendation for the removal of Los Adaes and the East Texas missions appeared to offer one solution to contraband trade with Louisiana. On the other hand, the Adaeseños evidently wanted to stay on the Texas-Louisiana borderlands, with markets free of government regulation.[33]

By 1750, the Spanish began to suspect the implicit involvement of Gov. Pedro del Barrio with contraband trade and lax vigilance on the Texas-Louisiana border that could have a domino effect on New Spain. The viceroy expressed concern over the arrival of French vessels the previous year on the Mississippi River for colonization and trade with Spanish soldiers. He believed that the French, who inched closer each day toward Los Adaes, could easily penetrate the adjacent provinces of northern New Spain, including New Mexico, Coahuila, Nueva Vizcaya (present Chihuahua), and Nuevo León, where "they could take advantage of their rich minerals and introduce illicit commerce." According to information from Capt. Antonio de Mederos at San Antonio, the viceroy stated, "It has been secretly rumored that Governor don Pedro del Barrio [y Espriella], who is completing his term, conducted trade in the French colony and placed goods into his store through the hands" of his lieutenants—Joseph Gonzalez, Antonio Losoya, and Marcos Ruíz. The viceroy ordered Barrios Jáuregui, the new governor of Texas, "to investigate those accused of said illicit commerce, apprehend the ones found guilty, and confiscate all their goods."[34]

Governor Barrios Jáuregui investigated smuggling at Los Adaes after his arrival in 1751 but did not punish anyone. The Adaeseños who were interrogated, in fact, did not accuse former governor del Barrio of any wrongdoing. All of the Adaeseño witnesses, including Felipe Muñoz de Mora, Domingo del Río, Manuel Losoya, Joseph Gonzalez, Juan Antonio Amorín, Pedro de Sierra, and Domingo Chirino, testified that their previous governor did not engage in illicit commerce with the French and that they "[did] not know, or had even heard said" that he introduced goods into his store at Los Adaes with the help of other Adaeseños.[35] The Adaeseños and especially officers certainly wished to avoid implicating themselves as collaborators or agents of the governor in this border trade.[36]

Mexico City officials, however, had evidence to the contrary and noted how deeply entangled the Adaeseños had become with commerce on the Texas-Louisiana borderlands. A *consulta* (council) of the viceroy's advisors became particularly concerned about Texas and "the annual revenue the French obtain in the area of Los Adaes, introducing clothes in exchange for meat, silver, and other convenient items." They declared that "soldiers from the Spanish presidios, like the [Spanish] citizens, reciprocate with conveyance in rafts of all these goods in addition to saddles from their own horses which they bring to New Orleans" and that "on their return trip take clothes back to the Spanish places from where they came."[37] The Adaeseños welcomed French traders, since contraband trade allowed them to clothe and feed themselves—even indulge a bit—and to fight poverty, corruption, and mercantilist policies against free trade. French merchants used the pretext of trading vegetables at Los Adaes to introduce contraband goods, including alcohol.[38]

Indeed, perhaps the most abused items for the Adaeseños and Indians on the Texas-Louisiana borderlands were wine and brandy. In November 1751, Mexico City officials were particularly appalled that Adaeseño soldiers "bartered horses and saddles with the French from Natchitoches in exchange for 150 pounds of brandy and 18 barrels of wine."[39] The smuggling of alcohol into Los Adaes began as early as the 1730s, if not sooner, when the viceroy first permitted legal trade in foodstuffs from French Natchitoches. The regulation of alcohol remained difficult for the Spanish on the Texas-Louisiana border, as it did with guns, ammunition, and powder. As the late historian Jack Jackson surmised, Governor Barrios Jáuregui likely "made the most money" from contraband trade.[40]

Barrios Jáuregui not only concluded that his predecessor was innocent of smuggling, but after investigating the boundary issue between Texas and Louisiana, he apparently expanded on his predecessor's illicit trade and punished the Adaeseños who dared to challenge his own monopoly and power.[41] For example, Manuel Antonio de Soto Bermúdes, the immigrant from Spain mentioned earlier, conducted business at French Natchitoches and drew the ire of the governor for reasons beyond just trade. De Soto's marriage to St. Denis's daughter at Natchitoches in 1754 and his attempts to rally the Adaeseños against the governor stoked memories of St. Denis nearly twenty years before. Worse yet, Manuel de Soto had deserted Los Adaes on January 21, 1753, because of his alleged outrage that Barrios Jáuregui did not retain him as his personal secretary.[42] Those Adaeseños who transferred their loyalty to Governor Barrios Jáuregui remained silent, perhaps hoping to retain their trade ties with Natchitoches. Those individuals who traded independently without a license from the governor faced possible prosecution, imprisonment, and banishment.

Curiously, however, the residencia of Barrios Jáuregui did not unveil incriminating evidence about his contraband trade with the French between 1751 and 1759. The Adaeseños did not indict him, just as some of them had claimed to know nothing about the illicit trade of his predecessor. The eighth question from the residencia asked whether Barrios Jáuregui had prevented any foreigners in nearby Louisiana from introducing any goods except those foods and supplies permitted under Spanish law and if he punished any persons engaged in the trafficking of contraband. Felipe Muñoz de Mora testified that the governor "prevented the French from introducing any goods, except corn for the maintenance of this company [Los Adaes] and community, and whenever convoys occurred he sent persons to register them to his satisfaction." Muñoz de Mora, by then seventy-five or eighty-one years old (depending on the documents), was "unable to sign his own name because of the trembling in his hand due to his advanced age," so the residency judge, Gov. Angel de Martos y Navarrete, signed on his behalf.[43] Domingo Chirino, forty-five years old, also testified that Barrios Jáuregui did not allow illicit trade with the French colony and punished those individuals who did.[44] In fact, none of the twenty-four witnesses, consisting of twelve soldiers and twelve residents from Los Adaes, incriminated Barrios Jáuregui.[45]

His successor, Martos Navarrete, contradicted this residenica at the end of his own term when he disclosed that Barrios Jáuregui actually did engage in contraband trade. Martos Navarrete also blamed Barrios Jáuregui for the delays of postal deliveries at Los Adaes due to his nonpayment of such expenses.[46] Most governors did not hesitate to make themselves appear better than those whom they replaced, especially regarding smuggling, border disputes, Indians, and just about any other administrative matter. Governor Martos Navarrete, however, added that Barrios Jáuregui actually engaged in illicit trade with *indios bárbaros* (savage Indians).[47] In 1761, during Martos Navarrete's investigation of his predecessor at Los Adaes, Juan Antonio Maldonado, an Adaeseño muleteer and freighter, testified that "from the time don Jacinto maintained trade [in 1751] with the Bidais, Tejas, Nabedache, San Pedro [Orcoquiza], Tonkawas, and Illinois[?] Indians, the declarant [Maldonado] was always with his son-in-law, Ignacio de San Miguel." Maldonado testified that Pedro de Sierra, from Los Adaes, carried on such Indian trade with the help of his son, Bartholomew, and another person named Joseph Valentín. Furthermore, Jacinto de León *traficaba* (trafficked) with Indians farther north by order of Sierra but apparently died while doing so, and the Indians returned his body to Mission Nacogdoches. Sgt. Domingo del Río, from Los Adaes, also traded among the Indians with the help of his son Joaquín and his brother Cristóbal, who passed away at

San Antonio.[48] Apparently, smuggling on the Texas-Louisiana borderlands became somewhat of a family business for Adaeseños, especially mixed with elite family networks at Natchitoches.

Maldonado described a rather brisk illicit commerce. Among the items he traded with the Indians were twenty-five pounds of gunpowder, fifty pounds of ammunition, six guns, vermilion, knives, beads, tobacco, combs, *eslabones* (steel links or strike-a-light), sacatrapos (wad hooks), and other small items. Besides the help of his son-in-law, who died before the investigation, Maldonado received assistance on another occasion from Pedro Granados. Significantly, Maldonado testified that he "many times brought the guns, ammunition, gunpowder and the rest of the trafficked goods from Natchitoches for them to take to the Indians" and that on a "couple of occasions," he had returned with "hides, chamois of buffalo, and horses, which were distributed among the company [Los Adaes]." However, he did not know "how many of each species [of skins and furs] there were," though he claimed that the other soldiers he mentioned "also brought the same." Maldonado added that every time he transported the hides and furs for sale to the French at Natchitoches—"and it was many times"—he returned twelve mules loaded with these items.[49] Adaeseño soldiers did the governor's bidding, yet how many side deals they made with the Caddos, French, or other Spanish subjects may never be fully known, especially if they were never apprehended.

Lt. Joseph Gonzalez evidently estimated the number of buffalo hides and furs that the Adaeseños obtained from the Indians and transported to French Natchitoches. He stated that "on several occasions they took 1,500, other times 1,000, and still other times 800."[50] The chamois and horses again were distributed among the company at Los Adaes, though the lieutenant did not say exactly how many. Lieutenant Gonzalez probably knew better than anyone else the number of buffalo hides and furs because he managed the governor's store at Presidio Los Adaes. Based on his testimony, in nine trips to Natchitoches for one year alone via Adaeseño freighters, Barrios Jáuregui sold approximately 9,900 hides and furs at French Natchitoches. The multiplication of this figure over the eight years Governor Barrios Jáuregui remained in power at Los Adaes results in nearly 80,000 animal hides during the 1750s, a figure that is likely an underestimation of the total hides and furs smuggled. Since this fur trade involved the Orcoquiza and Tonkawa Indians in addition to the Caddos, the governor also likely used Adaeseño soldiers who were assigned to Presidio San Agustín on the lower Trinity River for barter with the Orcoquizas once this fort and mission were built in 1755. The same arrangements likely occurred with Adaeseños temporarily garrisoned at Presidio San Xavier in Central Texas for barter with the Tonkawas around the same time. Whether or not the governor used Spanish soldiers at the presidios of San Antonio and La Bahía in a similar fashion with other Indians remains unknown. The archival records suggest that Barrios Jáuregui engaged in a relatively significant fur trade together with cattle and horses on the Texas-Louisiana borderlands while moving out Adaeseño troops from Los Adaes to other presidios in Texas.

Lieutenant Gonzalez mentioned that Maldonado, along with Sgt. Pedro de Sierra and Sgt. Domingo del Río and his brother Cristóbal, in fact did the governor's bidding. There was an Adaeseño resident, Jacinto de León, who also assisted, but Gonzalez said that all the soldiers who usually accompanied them were not present. He added that the governor prohibited residents from trade with the Indians "because he did not want to harm those [Adaeseño soldiers] that the governor used [for trade]." He also confirmed that the Franciscan missionaries from the Nacogdoches and Ais missions exchanged gunpowder and ammunition with the Caddos for bear grease.[51] Other Adaeseño officers, such as Lieutenant Gonzalez, testified to how important contraband trade was to the local Spanish economy. While Gonzalez played a role in the governor's trade, he was not directly implicated and continued to serve at Los Adaes together with a new generation of Adaeseños, including his own grandson, such that military service, ranching, and trade became a family business regardless of whether it appeared illicit to Mexico City officials.

The captains of various Indian nations followed Gonzalez's testimony a week later and appeared before Governor Martos Navarrete at Los Adaes to stress the importance of contraband trade. These representatives were from the nations of the Nabidachos, Ais, Adaes, Caddos, Bidais, and Orco-quizas. They reportedly told the governor that "their sustenance derives from hunting upon which they eat and dress while it was indispensable they barter guns, gunpowder, and other necessaries" as well as that "the French came among them and drank to a toast for the Indians to seek their relief by going to Natchitoches."[52] In order to block this French trade with the Indians, Martos Navarrete stated that he "had no other way of securing [the loyalty of] so many Indians than to give licenses to Joseph de Acosta and Antonio Morales, residents of Los Adaes, to go traffic among these Indians . . . and that with this superabundant barter the Indians will fall under our devotion." He had Sgt. Domingo del Río, Domingo's brother Cristóbal, and his son Joaquín assist in this barter with the Indian *tamas* (captains) "to calm them down and establish their obedience."[53] Interestingly, the investigation showed that the French enticed the Caddo nations away from the Spanish governor just as St. Denis did many years earlier when he tried to lure Pedro de Sierra and other Adaeseños into desertion from Los Adaes. Trade among the Adaeseños, Caddos, and French proved vital to survival for each regardless of political loyalties. Unlike del Barrio and Barrios Jáuregui, however, Governor Martos Navarrete ran into legal troubles with the Adaeseños, many of whom perhaps felt like "handcuffed colonists" in Latin America, just as they did under Governors Sandoval and García in East Texas.[54]

The Franciscan missionaries indeed actively engaged in commerce, though they were more often in league with the governors than in opposition to their rule. The lack of Indian converts in the East Texas missions did not imply that missionaries simply watched trade bypass them while they administered the sacraments at Los Adaes and Natchitoches. They participated in local and regional trade networks to keep the missions functioning and methodically awaited the chance that the Caddos someday might gather voluntarily in the East Texas missions in the event of some calamity. Meanwhile, the Franciscans used the missions like trade posts either in collaboration with Spanish governors at Los Adaes or clandestinely on their own. Informal trade between governors and missionaries was a fairly common occurrence elsewhere in northern New Spain and was no less practiced in East Texas.[55] The isolation and lack of overland convoys compelled the missionaries to trade readily with the French and Indians. French Natchitoches continued to serve as a hub of contraband activity with the Spanish missions, and Presidio

Los Adaes increasingly oriented toward Louisiana and integration into an emerging Atlantic economy through New Orleans.[56]

In 1761, during another investigation into smuggling, Mexico City officials became alarmed about the complicity of the friars upon learning that St. Denis's son had incited the Caddos against the Spanish while former governor Barrios Jáuregui traded illegally with the Indians. Asked if Franciscans from the missions at Nacogdoches, Ais, Adaes, and Orcoquiza traded with "barbarous Indians," Juan Antonio Maldonado, the muleteer for the governor, answered in the affirmative. Maldonado stated, "When the missionaries from Mission Nacogdoches and Ais no longer have any lard, they send some hides over to Natchitoches to buy more" in addition to other goods, including "four to six pounds of gunpowder and eight to twelve [pounds] of ammunition," for distribution among the Indians near the missions "in exchange for bear grease for their yearly maintenance," all done during Barrios Jáuregui's governorship.[57] The Adaeseños not only provided guard duty at the East Texas missions; they assisted the missionaries with security in their trade with the French and Indians.

Lt. Pedro de Sierra's testimony, which collaborated Maldonado's declaration, revealed that local and regional trade expanded from Coahuila to Louisiana with the involvement of Spanish missions along the Camino Real. Sierra stated that Barrios Jáuregui traded such goods as horses, corn, gunpowder, ammunition, knives, beads, combs, and vermilion with the Indians of Texas and used Mission Nacogdoches to store five hundred to six hundred *cueros* (hides) and 250 to 300 gamuzas, some of which the Adaeseños Domingo Chirino and Joseph Arredondo transported and sold in Saltillo, Coahuila. Historian Frank de la Teja describes the Saltillo market as "part of a hierarchy of fairs" that emerged in Mexico during the seventeenth century but did not get royal approval until the late eighteenth century. According to Lt. Pedro de Sierra, the former governor also had his muleteer, Maldonado, transport five hundred to six hundred hides and 60 to 70 gamuzas for sale at Natchitoches.[58] This investigation uncovered a complicated web of illicit trade among governors from Los Adaes, Franciscans from the East Texas missions, French Natchitoches, and the Caddos. The extent of such contraband activity cannot be determined precisely, but it continued long after the death of St. Denis under the auspices of his son and other elite French merchants from Natchitoches. This east-west trade connection from northern New Spain and Louisiana strengthened over time. De la Teja explains how Saltillo developed into a large center for trade with annual fairs that attracted residents from Coahuila, Nuevo León, Texas, and eventually Nuevo Santander (present Tamaulipas), much like north-south trade from Santa Fe, New Mexico, to Chihuahua (Nueva Vizcaya).[59]

Evidently, the complicity of Franciscans in smuggling extended to the Spanish mission at La Bahía in the aftermath of the Louisiana transfer from France to Spain and conclusion of the Seven Years' War. In 1766, Sgt. Domingo Chirino, from Los Adaes, appeared before Governor Martos Navarrete and revealed that friar Francisco Zedano from the East Texas missions trafficked goods with the French and Caddo Indians (see appendix D). Sergeant Chirino went on patrol with four other soldiers from Los Adaes when he encountered Father Zedano with contraband in East Texas near the home of a Bidai Indian named Thomas. Chirino asked the friar if he had an order from the president of the missions for the goods, and the missionary said he had permission from the governor. Chirino, however, seized the goods and took these to Los Adaes along with the other individuals, Cristóbal Casillas, Agustín Rodríguez, Juan Palacio, Joseph de Anda, and two others (Isidro and Joseph Antonio), all caught with a string of pack animals among Father Zedano.[60] These men were muleteers, yet their residence went unrecorded in the investigation. De Anda sought refuge at Mission Los Adaes before he was called to testify and corroborated what Chirino had declared. Some of these men, however, were apparently from Los Adaes and might have traveled back and forth from Natchitoches to San Agustín to La Bahía. The length of time they had been engaged in smuggling also went undetermined.[61]

Meanwhile, Louisiana tobacco gained a reputation as the best weed and was greatly desired at Spanish missions in Texas. During the same investigation at Los Adaes, friars Bernando de Silva and Ygnacio Maria Laba, both Franciscans from Mission Adaes, certified the testimony of Father Francisco Xavier de la Concepción from Mission Ais about Father Zedano's contraband. Father Concepción stated the nearly three hundred pounds of French tobacco that Sergeant Chirino seized along the lower San Antonio road was intended for Mission La Bahía because the Indians there "found it most desirable." Apparently the Karankawas became "apostate" when this tobacco they expected fell into short supply. He added that because this tobacco is "only for the goal of recovering the Indians to the mission, it should be returned," as Governor Martos Navarrete wished to dispose of it.[62] The governor valued the tobacco at 163 pesos and made a bill of sale at the company store inside the presidio at Los Adaes, while the total amount of all the contraband was estimated to be worth 660 pesos.[63] The governor asked Lt. Joseph Gonzalez and Bernardo Cervantes to sell the tobacco before it spoiled.[64] By mid-1767, Spanish officials learned of Father Zedano's confession that the tobacco was indeed of French origin for use at Mission La Bahía. The officials ordered Governor Martos Navarrete to auction the other goods to the highest bidder and then recommended that another missionary replace Father Zedano at Mission Ais.[65]

The other contraband items taken from Father Zedano reveal that British cloth or threads filtered through East Texas from Louisiana long after St. Denis initially introduced similar goods into northern New Spain. Desperate times called for drastic measures; thus the efforts of Franciscan missionaries to sustain Texas missions led to their dependence on French and Indian commerce. Whether this trade was legal mattered little to the missionaries in the East Texas missions as long as potential Indian souls could still be saved and the flock gathered. Contraband trade among the governors and Franciscans, however, was not unique to the Texas-Louisiana borderlands. Historian Henri Folmer remarks that governors and missionaries in New Mexico "were as much a part of illegal commerce as the tradesmen."[66] The smuggling frontier evidently became more extensive across northern New Spain despite occasional Spanish interdiction and prosecution of illicit trade across the border with Louisiana. Regional trade increasingly pulled the province of Texas in opposite directions—one toward Natchitoches, which became part of greater Franco-Indian trade on the Southern Plains and Louisiana, and the other toward Saltillo, as de la Teja notes, where San Antonio merchants increasingly found themselves in the latter part of the eighteenth century.[67]

II

By the 1750s, the French controlled the fur trade on the Texas-Louisiana borderlands and Upper Louisiana (Missouri country). A French trader named Pedro Malec provided a perspective on its scale when he claimed that the French "obtain annually about 100,000 pounds of fur, as well as tallow and oil derived from bears, buffaloes, and deer" in trade with the Kadohadacho of southwestern Arkansas. This volume was approximately 10 percent of the total amount of goods exported from Louisiana by 1758, when it declined rapidly until the Louisiana transfer to Spain in 1762. The amount of French gifts to non-Caddoan groups became greater than presents to the Caddos, and this shift in diplomacy reflected the growing importance France placed on other Indians from Upper Louisiana in response to the bitter imperial rivalry with the English fur trade during the Seven Years' War. The trade in hides remained a viable business for French Louisiana but was less significant than the production of cash crops. The contribution of tobacco, indigo, sugar, and other products to Louisiana's exports rose dramatically as the colony's economy matured, with a greater emphasis placed on plantation agriculture under Spanish sovereignty and increased African slave trade with Havana, Cuba. While the fur trade in Louisiana grew steadily by the mid-eighteenth century, the Caddo share increasingly came into competition with other Indian nations and the French.[68]

The Caddos, however, continued to specialize in the supply of horses to the French at cheaper prices than the Spanish. The Hasinai of East Texas, whom the Spanish called Tejas, first acquired horses in the late seventeenth century through trade with the Jumanos, a seminomadic group from present West Texas, who obtained Spanish horses in New Mexico through raid or trade. The Caddos added livestock and horses following the initial Spanish attempts at settlement of East Texas and traded horses/mules to the French in Louisiana and the Illinois country. Domesticated Old World animals became an "eco-species" that thrived in the vast Southern Plains environment. In exchange, the Caddos received guns, ammunition, powder, hatchets, knives, clothes, and other goods, while Frenchmen in turn sold newly acquired horses in New Orleans for profit.[69]

French merchants from Natchitoches simultaneously made important links with Los Adaes through kinship and trade, as discussed in previous chapters, but the contribution of the Spanish from East Texas to the fur trade in the Louisiana economy naturally remained less overall than from the Caddos and other Indians. The trade in deerskins and buffalo hides for the Adaeseños, with the exception of the governor, was done more for subsistence than profit in order to pay off debts and fight poverty at Los Adaes. The Adaeseños still looked to wages from soldiering, stock raising, and farming in addition to contract work in Louisiana as vaqueros within the frontier exchange economy. Even the livestock trade between Texas and Louisiana, which required the permission of Spanish officials, remained illegal until Spain allied with France in 1779 during the American Revolution against Britain. The lack of free trade propelled the Adaeseños to continue their pursuit of opportunities across the border and, in the process, extended the Camino Real into Natchitoches even though its terminus was Los Adaes.

One of the most popular sites for smuggling operations near the Texas-Louisiana border became Bayou Pierre, located along the lower Red River in a highland district about forty miles northwest of French Natchitoches. In the early eighteenth century, one of the main villages of the Yatasi Indians, a small, sedentary Caddo nation, was on a high point that overlooked this spot. In 1722, the French established a trade post among the Yatasi called La Pointe, which formed, as historian Robert Vogel explains, "the nucleus of a polyglot community of Frenchmen, Spaniards, Caddoans, and mixed bloods." It eventually became known as the Bayou Pierre settlement around 1750. The commandants at Los Adaes and Natchitoches tacitly recognized the Bayou Pierre community as a dependency of French Natchitoches even though it also bordered on the ranches of the Adaeseños.[70] French traders from Louisiana first passed through the Yatasi village and Bayou Pierre on their way to smuggling goods into Spanish Texas and sometimes as far as New Mexico and Coahuila in northern New Spain.[71]

French merchants in turn created greater mistrust among Spanish officials in Mexico City, who were ever mindful of La Salle's efforts to claim Texas for France and St. Denis's smuggling along the Rio Grande in Coahuila. Periodic residencias of governors, investigations into trade with Indians in East Texas, and the strengthening of French settlements along the Mississippi by the early 1750s stirred passionate defense-of-sovereignty claims among viceroys and their advisors, which added fuel to counter-European movements with the expansion of Spanish fortifications in Texas. For instance, the French attempted to settle traders near the Bidai just south of the Tejas and the Orcoquiza Indians on the lower Trinity River northeast of present Houston, which drew a response. The Spanish adamantly prohibited commerce with "foreigners" anywhere in Spain's dominions, including Texas, where the governors from Los Adaes—such as del Barrio, Barrios Jáuregui, and Martos Navarrete—engaged in illicit trade with the French and Indians during the middle decades of the eighteenth century.[72] French merchants became targets for prosecution despite duplicitous Spanish governors while the Caddos played off each side in pursuit of their own interests.

Spanish interdiction against smugglers arose periodically whenever traders from Louisiana appeared among the Indians in Texas even as governors incorporated French-style diplomacy, which valued commerce over conquest. Governor Barrios Jáuregui wrote the viceroy in 1751 about the heavy influence of French trade among all the Indians of Texas, not just the Caddos. The French continued to provide Indians with muskets, gunpowder, vermilion, beads, and other goods. The Spanish engaged in similar trade but could not compete with the quality of goods, transportation, and cost issues from New Spain.[73] Barrios Jáuregui later reported about French trade again with the Indians, especially the Hasinai of East Texas, and noted the same goods as before in addition to shirts, blankets, and breechclouts. The French gifted Hasinai chiefs with braided hats, military coats, and other distinguishable wares. Before removing Manuel de Soto Bermudes as his personal assistant, Governor Barrios Jáuregui ordered him to visit these Indians, investigate where the French entered Texas, and discern the number of armed Indians in the province. The governor assigned another Adaeseño, named Antonio Barrera, as de Soto's interpreter because he spoke the Caddo language after having lived among them for many years.[74] Mexico City officials became alarmed that the French had been "making a silent conquest" of Spanish territory through trade and that, in the event of war between Spain and France, the Indians of Texas might side with the French.[75] The governors of Texas became aware of the need for a more practical Indian policy. Spain eventually adopted the French model of "trade, treaties, and toleration" from Louisiana in the late eighteenth century.[76]

De Soto's investigation of French activities in East Texas revealed that the goods exchanged were similar to items sold to the Adaeseños. Guns, ammunition, and clothing remained in great demand among the Spanish, not just the Indians. Impoverished Adaeseños also bartered furs with the French whenever possible, especially if livestock or saddles were unavailable, for lack of silver pesos. De Soto added that French traders ventured among the Nacogdoches Indians in East Texas along a route through the territory of the Yatasi Indians, who lived on the Spanish side of a river or lake known as Los Adaes.[77] De Soto's report only heightened concerns of the viceroyalty as they learned from the Spanish commandant at Presidio Santa Rosa in Pensacola that French naval ships and merchant vessels had arrived on the Mississippi River. French commerce enticed Spanish troops and residents from East Texas and West Florida through Natchitoches and Mobile, respectively, with New Orleans acting as a nexus connecting multiple regional trade networks with transatlantic commerce. The French held annual trade fairs much like the one in Saltillo at the other end of the Camino Real such that the Adaeseños found greater opportunities and accessibility with the French and Indian trade in closer proximity.[78]

By October 1754, the Spanish decided on colonization in southeast Texas rather than free trade after the arrest and imprisonment of Joseph Blancpain, a French trader from New Orleans.[79] Governor Barrios Jáuregui dispatched Sgt. Domingo del Río and twenty-five soldiers from Los Adaes under the command of Lt. Marcos Ruíz to verify whether the French had established houses at the mouth of the Trinity River among the Orcoquiza Indians with assistance from the Bidais. A Franciscan friar named Father Mariano de Anda accompanied the Spanish troops to retrieve some apostate Indians who had fled Mission San Xavier in Central Texas. On October 22, the governor recorded the return of four soldiers to Los Adaes with a letter from Lieutenant Ruíz and an inventory of provisions the French supplied the Orcoquizas.[80] Among the seized items were seventeen rifles, eight pistols, two thousand rounds of ammunition, twenty-three hatchets, seventeen iron pots, ten shovels, two hundred sombreros, nineteen blankets, some shirts, and 1,600 hides.[81] Perhaps the Tonkawa Indians, for whom Mission San Xavier was established, desired French tobacco like the Karankawas did at Mission La Bahía, but the weaponry surely raised suspicions among the Spanish.

The Council of War and Estates in Mexico City deliberated this disturbing news from November 1754 through October 1755 and learned that Blancpain had been arrested along with his brother, another Frenchmen, and two black men. One of the viceroy's advisors stated, "Governor Barrios y Jáuregui had the munitions, merchandise, and drugs confiscated then routed these through Presidio San Xavier de Gigedo, near Mission San Xavier, and distributed the items among the auxiliary troops as plunder." When the Spanish first took the prisoners to the presidio's jail, around fifteen Indians emerged and protested Blancpain's arrest, suggesting either he or other French traders were already accustomed to trade with Indians in the region. One of the French prisoners told the Spanish they expected the arrival of fifty families from New Orleans at the mouth of the Trinity River under the direction of Captain Monsieur de Sacreu.[82] Mexico City officials interpreted this news as an imminent French attack on Spanish Texas despite the preoccupation of France with the English threat east of the Mississippi. Governor Kerlérec of Louisiana aggressively pursued expansion of French settlements, and Blancpain served as one such agent whose trade with the Indians upset distant Spanish officials.

An equally important reason to establish a presidio and mission on the lower Trinity River was to check the Adaeseños from joining smuggling operations with the French and Indians of Texas. One of the royal advisors in Mexico City expressed the council's concern about the risk of Lieutenant Ruíz and Sergeant del Río bartering goods with French traders and the Indians. The temptation proved great for Governor Barrios Jáuregui to take control over Indian trade from the French and extend his own fiefdom. The advisor stated that missions and a presidio at the mouth of the Trinity River on the Gulf of Mexico would also "maintain the honor of the state and Nation" in an area of "fertile and beautiful lands" while avoiding any harm that could derive from French colonies.[83] By late 1755, another of the viceroy's advisors reiterated his predecessor's opinions to the Council of War and Estates but urged even greater caution. He believed the Spanish should "maintain peace with the Indians and slowly introduce the light of Evangelization until their hearts swell with the love for our true God by means of knowing our Religion." For the establishment of a Spanish civil settlement, he proposed "taking twenty or more families from Los Adaes and providing them with goods in the custom of our settlers."[84] The specific details for settlement in the coastal region of Texas near Louisiana followed the rhetoric of defending Spanish territory from "foreigners." Mexico City officials, however, still overlooked the problem of restrictive mercantile policies on the Texas-Louisiana frontier, where Spanish conquest, evangelization, and border enforcement remained illusory.

Meanwhile, Joseph Blancpain was transferred to prison in Mexico City and suffered an interrogation similar to that of St. Denis. Blancpain apparently had been imprisoned at least eight months as the Council of War and Estates deliberated his fate, which followed nearly four months of confinement that he had already endured in Texas. In February 1755, Domingo Valcarcel, an advisor to the viceroy, interrogated Blancpain at the Royal Prison of the Court and Hall of Confessions through an interpreter. After stating his name, Blancpain said he was a native of Mons(?) in Flanders (France), was married to María Anna Lambrote in Mississippi, and held an appointment from the French king as interpreter of Indian languages for eight nations. He also declared he was fifty-seven years old, owned a *tienda de mercancia* (goods store) at Natchitoches and Hacienda les Lanor(?), or Estate Lanor, located twenty-two leagues outside New Orleans, where he resided.[85] Blancpain, however, did not follow St. Denis's example of marrying into a Spanish family to create a network or feign loyalty to Spain but rather brought an entourage at a time when tobacco production became more stable in Louisiana. Spain distrusted their own Bourbon cousins on the Texas-Louisiana border despite sharing a common enemy in England.

Blancpain only fueled Spanish anxieties as he found his way to the mouth of the Trinity River for commerce seemingly on his own accord and arrived there around August 1, 1754, where he stayed for two months and two days before being apprehended. To be sure, however, he added that Governor Kerlérec from New Orleans gave him permission and a license to trade in the southwestern portion of the Louisiana colony. The goods he brought from New Orleans had an estimated total value of six thousand pesos, which included four and a half barrels of gunpowder, each weighing one hundred pounds; one thousand pounds of ammunition; two hundred pounds of munitions; a number of rifles, pistols, and axes; clothing of various types for men and women; thread; cotton linens; cauldrons; cutlery; and smaller items such as beads.[86] Blancpain declared that "at the time of my imprisonment and confiscation, I bartered some of the goods for deerskins, which had a value of 300 or 400 pesos."[87] The sheer quantity of trade goods and weapons he transported into southeast Texas without a proper license perhaps troubled the Spanish.

Blancpain also admitted to providing gifts to Indian chiefs from the Bidais and the Orcoquizas, which consisted of five to six guns, gunpowder, ammunition, knives, and small mirrors. He gave a greater quantity of beads, bells, and some *bayetas* (woolen cloth) specifically for Indian women. He adamantly declared that he had no trade agreement with these Indians but instead "bartered only with the nation of the Atacapas with whom I have traded for twenty-five years with a license."[88] According to him, the Atacapas, a semisedentary coastal nation on both sides of the present Texas-Louisiana border, went "to New Orleans for trade, taking horses, deerskins, and bear oil," and the French conducted business with this nation for thirty-two years in their many rancherías. Upon hearing from the Indians that Spaniards had arrived five or six days earlier and ordered them not to flee, Blancpain allegedly told the Orcoquizas he would ask "the Spanish governor if this was just," and he told the Indians "to calm down" because "the French and Spanish governor were one and the same." Interestingly, Blancpain refuted the rumor about the arrival of fifty families from New Orleans with a priest to establish missions.[89] Perhaps Blancpain knew more than he actually divulged.

Significantly, Blancpain's responses to the Spanish interrogator revealed more detail about French trade along the coastal region of southeast Texas that extended from the mouths of the Trinity and Brazos Rivers, near present Houston, eastward approximately 150 miles across the mouth of the Sabine River into present southwestern Louisiana. This broad range fell within the commercial network of French merchants at least since 1723 but was beyond any imagined border with Los Adaes, which was much farther north near Natchitoches between the Sabine and Red Rivers. The French fur trade with the Atacapas expanded into trade with the Indians of East Texas, including the Caddos, Bidais, and Orcoquizas. The French simultaneously skirted Los Adaes for commerce with the Caddos, Wichitas, and Comanches. From a French perspective, the Spanish encroached into territory along the coast that fell under the sovereignty of France. In fact, after learning of French traders on the lower Trinity River, Governor Barrios Jáuregui promptly sought an embargo against their commerce and took over trade with the Indians. In this manner, the governor forcefully expanded his personal fiefdom by monopolizing "smuggling" operations and continued gift giving with Indian chiefs, as did his French counterparts.

By late 1755, a Mexico City official ordered Blancpain from his prison cell to write a *memoria* (list) of the goods at the time of his arrest along with a diary of his journey to the lower Trinity River. He also had to submit his passport and any other papers he might have possessed.[90] The number of goods was much lengthier than the ones he initially reported during his interrogatory earlier that year. Blancpain listed 180 different items as before, but also tools and parts for repairing guns, screws, Flemish knives, crystal glasses, British cloth, a boat, an iron frying pan, plenty of wine and brandy, vinegar, sugar, chocolate, silk masks, a cane with a silver top, new pairs of shoes, and many other goods.[91] Blancpain's list only proved to the Spanish that the French intended to make a settlement in Texas and resume the imperial designs that La Salle held for France long ago.

Blancpain's diary revealed the complexity and difficulty for the Spanish to impose a Texas-Louisiana border when foreign traders could just travel to the north of Los Adaes along the Red River or to the south along the coastal region. Blancpain described his journey to the lower Trinity River and noted his arrest along with four of his servants—two white and two black—and the confiscated goods. The diary began with their departure from New Orleans and arrival at Blancpain's residence in Houmas, 22 leagues (55 miles) upriver. From there, they traveled 10 leagues (25 miles) to a place called Plaquemina. From this point, his words described how "they walked another five leagues before descending upon a lake named Chettimacha in whose frontier are the Atacapa nation." They then marched to the sea and, after traveling 30 leagues (75 miles), arrived at another lake, which Blancpain believed was very deep and belonged to the Atacapas. From this lake, his diary continued, "we went another 25 leagues before arrival at the Bay of the Atacapas, which is probably 15 leagues deep and forms two branches, one to the west and another to the east, where we were apprehended." The eastern branch formed a lake about 2 leagues from the Bay of the Atacapas, while the Atacapa settlement was located some 5 leagues east of the mouth of the Trinity River. Lastly, Blancpain figured that the distance from the Mississippi to the easternmost side of the Atacapa's territory in southwestern Louisiana was approximately 55 leagues (110 miles).[92] Unfortunately, Blancpain died tragically in the Mexico City prison shortly after he wrote the memoria and diary. His two white companions, George Elias and Antoine de la Fars, were transferred to Spain the following year and sentenced to life imprisonment. The fate of Blancpain's black servants went unrecorded.[93]

Governor Kerlérec of Louisiana protested Blancpain's arrest and imprisonment for contraband trade from the beginning. He told Governor Barrios Jáuregui that Blancpain's trade post among the Orcoquizas was in French territory. Kerlérec also proposed a joint commission to determine the boundaries of the lower Trinity River. Barrios Jáuregui, however, rejected the idea and counterclaimed that the Texas border extended to the Mississippi River. He also threatened to fortify its west bank with a Spanish presidio against French encroachment.[94] Interestingly, historian Father Juan Morfi, who visited Texas in the 1770s, stated that Blancpain actually worked for Barrios Jáuregui, who gave him permission to enter Texas but then abruptly persecuted the Frenchmen out of fear that their illicit trade might be discovered in a residencia proceeding someday.[95] Barrios Jáuregui's actions more than likely proved him capable of doing such a thing, considering his restrictions against the Adaeseños from trade while seizing opportunities to expand his own commercial operations.

Oddly, at some point during the Blancpain affair, a French priest named Didier, along with another individual (Massé), requested permission from

Governor Barrios Jáuregui to settle among the Orcoquizas, but he denied their request.[96] In July 1756, Father Didier wrote the viceroy from Los Adaes about the intentions of Monsieur Massé to settle at Presidio San Agustín. He described Massé as a distinguished gentleman by birth and merit who resided on his ranch at Atacapas under the jurisdiction of New Orleans. Massé was advanced in age, and for some unstated reason, said he wished to free his slaves and leave them his wealth after his death. Father Didier identified himself as a secular priest and companion of Massé at his ranch.[97] Father Didier's intentions recall the attempts of Father Hidalgo, who worked behind the scenes to interest the French from Louisiana into helping restore Spanish missions in East Texas.

Father Didier indeed mentioned the advantages of permitting Massé and himself to come to Texas and settle at Presidio San Agustín. First, Massé had a great number of livestock that could be easily transported to San Agustín and provide great relief to the new Spanish inhabitants of that fort. Second, Father Didier claimed that the *grandes* (large) and *pequeñas* (small) Atacapas were entirely devoted to Massé and were certain to follow him to Texas such that Spain would have no enemies in that part of the province. Third, Didier said that Massé's *negros* (blacks), the majority of whom were married with their *negras* (black females) and had children, "are a seed" for settlement and could reinforce the Spanish population on the lower Trinity River. Fourth, Massé knew "the essence and weaknesses of the Nations of the North, like the Tabayages, Letas, Patoca, Ycarra, and Paris, having been among them." Father Didier believed that Massé's familiarity with these Indian enemies in Texas could help persuade them to be loyal to the Spanish. Didier requested no other recompense than His Excellency's protection and his own satisfaction in performing zealous service to God and the growth of Spain.[98] Didier thus offered a solution to the lack of coerced labor in East Texas that was so critical to Spanish colonization.

A few days later, however, Governor Barrios Jáuregui wrote the viceroy and presented him with a different version of events than Father Didier, whom the governor believed had arrived under the pretext that he was lost. The governor remitted papers to the viceroy requesting his counsel on the matter, adding the description of Massé's character, the devotion to him by the Indians, and the number of slaves and livestock in his possession. Meanwhile, the governor said he denied Didier's request to go to Mexico City and that Massé wanted no recompense other than to place his goods in a temporary place on the west bank of the Trinity River. Barrios Jáuregui suggested that the viceroy should distrust Father Didier and Massé because they did not appear to be who they said they were and not truly wealthy; instead, they might be *adivinos* (fortune-tellers) or *hechizeros* (sorcerers). He ended his letter by politely asking the viceroy to order whatever he considered best in this matter.[99]

Father Didier's request revealed French interest in the lower Trinity River by virtue of their trade with the Atacapas and the Orcoquizas for more than thirty years. Spanish colonization along the upper Texas Gulf Coast was nonexistent prior to the arrival of French merchants. The recently established Spanish presidio and mission at San Agustín among the Orcoquizas, on the other hand, lent immediate credibility to the view that territorial conquest and occupation trumped any previous French commercial ties with the Indians. Mexico City officials had no knowledge of these other woodlands Indians when they first contemplated the colonization of southeast Texas during the 1740s after rumors surfaced that French traders had already settled on the lower Trinity River.[100]

Governor Barrios Jáuregui naturally suspected his Louisiana counterpart's territorial ambitions. In October 1753, Governor Kerlérec proposed seizing Texas, but the French minister of the Royal Navy rebuffed this idea. Kerlérec dreamed of expansion to New Spain and its silver mines, believing that "a large Indian war party, well led, would without doubt carry destructive war" to Mexico. Had distant French officials not been consumed with English aggression to the east, perhaps they might have shown greater enthusiasm about westward expansion and the Louisiana governor's designs on Texas.[101]

Governor Kerlérec's best opportunity to attack Spanish Texas arose when the Hasinai of East Texas planned a revolt. In early 1753, as part of de Soto's investigation, Father Calahorra from Mission Adaes informed Governor Barrios Jáuregui about Calahorra's visit with a chief from the Nacogdoches Indians and his witness of a Caddo council composed of Tejas, Navidachos, Nazones, and Tehuacanas nations with five hundred warriors. These groups were upset that the Spanish attempted to cut off their trade with the French. As Calahorra reported, the Caddos clamored for retaliation and suggested such an action to Louis St. Denis, commandant at the Natchitoches post after his father (St. Denis the elder) passed away. The Caddos reportedly enticed St. Denis (the younger) to take advantage of "becoming lord of these lands for which purpose they were ready to kill all Spaniards found in them." They first targeted Mission Nacogdoches for attack, then would look eastward until Los Adaes was destroyed.[102]

St. Denis (the younger) declined, however, and stated that those parts of East Texas belonged to the Spanish, from whom the French needed permission to pass. Since the Spanish and French were close allies, St. Denis told the Caddos that the French, in such an event, "could not fail to take up arms in their [Spain's] defense." Calahorra was glad to learn that the Nacogdoches chief also dissuaded the Caddo council from destroying Mission Nacogdoches because the missionary treated his people nicely.[103] Kinship, religion, and trade ties with St. Denis (the younger) at Natchitoches also gave Governor Barrios Jáuregui confidence when Governor Kerlérec disputed Spanish claims to the lower Trinity River following Blancpain's arrest. Perhaps St. Denis heard stories in his youth about Spanish troops from Los Adaes defending his father's post during the Natchez revolt. Evidently, local elites from Natchitoches, such as St. Denis (the younger) and his mother, Manuela, still wielded great influence among the Caddos and French that could make or break the Spanish presence in East Texas.

Concern over the imperial boundary between Texas and Louisiana, the Indian trade, and the fateful end to Blancpain's commercial venture carried over into tense relations between Barrios Jáuregui's successor, Governor Martos Navarrete, and Governor Kerlérec. In March 1760, Governor Kerlérec wrote a letter to Martos Navarrete and expressed his surprise and indignation at how the Spanish treated St. Denis (the younger). Apparently, Governor Martos Navarrete wrote Kerlérec in January about news from the commandant at Presidio San Agustín and how St. Denis allegedly "sent a savage Indian of the *Ados*[?] nation to oblige the *Orcoquisa* chiefs (whom you provided lodging)" and received gifts of gunpowder, ammunition, guns, tobacco, vermilion, and other goods on the condition that they kill the Spanish soldiers at San Agustín and destroy its fort. In return, Kerlérec added, the French "would forgive what happened with Blancpain."[104] The Spanish believed St. Denis had trespassed into Texas among the Orcoquizas along the lower Trinity River, while Governor Kerlérec sought to protect the honor of France and the reputation of the St. Denis family. Kerlérec tried to blackmail his counterpart when he told Martos Navarrete not to be "afraid of being exposed to a residencia" if such slander against St. Denis did not end. Kerlérec suggested instead that Martos Navarrete maintain close and open communication with Sir Le Blanc, the new commandant at Natchitoches, on future border issues, Indian relations, and trade that were important for preserving the Family Compact of alliance between Spain and France, especially as the latter lost major military campaigns against the English in North America during the Seven Years' War.[105]

Even so, Governor Kerlérec continued to lecture Martos Navarrete about best practices on the Texas-Louisiana borderlands for Spanish, French, and Caddo relations that challenged Spain's mercantilist policies. Kerlérec reminded him that former governor Barrios Jáuregui traded all kinds of goods with the "*Tankaoneys* [Tawakonis] and other Savages, who would have become your enemies without this interesting business." Ironically, the Tawakonis were Wichita Indians who had asked the Spanish for a mission on the Red River after they had joined the Comanches in the destruction of Mission San Sabá, near present Menard in the Texas Hill Country, in March 1758. The Tawakonis migrated to the Red River after abandoning their home on the Arkansas River due to Osage raids from the north and, in alliance with Comanches, warred against the Apaches, for whom the Spanish established Mission San Sabá. Historian F. Todd Smith notes that the Seven Years' War negatively impacted French trade with the Tawakonis and other Wichitas uninterested in Christianity, but acceptance of a mission and presidio would cement friendship with Spain and improve trade. For good measure, Kerlérec stated that Governor Martos Navarrete should "equally recognize that his Missions *Ais*, *Nacogdoches*, and *Orcoquisas* purchase goods daily from Natchitoches for money, a distribution which you do not even approve among your residents whom you well know carry on commerce publicly with the Hasinais, Nadacotes, and Nacogdoches." Kerlérec reminded Martos Navarrete that whenever he wrote complaining about abuses over trade, these originated from the governor's own Spanish subjects.[106] The French governor evidently heard about the plight of the Adaeseños and their rumblings against Spanish governors and suggested that the Spanish governor could make everyone happier if only he loosened Spain's trade restrictions.[107]

Governor Martos Navarrete needed to be apprised of consequences for Spain if France lost its North American possessions to England. "I should not omit to tell you," Governor Kerlérec wrote him, that the Indian "nations who have rebelled, communicate in the North with the *Oragos*, *Arkansas*, *Illinois*, *Peanguichias*, *Viatones*, *Choanones*, *Miami*, *Potuamises*, *Missouri*, *Kansas*, *Naytanes*, *Picaras*, *Pawnees*, *Blacks*, and *Whites*," plus many other allies, "in the present turbulences which we see ourselves fighting the English, are spilling their blood, life, and liberty for us." Kerlérec added that rather than complaining about their aid to these Indian allies, the Spanish should promote and encourage their support for the sake of both France and Spain.[108] Governor Kerlérec expressed his desire that both Catholic monarchs maintain their Family Compact and not permit Martos Navarrete to cut off vital supply lines through Texas that lay beyond the reach of British forces and their native allies.[109] The Spanish had been preoccupied with punitive expeditions against the Comanches in the aftermath of the San Sabá fiasco and were slower to respond to French needs after Spain declared war against England in 1758 and joined their Bourbon cousins in the Seven Years' War. Governor Martos Navarrete assumed command at Los Adaes in late 1759, when France lost to Britain in Canada and in the Ohio River valley, so he needed counsel from his superiors in Mexico City over how to proceed with events on both sides of the Texas-Louisiana border. In Martos Navarrete's defense, a translation of Governor Kerlérec's letter, which required certification in Mexico City, delayed his course of action, much to the chagrin of Kerlérec.[110]

The Marqués de Aranda, as the viceroy's *fiscal* (attorney general), reacted negatively to Kerlérec's correspondence with Governor Martos Navarrete. First, Aranda instructed Martos Navarrete to investigate dealings between the commandant at San Augustine and St. Denis (the younger) and to offer gifts to the captains of the Orcoquiza Nation, particularly gunpowder, ammunition, guns, tobacco, and vermilion. Martos Navarrete was to remind the Indian captains about Blancpain's imprisonment and to verify whether the French still wanted the Indians to kill Spanish soldiers and residents at San Agustín. Second, the Spanish governor was to check whether anyone else, presumably discontented Spaniards or mission Indians at San Agustín, also wished for the Indians to destroy the fort and mission, as St. Denis allegedly desired. Aranda added that Martos Navarrete had better "make sure the aforementioned Orcoquiza Indians and others from those frontiers do not assemble in any manner whatsoever with said French, which can disturb the public peace." Aranda remained under the impression that the mission Indians on the lower Trinity River sought Christianity under Spanish arms and no longer needed the French, but he still feared disruption to Spanish colonization on the border of New Spain with Louisiana.[111]

III

The Marqués de Aranda was equally adamant about stopping Spanish contraband trade with the Indians and French. He ordered Governor Martos Navarrete to investigate the alleged trade that former governor Barrios Jáuregui had with the Tawakonis and other "Savages" during his governorship of Los Adaes. Aranda specifically wanted the investigation done separately from the residencia and sent immediately to Mexico City for the government's prosecution against Barrios Jáuregui. Finally, Aranda directed the governor to investigate "the missionaries of the Ais, Nacogdoches, and Orcoquisas Indians, who trade daily with the Natchitoches Indians . . . and to prevent said missionaries from having commerce, and contracts, with said Indians." Aranda asked that the translated copy of Kerlérec's letter be sent to Governor Martos Navarrete in case he did not fully understand the French language. Aranda then ordered "a soldier or resident from there [Los Adaes], who knows the French language, to translate such letters" in the future and thereby avoid delays in response to correspondence and, presumably, investigations into possible wrongdoing.[112] Although few Adaeseños could read or write Spanish, much less French, they likely came to understand local

French and Caddo dialects through frequent transactions on the Texas-Louisiana borderlands.

Governor Martos Navarrete's investigation for the moment dispelled rumors that St. Denis (the younger) incited Indians to rebel against the Spanish at San Agustín. In the spring of 1761, Captain Calsones, from the Orcoquiza Nation, appeared before Domingo del Río and Juan Prieto, both Adaeseños garrisoned at San Agustín, and testified that two Bidais had implicated St. Denis with having made the offer. Captain Calsones, however, asserted that "it was not true because Sir San Denis never actually said so, and that they [Bidais] said it just to see if we would laugh at the Spaniards." A few days later, Captain Gordo, from the Orcoquiza Nation, appeared and also stated that the Bidai Indians were just "playing" for laughs at the Spanish.[113] Four other Indians testified in the same manner: Famages, probably an Orcoquiza chief; Bocaflores, an Orcoquiza *tama* (captain); and two Bidais captains named Thomas and Antonio.[114] While their testimony seemed genuine enough to Governor Martos Navarrete, Mexico City officials likely became increasingly anxious about the overlap of imperial warfare with Indian troubles in northern New Spain and were not in the mood for jokes from anyone, much less independent Indians on the frontier.

Meanwhile, the Spanish contemplated opening ports on the Texas coast to guard against penetration inland from foreign traders, but they ultimately shelved the idea. By 1762, the auditor in Mexico City, Domingo Valcarcel, had weighed this possibility in light of several other matters, including the Blancpain affair, the inability to evangelize the Indians, Capt. Joaquín Orobio Basterra's "discovery" of the lower Trinity River, and the prevention of French-Indian commerce with other Spanish presidios. Although the establishment of a "legal" port on the Texas coast might have facilitated commerce with other provinces in New Spain, the auditor feared that more ports would only exacerbate smuggling and thus make enforcement against it even harder, as in the case of Peru.[115] Mexico City officials recognized the impediments of Spain's mercantilism but stayed the course, believing "free trade" to be the greater threat to the security of New Spain's enterprises. Fortunately or not, their counterparts in Madrid negotiated the transfer of Louisiana from France to Spain in late 1762, which moved the border of New Spain farther east to the Mississippi and shifted the Spanish focus to containing the English.[116]

Governor Martos Navarrete from Los Adaes and Commandant McCarty at Natchitoches also discussed broader imperial concerns and a desire for harmony on the Texas-Louisiana borderlands.[117] McCarty informed Martos Navarrete about the history of French and Spanish claims to the country west of the Mississippi following La Salle's venture into Texas and mistakenly believed Mission Nacogdoches was located near French posts in Illinois country, among other geostrateigc concerns.[118] Regardless of past tensions over territorial limits between their respective kingdoms, peaceful relations remained imperative, especially as French residents at Natchitoches initially resisted the transfer of Louisiana to Spain, and rebellion arose against Spanish rule in New Orleans for the remainder of the 1760s. Both Martos Navarrete and McCarty kept open lines of communication between their respective posts amid great challenges to Spanish rule in Texas and Louisiana.

Meanwhile, the familiar pattern of French trade continued with the occasional Spanish interdiction and prosecution of contraband trade in Texas. In August 1766, Lt. Joseph Gonzalez became alerted to potential trouble from the French once again when he found himself in temporary command at Los Adaes, as in the mid-1730s. This time around, an interim governor named Hugo O'Conor investigated Governor Martos Navarrete for illicit commerce. "Around prayer time in the evening," Lieutenant Gonzalez wrote, "Francisco Ramírez, alias *El Badeño* and resident of this royal presidio [Los Adaes], arrived at my home with the news that around sunset, near the Ranch called Bermúdez in this presidio's jurisdiction, he saw ten Frenchmen marching with horses carrying gunpowder, ammunition, guns, and other goods for commerce with our Gentile Indian Nations."[119] Interestingly, Gonzalez declared that smuggling became "more daring and audacious" and linked it with "the occurrence of so many robberies and deaths in this province [Texas]." He ordered Ramírez to return to said place and determine where the Frenchmen hid their horses. He also dispatched a squadron of soldiers into the night under the command of Sgt. Domingo Chirino, who was instructed to select ten men of his choosing from Los Adaes to pursue the French smugglers.

The following day, Sergeant Chirino returned with the Frenchmen and their goods, whereupon Gonzalez ordered the smugglers to confirm their contraband items before he had them imprisoned.[120]

This smuggling case, like others before it, ended in legal troubles but left more doubt than ever about the volume of contraband trade that flowed across the border and the loyalty of Spanish subjects. On August 14, 1766, a Frenchman named Duzan Lodre appeared with the others apprehended before Lieutenant Gonzalez and several Adaeseño soldiers, declaring that "all of the goods belonged to him." Lodre also stated that four of the Frenchmen were actually his servants, whom he paid to help him trade the goods among the Indians, but that "the other Frenchmen had passports from don Louis de la Perierre [Natchitoches commandant] to take a canoe near Bermudez [Ranch] they hid in a creek that empties into the lake of this presidio [Los Adaes] and flows from the Red River at Natchitoches."[121] Lodre mentioned many goods, including guns, ammunition, gunpowder, blankets, shirts, beads, soap, and kettles (see appendix E).[122] Many similar French goods also appeared on the account books for the soldiers at Presidios Los Adaes and San Agustín during the 1760s. Some of the contraband items allegedly intended for the Caddo and Plains Indians were evidently diverted, intentionally or not, past the scrutiny of Mexico City officials.

Lieutenant Gonzalez at least arrested French traders, which ostensibly left no doubt that his loyalties remained with Spain despite his daughter's marriage into the Derbanne family at Natchitoches many years before. After all, Lieutenant Gonzalez's daughter and her French husband had a child who eventually served under him at Los Adaes. This made it appear as if he had everything under control, including trade and his own family. Lieutenant Gonzalez decided to placate interim governor O'Conor (known as "Red Beard") and his superiors in Mexico City by ordering five of the Frenchmen to remain under the company guard at Los Adaes until O'Conor's arrival, yet he freed two of the smugglers who surrendered their guns and ammunition. Gonzalez at last dutifully submitted his orders to O'Conor for his determination in this matter.[123] In May 1767, former governor Martos Navarrete was transferred to Mexico City to stand trial on charges drawn up by O'Conor, who then assumed command of Los Adaes, where he found much lacking.[124] Meanwhile, Martos Navarrete was likely reassigned to another government position yet was spared a forced run through the gauntlet at Los Adaes like Sandoval. For his part, Gonzalez displayed a consistently loyal presence at Los Adaes, with greater local concern about his own family's livelihood and the Adaeseño community rather than smugglers and deserters over the years.

Governor O'Conor soon complained to the viceroy about the lack of military forces in Texas to contain Indian hostilities. He recounted Father Juan de Gumiel, from Mission Concepción at San Antonio, who told him how enemy Indians had stolen all the horses and several pack trains from this mission. The governor led a combined squadron of thirty troops from the presidios at Los Adaes and San Antonio in pursuit of the Indians. O'Conor and his men went as far as the Brazos River but had to return "because of the impossibility of their horses being able to travel any farther." The governor described how on their return to San Antonio, the day before the Feast of the Immaculate Conception (December 8), he encountered two hundred Indians armed with guns on the Guadalupe River. Without declaring whether they were friend or foe, the Indians gave the governor a *carga cerrada* (close charge). The governor left behind one officer with ten soldiers to guard the small herd of horses while he and the remaining twenty troops "attacked the enemies with great vigor." This "fight lasted from three in the afternoon until five-thirty without the enemies gaining any advantage, besides wounding two soldiers and six horses that died during the struggle." O'Conor witnessed at least seven dead Indians and many wounded but feared another attack and took advantage of the night to hide by the river. The governor ended his account by extolling the valor and courage of Luís Antonio Menchaca, captain of Presidio San Antonio de Béxar, in the *refriega* (combat), yet O'Conor stressed the need for increasing the number of troops, especially at San Antonio, which he felt to be the only fort in Texas that merited attention.[125] In essence, Governor O'Conor sounded like General Rivera and foreshadowed more base closures under the Bourbon Reforms and the redeployment of troops and resources to the violent borderlands of the Southern Plains and South Texas rather than to the border with Louisiana.

During the late 1760s, San Antonio in fact came under incessant attack from Norteño Indians, Wichitas among them, allied with Comanches, who obtained weapons through French traders and Caddo intermediaries. In response to Captain Menchaca's reports about continued Indian warfare at San Antonio, Governor O'Conor moved his headquarters there closer to the action, much like Sandoval did in the 1730s to combat the Apaches. The viceroy promptly approved the detachment of twenty-two soldiers from Los Adaes to San Antonio.[126] Lieutenant Gonzalez, however, stayed behind in at Los Adaes, presumably to keep watch over French and Indian movements from Louisiana, where the rebellion against Spanish rule continued.

Besides harping on the lack of troops at San Antonio, Governor O'Conor complained about Los Adaes and trade that some Adaeseños had with enemy Indians. He told the viceroy he had to request a squadron of twenty troops from the captain at Presidio La Bahía, which was promptly sent for the defense of San Antonio. The governor still could not protect the missions, ranches, and *bienes* (goods)—namely, livestock—in San Antonio because there were insufficient troops to contain so many enemies who were well stocked with gunpowder, ammunition, and guns. The governor lamented how "useless Presidio Los Adaes is to the King and its settlement never fully developing" and said that the "enemies [Indians] offend [San Antonio residents] through commerce with some [Spanish] subjects."[127] Governor O'Conor essentially blamed French contraband trade and Adaeseño illicit commerce on the Texas-Louisiana borderlands for Indian troubles at San Antonio aside from the shortage of troops. How could the governor contain Indian raids when his own subjects indirectly helped the enemies through trade with French traders and their Caddo allies? The governor's link between smuggling and continued guerrilla warfare highlighted the inability of Los Adaes to stop contraband trade even as French officials from Louisiana encouraged the loosening of Spanish trade restrictions. O'Conor's comments to the viceroy reinforced the Marqués de Rubí's negative impression of Los Adaes during his military inspection that year (discussed in chapter 7).

In January 1768, the viceroy responded to Governor O'Conor, and the contraband case against Duzan Lodre, with an emphasis on exerting control over the Texas-Louisiana borderlands—especially Natchitoches—now that the Louisiana territory came under Spanish sovereignty. He ordered the governor to arrange the sale of the illicit goods and to give notice that Spaniards keep a watchful eye for similar smuggled items entering Texas. The remaining five French prisoners were to be freed, but O'Conor warned that continued contraband trade would result in their arrest and imprisonment at Los Adaes for ten years. The viceroy forewarned specifically about "getting caught trafficking in guns and ammunition with Indians at war which means the ultimate punishment of torture and execution." He instructed Governor O'Conor to publish his decree of resolution "on the frontiers" and send it with an official to the governor at Natchitoches for him to do his part in making sure the resolution arrived and notice was given to everyone so they could not plead ignorance of the law.[128] The viceroy and Governor O'Conor considered Los Adaes and the surrounding Adaeseño ranches within the orbit of contraband trade emanating from Natchitoches. The viceroy and his advisors in Mexico City likely did not know yet about other settlements, such as Bayou Pierre, that functioned as safe havens for smugglers, deserters, and vagabonds who sought refuge from French and Spanish laws.

The viceroy, Marqués de Croix, also informed the Spanish governor of Louisiana, Antonio de Ulloa, about the contraband case against Lodre at Los Adaes. Viceroy de Croix impressed upon Governor Ulloa the great harm that French smugglers caused, especially the "supply of guns and war munitions to the Apache and Comanche Indians with which they commit many robberies and deaths in the province of Texas." The viceroy said that he freed the French *contrabandistas* with warnings and prohibitions under the law, which was simply more convenient. He also stated that the guns, ammunition, and gunpowder the Indians used were obtained from the French in exchange for deerskins and lard. Viceroy de Croix then stressed to Governor Ulloa the ineffectiveness of Los Adaes, located only seven leagues from Natchitoches on the Texas-Louisiana border. The viceroy stated that Los Adaes, along with some presidios in other parts of both kingdoms, were "today, under our monarchy, useless, and can free up the *Real Herario* [Treasury] of expenses" if closed. The viceroy wished to learn the Louisiana governor's thoughts about the "advisability of extinguishing some of these presidios."[129] Governor Ulloa, who had arrived at New Orleans in March 1766, however, was consumed more with the revolt of French colonists against his own rule and leaned instead on the Spanish government in Havana, Cuba, for additional troops and financial support.[130]

Meanwhile, another insidious "foreign" menace increasingly occupied Viceroy de Croix's attention. By late summer 1768, the viceroy wrote Governor O'Conor about a notice from New Mexico's governor that Comanche Indians were well stocked with guns and ammunition through trade with the Jumano Nation. The governor of New Mexico suspected that these Indians, situated at the intersection of the Arkansas (Napestle) and Colorado Rivers some two hundred leagues southeast of Santa Fe, had commerce with English traders by means of the Mississippi River. The viceroy wanted Governor O'Conor to confirm the accuracy of these reports.[131] The Jumanos of West Texas and the Caddos of East Texas were gatekeepers of trade in their respective border regions and continued to play off European powers while negotiating with more powerful Indian nations. The Spanish governors in Louisiana, Texas, and New Mexico certainly had their specific internal problems, but contraband trade crossed boundaries in multiple directions and fueled Spanish-Indian warfare at San Antonio and Santa Fe. European traders pumped their wares into northern New Spain as long as El Dorado remained at the end of the Camino Real, with silver mines as the ultimate prize.

Spain's concern over an emerging Comanche empire on the Southern Plains coincided with greater alarm over illicit tobacco from Louisiana mixed with guns and ammunition. Under the Bourbon Reforms of King Carlos III (1759–88), whose reign became the apogee of the Spanish Empire, Spain sought to increase annual revenues from its monopoly of tobacco.[132] In 1766, the Mexico City viceroy Marqués de Croix wanted greater accounting of tobacco in Texas and whether Spaniards, friendly Indians, or "the barbarous enemies" grew any quantities of this cash crop. De Croix wished to learn the quality, size, and price of the tobacco. He also wondered whether "free trade in tobacco" with Indians hurt the friars' ability to convert them in the missions.[133] By 1770, the viceroy promulgated a fine of double the value of tobacco against those who sold it—unless they were authorized *cigarreros* (tobacco rollers) or merchants.[134] This measure also reflected missionary extralegal enterprises, such as Father Zedano's.

Evidently, the higher-quality French tobacco was desired so much that it caught the attention of Mexico City.

Tobacco, however, also undercut the value of the silver peso as de facto currency, especially for cash-strapped soldiers and their families. Historian Marcy Norton explains that tobacco and chocolate had been the basis for tax revenues in a downward economy dating back to the Hapsburg monarchy of the previous century. In fact, tobacco came to generate more wealth than silver by the time La Salle made landfall in Texas.[135] Historian Amy Bushnell notes that in Spanish Florida, the Indians bartered items due to the lack of currency among Spaniards and that gambling also occurred at Indian ball games. Soldiers in Florida were only legally allowed to buy their own food from the Indians.[136] Archival records do not refer to gambling at Indian ball games on the Texas-Louisiana borderlands, but the Spanish soldiers at Los Adaes were forced into gambling away their pesos or in advance of payment of their wages. Adaeseño troops were allowed trade in foodstuffs legally only with the French from Natchitoches, but not with non-Christianized Indians. Interestingly, chocolate held trade value because it could be used for sustenance, for medicinal purposes, or as an aphrodisiac. An Adaeseño soldier named Joaquín Ruíz, who was dispatched for duty at San Antonio, paid a three-peso debt to fellow Adaeseño Joseph Hidalgo in chocolate.[137] The accounts of many other Adaeseño soldiers showed purchases for chocolate, though how many used it to pay off debts is unknown. The power of tobacco and chocolate, however, went beyond trade, as Norton describes how these two goods "trespassed into the Christian Mass" and competed with the devotion to Catholicism as well as matched Mesoamerican descriptions of the Eucharist as a "life-infusing elixir."[138] Tobacco and chocolate mixed with contraband trade in guns, furs, and alcohol did not bode well for Spanish control over any frontier or border, much less Texas and Louisiana, especially when it involved gambling and raised the specters of corruption, crime, and rebellion.

The gravest concern of Spanish officials during the early 1770s, even more than tobacco, was the smuggling of alcohol on the Texas-Louisiana borderlands among Adaeseños, Indians, and Africans, mixed with the barter of horses, clothing, and captives. Athanase de Mézières, commandant at Natchitoches, alerted Gov. Luís de Unzaga y Amezaga in

New Orleans that the contraband in liquor and wine with Indians and Africans was "cause for very serious consequences, and now the barter of horses and clothing which, at all hours of every day, the soldiers of Los Adaes secretly conduct." According to de Mézières, who married a daughter of St. Denis (the elder) and Manuela Sanchez Navarro, complaints from the interim commandant at Los Adaes (Lt. Joseph Gonzalez) rained down on him, but there was no solution. De Mézières asked the Spanish Louisiana governor, "For what is authority unsupported by force? Only if I were endowed with as many eyes as it is claimed Argo had, and with a hundred arms, like Briareo, could I watch and suppress these abuses."[139] Spanish officials in Mexico City and Madrid could do little to stop smuggling aside from occasionally prosecuting unlicensed French traders and punishing corrupt governors. An alternative involved closing Los Adaes and withdrawing from East Texas entirely, as King Carlos III ultimately commanded (chapter 7).

CHAPTER SIX

Apachitos and Africans

Captivity and Slavery

Soldiers from Los Adaes at times illegally trafficked Indian captives virtually anywhere the governor sent them for duty while Southern Plains Indians in turn took captives whose return the Caddos and French negotiated with the Spanish. The Adaeseño community itself, however, owned few, if any, Indian or African slaves and remained overwhelmingly poor compared to Spanish settlements elsewhere in northern New Spain. The governors of Texas proved the exception, as did Adaeseños who joined in kinship and trade at French Natchitoches, where masters increasingly grew dependent on African slave labor for cash-crop agriculture, especially tobacco, despite the continued presence of Indian slavery in Louisiana. French slaveholders, meanwhile, expressed concern about runaway slaves from Louisiana who fled across the "border" into Texas and sought asylum in the Spanish missions. African slavery also revealed another form of labor by which the Adaeseños measured their own poverty and lack of freedom under autocratic rule at Los Adaes. Indian captivity, African slavery, and impoverished settlers proved a volatile mix, especially on the borderlands, where anxious Spanish officials could never be certain against frontier rebellion as they attempted to coerce labor and enforce a border that Spain could never entirely control. The Spanish, Indians, Africans, and French on the Texas-Louisiana borderlands experienced what historian Thomas Hall calls "a time of changing relations between a region of refuge and the state," when local and regional elites on the periphery of empires challenged the power of distant officials.[1]

The transformation of the Texas frontier followed the capture of Indians in New Spain and their subsequent slavery through the capture of those who resisted Spanish colonization and forced labor in the silver mines. This common practice had deep roots in medieval Spain with the Christian Reconquest against the Moors and developed out of Spanish legislation in the *Siete Partidas* of King Alfonso X during the thirteenth century.[2] Following initial conquests of the Caribbean, Mexico, and Peru, Spain prohibited Indian slavery under the New Laws of 1542 and called for an end to the *encomienda* system, which involved grants of Indian tribute to Spanish overseers obligated to care for the natives in exchange for their labor.[3] In 1573, after decades of unsuccessful warfare against the Chichimecas, who blocked Spanish colonization northward from Mexico City in the central mining districts, the king enacted the Royal Orders for New Discoveries, forbidding military campaigns, and placed emphasis instead on missionaries to lead expeditions for the pacification of new lands.[4] The only legal slavery in New Spain after the New Laws involved Africans, who became more predominate on sugar plantations in Veracruz along the southern Gulf of Mexico and in the silver mines of Zacatecas in central Mexico, while Indian captivity became more common in northern New Spain, where many indigenous peoples continued to resist the Spanish. By 1672, under a royal decree, the Spanish Crown found it necessary to reiterate its prohibition "against making Indians slaves under any pretext whatsoever, neither selling nor alienating them." In addition, the decree stated that "the conversion of the Indians be made through their congregation into pueblos and distribution of land to them."[5] In theory, the encomienda system of tribute labor was finally abolished and replaced by the *congrega* (congregation), and the term *encomendero* (Spanish overseer) was replaced with *capitán protector* (protector of Indians), whose interests in frontier regions actually aligned more with the Spanish than the Indians.[6]

Although no encomiendas per se existed in Texas, Spanish raids against the Coahuiltecans and Apaches supplied workers for haciendas and mining operations in northern New Spain or for congregation into missions.

Apache captives were also sold at slave markets in Louisiana and Cuba, while Apache children taken in war were raised as servants in Spanish households. Historian Juliana Barr argues that by calling those Apache children *criados* (from the Spanish verb *criar*, or "to raise"), Texas colonists circumvented legal prohibitions against Indian slavery, especially through baptism, as discussed in chapter 2. Franciscans opposed this practice and called these military tactics into question, since the missionaries preferred to establish missions for the Lipan Apaches, if not place captives in the missions, as they did for the Coahuiltecans in San Antonio.[7] Women captives in particular held diplomatic significance in Spanish Texas as symbolic peace offerings, yet they also became spouses, concubines, and servants.[8]

Meanwhile, the governor-commandants at Los Adaes frequently utilized the king's troops as de facto servants in a largely subsistence-based society of small ranchers and farmers, which involved tasks that cowboys, domestic servants, or day laborers performed.[9] Historian Susan Deeds explains that a "chaotic mix of free and unfree labor persisted" in the province of Nueva Vizcaya (present Chihuahua and Durango) in northern New Spain.[10] The labor situation at Los Adaes could be described similarly as chaotic due to the improper use of troops in virtual debt peonage without a dependable source of mission labor, Indian captives, or African slaves.

Spanish troops at San Antonio, which included the Adaeseños who were intermittingly garrisoned there, dealt forcibly with any Lipan Apaches whom they imprisoned, enslaved, or banished. In 1741, during the residencia of Gov. Prudencio Orobio Bazterra, Mateo Ybarbo testified that "only on one occasion, at Presidio de San Antonio during wartime, did the said don Prudencio take sixteen Apache prisoners, whom the governor sent abroad upon orders from his superior."[11] Specifically, Orobio Bazterra "sent some Apache Indians to the prison in Mexico City by order of his excellency," while witnesses declared that they did not know whether he actually punished the Indians.[12] Apache captives taken in war were sold to the military and civilians throughout New Spain and beyond its borders. The New Regulations of 1729, however, forbade this practice such that Indian captives (in theory) were to be sent to prison in Mexico City and presumably "recruited" for labor.[13]

Most soldiers and residents from Los Adaes either genuinely did not know about slave expeditions elsewhere in Texas or simply denied such activities if they knew about Indian captivity.[14] Question number six of the residencia proceedings routinely asked witnesses to declare whether the governor "has condemned any Indians to personal servitude, temporarily or in perpetuity."[15] In 1748, for example, Marcos Ruíz, a fifty-two-year-old former soldier who became a resident at Los Adaes, declared that he had not heard "that Governor General don Francisco García Larios ever condemned any Indian with punishment"; rather, Ruíz said that the governor treated the Indians "with all his love and provided them gifts out of his own pockets."[16] Another witness, Domingo del Río, a thirty-eight-year-old sergeant from Los Adaes, testified that Governor García Larios "received the Indians of this immediate vicinity with all his affection and gave them what they wanted, like tobacco and sometimes corn," and that he did not know whether the governor had condemned Indians to servitude.[17] Juliana Barr, however, explains that by 1749, the Apaches and Spanish finally reached peace accords at San Antonio, where the presidial commander, Toribio de Urrutia, forced residents to turn over Apache women and children held as slaves in their homes in order to forge a truce. Garcia's successor, Gov. Pedro del Barrio, actually received orders from the viceroy and freed two Apache girls and one boy after taking them to Los Adaes before deporting them with promises of freedom for all Indian captives.[18] Such diplomatic overtures revealed that the Spanish did hold Apaches captive despite testimony to the contrary given in residencias of governors.

During the 1750s and 1760s, Bourbon reformers grew suspicious that Indian captives were indeed sold as slaves. In 1760, the residencia of Governor Barrios Jáuregui asked whether the Spanish governor sold any "barbarous Indians and removed them from their rancherías or if he refrained from punishing those who have committed this excess."[19] Phelipe Muñoz de Mora, an eighty-one-year-old veteran at Presidio Los Adaes who helped the Marqués de Aguayo establish the fort in 1721, declared that the governor "has not had motive to sell any Barbarous Indian, no less permit anyone to overstep boundaries in bringing them from their rancherías."[20] Cristóbal Santiago, another Los Adaes resident who arrived with Aguayo, testified that he "did not know nor has heard said" that the governor sold any Indians as slaves or removed them from their rancherías.[21] As to whether governors condemned Indians to perpetual servitude, witnesses from Los Adaes denied any knowledge of this practice. However, the taking of Apache captives likely continued in Texas. Most Indian captives generally were women and children sold in the markets of northern New Spain, Natchitoches, and New Orleans like commodities across North America and Caribbean.[22]

The number of Indians taken captive during war or removed directly from their rancherías through slave raids cannot be quantified from the residencia proceedings.[23] The questions led witnesses to answer in the negative. The declarations also appeared nearly identical, since most of the soldiers and residents from Los Adaes were illiterate, gave short responses, or likely feared retribution from the governor if they spoke against him. The governors normally used the same assistants, mostly Adaeseño officers, to sign on behalf of the soldiers and residents. No person willingly admitted anything more than the bare minimum required for the official investigations. Perhaps because Los Adaes served as the official capital of Texas, most of the testimony about the governor's administration and command came from Adaeseños, which is part of the problem because oftentimes, the governors resided at San Antonio instead of the Texas-Louisiana border. There were also no census records taken at Los Adaes in Spanish Texas. The number of Apache captives or servants likely had been less than those traded at French Natchitoches or San Antonio, where they perhaps numbered in the hundreds.[24] Barr notes that women and children held in bondage in Texas were few in number compared to the large *genízaro* (detribalized and enslaved Indian) population in New Mexico, where the Comanches often sold their own Apache captives while the Hasinai Caddos had raided Apache settlements since the late 1730s and sold captives to French traders in Louisiana.[25]

The residencias, however, contrast friendly Spanish-Caddo relations in East Texas with violent Spanish-Apache clashes at San Antonio, where Apache servants were likely traded more frequently due to proximity. The testimony of witnesses together with other archival records suggest that captivity and slave raids had everything to do with this difference. The Caddos were not subjected to the slave trade like the Apaches, who became enemies of the Comanches and Norteños on the Southern Plains. Different modes of social organization, geography, and alliances influenced the degree to which groups became targeted. In the cycles of warfare, raiding, and captivity, the Apaches in turn took Spanish captives from San Antonio.[26] Significantly, no separate class of captives existed at Los Adaes that was comparable to the *genízaros* in New Mexico or quite possibly San Antonio.[27]

In 1761, Governor Martos Navarrete wrote Viceroy Cruillas that the French commandant at Natchitoches, don César de Blanc, sent one of his officers to Los Adaes along with six captives—adults and children of both sexes. The Spanish governor informed the viceroy that de Blanc rescued them from among their Caudacho (Caddo) allies after being "captured along with many more Indians by the *Alitanes*, or Apaches Pelones, at the Ranch of Santa Fé."[28] One of the viceroy's advisers suggested that if these captives were Indians, the Spanish governor should deliver them to their pueblos or the missions, but if they were of other *calidades* (class or character), then they should be returned to their place of residence.[29] The viceroy instructed Martos Navarrete to let him know the fate of the six "prisoners" from Natchitoches.[30] Spanish men were less likely than Indian women to be taken captive if one believes residencia proceedings and other Spanish archival records. The captives to which Martos Navarrete referred were likely sedentary Pueblo Indians from New Mexico or *genízaros*.[31]

In 1763, following Louisiana's transfer from France to Spain, Governor Martos Navarrete petitioned Commandant McCarty of the Natchitoches post about returning a Christian Apache girl, named Isabel, held captive in the Tehuacanas village. McCarty said the Spanish governor was hypocritical to ask on behalf of the mission priests for the redemption of this Indian captive, whose French owner wished to sell her in New Orleans. McCarty reminded Martos Navarrete about "safe passage the Spaniards invariably grant our Indians in the interior [Norteños] to go make war on the Apaches to such visibly ill effects" and that "[our Indians], after being lodged and attended to by individuals of said town [San Antonio] do not return captive Apache children to their people." Instead, individual Bexareños "intend to sell them and profit with certain residents of Los Adaes, who promote the avarice and bloody deeds of the very same natives of your kingdom."[32] Apache captives evidently were present at Los Adaes but were not a dependable source of labor there, where poverty and the subsistence-ranching economy mitigated demand.[33] The few known Indian slaves at Los Adaes became domestic servants who conveyed status and wealth mostly for the Spanish governor, if not the officers.[34]

The Spanish rescue of captives with Caddo intermediaries appeared to be in the best interests of Indians and Europeans.[35] Caddos had to preserve their own relations with the Tehuacanas from Central Texas, who were allied with the Tawakonis, Wichitas, and Comanches and deeply interested in any Spanish-Franco negotiations concerning captives. In 1763, no ransom came from Governor Martos Navarrete in response to Commandant McCarty's request of two hundred pesos for Isabel. For some reason, McCarty, while awaiting word from the Spanish governor, decided against returning her in order to preserve the French flag that flew above the Tehuacana village for forty years. He informed Governor Martos Navarrete that this should not overshadow friendly Spanish-Franco relations, believing that such "controversies waste time that might be better dedicated to the pleasure and happiness with which we celebrated the family pact that intimately binds our nations [France and Spain]."[36] McCarty's reluctance to return Isabel perhaps signaled the need to reassure French ties and security with the Caddos as well as to show the Spanish that they still needed the French. According to McCarty, the Texas-Louisiana borderlands remained tranquil with the French and Caddo presence, insinuating that the Spanish alone were capable of disrupting the political and commercial balance with the Indians and inciting violence.

The circumstances surrounding Isabel's captivity arose from the belief among the French that only they properly understood the complexity of dealing with so many different Indian nations. McCarty's history lesson about Franco-Indian relations reminded the Spanish of the French claim to Texas since La Salle and subsequent trade with the Hasinai in East Texas. McCarty claimed that the Hasinais still belonged to France and told Governor Martos Navarrete that the Spanish did not know the Hasinai like the French did. He rhetorically asked if the Spanish even understood the Hasinai "because of the little attention you [Spaniards] view the meanings, inclinations, and laws of such diverse peoples [Indians] or the manner with which they arrange their hair? Why they paint their faces and bodies? Are settled or are vagabonds? Whether they engage in planting or are content with wild fruits? How some burn their dead while others give burials?"[37]

McCarty subsequently referred to intertribal warfare over contested homelands before St. Denis, who convinced the Indians to live in peace after great misfortune and hostility threatened to wipe them all out. According to McCarty, Governor Martos Navarrete should have realized more than anyone the importance of French diplomacy among the Caddos, since "the Bidais, Hasinais, Nacogdoches, Nazones and Ais beseech us to take care (using their expression) that the roads Saint Denis blazed do not develop new thorns, and that the blue sky above does not become cloudy, [ominous] and frightening precursors to the tempests that have befallen them."[38] McCarty conveyed a Caddo perspective, keenly aware of the need to maintain harmony rather than warfare on the Texas-Louisiana borderlands. He believed Spain should forever be grateful for the likes of St. Denis, who brought the Spanish and Caddos together in peace. In essence, McCarty justified Indian captivity so long as it preserved political and commercial alliances with the Caddos and hoped the Spanish continued this practice after Louisiana came under the sovereignty of Spain. Perhaps he would have returned Isabel if a ransom came from the Spanish—but only if such transfer did not upset the Caddos and their Tehuacana allies.

Although the Adaeseños likely possessed fewer Indian servants, they nonetheless participated with the Bexareños in taking captives on distant military expeditions to assist missionaries in search of apostate Indians or potential neophytes. In 1773, Juan Feliciano Casanova, a twenty-four-year-old soldier from Los Adaes, testified as such before Gov. Juan María Barón de Ripperdá in the investigation of Spanish citizens from the neighboring province of Nuevo Santander (present Tamaulipas) who were charged with selling Indian children as slaves. Casanova declared that he was part of "said detachment last summer that, after thirteen or fourteen days travel in the remoteness between the coast and this side of the Rio Grande, caught nineteen pagan souls, among them men, women, and children, the majority of the ranchería having escaped into the thickness of the wilderness, which we could not penetrate even on foot." Three other witnesses, including two soldiers, Joseph Manuel Martínez from Presidio San Antonio de Béxar and

Lt. Cristóbal Córdova, and an Indian interpreter named Juan Nicolás from Mission Concepción at San Antonio testified to accompanying Friar Francisco Durán, minister at Mission Concepción, and seizing Indians while the Spanish from the colony of Nuevo Santander took Indian children.[39]

Juan Nicolás apparently was not the only Indian from the San Antonio missions in the expedition. He stated that five fellow Indians from Mission Concepción joined him, as did two more Indians from Mission San Francisco de la Espada and two from Mission San Juan Capistrano. All three of these missions transferred from East Texas to San Antonio in 1731.[40] The viceroy ordered an investigation into "the excesses committed by the residents of the colony of Nuevo Santander, taking children from friendly Indians and selling them as slaves to the detriment of their settlement, which is in opposition to the humanity with which they should be treated and united with the motherhood of our Holy Faith, and in contravention of the practical intentions of the Majesty."[41] While the governor at Los Adaes likely benefited from slave traders who used his Adaeseño soldiers for the capture of nonsedentary Apache or Coahuiltecan Indians, royal investigations often failed to prosecute a governor based on inconclusive testimony about his complicity in Indian slavery, which became standard practice despite its official prohibition in New Spain.

II

The Spanish also negotiated the return of their own from captivity on the Southern Plains. The case of Antonio Treviño particularly sheds light on trade, diplomacy, and intimacy among the Indians, French, and Spanish along the Texas-Louisiana borderlands. In July 1765, Taovaya chief Eyasiquiche brought Treviño, a Spanish soldier from Los Adaes, from the Wichita fortress on the Red River to Friar José de Calahorra Sáenz, a Franciscan missionary at Mission Nacogdoches. Governor Martos Navarrete informed Calahorra that the return of Treviño left "no doubt of the friendship which this nation professes and their wish to maintain peace with us." Chief Eyasiquiche also offered five captive women and two Spanish cannons, which the Taovayas tried returning to the Spanish during Calahorra's negotiations for a mission among the Tehuacanas, who ironically captured the cannons during one of Col. Diego Parrilla's military campaigns against the Norteños following the destruction of Mission San Sabá. Governor Martos Navarrete dispatched Lt. Pedro de Sierra to escort Friar Calahorra from Mission Nacogdoches and presented gifts to Chief Eiasiquiche, including two rifles, six pounds of gunpowder, twelve pounds of ammunition, ten bundles of tobacco, several horses, twenty-four chains, a dozen knives, and an honorary fur coat trimmed with braids (see appendix F).[42] Governor Martos Navarrete followed the customary Spanish practice of gift giving but included guns, which were usually associated with the French-Indian trade. The chains could be used for binding captives, slaves, or fugitives, which made the Spanish governor complicit with the taking of Indians for servitude or slavery and perhaps explains why the Adaeseño residents generally might not have known the extent of such dealings as well as the crucial role of missionaries as brokers.

By asserting solidarity with the Spanish at San Sabá and the threat of military force, Governor Martos Navarrete did not fully heed McCarty's treatise on French-Caddo relations. The Spanish governor told Friar Calahorra that the Taovayas must keep peace with the Spaniards at Presidio San Sabá; "otherwise we cannot be their friends, this being indispensable for us to defend those [Spaniards] when confronted by hostilities."[43] Calahorra and Hasinai Caddo representatives acted as liaisons between Governor Martos Navarrete and Chief Eyasiquiche, specifically through Tawakoni and Iscani intermediaries who lived on the boundaries of the Hasinai Caddos, with whom they traded. The chief knew that the Caddos in turn traded with Los Adaes and the French while maintaining peaceful relations. Two Tejas Caddo captains, el Sanches and el Canos, knew the Taovaya language, while Calahorra spoke the Caddo dialect. The exchange of Treviño for the gifts took place at Mission Nacogdoches, where each Tejas captain was also offered a horse, with another presented to Chief Eyasiquiche.[44]

The fact that Antonio Treviño survived his captivity was atypical especially because of his gender. Historian Juliana Barr explains that Spanish men "captured in battle were destined for torture and death rather than adoption" compared to Hispanic women and children.[45] Friar Calahorra asked the Tejas captains what motives Chief Eyasiquiche had for keeping Treviño alive for six months before returning him. They responded that "in one spot not too far from San Saba, he [Treviño] defended himself with courage against forty-seven Indians from his [Chief Eyasiquiche] nation with whom they were at war . . . while three of those with Treviño, two men and a woman, were killed . . . and [Treviño] badly wounded from four bullets and two lances he received." Chief Eyasiquiche wanted his assistance with upcoming campaigns against Osage enemies, so Treviño "was well received by the [Taovaya] people, both adults and children, who cared for, and attended, to him even more meticulously after Eyasiquiche learned Treviño was from Los Adaes," whose residents had been at peace with the Indians. Chief Eyasiquiche returned Treviño "in person to Mission Nacogdoches, despite the extreme love and affection all his people had toward him, to show by this act the benevolence they profess for the Spaniards [from Los Adaes] and their wish to maintain peace with them."[46] From Chief Eyasiquiche's perspective, Treviño's bravery affirmed the general respect Indians held for the Adaeseños and their close relationship with French Natchitoches.

The Taovayas apparently made distinctions among the Spanish in Texas and viewed those at Los Adaes more favorably because they lived in relative peace with their neighbors among the Caddos and French. This point was lost on Governor Martos Navarrete when he asked why peace was preserved with Presidio Los Adaes and not San Sabá. Chief Eyasiquiche responded through Caddo interpreters that the residents of San Sabá "promised to protect and defend the Apaches who they escorted when they left to hunt, knowing that they were their [Taovaya] mortal enemies and, being the thieves they are, dared to offend their [Taovaya] pueblos and steal their horses like what just occurred among the Teheucanas, where they [Apaches] entered, killed and seized Indians, taking all the horses they found."[47] Barr says this suggested to the Wichitas that the Spanish also lived in bands, and though they "might speak the same language, wear the same clothes, and share the same culture," they had "individual political identities and affiliations, as did many Indian peoples."[48] This last point underscores the Adaeseños' greater sense of security as they traveled back and forth along the Camino Real and Indian trails in the Piney Woods of East Texas.

As it turned out, Treviño had been detached from Los Adaes to perform escort duty at San Sabá, where he accompanied the Apaches on one of their winter buffalo hunts.[49] Although Treviño knew his job was dangerous, he might not have imagined becoming a captive—much less being well treated by his captors. Treviño likely enjoyed hunting buffalo with the Indians because it was certainly more adventurous and thrilling than farming or ranching at Los Adaes or serving guard duty at a Spanish mission. In August 1765, Governor Martos Navarrete ordered an investigation into Treviño's captivity and return. First summoned was Pedro de Sierra, the seventy-year-old lieutenant from Los Adaes and the same individual whom Lt. Joseph Gonzalez wrote about thirty years earlier concerning the attempt of St. Denis to persuade Lieutenant de Sierra and the Adaeseños into desertion. Lieutenant Sierra testified to the truth of Father Calahorra's own testimony about his meeting with the Tejas captains. The thirty-four-year-old Treviño then appeared before the governor and also certified Father Calahorra's account.[50]

A few days later, Governor Martos Navarrete ordered Treviño to appear again before him and provide information about his Taovaya captors. Treviño said the Taovayas were a settled people whose village was located 140 leagues (350 miles) northeast of Presidio San Sabá on the other side of the Red River (present Texas-Oklahoma border), where they built their fort to resist the military campaigns of Colonel Parrilla from San Sabá. Treviño stated that the Taovaya kept hidden "the guns they use[d] as weapons" and that he saw trade goods during the six months he lived there, such as "powder, ammunition, cloth, shirts, and other things they use in their wardrobe from the French, who bring these items in exchange for skins of buffalo, deer, *apachitos* [Apache children], and Apaches [adults] who they seize in war along with the horses, mules, and all the rest stolen from the Spaniards."[51] Treviño witnessed this frontier exchange economy whereby Southern Plains Indians sold Apaches and possibly scalps as part of the fur trade with French traders from Louisiana.

According to Treviño, the Taovaya settlement was well defended, surrounded by friends and foe alike, who were all equally armed. To the east and west side of their fort were trenches, split-log picket walls all around for firing rifles, and an earthen rampart in between the trenches. The interior had four subterranean houses that sheltered women, children, and the infirm from attack. To the north, contiguous to the Taovayas' settlement, was the nation of the Wichita, who were not numerous. Nearby to the south were the Yscanis (Iscanis), who were allies of the Tawakonis. Altogether, a force of around five hundred armed warriors protected their own native boundaries.

There were many other Indian nations that encircled the Taovayas in an outer perimeter. To the northwest about eighty leagues (200 miles) were the Gnazas, Cuitaranches, Huitaguiras, and still more enemies whom the Taovayas feared, as these were also skilled with rifles and had recently occupied land that the Apaches abandoned eight years earlier following hostilities they suffered from Taovayas, who began to use firearms. To the west were enemy Apaches at some distance north of Presidio San Sabá. Most disconcertingly to the Spanish, Treviño said, "To the north live Comanches with whom they [Taovaya] are allied, but have no fixed dwelling, are numerous in some parts, and began using guns acquired from the French who transport these goods in exchange for all the same things expressed above." Finally, about fifty leagues (125 miles) to the south were the Tehuacana allies of the Taovayas, who "live off buffalo meat," which Treviño "witnessed many times as [he] went out with them to hunt the abundant meat in that country of the plains with its substantial pastures from the many rains that bathe them, providing corn, beans, and pumpkin in abundance, and whose graveyards they maintain in the vicinity of the settlement."[52]

Treviño ended the governor's interrogation with a declaration that he saw the two cannons the Taovayas had acquired in the military campaign against the Spanish from San Sabá and "discarded on the ground in two houses next to the [Taovayas] fort ... which they showed to a Frenchman."[53] Governor Martos Navarrete closed the proceeding and recognized the obvious misfortunes of San Sabá and the dominance of the French trade with the Indians. The governor then stored the records in his residence and sent copies to the viceroy to await further orders.[54]

Chief Eyasiquiche's peaceful overtures, however, ultimately proved too difficult to sustain, as his people resumed raids at San Antonio and San

Sabá to the disdain of Spanish officials who were more intent on closing Los Adaes and possibly withdrawing entirely from East Texas.[55] Treviño's testimony about French and Indian trade in furs, horses, and captives in exchange for European weapons and other goods was significant because it revealed that the Spanish at Los Adaes failed to guard the border against the encroachment of French traders from Louisiana, who easily skirted around the fort and into western trade routes.[56] The locations Treviño gave of Indian villages showed the growing power of Southern Plains Indians and their reliance on the horse to cover vast territory. Governor Martos Navarrete remained powerless to prevent covert arms trading. Paradoxically, such commerce ultimately lured him and other governors from Los Adaes into the frontier exchange economy in pursuit of more profitable, often illicit, activities and perhaps to establish a cartel in East Texas across the border from Louisiana.

In this aspect, the Texas-Louisiana borderlands in the eighteenth century offer a fascinating comparative perspective with Latin America. Historian Matthew Restall notes that amid the attempts of sailors and slaves to obtain freedom in the Yucatán-Belize borderlands, the Spanish unsuccessfully prevented the British from penetrating the logging trade into this peninsular region of New Spain on the southern Gulf of Mexico and Caribbean. Restall states that "most of the trade was illegal, and occasional arrests of smugglers hint at the extensive and complex networks of illicit commerce across the frontier."[57] In Spanish Texas, as explained in the previous chapter, the governors only intermittingly prosecuted French traders for smuggling from the 1730s through 1750s, but by the 1760s and into the early 1770s, after Spain acquired Louisiana from France, Spanish investigators found even more disturbing news of governors and Adaeseños being increasingly involved with illicit trade in guns, tobacco, furs, and captives. Such involvement of their own officials and soldiers made any Spanish border against the French or Indians practically unenforceable.

In effect, a "shadow economy" emerged on the Texas-Louisiana borderlands in connection with markets in New Spain and New Orleans. Historian Andrew Konove describes the Baratillo marketplace in eighteenth-century Mexico City, where legal and illegal commercial activities blended with each other. He argues that the Baratillo (from the Spanish word *barato*, or "cheap"), "more than a colonial-era flea market, was the nexus of Mexico City's larger underground economy" that "linked some of the most elite traders in New Spain to some of the lowliest through a far-reaching credit network."[58] Among items in this marketplace were imported British linen and silver plates that belonged to members of Mexico City's *consulado* (merchant guild) and jewelry that was secondhand, stolen, counterfeit, contraband, or untaxed. The Spanish attempted to regulate this market by issuing licenses to importers to ensure that the government received its *alcabala* (Arab-origin tax from Spain) income and to prohibit *hombres del color quebrado* (mixed-bloods) from participating. The Spanish could not totally abandon the marketplace precisely because elite merchants needed somewhere to dump secondhand items and make more profit even though the government tried to stop it.[59] British linen also filtered through the Texas-Louisiana borderlands as the Atlantic world trade increasingly penetrated northern and southern New Spain from various frontiers during the eighteenth century.

Treviño's captivity, moreover, underscored human trafficking and the multiple challenges governors and missionaries faced on the Texas-Louisiana borderlands. Convincing Indians to settle in the East Texas missions, gifting Caddo and Bidai leaders, negotiating peace through trade with Norteños at war with the Apaches and Spaniards from Presidio San Sabá altogether compromised Spanish military, diplomatic, and missionary objectives. Governor Martos Navarrete's gift giving reflected Spain's efforts at asserting dominion over the region following the Seven Years' War, but he also sought opportunities to expand his personal empire through surrogates at Los Adaes, especially when he resided at San Antonio. In addition, stiff competition came from powerful French merchants and slaveholders in Natchitoches even after the Louisiana transfer from France to Spain in 1762. St. Denis (the younger) and Commandant McCarty and his successors, César de Blanc and Athanase de Mézières—all among the town's leading figures—retained strong influence among the Caddos, Southern Plains Indians, Adaeseños, and African Creoles.[60] The mix of captivity and slavery blurred the distinctions between legal and illicit trade at the expense of the Spanish government's ability to collect tax revenue from the frontier for the treasury in Mexico City.

Meanwhile, Martos Navarrete's concern over his two cannons in the hands of "savage" Indians represented a final challenge to his manhood and the inability to control the flow of goods and people on the frontier. The cannons symbolized absolute power, but their loss drained the virility and strength of Spanish conquest in the minds of royal officials. There was no tactical advantage to using such heavy artillery against highly mobile warriors other than intimidation and psychological impact. Commandant McCarty, having contemplated the recent British defeat of the French, likely preferred the governor to reposition the cannons and focus eastward instead on the greater threat that England posed to Spain in North America. McCarty sought to preserve Caddo alliances and French commerce and improve relations with the increasingly powerful Comanche and Norteño nations. The Apaches, on the other hand, appeared doomed to remain in captivity or be completely annihilated through war if they did not find salvation through mission settlement. Antonio Treviño's captivity highlights the fact that Indians dominated Texas and that the purpose for Los Adaes's existence—indeed, Spanish defenses and policies overall—needed major adjustment, especially after the transfer of Louisiana from France to Spain.

III

Meanwhile, in contrast to Spanish settlements in Texas, French Natchitoches rapidly became a "slave society" by the late 1730s, with a combined African and Indian population that formed a majority of the local population.[61] The danger that African slave rebellions, like Indian rebellions, posed to domestic tranquility became another reason for the French to keep ties with Los Adaes. The memory of the Natchez revolt was ingrained in French merchant slaveholders' memories. They wanted to keep Louisiana's western boundary quiet from insurrection, but the English threat east of the Mississippi proved more dangerous over time.[62] The British, along with Iroquois allies in the New York–Canadian borderlands and Chickasaw friends in the southern borderlands, increasingly threatened French commercial interests on the North American frontier. Meanwhile, African slave revolts arose periodically in New Orleans and the French Caribbean while more rebellions from Indians broke out in the lower Mississippi valley concurrently with the Fox Wars in the Illinois Country.[63] French Natchitoches needed to ensure its own safety deep in the backcountry of Louisiana and as an emerging plantation society in the wilderness.

Distant Spanish officials viewed the Texas-Louisiana borderlands as an impoverished region. The lack of silver mines, large haciendas, and plantations found elsewhere in New Spain lessened the need for African slave labor in Spanish Texas. The Spanish assigned African and mulatto slaves and Indian captives largely to domestic servitude among a small class of elites who could afford this luxury. Few such legal slaves could be found at Los Adaes compared to French Natchitoches or even San Antonio. According to historian Frank de la Teja, the prohibitive cost of labor at San Antonio, however, was one reason "ranchers themselves took to the field" and were dependent on the help of their children.[64] The same applied to the Adaeseños, like many frontier settlers in northern New Spain, who were "working people, doing their own manual labor."[65] Had the original Spanish explorers found gold or silver in Texas, the labor situation might have been different, with a much greater need for African slaves or Indian captives.

The governor at Los Adaes usually remained the only Spaniard with any considerable personal wealth on the Texas-Louisiana borderlands. The social status of the governor's officers, however, was not much above rank-and-file soldiers except perhaps those Adaeseños with French connections at Natchitoches. There were no Canary Islander families settled at Los Adaes, as there were in San Antonio, where the Isleños established a cabildo and, in effect, acted as a counterbalance to the governor's power.[66] The political and economic interests of the Adaeseño community were submerged entirely beneath the whims of autocratic governors, and the only avenues to escape included desertion or open rebellion against Spanish rule.

The legal trade in black and mulatto slaves remained insignificant at Los Adaes, where only two known bills of sale were recorded, and both involved governors with Mexico City connections. On September 6,

1748, former governor general Francisco García Larios appeared before Gov. Pedro de Barrio Junco y Espriella and sold "from today forward and forever, a black slave, named Luis de Urrutia Cofre de Pazas," to don Joseph Carvallido Villarino, a resident of Mexico City, in the amount of two hundred pesos. Interestingly, Governor Barrio sold Luís as "a captive slave subject to servitude and free of mortgage bond, or other alienation, and without assuring illness, fault, nor any other public or secret defect." Carvallido acquired Luís from the estate of Lt. Col. Justo Boneo Morales through a power of attorney from don Diego Giraud, the same agent from Mexico City who collected salaries for the troops.[67] Boneo Morales had preceded General García as the governor of Texas but passed away in 1745 shortly after assuming command at Los Adaes.[68] The next day, September 7, General García Larios sold another black slave, named Antonio Nicolas Patricio Cafre de Passa, to don Manuel de Villanueva, a resident from Los Adaes, for two hundred pesos as a "captive slave"—also previously owned by Carvallido—which included a power of attorney to Giraud.[69]

Although the origins of these two slaves, Luís and Antonio, are unknown, the sales provide hints about their background. Both men were previously owned by the same master and had the same last names despite the slight difference in spelling. Both had been slaves in Mexico City, which suggests they were household servants rather than field hands.[70] The language in the contracts, "captive slave," likely referred to Luís and Antonio as alienable property, such as land and chattel, which could be sold or mortgaged. Perhaps both men were brothers and the second generation of Atlantic Creoles from parents or ancestors originally brought to work the sugar plantations in Veracruz or the silver mines in Zacatecas.[71] Their presence at Los Adaes highlighted the wealth and status of Spanish governors in contrast to the impoverished Adaeseños and served to remind settlers of their own subservient status on the frontier, which fell somewhere between captivity and slavery and was more like indentured servitude.

Some of the Adaeseños closely followed in the footsteps of St. Denis and his wife as role models on the frontier. One such individual was don Manuel Antonio de Soto Bermúdez, mentioned in the previous chapter, who had many children of his own and also became the godfather to his African slaves. In November 1754, six months after marrying into the St. Denis family at Natchitoches after his desertion from Los Adaes, de Soto became the godfather of a black child named Manuela Marianne, the daughter of Nanette and Pierrot, who were African slaves owned by Madame (Manuela) St. Denis. Manuela outlived her husband and essentially became the matriarch of French Natchitoches society. Several years later, de Soto also became the godfather of a mulatto slave named Louise Cirena, who was property of Monsieur de Blanc, the commandant at Natchitoches who succeeded St. Denis (the younger). De Blanc's wife was the slave's godmother.[72] Less than two years before she married Manuel de Soto, Marie des Nieges de St. Denis was named the godmother to at least three black slaves, apparently as part of a dowry. Other slaves owned by de Soto and his wife were also baptized. Indeed, de Soto married into the most powerful and wealthy family at French Natchitoches, where archival records referred to him as the "Spaniard." Black slaves at Natchitoches continued to receive baptism following Louisiana's transfer to Spain, which Gov. Alejandro O'Reilly affirmed in 1769, when he declared the French Code Noir of 1724 be "observed with exactitude."[73]

Manuel de Soto and Marie also had many children of their own whose baptisms tied Natchitoches with Los Adaes, just as baptisms of slaves brought them into kinship across race and class at Natchitoches. They had three daughters and three sons at Natchitoches over a ten-year period from 1756 to 1766, and Franciscans from Mission Adaes performed baptisms for their first four children. In the baptism of their fifth child, Father Ignacio Laba, a priest from Los Adaes, recorded in Latin and listed an Adaeseño named Juan Prieto as the godfather. Francisco Solís, Governor Martos Navarrete's secretary, witnessed the baptism of their last child.[74] During the 1750s, other Spaniards had their children baptized at French Natchitoches and became fictive kin of the St. Denis and de Blanc families.[75] Spaniards also became godparents for French children.[76] French Natchitoches evidently had been more connected with Los Adaes through baptismal ceremonies prior to the Louisiana transfer to Spain and interdependence resulted in greater numbers of Spanish-Franco baptisms at Natchitoches than ever before. By 1766, thanks largely to his wife's dowry and other purchases, Manuel de Soto owned eleven slaves and a small number of livestock, though he did not own great quantities of tobacco.[77]

He purchased land in Natchitoches from a Sieur Prodhomme and became the godfather to his slaves.[78] De Soto's rapid rise in stature, wealth, and power based on slavery and land at Natchitoches most likely would not have occurred at Los Adaes, where the Adaeseños still longed for land grants such as those that Spanish settlers eventually obtained under don José de Escandon along the lower Rio Grande valley in 1767 with *porciones* (rectangular tracts with river access).[79]

The majority of the baptisms for children from Adaeseño families, on the other hand, occurred at the chapel of Presidio Los Adaes. At that chapel, there were evidently no baptisms of Caddo or African children as there were in Natchitoches. During his inspection tour of the Texas missions in the late 1760s, Friar Gaspar José Solís noted 256 total baptisms performed at the fort of Los Adaes. He also mentioned that the Franciscan missionaries performed around 20 baptisms at the Natchitoches post because it did not always have Jesuit or Capuchin ministers, the same reason the Spanish cited in the 1730s.[80] Pervasive poverty of the Adaeseño community and arbitrary rule under their governors did not attract French residents from Natchitoches to Los Adaes to baptize their children. French visitors likely witnessed baptisms at Los Adaes, but their primary reason for being there remained commerce, worship, and festive occasions.

African slavery across the "border" at French Natchitoches became the dominant form of labor in contrast to the servitude of the Adaeseños as personal laborers at Los Adaes.[81] In 1763, Commandant McCarty at Natchitoches defended the institution of African slavery as a vital part of the Louisiana economy and reminded Governor Martos Navarrete that Spaniards enslaved both Indians and Africans. It was "nonsense," McCarty told the governor, that "every individual of either sex, whether black or other colors, devoted to manufacturing labor in the regions of the New World only remain slaves for a short time." McCarty thought development without slavery was "unsustainable unless under the condition that they [slaves] are instructed in the doctrine and enter the sacred fountain of Baptism if they were to become free of the services of their masters" and attained the benefits of "regeneration" through Christianity. McCarty, however, believed that emancipation "releases the tremendous captivity of the Devil, while tightening the law gives them a greater longing for their employer and they become good workers."[82] According to McCarty, African slavery was not only economically necessary but also morally justified because French society was strengthened if slaves remained in captivity and were baptized into the Christian faith. French and Spanish masters in the Americas held similar goals of incorporating Africans and Indians into colonial society with a rigid hierarchy based on race, caste, and wealth that varied across frontiers in Latin America. While Natchitoches continued to develop as a slave society, Los Adaes at the least can be described as a society with slaves like other Spanish settlements in northern New Spain.

IV

Aside from philosophical debates about Indian and African slavery, the French and Spanish entered into diplomatic discussions concerning the return of black slaves to their masters in Louisiana. The issue over the status of fugitive slaves would arise in the event that war broke out between imperial France and Spain prior to the Louisiana transfer. As early as 1753, Governor Barrios Jáuregui from Los Adaes wrote his superiors in Mexico City and explained that the French at Natchitoches were dependent on slavery, noting how one French official in particular owned forty-four slaves, while his poorer brethren had but one or two. He added that the French also needed the assistance and protection of loyal Indians, as if to suggest their need for assistance against potential slave revolt. "Although it is against military practice as your Excellency knows," Barrios Jáuregui suggested to the viceroy, "I would like your permission to allow me to issue a proclamation to the effect that all slaves who might come here can enjoy their freedom and protection of the king." The governor believed that many slaves "would come from as far as New Orleans since their owners do not provide for these wretched ones in any way and give them only Sundays off for themselves." He described how "punishment is to tie them naked to a ladder and to lash them with a whip until not a part remains on their bodies that is not bloody," followed by an equally cruel method of washing wounds with chili and vinegar.[83] Barrios Jáuregui finally stated that black slaves had twice attempted revolts in New Orleans, but they were horrifically defeated "due to the fact that they have no one to take their part."[84] For African slaves at Natchitoches in Louisiana and beyond, they discovered a possible road to freedom across the border in Spanish Texas inside Spanish missions.

The governor basically wanted to know whether he could apply the law of religious refuge established by royal decree on December 19, 1739, even though Louisiana was already officially Catholic. Historian Matthew Restall explains that this law of refuge, or religious sanctuary, granted freedom "to slaves who fled non-Catholic owners in rival colonies and requested baptism in Spanish colonies." He notes that this law, however, was applied rather inconsistently throughout the remainder of the eighteenth century.[85] While such a law proved significant for African slaves elsewhere in colonial Latin America, such as those who fled the English colony of Carolina to St. Augustine in Spanish Florida or from Belize (British Honduras) in Central America to the Yucatan Peninsula in southeastern Mexico, the law really had not been tested on the frontiers between Spain and France in North America, as both were under Catholic monarchs who were signees to Family Compacts of alliance.[86] Restall explains that for the Yucatan-Belize frontier of Mesoamerica, "borders between colonies were not obstacles but bridges, crossed by sailors and slaves in search of safety—sometimes with success, sometimes in vain."[87] The same applied to the Texas-Louisiana borderlands except with soldiers and slaves as deserters and fugitives who took the same routes along the Camino Real irrespective of religion in quest for refuge.[88]

Governor Barrios Jáuregui's proposal for emancipation divided the viceroy's advisors. One thought it was a good idea considering the small size of the Spanish military force and population of Texas. The other sounded alarm because the same measure could be used against Spanish colonies elsewhere, as England had done in Havana when the British captured this strategic Caribbean port in 1762 and held it for nine months during the Seven Years' War. Besides, French masters would only repress their slaves further to make sure they did not escape. This advisor also viewed the measure as premature, since he believed war between France and Spain was unlikely due to their "well-founded alliance, friendship, and harmony" and the current "state of peace and tranquility which the two nations are enjoying."[89] The Royal Council of War and Finance in Mexico City ultimately advised the viceroy against emancipation, having resolved that "it would rather serve to change the minds of the French and provoke the very war that he fears." The viceroy found this argument convincing, though Barrios Jáuregui apparently recognized runaway slaves from Louisiana who reached Spanish settlements as free.[90]

Spanish officials similarly considered the problem of granting immunity to a runaway slave from French Louisiana who sought freedom inside an East Texas mission, which appeared a closer fit to the notion of offering sanctuary. One such case went before the viceroy Marqués de Aranda in 1758. He considered legal precedents from a similar case eight years earlier, when a royal decree permitted the apprehension of a French slave, described as the *reo* (defendant), from a church sanctuary to avoid future harm that could arise from clandestine escape. The fugitive was placed in jail with a temporary *caución* (bond). The governor of New Orleans, Marqués de Kerlérec, and Commandant de Blanc from French Natchitoches demanded his return. However, the secular judge, a position the governor of Texas held jointly with his command at Los Adaes, could not immediately punish the offender, only detain the runaway before deciding if he should "benefit from local immunity" through a power of attorney. A final decision required a background check of any accompanying documents in the case, along with a determination of whether the refugee had any *delitos* (crimes) to justify his return. Such action was in accordance with the Recopilación de Leyes de Castilla (law 5 and 6, title 16, book 8), which applied to the return of delinquents from Portugal or other parts of the Spanish kingdom. Meanwhile, the slave remained in jail at Presidio Los Adaes. If the owner from the French colony made his request in the proper form with the appropriate paperwork, then the refugee could be returned regardless of whether crimes were committed.[91]

Aranda's successor as viceroy, Marqués de Amarillas, based his own decision on the earlier case as precedent when he ordered Governor Barrios Jáuregui to have the master establish ownership of the runaway slave from New Orleans.[92] Royal advisors told the governor to follow his superiors' orders despite the vague instructions, but it was too late.[93] Viceroy Amarillas wrote the governor and said, "I realize the black slave, who sought refuge of immunity in the Church of your Province, has been returned to the French of New Orleans." The viceroy added, "The delivery of the abovementioned slave was overlooked without awaiting my resolution in this case," so he instructed the governor only to prepare testimony in future cases without any evident reprimand.[94] The name of the slave appeared nowhere in the documents, and he was likely confined in the presidio's jail longer before returned to his owner from Louisiana. Barrios Jáuregui ultimately decided to return the slave without permission from Mexico City, a prerogative that governors sometimes took on the Texas-Louisiana borderlands to avoid notorious bureaucratic delays that hindered diplomacy in local and regional matters.

The governor from Los Adaes continued to weigh the concerns of merchants and slaveholders from Louisiana after its transfer to Spain, especially since the French did not suddenly relinquish power to the Spanish in New Orleans or Natchitoches. In 1768, Hugo O'Conor, the interim governor of Texas, requested an order from the viceroy, Marqués de Croix, concerning a mulatto runaway slave who belonged to a resident from Louisiana and took refuge at Mission Adaes. The French commandant at Natchitoches requested the return of the slave, claiming that it was the custom of governors in Spanish Texas to oblige with the return of fugitives.

Governor O'Conor did not consider local policy making as judicious until hearing the appropriate testimony that the fiscal in Mexico City ordered. The governor included copies of previous correspondence between Viceroy Amarillas and Governor Barrios.[95] The viceroy informed Governor O'Conor that he was aware of the governor's doubt about returning the slave and asked, "If the slave has not committed any crimes, why punish him by returning him to his owner?" However, if the slave had gone to the mission because he was fleeing a crime, then O'Conor "can advise the French commander to make a sworn pledge against immunity, and in doing so, return the slave, which you also can practice in the future."[96] Governor O'Conor's hesitation reflected the ebb and flow of Spanish concerns about the law of religious sanctuary for slaves who escaped into Texas. Whether the mulatto runaway slave in this case attained freedom was inconclusive, but he probably did not achieve it if officials followed local custom to remove the potential for rebellion.[97]

During the mid-eighteenth century, the problem of fugitive slaves from Louisiana became entangled with the rescue and ransom of Indian and Spanish captives, which further complicated political and economic relations on the Texas-Louisiana borderlands. After Governor O'Reilly established Spanish control over New Orleans in 1769, he outlawed Indian slavery, which had existed legally in Louisiana under French rule. Although the New Laws of 1542 that prohibited Indian slavery technically extended to Spanish Louisiana, the enslavement of Apache captives continued. The spirit of the French Code Noir of 1724 that applied to African slavery also remained in effect.[98] Indian captivity blended with a labor system in the lower Mississippi valley, where European settlers increasingly relied on African slaves for cash-crop plantations.[99] However, the fate of Indian and African slavery in Spanish Louisiana did not concern the governor-commandants at Los Adaes so long as they could exploit the labor of the Adaeseños and avail themselves of captives and slaves as status symbols whenever possible. The existence of African slavery at the Natchitoches post essentially became a mirror through which the Adaeseños measured their own servitude at Los Adaes. They also took opportunities to trade with Indians, Africans, and European deserters.

Spanish officials in Mexico City or Madrid likely did not know about slaves and deserters engaged in contraband trade at Los Adaes, which appeared to have been tolerated locally so long as it did not threaten the governor's rule or monopoly on trade. In 1757, for example, as the French and their Algonquian allies held off the British in the Ohio valley, an English deserter (named Chomure) made his residence at Natchitoches and engaged in smuggling with Los Adaes through the assistance of African slaves. Under interrogation, a slave named Etienne, who belonged to César de Blanc, commandant at Natchitoches, divulged to French officials that a slave named Marion and owned by the commandant's wife had sent stolen goods from another slaveholder to Los Adaes in exchange for silver pesos. Among the contraband items were cloth, a bottle of "wild cherry," and a box of undisclosed contents. Unable to obtain the silver, however, Marion deposited the items with Chomure, who paid with a horse "until the arrival of the Spanish army."[100] Perhaps the Spanish governors permitted, if not just tolerated, such illicit trade with the Adaeseños. On the other hand, had these contraband items included guns and tobacco, the governor likely would have arrested the smugglers and confiscated the goods, as was done with French smugglers.

In another example, during the fall of 1762, French officials at Natchitoches learned that a German deserter named Christophe Haische sold stolen goods to soldiers at Los Adaes. Haische bartered twenty-five pounds of gunpowder and thirty-four pounds of ammunition with Antonio Gil Ybarbo in exchange for fifteen cowhides as well as three hundred flints for three *piasters* (French currency).[101] With the formal conclusion of the Seven Years' War only a pen stroke away from eliminating French sovereignty in North America, the region between Texas and Louisiana increasingly attracted the movement of peoples and goods from completely opposite directions and cultures. The contraband trade of these goods proved significant and more troubling because Adaeseños such as Antonio Gil Ybarbo also drove cattle to Louisiana in exchange for African slaves. Ybarbo was later convicted for smuggling.

English traders also appeared in Texas along the Gulf of Mexico in the late 1760s as Comanche power expanded following their destruction of the Spanish mission at San Sabá in 1757. The Mexican silver trade that Spain initially denied other European and indigenous rivals access to would have placed the British and Comanches on a collision course with Spain over Texas were it not for the American Revolution, when the Spanish blocked English access to the Gulf of Mexico in the lower Mississippi valley. What these emerging powerful nations least expected was strong local resistance from Spanish, French, and Caddo regional elites who jockeyed for control of smuggling routes through the Texas-Louisiana borderlands as transatlantic commerce clashed against mercantilism. Apparently, both Haische and Chomure followed in the footsteps of other displaced deserters seeking similar opportunities on the Texas-Louisiana borderlands. As historian Restall says about the Yucatan-Belize borderlands, "Despite the regularity and disruption of frontier violence, there was also constant diplomatic communication, trade, and migration across the border" whereby "British merchants operated in Yucatan's Spanish

[port] cities of Mérida and Campeche."[102] French rather than English traders operated at Los Adaes, where the Spanish designated a small wooden building for official trade yet likely tolerated a shadow economy that operated simultaneously among poor Adaeseños, Indians, Africans, and Euro-Americans. The seemingly isolated instances of fugitive slaves together with deserters on the Texas-Louisiana borderlands appeared as by-products of warfare and contraband trade on a wider scale in North America while Spanish Bourbon reformers considered shutting down Los Adaes and the East Texas missions altogether. The Spanish wanted to dedicate more resources to holding the line against British settlement east of the Mississippi River while they reimagined the border and Indian policy across the frontier in northern New Spain.[103] Just as the Adaeseños seemingly turned the corner toward the sustainability of their community and sought free trade with foreigners and Indians, a royal order instead forced them to evacuate Los Adaes and abandon their adopted homeland on the Texas-Louisiana borderlands.

Trail of Sorrows

On June 25, 1773, the Adaeseño community began their forced march to San Antonio after Gov. Juan María Barón de Ripperdá arrived at Los Adaes earlier that month to initiate removal, then placed this task in the hands of Lt. Joseph Gonzalez to carry out the king's order. The governor informed the Adaeseños to be ready within five days, and after he granted their request for an extension, some thirty-five residents refused the eviction notice and fled into the forest. The majority obeyed, though not without a complaint against Lieutenant Gonzalez, who allegedly mounted a horse and rode from house to house forcing people outside. They abandoned their homes, furniture and lands and traveled on foot. They left behind livestock and corn untended. Heavy military equipment, including several cannons, gun cartridges, and most of the ammunition, was buried inside the fort at Los Adaes. A month into their exodus, they reached Rancho El Lobanillo, where twenty-four Adaeseños stayed behind due to sickness, including Antonio Gil Ybarbo's mother and sister-in-law. Traveling west along the Camino Real, they soon reached Mission Nacogdoches, where nine people, consisting of two families, remained apparently at the request of a Tejas chief named Bigotes, who wished to join the exodus to San Antonio and convince the governor to allow their return to East Texas along with a Franciscan missionary. On July 30, at Mission Nacogdoches, Lieutenant Gonzalez and two women passed away. After drought, heavy rains, and flooding, ten children also tragically died. Finally, on September 26, more than one hundred Adaeseño families entered San Antonio with four Franciscans from Missions Adaes, Ais, and Nacogdoches.[1] At no other time in the history of the Spanish conquest of the New World had the government forced its subjects to abandon their own settlement and suffer such sorrows, usually the fate of Indians.

❙

Los Adaes ironically became a casualty of violence that spilled across other frontiers as Spain harbored grave concerns about fighting two wars—one against more powerful Indians from the Southern Plains in Texas and the other against Britain east of the Mississippi as well as in the Caribbean, where the English made their smuggling stronghold and resisted Spanish enforcement against contraband trade. Meanwhile, France held commercial, political, religious, and kinship reasons for backing Spain in opposition to Britain. The French principal commercial interest remained with the port city of Cadiz, Spain, since anywhere from half to seven-ninths of all goods aboard galleons and shipped to Spanish America were produced in France.[2] The Caddos, meanwhile, defended native ground to preserve their benefits as gatekeepers of trade at the crossroads between Southern Plains and Woodlands Indians after having allowed the Los Adaes and Natchitoches communities into their vast political and economic alliances. Los Adaes became entangled with the overlapping spheres of mercantilism, the smuggling frontier, and transatlantic commerce as refugees, deserters, and fugitive slaves fled to the Texas-Louisiana borderlands.[3] Spain, however, did not have enough troops and resources to guard the border or to build a wall of forts inland and wanted instead to extract the Adaeseños, especially as Louisiana came under Spanish control after the Seven Years' War and the northeastern border of New Spain became the Mississippi. Los Adaes no longer served its primary purpose and could be sacrificed under the Bourbon Reforms in the effort to make the Spanish military more efficient and professional and to discourage smuggling.

Seemingly unrelated warfare in Texas and Canada ultimately outweighed whatever reservations the Spanish held against their French Bourbon counterparts over the territorial limits of Texas and Louisiana. In September 1759, while Britain achieved victory over France in the

Battle of Quebec on the St. Lawrence River, the Spanish colonel Diego Ortiz Parrilla arrived at Presidio San Sabá in the Texas Hill Country from San Antonio to launch retaliatory strikes against the Comanches and Norteño allies for destroying Mission San Sabá the previous year. From Madrid, this new Comanche menace played in the background as the wife of King Carlos III, who reigned over Spain and its dominions from 1759 to 1788, expressed her husband's sentiments that England "can become the owners of Mexico with the settlements they have made."[4] In 1761, Spain entered into the third Family Compact with France after the fall of Montreal to Britain. The English victory in the Seven Years' War not only eliminated French claims west of the Mississippi but also cut off French access to lucrative trade in New Spain. France secretly transferred Louisiana to Spain in 1762, however, just prior to the Treaty of Paris (1763) with the intention of blocking Britain's path to New Spain and regaining some of her lost possessions in the future. King Carlos III, in turn, wished to draw the eastern boundary of Louisiana as far east and north as possible to prevent the English from approaching New Spain through Texas and New Mexico from New Orleans or St. Louis.[5] Europeans and Indians in North America moved along parallel paths, as historian Daniel Richter describes, into "a single, ever more consolidated, transatlantic imperial world."[6] The British *and* the Comanches moved on such a course through Texas from opposite directions, and Spain could not let both these emergent empires make common cause, as no borderline of forts, missions, and settlements in northern New Spain could repel such an alliance of Anglo and native military forces.

Spain bled slowly at the edges of its empire in the Americas even as the Bourbon Reforms attempted to prevent smuggling on its frontiers, including Texas. In fact, two-thirds of all Spanish commerce was illicit. Contraband trade became more pronounced in the eighteenth century as the numbers of French and English traders increased.[7] One major reason for the illicit commerce remained the lack of a manufacturing sector in Spain, where smuggling of tobacco, salt, and raw silk became institutionalized.[8] According to historian David Weber, foreign-made goods at Los Adaes from Louisiana far surpassed those manufactured in Spain. Although King Carlos III considered smuggling an obstacle to growth, there was very little he could do overall except to consider loosening Spain's grip on mercantilism, permit "free trade" in cattle and tobacco, and promote greater immigration on the Texas frontier, where independent Indians continued to hold the upper hand against Spanish settlement.[9]

An enlightened monarch such as Carlos III indeed became aware of the call for economic and military reform throughout the Spanish Empire. A contemporary Spanish scholar named Manuel Antonio de Gándara argued in his *Notes on the Strength and Ills of Spain* (1759) that the root causes of Spanish troubles were smuggling and the lack of support for local manufacturing. Madrid's colonial policy had been to isolate New Spain from Jamaica, which the British utilized to smuggle goods not only into North America but throughout Spanish possessions in the Americas from present Venezuela, Honduras, Guatemala, and Yucatan to Florida, Louisiana, Texas, and the Pacific Northwest. The engine behind all this was the early Industrial Revolution with the sudden preference of consumers for relatively cheaper cotton fabrics instead of wool. England increasingly became a manufacturing rather than an agricultural nation, which necessitated new markets while its population and trade in the Caribbean and American mainland colonies boomed.[10] In his *Defense of the Spanish Nation* (1771), the intellectual writer José Cadalso, on the other hand, attributed Spain's decline to luxury that arose from commerce and the decadent Francophile character of the Bourbon dynasty in Spain. To open up Spain and its overseas territories meant growing possibilities for heresy, so Spanish officials, including King Carlos III, clung to the belief that Spain's survival required political and social control even though observers had argued that the removal of trade restrictions could end smuggling.[11]

The bleeding on the Texas frontier was due to internal and external causes, which the Marqués de Rubí discovered upon his inspection tour at Los Adaes in the late 1760s. Spain's inability to properly equip troops and an arsenal that was almost empty only added to many other problems. David Weber noted that presidios throughout the interior of New Spain operated as "local fiefdoms" under commanding officers, where little coordination of troop movements or standardization of weapons, ammunition, and uniforms existed between forts.[12] Los Adaes was featured in Rubí's scathing report, and on September 12, 1767, he wrote very specific instructions to Governor O'Conor. Rubí ordered the governor to have the company assembled at dawn two days later on horseback in the plaza of this presidio with all their armament, saddles, and uniforms so that he could "recognize the respective contingent of men, horses, and furnishings." Rubí warned against the troops appearing for inspection with borrowed personal effects, or else they might be punished. Second, before the inspection, Rubí wanted the company's horses brought closer and placed inside the presidio's corrals for each soldier, beginning with the sergeant, to transmit six horses into his *dotación* (endowment); afterward, those horses leftover would be included in Rubí's report. Third, Rubí ordered O'Conor to hand him the *Libro ministro de filiaciones*, which was an administrative book on the personal descriptions of the soldiers for comparison with the *Relación de alta y baja*, or the report on those individuals who were discharged from service, missing, or marked as casualties. Rubí also requested the *Libros ministros de caja* (administrative account book) to verify the debits and credits made during Martos Navarrete's governorship and commandancy. He wanted to see the *Cuadernos de abio* (notebooks of the equipment), which recorded the goods the soldiers received as well as the distribution of gunpowder, and copies of the *poderes* (powers of attorney) documents sent annually to Mexico City for the collection of troop salaries.[13]

Rubí also instructed O'Conor to see that the person who held power of attorney for former governor Martos Navarrete submitted the documents in the presidial archives. This information, Rubí said, might help him formulate an idea of the fairness with which the soldier was treated regarding the distribution of inferior-quality goods compared to those items mentioned in the regulations, invoices, or understandings of the lists brought for payment in goods to the troops.[14] Subsequent demands included a better formula to be used for settling the soldiers' accounts, which Rubí said should be done quarterly. O'Conor also had to show Rubí the weapons that Los Adaes had available on a daily basis. Lastly, Rubí asked O'Conor to let him know, as the interim governor, of his own situation, advantages, and usefulness for royal service because the king wanted Rubí to provide him with the most punctual and precise information about O'Conor's "zeal, intelligence, and military experience."[15] O'Conor dutifully followed Rubí's instructions—with perhaps much anxiety over the inspection and report to come.

Rubí indeed gave a most unflattering assessment of the soldiers, horses, and weaponry at Los Adaes during his inspection. He wrote that the presidio was composed of sixty-one troops. Its chain of command from the top down included (1) former governor Martos Navarrete, who was absent because Viceroy de Croix had ordered in July 1767 that he appear in Mexico City for trial, and O'Conor as interim governor; (2) Lt. Marcos Ruíz, who was also suspended by virtue of the viceroy's order; (3) Lt. Joseph Gonzalez, who was made interim commandant; (4) 2nd Lt. Pedro de Sierra and Sgt. Domingo Chirino; (5) four *cavos de esquadra* (corporals of the cavalry); (6) thirty soldiers; (7) three ill soldiers inside their homes; (8) two corporals posted elsewhere; and (9) eighteen soldiers posted elsewhere. Rubí remarked that Lieutenant Gonzalez was very advanced in age, which made him unable to perform his duties as acting commandant, while Lieutenant Sierra, who suffered from *enfermedades* (various illnesses) and the incorrigible vice of drunkenness, had retired. Since Lieutenant Ruíz had been punished recently for corruption and abuse of command at Presidio San Austín on the lower Trinity River, Sergeant Chirino was the only remaining officer whom Rubí said was "born in Saltillo, fifty-four years old, with an average disposition and intelligence for service, but without circumstances to become an officer." In other words, Domingo Chirino lacked the status or race that Rubí expected for officers despite Chirino's many years of loyal service at Los Adaes. Rubí held contempt for the chain of command, not to mention his abhorrence at the poor quality of recent recruits to the presidio, which included mestizos, mulattos, and Indians.[16] Rubí also stated that from the total of 117 company horses, 49 were *ynutiles* (useless), 43 were *medianos* (average), and only 25 were *bueno* (good). There were only two guns and seven swords in good working order, with the rest in disrepair or useless. No distribution was made of gunpowder. The same poor condition was noted of the *cueras* (leather-armored coats), with only two of any use, while most of the soldiers lacked proper uniforms and went about practically naked.[17]

Perhaps more damning were the account books that Rubí found in total disarray during the period that Martos Navarrete was governor-commandant from January 1759 to August 1767. The account books were not properly managed, as the troops and their families were poorly supplied with goods from the company store, and prices were manipulated in favor of the governor.[18] Rubí added that the distribution of the goods and comestibles for the troops and their families was disorderly "as evident in the repetitive and excess charges of the liquidated accounts" by Lt. Marcos Ruíz, his son Joaquín, and nephew Félix under Martos Navarrete. These charges were for such items as "wheat of the colony, coffee, piloncillo, tobacco, and bills of exchange in favor of the treasurer, Francisco Antonio, but items supposedly of the worst nature." During these years, the soldiers were collectively in debt for about 90,888 pesos and were owed nearly 10,000 pesos, while the difference of debts and credits favored Martos Navarrete. Rubí voided the excess charges for these items as well as for gunpowder and the debts of deserters and the deceased, which the Regulation of 1729 prohibited.[19] Indeed, Rubí discovered the old practice of extortion at Los Adaes, which occurred at other presidios of northern New Spain in the provinces of Nueva Vizcaya, Sonora, and New Mexico. The price controls instituted at presidios under the Regulations of 1729 obviously had been ignored and needed adjustment and enforcement.[20]

The condition at Los Adaes, however, went beyond even Rubí's worst nightmare. He was very critical of the corruption and abuses that occurred at Los Adaes under Governor Martos Navarrete. Besides his inappropriate use of soldiers for smuggling with the Caddos and the French at Natchitoches, Martos Navarrete made the troops his personal laborers, servants, and cowboys on ranches he established for raising cattle and horses. They also worked the governor's land for harvesting corn. In return, the governor cheated the soldiers by providing them with the worst horses and charging excessive prices for goods. The former governor left the company utterly destitute.[21] In reality, Rubí described problems that had plagued Los Adaes for decades. Los Adaes simply appeared too porous on the Texas-Louisiana borderlands, with its many entry and exit points for trade and travel—not to mention corruption (figures 7.1 and 7.2).

In his letter to O'Conor, dated September 23, 1767, Rubí offered recommendations for better management of the soldiers at Los Adaes, care, and admission of recruits. Again, he expressed concern that military veterans were replaced with troops of "bad quality." A provision for weapons in good working order was needed as well as the purchase of uniforms, saddles, cauldrons, needles, shoes, caps, and tools so that the troops could "maintain cleanliness as it should be." Rubí said their uniforms of quilted cotton were an embarrassment. He ordered that cartridge belts be purchased with the appropriate caliber bullets for the carbines to avoid fateful consequences. He told O'Conor to liquidate the account books in which Lt. Marcos Ruíz and his son and nephew had fraudulently charged troops. From Rubí's perspective, Presidio Los Adaes was in a "deplorable state" of "fatal decadence."[22] Rubí felt that keeping soldiers current about the state of their accounts could alleviate the difficulty of justifying their expenses after much time had elapsed. And he suggested that expenses be allowed only for such celebrations as the presidio's namesake, Our Lady of Pillar, and only certain other feast days.[23] In his final written report, dated April 3, 1768, Rubí commented again on the inferiority of the troops at Los Adaes. He stated that the presidio was "composed of

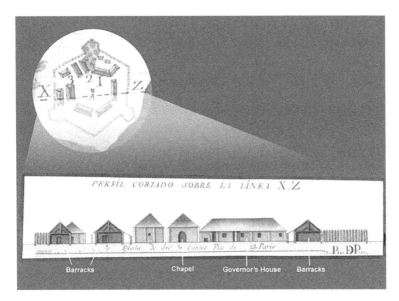

Figure 7.1: Don José de Urrutia drawing with cross-section detail of Los Adaes, 1767, on inspection tour with the Marqués de Rubí. Source: Courtesy of Texas beyond History, https://www.texasbeyondhistory.net/adaes/images/urrutia-1767-cross.html.

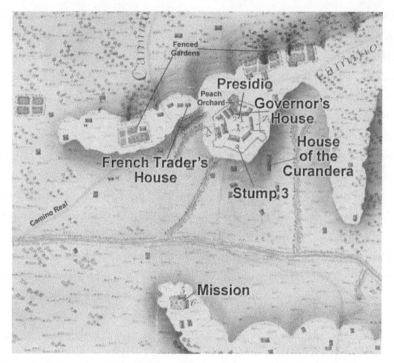

Figure 7.2: Don José de Urrutia drawing of Los Adaes, bird's-eye view with details. Source: Courtesy of Texas beyond History, https://texasbeyondhistory.net/adaes/images/urrutia-1767-presidio.html.

people collectively fugitives from other provinces, persecuted by Justice, with fourteen recruits in the year 1767 of the worst status and disposition, in place of the other various veterans, who used passports or deserted in exasperation at the bad treatment received from Martos Navarrete."[24]

Viceroy de Croix decided to micromanage Presidio Los Adaes from Mexico City while the king and his advisors in Madrid deliberated on Rubí's report.[25] The viceroy wrote to O'Conor in April 1768 instructing him to pay the salaries of the troops at Presidio Los Adaes "in cash" and to inform the viceroy afterward when this was done. The viceroy also addressed a letter the same day to the captain at Los Adaes without mentioning the name of Lt. Joseph Gonzalez, who assumed interim command following Rubí's inspection and O'Conor's departure to San Antonio. Viceroy de Croix warned Lieutenant Gonzalez, relayed from O'Conor, that only the captain general of New Spain had the reserved right to grant officer's commissions.[26]

By late summer 1768, O'Conor wrote Viceroy de Croix about the continued problems at Presidio Los Adaes, particularly the lack of expedited supplies to the troops, which left him no choice but to administer affairs at the king's expense.[27] Apparently, relief did not come fast enough for the Adaeseño troops and their families as Lieutenant Gonzalez's hands remained tied by superiors who prevented free trade with the Caddos and French. The viceroy sent instructions to Lieutenant Gonzalez before long about the management and distribution of tobacco from the government *estanco* (store) at Los Adaes, which governors habitually tapped for official and private business.[28] As Spanish officials deliberated upon Rubí's gloomy assessment of both Presidio Los Adaes and Presidio San Agustín, the death knell arrived from Texas with Rubí's final recommendation that Los Adaes be either annexed to the recently acquired Louisiana province or abandoned entirely and the Adaeseños resettled near San Antonio or somewhere in Louisiana if they wished.[29] In September 1769, O'Conor wrote Viceroy de Croix again about the deplorable conditions at Presidio Los Adaes and the need for repairs to the barracks and walls, which also drew Rubí's attention.[30]

In June 1769, before his arrival at San Antonio to replace O'Conor as governor, Ripperdá wrote to one of the viceroy's advisors about the "unhappy situation in which are found the few and weak populations in the province of Texas where I am destined." Ripperdá expressed concern over the suffering at San Antonio, La Bahía, and the surrounding missions from raids by armed Apache Indians that resulted in lost lives of Spaniards and much livestock.[31] The following year, the viceroy stated his objection to the idea that three hundred French hunters from Louisiana be formed into one or two companies to contain Indian hostilities around the presidio at San Antonio. Instead, he authorized the use of detachments from the presidios at Los Adaes, San Agustín, and San Sabá for the protection of San Antonio. Lt. Joseph Gonzalez was likely sympathetic when the viceroy instructed him to dispatch Adaeseño soldiers to San Antonio even though his troops appeared destitute.[32] Lieutenant Gonzalez realized over the years that Indian warfare at San Antonio consumed most Spanish resources. In fact, Viceroy de Croix sent shipments of ammunition to Governor Ripperdá at San Antonio to battle insurgent Apaches, while no relief arrived for Los Adaes.[33] Conversely, Lt. Athanase de Mézières, commandant at the Natchitoches post, proposed that various Indian nations be allowed to communicate and trade with Spanish presidios and towns all across the Interior Provinces of northern New Spain. Although Viceroy de Croix permitted Indians to enter Spanish settlements, he expressly forbade the sale of firearms to them.[34] Lieutenant Gonzalez and his fellow Adaeseños essentially had been left to their own devices and sustained their community far from the rest of New Spain and so close to Louisiana in what seemed worlds apart to outsiders, but the future of Los Adaes ultimately hinged upon an order from the king.

II

Indeed, King Carlos III's New Regulations of 1772 closely followed Rubí's recommendations as the Spanish sought to reform military defenses across northern New Spain, including Texas. These "new" regulations included a number of changes, most importantly the endorsement of Rubí's proposal for an impenetrable line of uniformly spaced presidios as a barrier or wall. Equally significant was the elevation of frontier forces to the equivalent status as the king's regular army, which meant similar duties, discipline, and consideration for promotions, honors, ranks, recompense, and retirement—in other words, the professionalization of troops who had been mostly conscripts, peasants, Indians, mestizos, or *pardos* (free people of color) across northern New Spain and throughout Spanish frontiers in Latin America. In order to curb abuses of presidial accounts, the soldiers were to receive salaries in advance and semiannually from one of three disbursement offices located more conveniently than Mexico City, while both payment of salaries and delivery of supplies were to be managed under a company supply officer elected by the troops rather than the governor-commandants. The pay scale was standardized, which actually reduced salaries from the rates established under the Regulations of 1729 following General Rivera's inspection.

The New Regulations of 1772 also standardized the weapons, uniforms, and saddles charged to the soldier's personal accounts. Each soldier now had to maintain a colt in addition to the six serviceable horses and pack mules stipulated under previous regulations. Each year the troops were to be issued cartridges to fit three pounds of gunpowder and undertake target practice at the presidios, while adequate amounts of gunpowder were to be kept inside the presidio under lock and key. However, according to historian Max Moorhead, the notion that a more equitable supply service would provide soldiers with greater purchasing power proved illusory.[35] With an interest toward domestic manufacturing in Spain to alleviate demand for clothing and competition from Britain, Viceroy Bucareli informed Governor Ripperdá of Texas about imperial decrees that ordered the export of cotton fabrics from the Spanish Philippines. Under the Bourbon Reforms, the viceroy explained, this cotton "can be sold and traded freely" for the time being, just like foreign-made colored linens.[36]

The blending of smuggling with transatlantic trade, however, dominated the Texas-Louisiana borderlands to supplement what the soldiers and retired veterans and their families lacked logistically, materially, and financially from the royal government. Los Adaes had become the poorest of the Spanish settlements across northern New Spain, as there were fewer "official" monied transactions. Years earlier, Lt. Joseph Gonzalez gave power of attorney to Thomas Ojeda, a soldier from Los Adaes, so that Ojeda could purchase some mules from don Ascencio Rasso for the Adaeseño troops at the "Villa of San Fernando and Presidio de San Antonio de Béxar."[37] In 1766, Juan Manuel de Bustamante, a resident from Los Adaes, appeared before Governor Martos Navarrete requesting payment in the amount of 140 pesos for hauling corn from the presidio at San Antonio to the commandant of the presidio at San Agustín, don Marcos Ruíz, who ordered this relief. Bustamante complained about the difficulty he experienced transporting said freight to East Texas.[38] The Adaeseños might have been materially poor, but they were resiliently faithful and open to trade with Indians, French, Africans, and Anglos on the border with Louisiana.

Amid the poverty of the Adaeseño community, the Spanish governors lived like feudal landlords through their personal use of mission lands, cattle, servants, slaves, and presidial labor and their monopolization of commerce with the French and Indians. During his military inspection of Los Adaes in 1767, the Marqués de Rubí lamented that Governor Martos Navarrete used his soldiers to escort convoys with goods from his house for "barter with the Indians" and commonly introduced other goods from San Antonio through his troops "without any other servant or muleteer than the same soldiers who lent their service." The governor repeatedly did this without the expense of freight charges or servants.[39] Governor Martos Navarrete utilized his soldiers, Rubí said, "for frequent trips, always using the same [soldiers] for pack trains in the class of servants and as agents of the governor to the Missions and those rancherías of the Tejas Indians, located 50 to 60 leagues from this Presidio [Los Adaes]." In this trade, the governor acquired the skins, bear grease, and other goods "trafficked almost daily to the Presidio of Natchitoches in the nearby French Colony," where they brought all the necessary goods for the entertainment of this company [at Los Adaes], which had not received any supplies in five years.[40] Rubí was concerned about soldiers being unable to perform their military duties, since the governor had them engaged in dubious work assignments.[41] In the absence of silver and Indian tribute that the conquistadors had exploited, the governors amassed a small fortune at the expense of the Adaeseños, whom they used like de facto servants and slaves. Indeed, many Adaeseños were designated mestizos or mulattos in the caste system of New Spain, which only reinforced their subservient status in the eyes of governor-commandants.[42]

In March 1768, Governor O'Conor informed the viceroy about Rubí's confirmation that Lt. Pedro de Sierra at Los Adaes not only sought retirement due to his advanced age and ailments; he also suffered from "drunkenness," which affected other soldiers as well as the "barbarous" Indians.[43] The record is silent as to other ailments that plagued Lieutenant Sierra, but he still earned the respect of Spanish officials for his loyalty to Spain as one of the original soldiers who arrived with Aguayo's expedition in 1721 and founded Los Adaes. Although the officers at Los Adaes were identified as "Spanish" and held a higher status than the rank-and-file soldiers, Bourbon reformers became concerned about the availability of alcohol and guns smuggled into Texas through Louisiana and the disastrous effects such illicit trade and corruption had overall on the behavior of the military and the implications for Indian warfare.[44] In 1769, following Rubí's inspection of the military forts across northern New Spain, the viceroy, Marqués de Croix, granted don Pedro de Sierra, an alférez and *vecino* (resident) from Presidio Los Adaes, permission to retire due to "his advanced age and ailments" after five decades of royal service on the Texas-Louisiana borderlands. Croix ordered that Sierra, originally from Celaya, Mexico, "remain in the class as settler."[45] This official pronouncement validated the gradual transformation of Adaeseño soldiers into ranchers, farmers, cowboys, and laborers with the expectation of land grants to follow for many years of military service and sacrifice.

Any dreams Lieutenant Sierra and his fellow Adaeseños had, however, about free trade with Spanish Louisiana were dashed. In November 1772, on the eve of Los Adaes's abandonment, Viceroy Bucarely wrote Governor Ripperdá about "not allowing commerce with the Natchitoches post for it being illicit, private, and against the established laws in these dominions." The governor could only legally supply Texas from settlements to the southwest along the Camino Real even though Louisiana was now Spanish.[46] The following month, the viceroy again wrote Ripperdá with his concerns about the penetration of English merchants on the Texas Gulf Coast. He reiterated to the governor that commerce with the Louisiana colony was absolutely prohibited and that Ripperdá would be held "responsible for any infractions due to lack of proper zeal and caution." The governor also had to keep the viceroy informed of any trade violations.[47] The viceroy dispatched yet another letter to Ripperdá and ranted about the detrimental effects of trade from Spanish Texas with the Indians and Louisiana. The viceroy asked Ripperdá, "What assurances have the Indians of the North given you for maintaining peace when they have broken it so many times?" He continued, "What confidence could you possibly have in your various ideas that they have not converted the auxiliary arms into facilitating the destruction of that province [Texas], introducing these [weapons] as far as the town of Saltillo, and even further to San Luis Potosi?" Viceroy Bucarely, exasperated, stressed, "What can you expect from some [Indian] Nations who, since the time of the conquest, have not given any sign of reducing themselves to the guild of our Holy Religion, in as much as His Majesty has claimed," that Presidio Los Adaes and the Spanish missions of East Texas "have not gained the conversion of a single Indian who, until now, freely obtain guns, gunpowder, and ammunition, which most effectively blocks their conversion ordered by law?"[48] Just when the Crown began to recognize first settlers at Los Adaes, such as Lieutenants Sierra and Gonzalez, an important step for obtaining land grants, the viceroy in Mexico City held disdain for the Adaeseños, who effectively subverted Spanish mercantilism and conversion on the Texas frontier through their frequent interaction with the Indians and the French from Louisiana.

III

Ironically, Rubí's inspection came after the Los Adaes community stabilized over the previous two decades due to successful harvests, the livestock trade with Louisiana, and population increase through natural reproduction and migration. In 1751, witnesses stated that the presidio had an abundant corn harvest, many residents plowed and cultivated the land, soldiers made repairs to the fort at the governor's expense, troops got married, and even a few foreigners became residents.[49] Lt. Pedro de Sierra and other witnesses strangely added that Gov. Pedro de Barrio actually "lost sleep in seeking relief for his soldiers."[50] Still, vaqueros drove livestock from Spanish Texas into Louisiana, and these cattle drives eastward anticipated much larger ones to come from South Texas during the American Revolution.[51] In fact, during the Seven Years' War, Viceroy Amarillas wrote Governor Barrios Jáuregui about the request from Governor Kerlérec in New Orleans for Texas cattle. Governor Kerlérec had been unable to get beef and wanted the viceroy's assistance in this matter. Barrios Jáuregui acknowledged the viceroy's order to send this "relief as soon as possible."[52] This aid proved critical for the Louisiana colony during the French imperial war against Britain, since France's attention and finances were consumed primarily in Europe and New France. All the while, the

Adaeseños' expectations had been raised when Spanish officials heard proposals during the 1750s that soldiers who served in the province of Texas should be allowed to remain as citizens, with land and access to water.[53]

The Adaeseños also worked as cowboys across the border and drove cattle in Louisiana for French merchants. In February 1767, don Luís Menard, a businessman from Natchitoches, sought justice from Governor Martos Navarrete at Los Adaes after he hired Adaeseños to move his livestock, which consisted of cows, bulls, horses, and mules, from Rapides to Pointe Coupe, Louisiana. Menard accused them instead with abandonment of his animals.[54] Marcos Hernández, a resident from Los Adaes, countered that Menard "hired him for fifteen pesos a month as overseer of his livestock, established at his place called *el petit écor* . . . and gathered 60 large beeves, 21 mules, 29 male and female horses." Hernández and his men, however, were "obligated to abandon said livestock because sir Perier [LaPerrier], Commandant of the Royal Presidio of Natchitoches ordered their return to Los Adaes."[55] Another Adaeseño, Joseph Luís Hernández, said Menard hired him for seven pesos a month and that on one occasion he helped conduct to said ranch [*el petit écor*] more than 100 cattle with 6 male horses and 7 mares, both recently delivered, plus 7 female mules and 8 males.[56] The remaining Adaeseños each testified the same, including Felipe de la Garza; Joseph Salazar, who was hired at 25 pesos per month; Joseph Torres, who was hired at the cheapest rate of four *reales* (less than a peso) to be a *vaquero de la vaqueria* (cowboy of the livestock); Salvador Esparza and his son, Andres Esparza; Dimas Moya; and Felipe Sanchez, a retired soldier turned cowboy. A few of these Adaeseño cowboys were considerably older than the others, such as Joseph Salazar and Salvador Esparza, who were each sixty-one years old, while Sanchez and Moya were fifty-seven and forty-nine years old, respectively, compared to Marcos Hernández at thirty-seven years old and the youngest ones in their early twenties. Regardless of age, all these men were illiterate and did not know how to sign their own names, which indicated their inferior caste status, such as the rank-and-file troops at Los Adaes.[57] The Adaeseño cowboys returned to Los Adaes in the hope of finding additional opportunities across the border in Louisiana, if not Texas, despite restrictions on trade and movement.

A parallel Spanish settlement emerged in East Texas during the mid-1750s, just as Los Adaes showed some signs of improvement and revealed further entanglements in the Piney Woods on both sides of the border. The Spanish considered establishing a town, presidio, and mission settlement on the banks of the lower Trinity River to check the encroachment of European traders from the Gulf of Mexico among the Texas Indians. While the Spanish exported cattle to Louisiana from Los Adaes, Governor Barrios Jáuregui recommended importing equipment from French Nathcitoches in order to build a new Hispanic community in the model of San Antonio. The governor ordered Francisco Xavier Hernández, a blacksmith from Los Adaes, to appear before him and declare the necessary tools for building a diversion dam, or acequia, but if such a structure could not be built, then he was to purchase whatever materials possible from the Natchitoches post, a job that Hernández said required wood shovels, axes, large-curved hoes, and beams.[58] Hernández, whose reputation for survey work in Saltillo and Mission Espada in San Antonio preceded him, informed the governor that clearing the land and building trenches and the wooden buildings required the help of forty *peones* (laborers) paid at four reales each.[59] The Adaeseños were one likely source of laborers, since at least a dozen were recently transferred from Los Adaes to the presidio at San Agustín de Ahumada on the east bank of the Trinity River, near where the civilian town was planned, but the fort itself was plagued with labor troubles. A civilian town did not emerge nearby despite the establishment of Presidio San Agustín and a mission for the Orcoquiza Indians between present Houston and Beaumont. This fertile area northeast of present-day Houston, with its abundant timber and waters from the Trinity and San Jacinto Rivers, necessitated a much greater influx of immigrant labor or African slaves than the governor could possibly provide or spare in Texas.[60] The presidio at San Agustín de Ahumada proved disastrous as the local commandant clashed with Adaeseño troops and the governor. The site was not helped any when a hurricane destroyed the fort and mission on September 4, 1766. Despite being rebuilt, this latest presidio-mission complex also drew sharp criticism from Rubí, and the king ordered its abandonment.[61]

The Spanish became alarmed at the growing incidence of desertions and the problems they caused for Texas and Louisiana such that the border between both colonies still mattered despite the sovereignty of the latter colony being transferred to Spain. On May 18, 1767, Gov. Antonio de Ulloa of Spanish Louisiana wrote Governor Martos Navarrete about various Spanish deserters "committing considerable robberies" and ordered the arrest of "anyone Spanish, French, or other from that colony [Texas] to this one [Louisiana]." They were to be brought directly to the capital of Louisiana in New Orleans.[62] The following month, Martos Navarrete refused Commandant LaPerrier's request for the return to Natchitoches of "seven Spanish maritime deserters who were in a convoy to the Illinois by order of a captain from this nation." Anxious about such deserters "in the vicinity of Los Adaes" stirring trouble for his own rule, the governor stated that he did not have an order expressly permitting their return to Natchitoches and that he only followed whatever the viceroy commanded.[63] Martos Navarrete added that besides detaining and severely punishing deserters, he would punish "any residents [Adaeseños] who might assist them from their ranches in this vicinity, as well as soldiers and missionaries at the three missions, Adaes, Aix, or Nacogdoches, who will suffer more than the penalty incurred for being disobedient to their superiors." Because the Adaeseño community was mostly illiterate, the governor, who wanted to be sure that none of the residents claimed ignorance, said he would command that "tomorrow, Sunday, after Mass, it be made public, and the order placed with the company guard of this Presidio [Los Adaes]."[64] The governors of Texas and Louisiana naturally worried about internal rebellions in their respective colonies due to outside agitators on the eve of Rubí's military inspection at Los Adaes.

The Spanish indeed investigated verbal threats made against the governor's rule at Los Adaes. In July 1768, interim governor don Hugo O'Conor, who investigated the corruption of former governor Martos Navarrete, examined witnesses from Los Adaes about an Adaeseño named Patricio Padilla and a French merchant named Pedro Simón. Both Padilla and

Simón allegedly had induced Caddo Indians to *acavar* (destroy) Presidio Los Adaes and its missions. The French commandant at Natchitoches secured Simón and sent him to New Orleans for trial, while Padilla sought refuge at Mission Nacogdoches.[65] Governor O'Conor astutely calmed the Caddos before he heard testimony from the Adaeseños about Padilla. The governor reported that on the previous day, a delegation of captains from seven Indian nations arrived at Los Adaes with the goal of ensuring peace between them and the Spanish. According to O'Conor, the meeting "concluded this morning with all the Indians leaving signs of their friendship," which he felt was good for the tranquility of Texas.[66]

Meanwhile, the Adaeseños testified to the actions of Simón and Padilla. Joseph Hidalgo, an alférez of the company at Los Adaes, declared before Governor O'Conor that the French at Natchitoches said Simón's "head was bad, and that all was well, that they all maintained peace with the Spaniards." As proof, the French wanted to come for a "dance" with the governor and "leave him a pen as a sign of peace." Hidalgo, on the other hand, said Padilla actually stated he wanted "to kill" the Spanish and destroy Los Adaes and the East Texas missions.[67] Another soldier from Los Adaes, Joseph Antonio Cruz, stated that Padilla had lived at Mission Nacogdoches. According to Cruz, the motive behind Padilla's plot with Nacogdoches Indians had something to do with his family. Padilla supposedly told the witnesses "he had three brothers and three sisters living among the Spaniards who he would remove after destroying the presidio and missions, then together with his brothers and the referenced Indians, return to kill all the Spaniards."[68] After he heard similar testimony from three other soldiers from Los Adaes, O'Conor requested that the priest at Mission Nacogdoches turn over Padilla to Capt. Melchor Afan de Rivera, whom the governor sent for the apprehension and detainment of Padilla.[69] Although the details of his subsequent prosecution remained unclear, the Spanish did not banish Padilla from Texas; instead, he eventually became a soldier at San Antonio.[70]

The concern over the desertion of Spanish troops and revolt led to Manuel de Soto's whereabouts once again following Rubí's inspection. In the spring of 1769, Marqués de Croix wrote Governor Ulloa of Louisiana and referred to the "scandalous event that befell" Presidio San Agustín, where seventeen soldiers fled as "fugitives" to Natchitoches, which resulted in the suspension of Captain Pacheco from his command. The viceroy declared, "Don Manuel Soto Bermúdez was the main perpetrator behind the incendiary extraction." Despite knowing about other causes for rebellion, the viceroy ordered the commandant at Natchitoches to arrest de Soto and return him to the governor of Texas so that he could be escorted to the capital of New Spain in Mexico City for trial.[71] The viceroy remained anxious about the spread of rebellion from Louisiana to Texas, as the presidios at Los Adaes and San Agustín already had enough internal problems. Meanwhile, the viceroy in Mexico City tried to assert jurisdiction over Louisiana perhaps to garner a potentially lucrative colony, but Cuba's viceroy also administered this Spanish colony as well as Florida.[72] The Spanish had expressed concern over deserters, slaves, and smugglers in their dominions—and much more so rebels on the Texas-Louisiana borderlands.

The Spanish remained adamant about de Soto's capture when news arrived that more deserters had fled to Los Adaes. In early December 1769, Lt. Joseph Gonzalez, interim commandant, who likely experienced déjà vu from his early career, wrote Governor O'Conor stating that eleven Spaniards appeared to be deserters and were held as prisoners at Los Adaes. He gave passports to two of them so they could appear at don Luís Menard's house and earn a living—the same Menard for whom Adaeseño cowboys labored in Louisiana—but the commandant at Natchitoches arrested them. Lieutenant Gonzalez also referred to some two hundred head of livestock, mules, and horses near Natchitoches that Indians allegedly had stolen from the Spanish.[73] Amid these reports, the viceroy wrote Governor O'Conor in late January 1770 about the arrest of de Soto and ordered him "sent with all security along the mountain range" to Mexico City.[74] By July, the viceroy wrote the new governor of Texas, Ripperdá, about sending de Soto to Mexico City and complained it took too long.[75] Two weeks later, the viceroy reminded Governor Ripperdá about transferring de Soto to Mexico City because he was worried about not resolving the case against de Soto without the cooperation of former governor Martos Navarrete.[76] Apparently, de Soto's competition in the Indian trade through his St. Denis in-laws had as much to do with the concern of Texas governors over his movements as with potential rebellion against Spanish rule not only in East Texas but also at San Xavier in Central Texas.[77]

A related threat emerged with Andrés Chirino's civil case before Governor O'Conor. Chirino exemplified many Adaeseños who actively participated in contraband trade on the Texas-Louisiana borderlands either with the governor or against him. In Chirino's situation, he went against the governor and stated in his own defense that former governor Martos Navarrete entered into the fur trade at Natchitoches "using a squadron of soldiers like the one Sergeant Domingo del Río commanded, living for a time on foot among the barbarous nations with the goal of acquiring increased numbers of hides, which [the governor] needed for his burgeoning trade."[78] In the spring of 1768, Andrés Chirino received a sympathetic hearing before Governor O'Conor following several imprisonments and confinement to shackles under the two prior governors at Los Adaes. Chirino's troubles began thirteen years earlier, when don Juan Antonio Amorín, an original settler at Los Adaes, alleged that Chirino illegally sold one of Amorín's cows to the father president of the East Texas missions. According to Chirino, however, the case against him arose from a one-peso debt that de Soto owed him following a transaction at Natchitoches.[79] In his petition, Chirino argued that the "principal motive behind all his legal troubles was the economic offense he committed in acquiring deerskins, the same ones through various means the governor [Barrios Jáuregui] had acquired in his trade with the French in Natchitoches." Chirino asserted that his dealings in deerskins were only "in order to maintain [his] family and not for enriching [himself] with this commerce, but to fight poverty."[80] The Adaeseños felt virtually handcuffed by the governors at Los Adaes under Spanish mercantilism.

Governor O'Conor's investigation of illicit commerce coincided with Rubí's inspection at Los Adaes. Rubí wrote about the inappropriate trade at Los Adaes in goods from the neighboring post of French Natchitoches for such items as coffee, flour, and grease as well as *brettañas*, blankets, and cloth used to supply shirts, breeches, and petticoats for the women. In particular, Rubí noted bills of exchange made in order to satisfy the company's treasurer, various French merchants, and other individuals with whom soldiers entered into contracts. This practice created legitimate dependence and charged prices three times their import, or at least double, in considerable amounts and repeated with great frequency.[81] Upon learning of Rubí's inspection, the king ordered his viceroy and royal council in Mexico City to quickly finish their investigation of Martos Navarrete's contraband trade with the French and Indians as well as his payment of only one-fifth the soldiers' salaries while charging them three or more times the regular price for goods in lieu of wages.[82]

Andrés Chirino and Manuel de Soto understandably hoped the fur trade might alleviate them of debts to the governor, the French, or other Spaniards. In his petition before Governor O'Conor, Chirino said he was punished for not having a license to trade, which he could not get from the former governors. His crime appeared to be a more serious offense than Amorín's complaint about Chirino stealing his cow. Chirino requested justice from O'Conor, especially the return of the cow that rightfully belonged to him and for back pay during the time he spent in prison. He dramatized his plight by requesting permission to plead his case before the viceroy in Mexico City.[83] Chirino's petition, however, revealed a deeper subplot. Chirino again felt his only true crime was his own poverty, which affected his duty and status. He stated that he went to the home of Lt. Juan Prieto at Presidio Los Adaes in search of Lt. Marcos Ruíz to sign a list Chirino had made of his horses so that he could retrieve them from the company's herd. Prieto objected because Chirino was an *hombre pobre* (poor man) and said that in lieu of the horses, he would find Chirino *mala obra* (bad or harsh labor) befitting someone of his status. Chirino added that Lieutenant Prieto subsequently called upon the company guard and ordered Chirino "to place his head in the stocks with a pair of shackles." Chirino shot back that "he was not frightened, afterall, it was the same thing that don Manuel [de Soto Bermúdez] told him at Natchitoches."[84]

Chirino's defiance, his accusers alleged, was made public when he shouted offending words from the balcony of Prieto's home. But Chirino responded that his accusers never stated the words he purportedly said aloud and that there was no balcony or even anyone present except for Ruíz. "*Omnes ad unum*," the petition added, his accusers allegedly declared "my continued presence has been prejudicial to society, as my pride and arrogance, combined with all my vices, the one most excessive and longstanding being drunkenness and lack of respect for the whole world."[85]

Lastly, Chirino requested an order to make former governor Martos Navarrete pay him the one-hundred-peso allowance so he could satisfy his creditor, de Soto. Although the bill of exchange Martos Navarrete gave Chirino was for the entire amount, it was for expenses from New Spain and not for de Soto. Martos Navarrete had ordered Chirino's "imprisonment and banishment to the Castillo del Morro," the infamous prison fortress in Havana, Cuba. Chirino also requested the return of six horses that remained from the original thirteen he had with him at Presidio San Agustín, which were appropriated by order of Lieutenant Prieto. Chirino then asked for the return of his weapons, particularly a rifle with its cover and a sword that were also taken from him upon his most recent arrest.[86] Governor O'Conor ordered that the testimonies in Chirino's case be sent to the viceroy in Mexico City for his deliberation.[87] Perhaps Andrés Chirino's biggest crime other than contraband trade or poverty had been his womanizing and insolent behavior, which the governors also tried to control. Aside from allegedly having stolen a cow, Chirino was denied a license to go to Mission Nacogdoches because along the way, "over at Mission Ais was Juana María Berbán [Derbanne] with whom Chirino had an illicit relationship, climbing up her mother-in-law's house and doing other scandals." The governor's denial of the license was meant to keep Chirino from trading with any Indians at the missions and to check further scandalous conduct.[88] Chirino's legal imbroglio over petty smuggling, stealing, lack of deference, and public intoxication might have been pardonable, but he was also romantically linked with higher-class women, especially María Padilla, the wife of Antonio Gil Ybarbo.[89] Illicit sex and lewd behavior were great offenses, like contraband trade, if done in disturbance of the peace or against the governor's rule.

During the government's investigation of Andrés Chirino's behavior, Lt. Marcos Ruíz declared that Chirino "intended to kill" Joseph Acosta, the uncle of Juan María Berbán (Derbanne), at Mission Los Ais. Chirino supposedly "hid in the forest of this mission waiting for the night to gain his wish."[90] This charge was never substantiated yet, combined with his other purported crimes, had earned Chirino several trips to prison over the years. Back on Christmas Eve of 1765, because of Chirino's alleged "interest" in María Padilla and other scandalous acts, Governor Martos Navarrete ordered his transfer in a pair of shackles from El Lobanillo Ranch to Los Adaes, where he disrespected the royal justice of the company guard and remained in prison.[91] The following summer, on July 2, 1766, Ybarbo petitioned the governor and requested he send Chirino into exile from Presidio Los Adaes. In his petition, Ybarbo stated, "The uneasiness and discord with which my wife and I continuously live because of Andrés Chirino, resident of this said presidio, and it serves you to banish him . . . or grant me license to retire with my family from this presidio if my petition has no merit." Ybarbo said Chirino was already imprisoned at Presidio San Agustín "for his pride and accustomed excesses" after his previous release from prison, so Ybarbo recommended the presidio at La Bahía. The governor went further and stated that it served his majesty more if Andrés Chirino were sent to prison in Havana for four years on ration without salary as his punishment. He ordered Chirino to be well secured by his troops and transported to New Orleans for passage to Cuba.[92]

However, on July 26, Governor Martos Navarrete received a letter from the commandant at French Natchitoches reporting that Chirino somehow "broke free from his shackles . . . and in his liberty sought refuge in the home of San Luis de San Denis." The French commandant stated that he ordered Chirino's return to Lt. Joseph Gonzalez and sent two soldiers to retrieve him, but "St. Denis said that since the morning of the 22nd, Chirino had disappeared."[93] Martos Navarrete became so concerned that he ordered any residents and soldiers of Presidio Los Adaes, who helped Chirino in whatever way or did not report his whereabouts, to be punished with "banishment forever from this province [Texas]."[94]

Andrés Chirino's personal saga, amid Rubí's inspection tour, revealed a lack of social control at the Los Adaes community on the Texas-Louisiana borderlands and the prevalence of smuggling, poverty, and rebelliousness. Spanish officials placed the burden on the governors of Texas to remain vigilant over the behavior of its subjects while guarding against illicit trade. In particular, this meant that the Adaeseños could not engage in illicit sex with either fellow Spaniards or their French and Caddo neighbors, which evidently had occurred.[95] Meanwhile, the Franciscans from the East Texas missions were expected to assist the governors with keeping in check the Adaeseño community whether at the fort, the missions, or Natchitoches through church attendance and administration of the sacraments. Otherwise, Spanish colonization in East Texas was doomed to failure with so many internal and external problems. Individuals such as Manuel de Soto and Andrés Chirino became scapegoats for any problems at Los Adaes.

Meanwhile, Governor Martos Navarrete actually held de Soto responsible for the plot to assassinate Captain Pacheco at Presidio San Agustín. He also believed de Soto was behind the unrest of the Orcoquiza Indians because he allegedly provided them guns in common cause with French traders and Spanish deserters. The former governor also implicated de Soto with the murder of a Spanish missionary at San Xavier. Thus the problems Rubi noted reached beyond East Texas and affected settlements elsewhere.[96]

Viewed from another perspective, Andrés Chirino, a soldier-resident from Saltillo at Presidio Los Adaes since 1741, exhibited agency and finally stood up to the commercial monopoly and exposed abuses of the governors and high-ranking officers who took advantage of the poor Adaeseño community. Had it not been for the loyalty of his older brother Domingo in service to all the governors over the years, Andrés's life might have ended in Cuba, like the Apache captives, or somewhere in the wilderness. Many Adaeseños bottled up the same contempt as Andrés Chirino and grew tired of authoritarian rule under governors in Spanish Texas. Ironically, Governor O'Conor also imprisoned Antonio Gil Ybarbo for smuggling until Governor Ripperdá secured his release—an indication, perhaps, of zero tolerance for smuggling or misbehavior at Los Adaes under the Bourbon Reforms.[97] Such trials and tribulations confirmed the storm of protest against corruption and abuse at Los Adaes. The net effect of worship, kinship, and commerce had been further entanglement of various border peoples into a web of intimacy that Rubí ranted against in reference to the "multitude of fiestas" that brought everyone together.[98] Chirino's petition revealed sharp class distinctions made among Adaeseños, the Spanish governors, and the military officers on the Texas-Louisiana borderlands. The former governors manipulated salaries and goods in connection with their own trade with the French and Indians through their officers while monopolizing commerce. Chirino symbolized Adaeseños who attempted to break free from the indebtedness, coercion, and expected norms of Spanish society at Los Adaes.

At the same time, the Adaeseño community could only tolerate so much about Andrés Chirino, especially since his siblings Domingo and Manuel modeled good behavior. Evidently, Andrés Chirino became disaffected with life on the frontier at Los Adaes and ultimately was considered a social deviant. While the behaviors of Manuel de Soto, Andrés Chirino, and even governors could be handled on an individual basis, what did that mean for the entire Adaeseño community, which had a reputation for contraband trade, rank-and-file troops of inferior quality, and too much movement across the border? Historian Frank de la Teja explains, "When entire groups choose to subvert or disregard social norms, or when the values and standards of a society are in a period of transition, the group or society's behavior might be termed chaotic, decadent, rebellious, or revolutionary."[99] For Bourbon reformers, such as the Marqués de Rubí, the Adaeseños indeed represented potential rebels against Spanish rule in Texas if left unchecked with too much autonomy and freedom to trade with whomever they wished.

V

Rubí's inspection at Los Adaes and East Texas evidently occurred at a time when farming went through a bust cycle after some progress, and the Adaeseño community remained dependent on cross-border trade. In late April 1770, Lt. Joseph Gonzalez petitioned his superiors for food relief due to the "total misery" of the troops, which echoed similar complaints he made thirty-five years earlier. He specifically requested two hundred bushels of maize, but if not corn, then wheat, rice, or similar harvests to this post.[100] This time, Lieutenant Gonzalez, impatient with officials in Mexico City, instinctively sent Adaeseños to New Orleans for corn and other seeds. The following month, Luís de Vergara, a Spanish official in

New Orleans, asked Athanase de Mézières, the commandant at Natchitoches, whether he had sufficient food for the relief of Presidio Los Adaes without hurting the inhabitants of Natchitoches and, if so, to provide the necessary supplies in anticipation of the "prices established by the tariff" in compliance with the order from the new governor of Spanish Louisiana, don Alejandro O'Reilly.[101] With Louisiana under Spain, Lieutenant Gonzalez likely figured his requests of Spanish officials in New Orleans and Mexico City had been reasonable and would not raise any trouble.

Señor Vergara sent goods, along with his letter to de Mézières, for sale in Natchitoches and told him "to make sure these do not end up in the hands of enemy Indian nations, but if to our [Indian] friends, then by the routes decided."[102] Vergara then granted licenses to de Mézières's troops from Natchitoches to transport relief supplies to Los Adaes. Spanish officials in Louisiana scrutinized the origin of these individuals out of concern that they might be foreigners in their territory without permission, which the Spanish also feared in New Spain. Among those persons granted licenses were Pedro Primo and Juan LeBlanc, both from seven Acadian families whom Vergara said "should go down and settle on the coast of Iberville." Another one, named Juan Crux (Cruz, Croix, or Crow), had been "living for five years in Natchitoches and is an Irishman, but naturalized so his residence in our Kingdom is not against the laws of the state." The remaining men, Guillermo Ovarden and Jamien Peret, had to leave Louisiana after finishing their business in Natchitoches because "they are of the English nation and not admissible in our Dominions."[103]

The Spanish also dealt with yet another Adaeseño from the Chirino family who raised suspicion in San Antonio about settlers from East Texas as Indian warfare raged in the wilderness. On a chilly winter morning in 1772, Juan Chirino, an Adaeseño soldier and third-generation Chirino to serve in Spanish Texas, murdered another soldier, named Cristóbal de Carvajal, on the outskirts of San Antonio. Their assigned duty had been the protection of San Antonio's settlers from enemy Indians, but notions of honor ostensibly came first. In the criminal proceedings that followed, the defendant, Juan Chirino, claimed self-defense after Carvajal suddenly cursed and attacked him for no apparent reason. The defendant stated there had been no previous animosity between them other than "the deceased having a lot of debts," which might have upset him after Chirino appealed to the governor on his father's behalf, ordering Carvajal to make payment for three horses.[104]

Later that year, the viceroy ordered Governor Ripperdá of Texas to declare the defendant "completely absolved, and free" to continue his royal service based on the legal claim of self-defense, a command the governor obeyed.[105] The judge stated, "There was no doubt that Chirino, having rightly used self-defense, did not commit any crime, since Law 4, Title 23, Book 8 of the *Recopilación de Castillo* states that any man who consciously kills another will die for it, except if he kills his enemy in self defense, and the Doctrines are well established that one can legitimately kill another when pursued by another armed with the intent of committing harm."[106] Perhaps Chirino's *machismo* (manhood) displayed what Viceroy Bucareli wanted for soldiers, among other qualities, on the Spanish frontier when Governor Ripperdá obeyed orders and set Chirino free to continue his military service.[107] Juan Chirino and his fellow Adaeseños who were sent to San Antonio knew that fighting each other over one's debts and family honor did not help the Spanish cause against Southern Plains Indians. This murder case illustrated larger problems throughout Spain's empire that had much to do with the failure of mercantilism and the inability to crack down on the illegal entry of foreigners or Indians interested in smuggling.

No one from the Adaeseño community likely expected, however, the manner in which they would be forced to abandon East Texas altogether, as most wished to stay far away from the warfare of South Texas and Southern Plains. In February 1773, Viceroy Antonio Bucarely Ursúa at last expressed his eagerness to Governor O'Conor's successor, Ripperdá, about putting into effect the king's new regulations from the previous year, which were based on Rubí's recommendations. By April, Governor Ripperdá had informed the governor of Spanish Louisiana, Luís de Unzaga y Amezaga, about closing Presidio Los Adaes, Presidio San Agustín, and the East Texas missions to ensure a smooth transition and avoid resistance to the removal of Hispanic settlements from the Texas-Louisiana borderlands. The Adaeseños were to be distributed lands upon their arrival in San Antonio to ease their resettlement. Governor Ripperdá expressed his desire to notify the Adaeseños promptly of the king's abandonment order because they were about to begin their planting season. He also related his concern to Governor Unzaga Amezaga about negative responses from surrounding Indians to the Spanish withdrawal. Ripperdá specifically asked Unzaga Amezaga to keep the commandant at Natchitoches, Athanase de Mézières, vigilant against any trouble by making sure the Indians understood that the settlers of Louisiana were as much Spanish as those at San Antonio. Governor Ripperdá also referred to Comanche depredations against San Antonio, which only heightened concern about potential Indian disturbances across Texas.[108]

By this time, Antonio Gil Ybarbo had emerged as the most influential Adaeseño. Born and raised at Los Adaes into a military family, he followed in his father's footsteps and eventually gained possession of El Lobanillo Ranch, located between present Nacogdoches and San Augustine, Texas, where he spent time managing a growing number of livestock and drove cattle into Louisiana. In addition to soldiering and ranching, Ybarbo became a merchant through his kinship and commercial relationships at French Natchitoches. In particular, he had a business partnership with Nicolás de la Mathe, a French resident from Point Coupée, Louisiana, to the south of Natchitoches. Despite his recent troubles with O'Conor over contraband trade, Ybarbo was well regarded by Governor Ripperdá, who placed him in charge of accounts for the purchase of presidial supplies. The governor had never met Ybarbo but caught wind of his local prominence.[109] While Lt. Joseph Gonzalez simply obeyed the abandonment order of his superiors, Ybarbo opposed the closure of Los Adaes. His father was buried there in 1744, and his elderly mother was too weak to travel as far away as San Antonio—not to mention he would lose lucrative trade opportunities for himself on the Texas-Louisiana borderlands.

By early October 1773, barely a week after their arrival at San Antonio, a majority of Adaeseño families requested permission from Governor Ripperdá to return to the Texas-Louisiana borderlands. Their petition, which Antonio Gil Ybarbo and seventy-five of his fellow Adaeseños signed, specifically asked the governor to grant them a license to establish a new town at the former East Texas mission for the Ais Indians near present-day San Augustine (see appendix G). They believed this place was the "most comfortable for our establishment, planting, ranching, and other things for our well being without causing harm or inconvenience to the residents and settlers of said Presidio and Villa [San Antonio de Béxar] and in this manner preserve general harmony."[110] They enticed the governor by adding that this could be done at minimal cost to the king, having asked only that they be given a chaplain to administer to their spiritual needs, paid for by the Crown over a ten-year period and then covered by the town thereafter. The Adaeseños made this solemn request of the governor, who knew "the lamentable misery [they] suffered on such a prolonged road, enduring thirst, drought, lacking mounts, death of children and adults, and abandonment of most of [their] goods."[111]

By December 1773, Governor Ripperdá gave these Adaeseños his permission to return to the Texas-Louisiana borderlands at former Mission Ais. He had previously instructed that if "these residents could not get *solares* [lots] and lands conveniently in San Antonio, Fort Santa Cruz de Cíbolo [Fort Cibolo], or in other immediate old ranches and sites with the security that can be permitted in a country of war," then they could seek what their petition asked. In the meantime, the Adaeseños gave Antonio Gil Ybarbo and Gil Flores power to speak for them. Evidently, the Adaeseños did not wish to burden San Antonio while many were eager to see family and friends back in East Texas and Louisiana.[112]

Interestingly, on December 10, after declaring his sympathy for the Adaeseños' plight, Governor Ripperdá informed the viceroy that he had given passports to Ybarbo and Flores so that they could "go before you at your feet" and implore your support for their cause. He repeated the petition that the Adaeseños made earlier that fall and added that they were unable to stay at San Antonio and "work the land, make a water well, or request solares in security and quiet from the surrounding Indian nations." They also did not wish to jeopardize the Bexareños or mission Indians. Besides, O'Conor, who was promoted to inspector in chief of the Spanish frontier army, prevented Governor Ripperdá from granting lots along the San Antonio River to the Adaeseños. Similarly, those few Adaeseños who had stayed behind at Fort Cibolo did not wish to be admitted to San Antonio without permission to leave whenever they wanted.[113]

As further incentive for the viceroy to grant the Adaeseños permission to establish a new town in East Texas, Governor Ripperdá told him that they could keep watch on commerce between the Norteños and the Natchitoches post while remaining vigilant against the English arriving from the Mississippi. He added how the Adaeseños had abandoned many fields at Los Adaes and that Rancho El Lobanillo was already a de facto *pueblo* (town), located thirty leagues (seventy-five miles) west from Los Adaes, where many ill evacuees were left behind.[114] Governor Ripperdá played on the distant Spanish officials' fear of the English threat, as Father Hidalgo had done long before to populate Texas in reaction to an imminent French attack from Louisiana. But the governor also shielded himself against a potentially unfavorable residencia for granting permission to the Adaeseño petition prior to the viceroy's approval. Meanwhile, the Adaeseños longed for grants to lands they had settled in East Texas in addition to payment of their salaries as soldiers.

Epilogue

Rebirth, Borders, and Freedom

I n February 1774, Antonio Gil Ybarbo and Gil Flores appeared in Mexico City with their petition to return to East Texas, which the viceroy handed over to the Council of War and Estates for consideration. The viceroy and his advisors, sympathetic to the plight of the Adaeseños, agreed that they could resettle at former Mission Ais, "making sure to establish the rest of the population closeby, secure the peace and calm of the Indians, and avoid communication with the English or other foreign nations." The following day, Viceroy Bucarely signed an *auto* (decree) approving the results put forth by his council.[1] Inspector in Chief Hugo O'Conor could not dissuade Spanish officials from making what he saw as a fateful decision. In a letter dated March 28, written from his headquarters in Chihuahua, O'Conor expressed to the fiscal in Mexico City his concern over "the abominable illicit commerce" in guns, powder, and ammunition in that part of Texas and the surrounding country.[2] The viceroy's order to Gov. Juan María Barón de Ripperdá, which commanded him to transfer the cannons from Los Adaes to the town of Monclova (Coahuila), near Saltillo in northern New Spain, was not good enough.[3] The Adaeseños remained intent on defying the odds and challenged their own government as they looked to resettle in the Texas-Louisiana frontier. Above all, the Adaeseños infused what late historian James McCorkle Jr. described as a "significant independent spirit" in the Piney Woods region, where diverse communities of people learned to accommodate each other and adapt to the environment far from Mexico City. Those Adaeseños determined to reconstitute their lives in East Texas eventually found their way back, while those who remained in San Antonio sought to settle into their new environs in the eternal quest for justice, land, and liberty with or without governors and missionaries.[4]

Exasperated, O'Conor understandably worried about the weapons and other munitions left behind at Los Adaes and the insufficient efforts of Governor Ripperdá to gather these items through the assistance of the commandant at the Natchitoches post. The weight of the viceroy's office, however, superseded O'Conor's newly created position under the Bourbon Reforms and his stance against the return of the Adaeseños to East Texas.[5] O'Conor tried to execute his command to oversee the defense of the entire northern provinces against Indian raiders, whom he believed acquired weapons smuggled from the Texas-Louisiana borderlands to New Mexico. Ybarbo actually informed O'Conor that once the Spanish left Los Adaes, the surrounding Indians allegedly ransacked the place, having carried away part of the ammunition and other goods buried inside the presidio. The Adaeseños who stayed behind at El Lobanillo returned to Los Adaes and recovered what had remained. Lieutenant Monsieur Périer from the Natchitoches post also reported that "fugitives" from Los Adaes sought refuge at El Lobanillo and arrived later at "my post in search of *aguardiente* [liquor] with the purpose of introducing it into the tribes." Despite the New Regulations of 1772 and O'Conor's concerns, the "frontier was never wholly abandoned," as historian Herbert Bolton argues.[6] Adaeseños under Ybarbo's leadership perhaps also stood to lose ranches and trade opportunities after their removal to San Antonio while praying for land grants someday.

The true intentions of Ybarbo and Flores were made clear in Mexico City, where they took the initiative of asking for the viceroy's permission to settle the Adaeseños at the Natchitoches post. Viceroy Bucarely, however, proved unwilling to allow their return that far eastward.[7] In early 1775, the viceroy wrote Governor Ripperdá about the damage caused to Inspector in Chief O'Conor by the governor allowing the Adaeseños to resettle in East Texas. After the Adaeseños left San Antonio and established the new town of Nuestra Señora del Pilar de Bucareli (Bucareli) on the lower Trinity River, in honor of Our Lady of the Pillar and the viceroy, O'Conor had informed Ripperdá about "the contraband they perpetuate, which can so easily be done there." In the future, Governor Ripperdá was to report to O'Conor about all matters regarding the resettlement of the Adaeseños.[8] In this regard, the viceroy's decision reflected O'Conor's concerns about the problem of smuggling and disputes over chain of command. Meanwhile, many Adaeseños hoped to trade freely with the Natchitoches post despite the viceroy's prohibition against resettlement across the border in Louisiana.

The Adaeseños again looked to their native son, Antonio Gil Ybarbo, for relief from resettlement troubles that plagued them at Bucareli over the next four years. In May 1779, Captain Ybarbo informed Teodoro de Croix, commandant general of the Interior Provinces, that on January 1 and 8, prior to abandoning Bucareli, all of its residents had appeared at Ybarbo's house to consider moving their families into the environs of the Tejas at the former mission of Nacogdoches, which was farther removed from enemy Comanches than Bucareli. Besides, families suffered from hunger at Bucareli, as they were unable to hunt for fear of Indian attacks on their settlement. Ybarbo said that a flood, which occurred on February 14, 1779, had been followed by a Comanche raid on Bucareli's horse herd, resulting in the loss of thirty-eight of these animals. Bucareli residents later came upon the bodies of six friendly Indians nearby, though two others had escaped to Bucareli. That night they also heard shots fired close by. Ybarbo claimed that had the remaining Bucareli families not left shortly thereafter, most likely they would have perished in the flood, especially those who were ill.[9]

On April 30, 1779, Father Joseph Francisco Mariano de la Garza, who had relieved Father Juan García Botello during the winter from his temporary assignment at Bucareli, also wrote Commandant General de Croix about the lack of security for the Bucareli settlers and their flight from the hostilities of Comanche enemies. Father de la Garza said that the last of Bucareli's citizens had decided on January 25, 1779, to resettle at the "depopulated" mission of Nacogdoches. They could ill afford to wait for Spanish royal permission to abandon Bucareli. They decided against travel westward across the Brazos, San Marcos, and Guadalupe Rivers because these were places of great *ensenadas* (coves/inlets) that served as entry and exit points for Comanches.[10]

By the summer of 1779, the Tejas visited Gov. Domingo Cabello, who had replaced Ripperdá as governor the previous year, and revealed close ties between their nation and the Adaeseños. Cabello informed de Croix that five Indians from the "Nation of the Texas" presented themselves in his home at San Antonio. Their chief had traveled with Ybarbo to Mexico City in 1773–74 to plead for the establishment of Bucareli. The viceroy honored this Tejas chief with "a suit and rod signifying captain for being a very acculturated Indian, both rational and capable." Cabello expressed his own pleasure at meeting him and the other Tejas Indians, using Pedro Gonzalez—a former Adaeseño soldier who became first sergeant at Presidio San Antonio de Béxar—as his interpreter. The governor also appeared content that many of the former residents of the extinguished Presidio Los Adaes knew how to speak the "Texas language." He even noted that Sergeant Gonzalez spoke their language with "a perfect accent and is well known by all of them [Texas Indians]." Governor Cabello recognized the Tejas chief with the name of "El Texito," who then stated that the Tehuacanas had given him notice that "Captain Pintado" (painted/colored), as de Mézières was known to all those Indian nations, sent word "advising that all the Indians come to this province [Spanish Texas] to make war against the Apaches" and to head out together with de Mézières. The Tejas chief added that de Mézières evidently spoke very poorly because of a tumor that protruded from a muscle after he allegedly fell from his horse and hit his head, which ultimately led to his untimely death.[11]

Meanwhile, for those Adaeseños who remained behind at San Antonio, the distribution of land to them, as Governor Ripperdá discussed, remained problematic for the Bexareño community, which was in the midst of its own land-related disputes. For many years, the Bexareños had claimed that mission boundaries limited the growth of their community. They desired the incorporation of the missions, including their structures, fields, and irrigation systems, for their own benefit.[12] Unlike Presidio Los Adaes, where Spanish governors held indisputable authority over the Adaeseño community, the local interests of San Antonio's cabildo could not be cast aside so easily. Governor Ripperdá had to carefully weigh his response to the Adaeseños in the context of current politics at San Antonio and the whims of Mexico City officials.

When Commandant General de Croix visited San Antonio in January 1778, sixty-three Adaeseños, led by Agustín Rodríguez, petitioned for lands where they and their families could subsist (see appendix H). They were upset that during their time in San Antonio since the abandonment of Los Adaes and forced removal, they had been treated "as if [they] were from some other foreign kingdom" despite having served their Catholic monarch with the same fidelity and love "as [they] are today about to spill [their] last drop of blood for [their] King." They remained impoverished and without land in San Antonio to farm for themselves, as did some Bexareños, and implored "the paternal love which His Majesty dignifies with protection for his vassals." Rodríguez signed the petition on behalf of all those Adaeseños who did not know how to sign their own names.[13] De Croix favored their request to form a new town in a place most suitable for them, believing that the Villa de San Fernando (Béxar) was sufficiently populated to defend itself from enemy Indians, and acknowledged that the best lands in San Antonio were already occupied.[14] For the time being, though, Pedro Galindo Navarro, one of the viceroy's advisors, believed that these Adaeseños should remain in San Antonio with their families and become industrious at farming, which would benefit the town until funds became available for a new settlement on the San Marcos River. He also suggested that Governor Cabello order the Franciscans to make an inventory of all their possessions and set aside fields "to be divided equally into lots, which by raffle can be distributed to the sixty-three Spanish residents [Adaeseños]."[15] De Croix agreed with Navarro and issued a decree in June 1779 for the secularization of Mission San Antonio de Valero.[16] More than a decade passed, however, before these Adaeseños received mission lands.

Until then, the Adaeseños in San Antonio and East Texas took a back seat as Spain became caught up in the tectonic shift of the American Revolution. The Spanish government sent dispatches to all its officers in the Americas, including viceroys, governors, and other government officials, to guard against illicit commerce. These communiqués coincided with the signing of the American Declaration of Independence in 1776 and Spain's declaration of war in 1779 against England in alliance with Bourbon France and the rebellious Anglo-American colonists.[17] The following year, royal dispatches to Governor Cabello in Texas authorized Spanish subjects in North America to carry out reprisals against Britain and to stop all communication with the English.[18] Among the dispatches sent to the governor of Texas was one from Bernardo de Galvez, governor of Louisiana and nephew of the secretary of the Indies in Spain, dated August 12, 1779, which reported the destruction of mail bound for America to keep it from reaching England.[19] Most importantly, Governor Cabello was informed about an attack the Spanish of New Mexico launched against the Comanches and was warned to guard against English influence on the Indians of Texas.[20]

Meanwhile, the resettlement of the Adaeseños from Bucareli to Nacogdoches during the winter and spring of 1779 along this lower road of the Camino Real opened more trade opportunities.[21] Having fled the Comanche threat from Bucareli on the lower Trinity River, Ybarbo and his fellow Adaeseños became ever more entangled on the frontier as revolutionary events from the east increasingly impinged upon the Texas-Louisiana borderlands. In May 1779, Ybarbo, now from Nacogdoches, built on previous trade connections at Natchitoches under the French when he sent fifty mules, eighty cows, and twenty bulls into Louisiana in exchange for black slaves. He certainly capitalized on the legalization of the Texas cattle trade to Louisiana as Spain contemplated joining its French Bourbon cousins in the American Revolution against Britain. Ybarbo and other Adaeseños, as with other ranchers from San Antonio and La Bahía, sent cattle to New Orleans in support of Spanish forces under Galvez. In September 1781, Ybarbo, by then promoted to captain, sold ninety cows to Athanese Poissot, a rancher with several operations in Opelousas, located about halfway between Natchitoches and New Orleans, in exchange for a twenty-two-year-old black Creole woman named Nanette. The following week, he sent Poissot around 155 cattle in exchange for two slaves, thirty-six-year-old Guillame and thirty-one-year old Louise. Captain Ybarbo's ties with Poissot and other local merchant slaveholders extended to New Orleans.[22] Ybarbo amassed a small personal fortune and once again drew the attention of Spanish officials for smuggling with foreign traders.

II

Nacogdoches survived in the Piney Woods with the spirit of Los Adaes under the protection of Captain Ybarbo's militia and friendly Tejas, while Governor Cabello's 1785 peace treaty with the eastern Comanches added to the relative tranquility of Texas—a peace that the Adaeseños had known among the Caddos on the Texas-Louisiana borderlands for several generations. Spanish Bourbon reformers had adopted a new Indian policy of trade, treaties, and toleration borrowed from the French model that served various economic interests.[23] The delicate balance, however, that emerged over the course of the eighteenth century among diverse communities on the Texas-Louisiana borderlands faced its ultimate challenge with the emergence of the United States of America and Napoleon Bonaparte in Europe. The determination of the border between Texas and Louisiana became a concern once again for Spain in the years before and after the Louisiana Purchase of 1803 due to religious boundary issues in addition to political, military, and economic factors. In 1797, the secular priest from Nacogdoches, Friar Francisco Vallejo, complained about the difficulty of defining his ecclesiastical jurisdiction over those communities east of the Sabine River who claimed they pertained to St. Francis Catholic Church in Natchitoches, not Nacogdoches.[24] These communities included ranches owned by French Creoles, such as Francisco Prudome, whose land was located "in the Pueblo of the Adaes Indians," and Manuel Prudome, whose ranch was "in the Arroyo Hondo of the Adaes." Other ranches, Spanish officials noted, belonged to "Morfil and Bouguier in the lagoon of the Adaes," "don Paul Laffitte in the Arroyo of the Rocks," and "Samuel the English in the Arroyo of St. John."[25] The Adaeseños who still had not received their salaries after the abandonment of Los Adaes were even more susceptible to illicit trade with Anglo-Americans, not to mention with mixed French, Indian, and African Creole communities.[26]

Ironically, Anglo-Americans became residents in the town of Nacogdoches as early as 1792 and engaged in commerce with Southern Plains Indians just like British and French traders. While Spanish officials in Louisiana could only promise to restrain Americans and other foreigners from entering Texas illegally, their counterparts in Texas permitted those with proper passports to stay, trade, and travel as far as San Antonio.[27] As long as Anglo-American immigrants remained a trickle and were listed as a separate category of foreign residents in the census records of Nacogdoches, the Spanish could monitor their movements within the Texas province—or so they believed.

The Spanish increasingly expressed concern, however, about US westward expansion following Charles Pinckney's famous treaty in 1795, whereby Spain abandoned its claims to the Ohio River and granted Americans the right to navigate the Mississippi into the Gulf of Mexico through New Orleans without paying taxes. Spanish officials in Madrid evaluated reports from Capt. don Luís Vilemont, a naturalist who served the French and then the Spanish government in Louisiana and made trips to Virginia, Pennsylvania, Upper Louisiana, Canada, and New Mexico. The Spanish sought the best maps possible, together with supporting accounts and other documents, for they believed Louisiana served as a barrier to "ambitious ideas of the Anglo Americans," against whom Spain needed to "defend its richest possessions of His Majesty in all of North America." Principally, they noted that the silver trade of New Spain could be captured through an invasion of New Mexico from the Great Lakes region, which required "Spanish occupation, especially from the St. Louis River and the mouth of the Missouri River northward." Although the Spanish agreed with Vilemont, who also advised Spain to wean the Indians from dependence on the United States and discourage them from engaging in commerce with British subjects, King Carlos IV, who succeeded Carlos III on the Spanish throne in 1789, did not act on these reports and instead secretly transferred Louisiana back to France in 1800.[28] By then, as historian Matthew Babcock shows, untaxed horses and mules surpassed cattle as Texas' main export, fueled in great part by demand from a young American republic. Historian Dan Flores remarks how this horse trade flew under the radar because it was a "concealed economy," taking place where the Spanish and American frontiers "touched at their edges," and involved "shadowy freelancers, Comanche and Wichita traders, Hispanic entrepreneurs, and Thomas Jefferson" during a most fluid time of emerging empires.[29]

The first show of force between Spain and the United States west of the Mississippi occurred by proxy in 1801 on the Texas frontier, where Spanish troops clashed with the infamous Irish American horse trader Philip Nolan and his small army. Formerly a resident of Nacogdoches, Philip Nolan garnered the attention of the Spanish with his horse trade among the Indians of Texas. Prior to his last foray in Texas, Nolan wrote Amigo Cook in Natchez, Mississippi, about his plans for a trip to the Rio Grande and requested Cook's loyalty to keep his secret.[30] Meanwhile, the Spanish arrested Paul Boüet Laffitte for smuggling livestock in exchange for African slaves with his brother-in-law, Athanase Poissot. A former resident of Natchitoches in 1779, Laffitte left to become the unofficial community leader at Bayou Pierre near present Mansfield, Louisiana (about forty miles south of Shreveport). The Spanish held Laffitte prisoner for seven months and then banned him from Spanish Texas after he allegedly gave information to American members of Nolan's expedition who had become imprisoned.[31] Poissot, of course, had been the one who sold African slaves from Louisiana in exchange for cattle from Captain Ybarbo in Nacogdoches. Ybarbo's own resumption of contraband trade got him into trouble again with Spanish officials investigating smuggling during the 1790s—precisely as American traders sold firearms to the Adaes from the Red River and British traders did the same with the Orcoquizas from the lower Trinity River.[32] Nolan ultimately suffered a fate opposite of the French pioneer St. Denis when Spanish forces under Miguel Francisco Musquíz, military commandant from Nacogdoches, shot and killed Nolan near the present-day town of Hillsboro, southwest of Dallas.

Spain and the United States followed a similar collision course after the Louisiana Purchase of 1803, which overlooked the mixed communities on the Texas-Louisiana borderlands with the increasing divide between the Spanish and Americans over territory, expeditions, and commerce. Spain and the United States avoided military conflict between the forces of Gen. James Wilkinson and Lt. Col. Simón de Herrera under the so-called Neutral Ground Agreement in November 1806, which included the area between the Sabine River to the west and from the Gulf of Mexico to the east at the mouth of the Calcasieu north through the Arroyo Hondo to the thirty-second parallel. Historian Dan Flores explains this agreement as "establishing a neutral buffer strip, claimed by both countries but governed by neither." For Wilkinson, wild horses and Mexican silver tempted American expansion while he lined his own pockets through double dealing as a secret agent for Bourbon Spain. Evidently, Wilkinson had counted on a clash earlier that year when Spanish forces under don Francisco Viana from Nacogdoches turned back the Freeman-Custis Expedition to Natchitoches. The latter had been dispatched into Texas under President Jefferson following the Lewis and Clark Expedition. These peaceful outcomes followed tense moments—for example, in February 1806, when a small force of eighteen men under José Maria Gonzalez (and namesake of the deceased Lieutenant Gonzalez) were forced to withdraw from their position at Los Adaes to avoid being attacked by a larger force of 150 Americans under Capt. Edward Turner from Fort Claiborne in Natchitoches, which only enraged Gov. Antonio Cordero, who subsequently ordered a surprise attack upon the Americans. Historian David Weber noted how "Texas had clearly resumed its historic position as a buffer province, with Anglo Americans having replaced Frenchmen." For good measure, Spain utilized documentary evidence to support its case on the boundary issue, especially the extensive report of José Antonio Pichardo, *The Limits of Louisiana and Texas*.[33] At the local level, Spain could also argue possession on the basis of prior occupation at Los Adaes in lands the Adaes Indians, French, and Adaeseños still claimed.

Meanwhile, Spain also sought more defensive measures in Texas through legal immigration, economic development, and additional settlements. In an effort to raise revenues, they allowed skilled foreigners into Texas. For example, in 1804, Vicente Micheli, an Italian immigrant who settled at Nacogdoches and then San Antonio, along with Oliver Clark, an Irish Catholic engineer from Opelousas, Louisiana, obtained permission to import cotton gin and mining technology, respectively, to develop plantation slavery and stimulate mineral extraction in northern New Spain. They also allowed the foreigners William Barr and Peter Davenport to establish their company in Texas for trade with the Indians. Spain even sought to entice friendly Indians into Texas from the United States, including the Alabamas, Cherokees, Chickasaws, Choctaws, Coushattas, Pascagoulas, and Shawnees, as another buffer. However, these possibilities coincided with a growing problem of fugitive slaves and US Army deserters arriving in Spanish Texas between 1803 and 1809.[34] The Spanish thus established a new defensive settlement, called Trinidad de Salcedo (1806–13), on the lower Trinity River at a crossing of the Camino Real between San Antonio and Nacogdoches, near where the Adaeseños had temporarily established Bucareli.[35]

For those Adaeseños who remained at San Antonio, the secularization of Mission San Antonio de Valero finally took place in 1793. They were one of four distinct groups to receive land of the former mission: the fifteen mission Indians, nearly forty individual Adaeseños, nine other Spanish residents from this mission, and two Bexareños. Evidently, the Adaeseños received the largest parcels.[36] Under Agustín Rodríguez's leadership, the Adaeseños each received a *suerte de tierras* (twenty-six acres of land; see appendix I).[37] Historian Frank de la Teja notes that the Adaeseños formed a small community at Valero with the other Spanish residents of this mission whose needs were more than met with room to grow in the future.[38]

Still other Adaeseños joined the civilian community in San Antonio and reconnected with those soldiers from Los Adaes who were transferred before the fort's abandonment. Adaeseños and Bexareños, including Canary Islanders, Spanish migrants, Hispanicized Indians, and Africans, came into greater contact as families grew in kinship with each other and the world outside. For example, in 1772, Juan Feliciano Casanova, a soldier from Los Adaes, gave a deposition in favor of the marriage between Jose Cristobal de los Santos and Maria Mendez, both originally from Saltillo, who became residents of the Villa de San Fernando in San Antonio. Don Ignacio Calvillo, a Spanish resident originally from the Villa de San Fernando, also gave a deposition in favor of this marriage, for which Father Pedro Fuentes Fernandez ordered wedding banns with three days of the festivities and gave permission for the ceremony to be performed at Mission Espada in January 1773. Other Spanish migrants included Pedro Joseph Texeda, originally from Mexico City, who made his way to San Antonio in 1768 after serving with the "Company of the Americas" in Havana,

Cuba, for six months and then moved to New Orleans, from where he traveled to Natchitoches, Los Adaes, and San Antonio along the Camino Real. Texeda obtained permission to marry Francisca Perez, a Spanish resident of the Villa of San Fernando, and they married on August 11, 1773. Texeda also gave a deposition in favor of the marriage between Aniceto Camaño, a native of Cuernavaca (located just outside present Mexico City) and a soldier at Los Adaes before his transfer to San Antonio, and Juana Bercuda Saucedo, a Spanish widow of the late don Francisco Xavier Galvan. Another soldier from Los Adaes garrisoned in San Antonio, named Joseph Maria Rodriguez, gave a deposition in favor of this marriage, as did a Joseph Patricio Suarez, an Indian from the town of San Francisco de Analco, who met Camaño in Havana, Cuba, before they left for New Orleans on a ship named *Valona* under Capt. don Antonio Correa. Many more examples of extended kinship appear among Hispanics and Indians, some from Los Adaes identified specifically as Tlascalans and mestizos, who lived among the Comanches, Apaches, other Indians, mulattoes, and blacks, all of whom are listed in the sacramental records for the Villa of San Fernando from the Catholic Archdiocese of San Antonio.[39]

Another Adaeseño, Manuel Berbán, mentioned previously as serving at Los Adaes under his grandfather, Lt. Joseph Gonzalez, joined the cabildo at San Antonio as a councilmember and then city attorney in 1801. After Los Adaes had been abandoned, Berbán moved to San Antonio along with his parents, Victoria Gonzalez Derbanne and Jean Baptiste Derbanne.[40] Apparently, not all transfers went smoothly, as some tension emerged between the Adaeseños and Bexareños. De la Teja notes how a "Santiago Seguín beat *alcalde* Manuel Berbán senseless because the latter stopped Seguín from irrigating his beans [crop] with water he had inherited from his aunt." This occurred as Seguín complained that Berbán had taken water illegally for himself despite the *acequia* being broken.[41] Such tension revealed just one more reason why it was imperative for the government to resettle the Adaeseños on their own lands with access to water from the San Antonio River or the San Pedro Springs.[42]

Some Adaeseños instead continued military service at Presidio La Bahía, most notably Juan Chirino, the same individual mentioned previously who was absolved of murder based on a self-defense claim. The son of the late Domingo Chirino and Micaela Saucedo from Los Adaes, Juan was granted permission to marry Xaviera Flores, a native from the presidio at San Antonio and the legitimate daughter of the late Pedro Flores and Juliana de la Garza, for whom Father Fuentes performed the wedding ceremony on January 26, 1780.[43] Juan Chirino's reassignment at La Bahía likely pleased some Bexareños amid the drama associated with the arrival of the Adaeseños and their resettlement while Indian warfare continued. De la Teja adds that San Antonio, the newly designated capital of Texas, "was not an entirely color-blind society" despite the fluidity of its social-caste labels and that the notions of race and class became more pronounced by the late eighteenth century when it came to whom could marry whom. Military service did not guarantee upward mobility or an elite status.[44]

The Caddos, however, largely continued to live in their ancestral lands long after the abandonment of Los Adaes, though in smaller numbers as they faced more challenges to their power on the Texas-Louisiana frontier. By the 1780s, the Spanish still sought to win influence over the Caddo and other Texas Indians through gift giving, especially weapons, clothing, tobacco, and farm tools that arrived from New Orleans following Louisiana's first transfer from France to Spain. In 1785, Mexico City officials estimated that around 394 Tejas, 238 Nacogdoches and Nazones, and 309 Bidais Indians received varying amounts of muskets, gunpowder, ammunition, farming hoes, axes, knives, chain links, bells, tobacco, skirts, and other products. They also listed the Adaes, Ais, and Saisitos Indians together, who numbered 213 people and received similar goods, as did other Caddo nations.[45] The Adaes Indians did not have a captain listed to whom the Spaniards presented gifts but instead received goods through the Ais captain.[46] Some Indian nations perhaps lost their tribal identities through association and intermarriage among Hispanics and other indigenous peoples, including the Comanches, Apaches, Choctaws, and Caddos. The Caddo Nation of present Oklahoma derived principally from the Kadohadacho Confederacy, originally from the lower Red River near the Oklahoma, Arkansas, and Texas border, where Chief Dehahuit emerged as the principal Caddo leader and powerbroker in the region from 1804 to 1815.[47]

On the eve of many tumultuous events, the Texas-Louisiana border ironically appeared potentially more dangerous for Spain than ever before because of the new threat from the United States, while South Texas seemingly benefitted from peaceful overtures with the Comanches. The Spanish census of Nacogdoches for 1809 reveals many foreigners settled within its jurisdiction on farms and ranches on both sides of the Sabine River. Immigrants came from Virginia, the Carolinas, Kentucky, Arkansas, Louisiana, Maryland, and Pennsylvania before Stephen F. Austin's well-known arrival. Still others came from Canada, Ireland, England, Italy, and Germany, as well as many migrants from towns in Mexico and Cuba. There were also a smaller number of Native Americans, including Tejas, Bidais, Apache, and Comanche, who married into Spanish or non-Hispanic families. Lastly, African slaves from Guinea are listed among both Spanish and Anglo-American families. The overwhelming proportion of residents in the census, however, were nonslaveholding farmers who grew mostly corn and wheat and owned relatively small numbers of cattle, horses, and pigs. Out of 153 total farmers listed in the Nacogdoches census, 37 of them (or 24 percent) were natives from Los Adaes, an indication that many Adaeseño families reconstituted their livelihood in East Texas as best they could for survival among many new neighbors.[48]

Whether or not Adaeseños reestablished familiar patterns of commerce, worship, and kinship on the Texas-Louisiana borderlands likely mattered less at the dawn of a new century—as long as they could claim titles to their own lands and obtain justice and economic freedom under Spanish mercantilism. They also had to move forward in Nacogdoches without Antonio Gil Ybarbo, who died in 1809 and left behind a lasting legacy.[49] The Adaeseños in East Texas eventually formed other communities on both sides of the border that emerged from farms and ranches. The present town of Chireno, Texas, between Nacogdoches and San Augustine, was named after Jose Antonio Chirino, a descendant of the Chirino boys from Los Adaes, who received a Spanish land grant in 1792.[50] Many other Adaeseños established ranches, including the Ybarbo, Mora, Padilla, Cordova, Flores, del Río, Procela, and Cruz families, all of whom also hoped for land grants they felt they had earned while making a living on the Texas-Louisiana borderlands over several generations.[51]

However, the loyalty of the Adaeseños and that of their counterparts in San Antonio and La Bahía hung in the balance as Mexico launched its struggle for independence from Spain in 1810 and pitted royalists against rebels. The Hispanic population of Spanish Texas peaked at around four thousand residents in 1803 only to decline sharply with less than two thousand residents ten years later. Following the Battle of Medina in 1813 and its reimposition of Spanish rule after a short-lived Republic of Texas, many Bexareños fled San Antonio and found refuge across the Texas-Louisiana border in Natchitoches—precisely where many Adaeseños had long been familiar—and Nacogdoches nearly abandoned altogether due to the revolutionary violence and fear of reprisals against Tejano rebels.[52] Meanwhile, the border between Texas and Louisiana remained in flux through the terms of the Adams-Onís Treaty, signed February 22, 1819, between the United States and Spain, which determined the Sabine River as the new border between Texas and Louisiana. By then, Adaeseños and their descendants evidently had been reestablished at Bayou Pierre in present De Soto Parish, Bayou Scie (or Vallecillo) in Sabine Parish, and the Adaes Village in Natchitoches Parish.[53] Along the Camino Real from San Antonio to Natchitoches, the Adaeseños became a "forgotten people" whose history at Los Adaes became lost amid the contest of empires, wars, and rebellions in Texas. While the loyalty and identity of the Adaeseños might have shifted over time and across nations and borders, they did not lose their spiritual faith.[54]

Rescued from oblivion in the national consciousness, the Los Adaes Commemorative Area grew over the course of the twentieth century. The Daughters of the American Colonists in Louisiana first recognized the presence of Presidio Los Adaes in 1933 with the donation of land for the site where it once stood and erected a tablet to honor another story that unfolded in the great North American wilderness. In the 1990s, old-timers of the area, descendants from multiple waves of US immigration, fondly recalled memories of youthful romance and family picnics in the hills and pine trees of the abandoned Spanish fort. Some even witnessed US troops practice secret military maneuvers during World War II in preparation for the forests of Europe. Little did they realize then that they walked among the spirits of Adaeseño soldiers and settlers from

Presidio Los Adaes.[55] The Louisiana Office of State Parks had planned aboveground restoration projects at Los Adaes, but Hurricane Katrina in 2005 (and later Rita) effectively wiped out the state's budget while it reeled from the horrific loss of life and property.[56] Mother Nature indirectly forced the closure of the archaeological station at Los Adaes, and its headquarters moved to Historic Fort Jean Baptiste in Natchitoches, which allowed entrance to Los Adaes through appointment. The gates to the Los Adaes State Historic Site are open once again to visitors, but the site remains largely dependent on the work of area volunteers.

Los Adaes is the spot where imperial Spain checked US expansion westward to the Rio Grande. Historian Matthew Babcock reminds us that it took another thirty-three years from the Louisiana Purchase for Texas independence from Mexico in 1836, while it took a war between the United States and Mexico ten years later to acquire the rest of the American Southwest and shape the present US-Mexico border. Los Adaes represented the colonial roots of the modern border that began as a Spanish fort with nearby mission strategically located at the end of a Camino Real that stretched from Mexico City through northern New Spain to the Texas border with Louisiana. Military service continued for many descendants from Los Adaes under different flags while the notion of a mission church emerged from grounds nearby as the foundation for local communities in the backcountry between Natchitoches and Nacogdoches (see figures E.1 and E.2).

This rich history of the Adaeseños in Texas and Louisiana has been overlooked in the narratives of the American Southwest and US South. Their story and those of other local peoples like the Adais Caddo and Choctaw-Apache nations add new tales that challenge our understanding of conquest, borders, and identity. For example, Mary Lucille Rivers (a.k.a. Betty) of Zwolle, Louisiana, corresponded with family and friends to say, "As far as we can tell, the Rivers, then known as Del Rios, were located in De Soto Parish" and "our heritage goes back to Antonio Del Rio and Manuel Del Rio." She adds how some of the Del Rios left Los Adaes in the 1770s and were sent to San Antonio; some stayed in present Madisonville, Texas; others returned to Nacogdoches; and then some eventually went back to Louisiana.[57] As David Weber explained, "Those who express fear that a new

Mexican reconquest is underway seem to overlook the significant role that accommodation has played along the border," which is an understandable oversight if all we are taught to believe is that the only thing Anglo-Americans and Hispanic Americans "shared was mutual contempt."[58] The history of local communities in the region indeed challenges the notions of state formation when viewed from the border.[59]

The frontera Spain imagined between Texas and Louisiana in Caddo country had been broken from the start, as the Spanish could not sever the ties of trade, religion, and kinship that were forged over the course of the eighteenth century. The Adaeseños sought a new homeland on the Texas-Louisiana borderlands against all odds, and their descendants continue to live in the region. Their story is not simply a revisionist history or counternarrative but one about the search for land, justice, and freedom that reverberates across time and place. The lives of the Adaeseños and their neighbors deepen our own understanding of modern borders and perhaps serve as the everlasting significance of Los Adaes for the history of the United States and Mexico. The irony is that today, East Texas and northwestern Louisiana are divided by the vast Toledo Bend Reservoir (from Highway 21 in Texas to Highway 6 in Louisiana), which the US Army Corps of Engineers created in the mid-twentieth century, rather than a mere creek as they were in the colonial era. The communities of this region between Nacogdoches and Natchitoches along the Camino Real all share much in common through commerce, worship, and kinship that continued beyond the cycles of violence and natural disasters to the present.

If anything, the Adaeseños and other subjects in Spanish Texas were likely unaware of events in distant lands that would affect their own future and border. Perhaps the Spanish had been too fixated on its northern frontier in New Spain when Herrera and Wilkinson avoided war between Spain and the United States in 1806 and were blindsided when Britain invaded Buenos Aires (Argentina) on Spain's southern frontier in the Río de la Plata region of South America and again in 1807. Nor could the Adaeseños imagine Napoleon's invasion and occupation of Spain the following year, sparking revolutionary movements against Spanish rule across its mainland colonies in Mexico and Venezuela.[60] The Adaeseños already had shown resiliency and the wherewithal to move beyond

Spanish conquest and borders for the sake of survival in search of a new homeland long before any revolutions. They hoped to remain in or return to the Texas-Louisiana borderlands time and time again, where they came to view the lands of the Caddos as a Garden of Eden and a refuge. In a literal sense, the Adaeseños never fully abandoned the region and felt instead that the Spanish government had abandoned them, only to pay attention when threats came from across the border or ocean blue. In effect, the Texas-Louisiana borderlands were not the only locations where the border was broken; indeed, this occurred viturally everywhere across Latin America where adversaries confronted Spain at the edges of its empire in the Americas.

Figure E.I: Signage at the "Old Catholic Cemetery" near Zwolle, Louisiana, about twenty-five miles off Louisiana State Highway 21, where many descendants from Los Adaes are buried. Photo by Francis X. Galán, October 13, 2012.

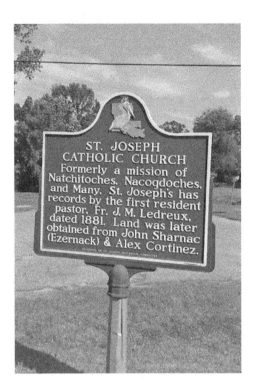

Figure E.2: Signage at St. Joseph Catholic Church in Zwolle, Louisiana, where many descendants from Los Adaes are buried. St. Joseph's oversees the "Old Catholic Cemetery." Photo by Francis X. Galán, October 13, 2012.

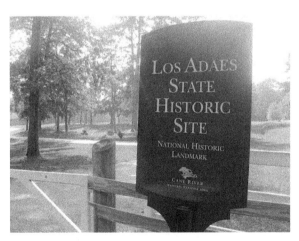

Figure E.3: Signage at the Los Adaes State Historic Site, US National Historic Landmark, the Spanish archeological site of Nuestra Señora del Pilar de los Adaes, located off Louisiana State Highway 485, about one mile from Louisiana State Highway 6 near Robeline. Photo by Francis X. Galán, October 10, 2012.

Appendix A

Mission Ranching/Farming in East Texas, 1727

Mission Adaes	Mission Ais	Mission Nacogdoches	Mission Concepción	Mission San Francisco	Mission San José
Hatchets	Large-curved hoes	Farm tools and equipment	*Rejas* (plowshares)	Many farm tools and equipment	Farm equipment
Large-curved hoes, etc.	Stew pans	Large livestock	Hatchets	Large livestock	Large livestock
3 corn seeds planted	1 yoke of draft animal (domesticated)	30 cattle	Large-curved hoes, etc.	64 cattle	48 cattle
Large livestock	9 cattle	3 yoke of oxen (domesticated)	Large livestock	2½ yoke of oxen for planting	4 yoke of oxen
26 cattle (big and small)	3 or 4 *almudes de maíz* planted	Planting done every year	120 cattle (big and small)	3 or 4 *almudes de maíz* planted each year	4 or 5 *almudes de maíz* planted each year
Some riding animals [horses?]	Usually unsuccessful planting due to lack of rain	5½ corn seeds are successful when it rains	5 yoke of oxen (domesticated)	Some seeds a successful w/ good season	Harvest proportionate crop following rain
A string of pack animals	—	Harvest 40 *fanegas* (60 bushels) of corn	Planting done every year	Harvest 18 to 20 *fanegas* (27–30 bushels) of corn	—

Mission Adaes	Mission Ais	Mission Nacogdoches	Mission Concepción	Mission San Francisco	Mission San José
One farm and ranch	—	—	6 or 7 *almudes de maíz* are successful when it rains	—	—
Sometimes the seeds are successful	—	—	Harvest 35 to 40 *fanegas* (52–60 bushels) of corn, wheat	—	—

Source: Father Muñoz's inspection of the East Texas Missions, October–November 1727, in Francisco Morales, "De la vida conventual a la vida misionera: Un acercamiento a dos formas de vida franciscana" (paper presented at the Franciscan Presence in the Borderlands symposium, Bishop DeFalco Retreat Center, Amarillo, Texas, September 17, 2004), 2–6 (courtesy of Father Morales).

* One *almudes de maíz* equals approximately seven dry quarts of corn.

Appendix B

Military Roster at Los Adaes, May 1731

Listta, y relacion jurada que yo Dn. Juan Antonio de Bustillo, y Zevallos, Governador de esta Provincia de Thexas hago de los Ofiziales, y soldados de este Presidio de Nta. Sra. Del Pilar de los Adais para remitir a el Exmo. Señor Virrey de esta Nueba España en cumplim.to de la Ordenanza Veinte y quatro del Reglamentto en la forma siguente—

1. Capi.n [Captain] Dn. Juan Antonio de Bustillo, y Zevallos de edad de quarenta años, y ocho de servicios en esta Prov.a, hidalgo notorio en las montañas de Burgos.
2. Then.te [Lieutenant] don Joseph Cayettano de Bergara de edad de trientta, y un años, onze de servicios en esta Provincia Español.
3. Alfz. [*Alférez*] Dn. Josseph Gonzalez de edad de treintta años, onze años de servicio en esta Provincia Español.
4. Sar.to Man.l Anttonio de Losoya. Español.
5. Andres de Espino. Español.
6. Manuel de Cos. Español.
7. Nicolas Hernz. [Hernandez]. Español.
8. Juan Hernz. [Hernandez]. Español.
9. Juan Gamez. mulatto.
10. Franco. de Napoles. español.
11. Franco. de la Zerda [de la Cerda]. español.
12. Juan de Armijo. mestizo.
13. Josseph de Arejo. mulatto.
14. Josseph Rossales. mestizo.
15. Blas de Villa Real. mestizo.
16. Gregorio Lopez. mulatto.
17. Juan Jph. De la encarnz.on [Encarnazion]. español.
18. Guillermo Rodriguez. mestizo.
19. Juan Anttonio Ramos. mestizo.

20. Josseph Sanchez. mestizo.

21. Agustin de Abila [Avila]. mestizo.

22. Josseph de Albarado [Alvarado]. Yndio.

23. Lazaro Ybañes. mestizo.

24. Anttonio de Pan y agua [Paniagua]. mulatto.

25. Juan Joseph Marquez. mulatto.

26. Xptoval de Santiago. mulatto.

27. Juan Sanches Tovar. español.

28. Pascual de Luna. coiote [coyote].

29. Anttonio de Luna. español.

30. Juan de los Reyes. mulatto.

31. Phelipe del Rio. Español.

32. Xptoval del Rio. Español.

33. Domingo del Rio. Español.

34. Juan de Villa Real. mestizo.

35. Juan Paulin. español.

36. Anttonio Gregorio Cordoves. Español.

37. Franco. Morillo. Lobo.

38. Andres Sanchez. mestizo.

39. Phelipe de Sierra. Español.

40. Juan Anttonio de Covarrubias. Español.

41. Josseph de Acostta. mestizo.

42. Juan de Padilla. Español.

43. Joachin de Torres. Español.

44. Xptoval Rodriguez. Coiote.

45. Julian de los Reyes. Coyote.

46. Josseph Ventura de Alcala. español.

47. Mateo Ybarvo. Español.

48. Franco. de Sn. Mig.l [San Miguel]. mestizo.

49. Juan de Torres. español.

50. Josseph Anttonio de la Vera. mestizo.

51. Phelipe Bermidez [Bermudez]. español.

52. Pedro Perez. español.

53. Franco. de Santiago. mulatto.

54. Ypolito de Montes. Coyote.

55. Man.l [Manuel] Luis de los Reyes. Coyote.

56. Mig.l [Miguel] Julian Flores. Coyote.

57. Franco. Xavier de Talam.tes [Talamantes]. español.

58. Nicolas Anttonio de Cordova. español.

59. Diego de Villa franca. mestizo.

60. Man.l Salvador de los Pozos. Coyote.

61. Joseph Anttonio de Acostta, y Arias. mulato.

Que haviendose manifestado en la forma expresada juro dha. relacion, y para que conste lo firme en dho. Press.o en veintte, y sitete Dias del mes de Maio de mill setec.tos y treintta, y un años—

Dn. Juan Antt.o de Bustillo y Zevallos. (Rúbrica)

Source: *Archivo General de México—Provincias Internas, CAT*, Austin, box 53.2a, pp. 32–34, transcription.

Author's Note: The following soldiers were not listed above yet appeared on a previous list that Governor Bustillo y Zevallos prepared at Presidio Los Adaes on April 30, 1731, regarding equipment and horses belonging to the troops: Lt. don Juan Antonio de Amorín, Alférez don Phelipe Muñoz de Mora, Sgt. Manuel Antonio de Losoya, Josseph de Trexo, Juan Muñoz de Mora, and Francisco de la Zerda. Joseph Gonzalez appeared on this list among the rank-and-file soldiers and evidently was promoted to the officer's rank of alférez the following month. Source: *Archivo General de México—Provincias Internas, CAT*, Austin, box 53.2a, pp. 29–31, transcription.

Appendix C

Inventory of Arsenal at Presidio Los Adaes, 1734

6 bronze cannons	3 *vota fuegos*[?]	12 lances and *media lunas*[?]
12 cannon balls	6 pounds of rope	6 pairs of shackles, plus 1 small one
1 "spoon" used for cannons	250 pounds of gunpowder	3 iron shovels
1 dresscoat	54 lead balls of caliber for the cannons	64 sickles to remove wheat
1 *atacador*[?]	3 *valeros*[?], 2 for cannons, 1 for rifle, bronze	6 *cureñitas*[?] covering the cannons

Source: "Certification of Inventory by Outgoing Governor, don Juan Antonio Bustillo y Zevallos," May 9, 1734, Presidio Los Adaes, *Archivo General de México—Provincias Internas*, vol. 236, *CAT*, Austin, box 53, folder 2b, pp. 115–16, transcription.

Appendix D

List of Contraband Goods among French, Caddos, and Franciscan Missionaries, 1766

299 bundles of good tobacco made in Natchitoches

One piece of *coteries*

8 varas of *pontibi* in two pieces

8¾ varas of *tersio pelo carmesi*

One small barrel of brandy of 10 to 12 *assenbres*[?]

4 *pañitos* more of the said

20 pieces of British ordinary *angostas*

10 *yslabones*

4 varas of red Indiana

2 pieces of *morles*

3 *masos* of white beads weighing three pounds

5½ varas more of Indiana with blue lines

25 *pañitos* of fine yarn

38 dozen of metal rings in 1 *pañito*

14 varas of more British in two pieces

3 packets of *galon de angosto* of fine gold weighing five pounds

4 more of the mentioned British pieces

7 mules with the mark of Mission de los Ais

Source: *Memoria de los efectos* (list of goods) that Sgt. Domingo Chirino, from Presidio Los Adaes, seized and confiscated, having recognized the items as contraband belonging to the Father Conductor[?] of the Texas Missions, Fray Francisco Zedano, about half a league before the place that is called *el durasno* (the peach) on the trail to the house or ranchería of the Bidais Indian named Thomas, November 25, 1766, Presidio Los Adaes, *Béxar Archives*, microfilm, roll 10, frame nos. 0443–0444.

Author's note: Since Chirino was illiterate, Joaquín Ruíz, another soldier from Presidio Los Adaes, actually wrote the list, *BA*, 10:0449.

Appendix E

Contraband Goods of French Trader Duzan Lodre Seized by the Spanish near Bermudez Ranch in the Jurisdiction of Los Adaes, August 1766

6 new guns *ordinaries*	1/3 with 6 pieces of royal	18 pounds of *ilo de Alambre amarillo*
1 *tercio* (1/3) lining in *cotense*[?] with 7 blankets	1/3 with a piece of blue cloth of *Lembur encarnado*[?]	Two pounds of *laños y lada*
11 pounds of vermilion	2 pieces of *morles*	200 *piedras de fusil* (gunflints?)
1 *talega* (sack) gunpowder in *cotense encerrado*	½ pound of beads	2 big *panes* of French soap
Another 1/3 with 7 blankets	100 pounds of gunpowder	4 pounds of blue and white beads
14 ounces of *ilo salon* (parlor thread or yarn?)	1 [?] of cloth of *Lembur encarnado*	Two brass kettles
Half-piece of black *listón* (lath)	12 dozen of *belduques*	42 medium axes, 20 of these small
2 striped shirts and 1 white	6 dozen of razors *cavos de cuerno*	

Source: *Declaration*, Duzan Lodre, a French trader, appearing before Lt. Joseph Gonzalez, in the Spanish investigation of French contraband trade, August 14, 1766, Presidio Los Adaes, *Archivo General de la Nacion—Cuba*, 149A, microfilm, reel 13, doc. 33, pp. 3–4, Old Spanish Mission Records, Our Lady of the Lake University, San Antonio, Texas.

Appendix F

Spanish Gifts to Taovaya Indians
for Ransom of the Spanish Captive
Antonio Treviño, 1765

1 fur coat trimmed with braids	6 pounds (lbs.) of powder	1 dozen knives
1 cane	12 lbs. of musket balls	1 dozen awls
4 fur braces	3 lbs. of beads	½ lb. of thick wire
4 mirrors	2 lbs. of vermilion	1 thin mallet
2 large curved hoes	2 dozen chains	10 bundles of tobacco
1 ax	2 dozen *sacatrapos*	[?] ½ dozen of baize
4 shirts	1 bolt (of cloth) red ribbon	3 horses
2 muskets	1 bridle (restraint)	

Source: Letter, Governor Martos Navarrete to Friar Calahorra, Presidio Los Adaes, March 21, 1765, *Béxar Archives*, microfilm, roll 10, frame no. 0735.

Appendix G

List of Adaeseños from Testimony and Request to Move from San Antonio to the Abandoned Mission Dolores de los Ais in East Texas, October 4, 1773

1. *don* Antonio Gil Ybarbo
2. Juan de Mora
3. Augustin Sanches
4. Juan Josef Sanches
5. Torivio de la Fuente
6. Jose Zepeda
7. Pedro Manzolo
8. Bernabé del Rio
9. Joachin Cordova
10. Christoval Padilla
11. Juan Manuel Padilla
12. Manuel Mendez
13. Calletano Gamez
14. Matias Sanchez
15. Marcos Martinez
16. Salvador de Esparza
17. Manuel Mora
18. Christoval Exis
19. Melchor Morin
20. Juan Josef Pacheco
21. Antonio del Rio
22. Miguel Ramos
23. Ygnacio del Rio

24. Mariano Padilla
25. Gaspar Ruiz
26. Diego Herrera
27. Francisco [de la] Zerda [Cerda]
28. Tomas Gutierres[z]
29. Gabriel Padilla
30. Francisco de Torres
31. Gil Flores
32. Lazaro de Torres
33. Francisco Guerrero
34. Bernardo Cervantes
35. Juan Josef Santa Cruz
36. Tomas YBarbo [Ybarbo]
37. Pedro Rincon
38. Patricio Padilla
39. Juan Martinez
40. Juan Ygnacio Guerrero
41. Dumas Moya
42. Ygnacio del Rio
43. Francisco Lozoyo [Losoya]
44. Juan Chirino
45. Candido San Miguel
46. Francisco Ramires
47. Pedro Sanches
48. Pedro de Luna
49. Manuel Lisardo
50. Francisco Cruz
51. Juan de Tovar
52. Pomuceno de la Zerda [Cerda]
53. Melchor Benites
54. Christoval Ballexo [Vallejo]
55. Josef Calderon
56. Manuel Trexo [Trejo]
57. Manuel Barela [Varela]
58. Christoval Garcia

59. Domingo Carmona

60. Josef Maria Camberos

61. Joachin Mansolo

62. Ambrocio Basques [Vasques]

63. Vicente Zepeda

64. don Pedro de Sierra

65. Bartolo Soto

66. Gregorio Soto

67. Juan de Torres

68. Jacinto Mora

69. Nicolas Mora

70. Josef Domingo Barcenas

71. Victor Manzolo

72. Augustin Morillo

73. Manuel Cruz

74. Miguel del Rio

75. Ysidro Eugenio

76. *don* Ramon Benero

con cuias familias hacen el numero de ciento veinte, y siete
[together with their families total 127]

Source: *Archivo General de México—Historia*, *CAT*, Austin, box 31.3, pp. 314–17, Spanish transcription.

Appendix H

List of Adaeseños Who Remained in San Antonio and Their Petition for Land to Subsist with Their Families, January 4, 1778

1. Agustin Rodriguez.
2. Miguel de la Cerda.
3. Bernardo Cervantes.
4. Vicente Gonzales.
5. Lorenzo Pozos.
6. Juan Joseph Pacheco.
7. Ignacio de el Raso.
8. Simon de Aragon.
9. Miguel Ramos.
10. Marcos Martinez.
11. Juan Martinez.
12. Manuel Ramos.
13. Manuel de Alcala.
14. Juan de los Reyes.
15. Manuel Barela [Varela]
16. Joseph Valentin.
17. Francisco de Torres.
18. Cayetano Gomez
19. Francisco Ramirez.
20. Cristoval Bayja.
21. Antonio de San Miguel.
22. Rafael de San Miguel.
23. Juan Antonio de los Reyes.
24. Joaquin Manzolo.

25. Lorenzo Ramos.
26. Lazaro de Torres.
27. Fernando de la Cerda.
28. Juan de la Cerda.
29. Joseph Antonio Acosta.
30. Joseph Antonio Salinas.
31. Domingo Carmona.
32. Diego Carmona.
33. Manuel Losolla. [Losoya]
34. Ciprian Losolla. [Losoya]
35. Pedro Hernandes.
36. Francisco Flores.
37. Pablo Flores.
38. Antonio Chiver.
39. Joaquin Benites.
40. Clemente Gonzales.
41. Manuel de la Cruz.
42. Juan Santos Aragon.
43. Manuel de Aragon.
44. Antonio Banuis.
45. Matias del Rio.
46. Francisco Romero.
47. Manuel Trexo. [Trejo]
48. Joseph de Lara.
49. Joseph feliz Guerrero.
50. Antonio de el Rio.
51. Joseph Eugenio de el Rio.
52. Antonio Rincon.
53. Joseph Luis Hernandes.
54. Prodencio de San Miguel.
55. Sebastian Camacho.
56. Antonio Brito.
57. Marcos Hernandes.
58. Francisco Antonio Medrano.
59. Antonio Cadena.

60. Francisco Villa-Real.

61. Juan Baldes. [Valdes]

62. Ignacio Montes.

63. Joseph _____ [?]

Source: *AGI—Guadalajara*, 267, microfilm, reel 2, doc. 25, Old Spanish Missions Research Library, Our Lady of the Lake University, San Antonio, Texas; see also *AGI—Guadalajara*, *CAT*, Austin, box 10.3, pp. 69–72, Spanish transcription.

Author's note: Agustin Rodriguez "signed for all without malice because they did not know how to" ("no de malicia alguna lo firma por todos por no saver").

Appendix I

List of Adaeseños Who Received *Suertes* of Land from Mission San Antonio de Valero, February 25, 1793

1. Manuel Martinez
2. Jose Maria Rodriguez
3. Manuel de los Santos
4. Joaquin Musquiz
5. Mariano Salinas
6. Juan Martinez
7. Manuel Franco
8. Bernardo Cervantes
9. Francisco Carmona
10. Luís de Castro
11. Nepomuceno San Miguel
12. Manuel de Alcala
13. Felix Guerrero
14. Francisco Antonio Guerrero
15. Luis Ramirez
16. Domingo Carmona
17. Juan de la Cerda
18. Jose Ramirez
19. Matias del Rio
20. Jose Antonio Acosta
21. Francisco Cerda
22. Francisco Cerda for the front
23. Gaspar Hidalgo
24. Miguel Losoya

25. Cipriano Losoya
26. Jose de Zepeda
27. Manuel de la Cruz
28. Manuel Losoya
29. Luis Hernandez
30. Jose Serafino Manzolo
31. Jose Alcala
32. Ambrosio Zepeda
33. Diego de Herrera
34. Tomas Maldonado
35. Teodoro de la Cerda
36. Pablo Flores
37. Antonio Chiver
38. Lorenzo Ramos
39. Xavier de Zepeda
40. Luis Cruz

Source: *Partition of the Suertes of Mission San Antonio de Valero to Adae-seños*, Bexar County Spanish Archives, Spanish Deeds, book 3, p. 312.

Glossary

Spanish Archival Terms

abonar. To credit; settle an account

acoger(se). To harbor, shelter (take refuge)

adivinos. Fortune-tellers

agrimensores. Surveyors

aguardiente. Liquor; brandy

altivez. Haughtiness; pride

amanuence. Amonuensis; scribe

amo. Master; head of household; owner, landlord

apropriar. Appropriate; take possession

arancelado. Ttariff, duty; list, guide

balas. Ammunition

barriles. Barrels

bastimentos. Provisions, supplies

bayeta. A kind of woolen cloth

cambalache. Barter; trade

caución. Bbond; insurance, for runaway slaves and release from jail

cigarreros. Tobacco roller

contrabando. Contraband; smuggling

contratar. Enter into agreement, contract

criado. Domestic servant (n.); (adj.) bred, raised

cuentas. Beads

cuero. Hide, animal skin; leather coat of armor

dadiva.	Grant; gift
dados.	Dice
delitos.	Crimes
desertar.	Desertion; abandon
desterrado.	Banished; exiled
deudos.	Kinsman
disimular.	To tolerate, overlook
embargo.	Seized (law); attachment
embriaguez.	Intoxication; drunkenness
escalfase.	To poach (eggs)
escrito.	Petition (law)
fardo.	Bale, bundle
fiesta.	Festival; communal celebration
frazadas.	Blankets
fusiles.	Guns; muskets
gamuza.	Chamois; deer
ganado vacuno.	Cattle
generos.	Commercial goods
hechizeros.	Sorcerers
huerta.	Large vegetable patch, garden
limosnas.	Alms
mercador.	Merchant
molinos.	Mills
moradores.	Residents
murmuraciones.	Gossip; grumbling
naipes.	Playing cards
negociante.	Trader; merchant
obsequiar.	Gift; present

paraje.	Place; spot
partidas.	Certificate (of birth, marriage, etc.)
patente.	Patent (n.); obvious (adj.)
peones.	Peasants
permutar.	Barter
piquete.	Picket
polvora.	Gunpowder
portillos.	Opening, gap; barnyard gate
recelo.	Fear; suspicion, distrust
reo.	Defendant; culprit; offender; runaway slave
residencia.	Review of a governor's administration
rifa.	Raffle
salinas.	Salt pits
sarao.	Soirée; informal dance
sombrero.	Hat
sosiego.	Peace; calm
suplicio.	Torture; execution
tama.	(Caddo) Indian captain
taparabo.	Dress coat
tasa.	Fixed; regulated
tasado.	Conduct in affairs; regulated, fixed
traficar.	To traffic, trade; travel, roam
vecindario.	Community; neighborhood
vino.	Wine
virtud.	Virtue; quality; power
yegua.	Mare

Notes

INTRODUCTION

1 Letter, Charles Pinckney to William Lee, March 4, 1804, Madrid, the Historic New Orleans Collection, Williams Research Center, MSS 356, p. 2. Pinckney, who had been one of the signers to the US Constitution from South Carolina, also expressed uneasiness about his letter's safety, informing Lee that there was no need for him to send the "two small boxes of Champagne I requested as I have received lately much wine from France."

2 David J. Weber, *The Spanish Frontier in North America* (New Haven, CT: Yale University Press, 1992), 291.

3 Ibid., 292–95. Although Spanish troops dispatched from Santa Fe did not find the Lewis and Clark expedition, which President Thomas Jefferson sponsored from 1804 to 1806, another Spanish force from Nacogdoches, Texas, stopped Freeman and Custis in eastern Oklahoma in late July 1806, the second of the American president's government-funded explorations that journeyed up the Red River to find its source, presumably near Santa Fe.

4 Letter, Spanish military officer, March 19, 1807, Nacogdoches, in Charles Wilson Hackett, ed., *Pichardo's Treatise on the Limits of Louisiana and Texas*, vol. 3 (Austin: University of Texas Press, 1941), 433.

5 For discussion of international rivalries and the silver trade, see Paul W. Mapp, *The Elusive West and the Contest for Empire, 1713–1763* (Chapel Hill: University of North Carolina Press, 2011); J. H. Elliott, *Empires of the Atlantic World: Britain and Spain in America, 1492–1830* (New Haven, CT: Yale University Press, 2006); Weber, *Spanish Frontier*; and Henry Folmer, *Franco-Spanish Rivalry in North America, 1524–1763* (Glendale, CA: Arthur H. Clark, 1953). For background on early Georgia, see Betty Wood, *Slavery in Colonial Georgia, 1730–1775* (Athens: University of Georgia Press, 2007); Harvey H. Jackson and Phinizy Spalding, eds., *Forty Years of Diversity: Essays on Colonial Georgia* (Athens: University of Georgia Press, 1984); and Trevor R. Reese, introduction to *The Most Delightful Country of the Universe: Promotional Literature of the Colony of Georgia, 1717–1734* (Savannah, GA: Beehive Press, 1972).

6 For discussion of the Natchez revolt of 1730–31 and its immediate threat to Natchitoches, see F. Todd Smith, *The Caddo Indians: Tribes at the Convergence*

of Empires, 1542–1854 (College Station: Texas A&M University Press, 1995), 49; and H. Sophie Burton and F. Todd Smith, *Colonial Natchitoches: A Creole Community on the Louisiana-Texas Frontier* (College Station: Texas A&M University Press, 2008), 11. On European and Indian rivalries in the North American borderlands, including the present southeastern United States, see Richard White, *The Roots of Dependency: Subsistence, Environment, and Social Change among the Choctaws, Pawnees, and Navajos* (Lincoln: University of Nebraska Press, 1983); and Weber, *Spanish Frontier.*

7 Letter, Lt. Joseph Gonzalez to Gov. don Manuel de Sandoval, August 29, 1736, Presidio Los Adaes, *Archivo General de la Nación* (hereafter *AGN*)—*Historia,* vol. 395, microfilm, box 5, 236v, 238, 240v, Mission Dolores Historical Materials Collection (hereafter *MDHMC*), Mission Dolores Research Center, San Augustine, Texas; Jesús F. de la Teja, *San Antonio de Béxar: A Community on New Spain's Northern Frontier* (Albuquerque: University of New Mexico Press, 1995).

8 Letter, Gonzalez to Sandoval, *AGN—Historia,* vol. 395, microfilm, box 5, 236v, 238, 240v; see also Hackett, *Pichardo's Treatise,* 3:490.

9 Pekka Hämäläinen, *The Comanche Empire* (New Haven, CT: Yale University Press, 2008); Juliana Barr, *Peace Came in the Form of a Woman: Indians and Spaniards in the Texas Borderlands* (Chapel Hill: University of North Carolina Press, 2007); Gilbert C. Din, *Spaniards, Planters, and Slaves: The Spanish Regulation of Slavery in Louisiana, 1763–1803* (College Station: Texas A&M University Press, 1999); Gwendolyn Midlo Hall, *Africans in Colonial Louisiana: The Development of Afro-Creole Culture in the Eighteenth Century* (Baton Rouge: Louisiana State University Press, 1992).

10 David J. Weber, "John Francis Bannon and the Historiography of the Spanish Borderlands: Retrospect and Prospect," in *Myth and the History of the Hispanic Southwest* (Albuquerque: University of New Mexico Press, 1988), 88. See also James A. Sandos, "From 'Boltonlands' to 'Weberlands': The Borderlands Enter American History," *Journal of American History* 46 (December 1994): 598, which agrees with Weber's conclusion that the perspective of borderlands historians, who "have a secure foothold in both English and Spanish-speaking America," will only become more valuable "as the juncture of those two worlds continues to grow in population and in economic and strategic importance."

11 Samuel Truett, "The Borderlands and Lost Worlds of Early America," in *Contested Spaces of Early America,* ed. Juliana Barr and Edward Countryman (Philadelphia: University of Pennsylvania Press, 2014), 300–324; Gary B. Nash, "The Hidden History of Mestizo America," *Journal of American History* 82 (December 1995): 941–64.

12 Gerald E. Poyo and Gilberto M. Hinojosa, "Spanish Texas and Borderlands Historiography in Transition: Implications for United States History," *Journal of American History* 75 (September 1988): 406, 416; de la Teja, *San Antonio*

de Béxar, 3–5. The province of Nuevo Santander (or the present state of Tamaulipas, Mexico) extended from present Laredo to Brownsville in the lower Rio Grande valley on both sides of the current Texas-Mexico border.

13 Felipe Fernández-Armesto, *Our America: A Hispanic History of the United States* (New York: W. W. Norton, 2014).

14 Juliana Barr, "There's No Such Thing as 'Prehistory': What the Longue Durée of Caddo and Pueblo History Tells Us about Colonial America," *William and Mary Quarterly* 74, no. 2 (April 2017): 207.

15 Gary B. Mills, *The Forgotten People: Cane River's Creoles of Color* (Baton Rouge: Louisiana State University Press, 1977).

16 Elizabeth Jameson, "Dancing on the Rim, Tiptoeing through Minefields: Challenges and Promises of Borderlands," *Pacific Historical Review* 75 (2006): 5.

17 For discussion about the multiple meanings of borders, borderlands, and frontiers, see Rachel C. St. John, *Line in the Sand: A History of the Western U.S.-Mexico Border* (Princeton, NJ: Princeton University Press, 2011); Alan Taylor, *The Divided Ground: Indians, Settlers, and the Northern Borderland of the American Revolution* (New York: Alfred A. Knopf, 2006); Jeremy Adelman and Stephen Aron, "From Borderlands to Borders: Empires, Nation-States, and the Peoples in between in North American History," *American Historical Review* 104, no. 3 (June 1999): 815–16; Donna Guy and Thomas E. Sheridan, eds., *Contested Ground: Comparative Frontiers on the Northern and Southern Edges of the Spanish Empire* (Tucson: University of Arizona Press, 1998), 10–11; Stephen Aron, "Lessons in Conquest: Towards a Greater Western History," *Pacific Historical Review* 63 (1994): 147; Weber, *Spanish Frontier*, 11; and Fabricio Prado, "The Fringes of Empires: Recent Scholarship on Colonial Frontiers and Borderlands in Latin America," *History Compass* 10, no. 4 (2012): 318, who states that the translation of *frontera* (in Spanish) and *fronteira* (in Portuguese) "is a complex task because the term carries multiple meanings such as frontier, wilderness, border, boundary, and limit" in both of these Iberian languages. In addition, "the meanings of these terms changed overtime and over different geographical areas."

18 Guy and Sheridan, *Contested Ground*, 4.

19 Richard White, *The Middle Ground: Indians, Europeans, and Republics in the Great Lakes Region, 1650–1815* (New York: Cambridge University Press, 1991); Taylor, *Divided Ground*; Juliana Barr, "Geographies of Power: Mapping Indian Borders in the 'Borderlands' of the Early Southwest," *William and Mary Quarterly* 68, no. 1 (January 2011): 28 ("borders and interiors"); Smith, *Caddo Indians*; Kathleen DuVal, *The Native Ground: Indians and Colonists in the Heart of the Continent* (Philadelphia: University of Pennsylvania Press, 2006); William L. Eakin, "The Kingdom of the Tejas: The Hasinai Indians at the Crossroads of Change" (PhD diss., University of Kansas, 1997).

20 Guy and Sheridan, *Contested Ground*, 11. See also Inga Clendinnen, *Ambiva-lent Conquests: Maya and Spaniard in Yucatan, 1517–1570* (New York: Cambridge University Press, 1987).

21 Pekka Hämäläinen and Samuel Truett, "On Borderlands," *Journal of American History* 98, no. 2 (September 2011): 338.

22 Max L. Moorhead, *The Presidio: Bastion of the Spanish Borderlands* (Norman: University of Oklahoma Press, 1975), 4; Burton and Smith, *Colonial Natchitoches*, 9.

23 The phrase "Caddo country" derives from Smith, *Caddo Indians*.

24 See Weber, *Spanish Frontier*, 235, who mentions such military communities as San Diego, San Francisco, Tucson, and San Antonio, as well as San Fernando (Memphis) and Nogales (Vicksburg).

25 De la Teja, *San Antonio de Béxar*, xiii–xiv, refers to the presence of the military establishment in San Antonio, Texas, as a type of "sub-community." See also Gerald E. Poyo, ed., *Tejano Journey, 1770–1850* (Austin: University of Texas Press, 1996), xiv, 4, who refers to Los Adaes as part of the "territorial triangle" of Spanish Texas communities at San Antonio, La Bahía (present Goliad), and Los Adaes. For another regional framework about communities, see Sarah Deutsch, *No Separate Refuge: Culture, Class, and Gender on an Anglo-Hispanic Frontier in the American Southwest, 1880–1940* (New York: Oxford University Press, 1987).

26 Tina Laurel Meacham, "The Population of Spanish and Mexican Texas, 1716–1836" (PhD diss., University of Texas at Austin, 2000), viii, states that the Spanish settlements of Los Adaes, San Antonio, and La Bahia "began as artificial communities, dependent on the military for their existence." See also Light Townsend Cummins, *To the Vast and Beautiful Land: Anglo Migration into Spanish Louisiana and Texas, 1760s–1820s* (College Station: Texas A&M University Press, 2019), 2.

27 Jimmy L. Bryan Jr., "The Enduring People: Tejano Exclusion and Perseverance in the Republic of Texas, 1836–1845," *Journal of the West* 47 (Summer 2008): 40–47.

28 Kevin Terraciano and Lisa Sousa, "Historiography of New Spain," in *The Oxford Handbook of Latin American History*, ed. Jose C. Moya (London: Oxford University Press, 2010), 34. For recent work on discussion of rank-and-file soldiers in the early Spanish conquest of Mexico, see Ida Altman, *The War for Mexico's West: Indians and Spaniards in New Galicia, 1524–1550* (Albuquerque: University of New Mexico Press, 2010).

29 Some of the classic works on Spanish colonization elsewhere in northern New Spain include Oakah L. Jones Jr., *Los Paisanos: Spanish Settlers on the Northern Frontier in New Spain* (Norman: University of Oklahoma Press, 1979); Ross Frank, *From Settler to Citizen: New Mexican Economic Development and the Creation of Vecino Society, 1750–1820* (Berkeley: University of California Press, 2000); and de la Teja, *San Antonio de Béxar*. See also Amy M. Porter,

Their Lives, Their Wills: Women in the Borderlands, 1750–1846 (Lubbock: Texas Tech University Press, 2015). On the comparison with Anglo-American rank-and-file soldiers, see Alfred F. Young, *The Shoemaker and the Tea Party: Memory and the American Revolution* (Boston: Beacon Press, 1999); and Fred Anderson, *A People's Army: Massachusetts Soldiers and Society in the Seven Years' War* (Chapel Hill: University of North Carolina Press, 1984).

30 Barr, "There's No Such Thing," 204–5.

31 See, for example, Robert S. Weddle, *Wilderness Manhunt: The Spanish Search for La Salle* (College Station: Texas A&M University Press, 1999). For background on the Spanish settlement of San Juan Bautista, see Weddle, *San Juan Bautista: Gateway to Spanish Texas* (Austin: University of Texas Press, 1968).

32 David Rex Galindo, "Propaganda Fide: Training Franciscan Missionaries in New Spain" (PhD diss., Southern Methodist University, 2010), 245, 261.

33 Barr, "Geographies of Power," 24, 28.

34 Andrés Reséndez, *Changing National Identities at the Frontier: Texas and New Mexico, 1800–1850* (New York: Cambridge University Press, 2005), 126; Porter, *Their Lives*, 6.

35 Eric Van Young, *Hacienda and Market in Eighteenth-Century Mexico: The Rural Economy of the Guadalajara Region, 1675–1820* (Berkeley: University of California Press, 1981), 245–46.

36 See Burton and Smith, *Colonial Natchitoches*, 53–54, who argue that the French created a hegemonic society at Natchitoches that dominated the Louisiana-Texas region.

37 Peter Sahlins, *Boundaries: The Making of France and Spain in the Pyrenees* (Berkeley: University of California Press, 1989), 129, 140; George T. Díaz, *Border Contraband: A History of Smuggling across the Rio Grande* (Austin: University of Texas Press, 2015), 6.

38 For discussion of smuggling in other borderlands and its significance, see Alan L. Karras, *Smuggling: Contraband and Corruption in World History* (Lanham, MD: Rowman & Littlefield, 2010); Diaz, *Border Contraband*; Elaine Carey and Andrae M. Marak, eds., *Smugglers, Brothels, and Twine: Historical Perspectives on Contraband and Vice in North America's Borderlands* (Tucson: University of Arizona Press, 2011); Linda M. Rupert, *Creolization and Contraband: Curaçao in the Early Modern Atlantic World* (Athens: University of Georgia Press, 2012); Paul Nugent, *Smugglers, Secessionists and Loyal Citizens on the Ghana-Togo Frontier* (Athens: Ohio University Press, 2002); Jesse Cromwell, *The Smugglers' World: Illicit Trade and Atlantic Communities in Eighteenth-Century Venezuela* (Chapel Hill: University of North Carolina Press, 2018).

39 Andrew Konove, "On the Cheap: The Baratillo Marketplace and the Shadow Economy of Eighteenth-Century Mexico City," *The Americas*, April 2015, 258.

40 Ira Berlin, *Many Thousands Gone: The First Two Centuries of Slavery in North America* (Cambridge: Harvard University Press, 1998), 7–8. For discussion of African slavery that developed in Louisiana, see Din, *Spaniards, Planters, and Slaves*; and Hall, *Africans in Colonial Louisiana*. On Indian slavery in North America, see Andrés Reséndez, *The Other Slavery: The Uncovered Story of Indian Enslavement in America* (Boston: Houghton Mifflin Harcourt, 2016).

41 For discussion of Indian captivity and slavery in Texas, see Juliana Barr, "From Captives to Slaves: Commodifying Indian Women in the Borderlands," *Journal of American History* 92 (June 2005): 19–46; and Reséndez, *Other Slavery*. On African slavery in Texas under Spain, see Francis X. Galán, "Between Esteban and Joshua Houston: Women, Children and Slavery in the Texas Borderlands," *Journal of South Texas* 27 (Fall 2014): 22–36. On African slavery in Natchitoches, see Burton and Smith, *Colonial Natchitoches*. See also Jesús F. de la Teja and Ross Frank, eds., *Choice, Persuasion, and Coercion: Social Control on Spain's North American Frontiers* (Albuquerque: University of New Mexico Press, 2005).

42 See Carlos Manuel Valés, *Esclavos negros en Saltillo* (Saltillo, Mexico: Universidad Autónoma de Coahuila, 1989); de la Teja, *San Antonio de Béxar*; Porter, *Their Lives*.

43 Anne F. Hyde, *Empires, Nations, and Families: A New History of the North American West, 1800–1860* (New York: HarperCollins, 2011), 219, 223, adds that these neighborhood communities in the early American West—Bent (Arkansas River), Vallejo (Northern California), and Austin/Seguin (central Texas)—operated as a "borderland" regardless from which starting point of territory one looks outward.

44 Tamar Herzog, *Frontiers of Possession: Spain and Portugal in Europe and the Americas* (Cambridge: Harvard University Press, 2015), 7.

45 Eric Hinderaker, *Elusive Empires: Constructing Colonialism in the Ohio Valley, 1673–1800* (New York: Cambridge University Press, 1997); Thomas M. Truxes, *Defying Empire: Trading with the Enemy in Colonial New York* (New Haven, CT: Yale University Press, 2008); David J. Weber, *Bárbaros: Spaniards and Their Savages in the Age of Enlightenment* (New Haven, CT: Yale University Press, 2005).

46 Gene Allen Smith and Sylvia L. Hilton, eds., *Nexus of Empire: Negotiating Loyalty and Identity in the Revolutionary Borderlands, 1760s–1820s* (Gainesville: University Press of Florida, 2010).

47 Weber, "Conflicts and Accommodations: Hispanic and Anglo-American Borders in Historical Perspective, 1670–1853," *Journal of the Southwest* 39 (Spring 1997): 17, adds that the contradiction between Los Adaes's defensive purpose and its legal/illegal accommodation is not unique when one considers the same applied to Spanish Pensacola and St. Augustine.

CHAPTER I

1   Letter, Lt. Joseph Gonzales to Governor Sandoval, April 11, 1735, Presidio Los Adaes, *AGN—Historia*, in *MDHMC*, San Augustine, Texas, vol. 395, microfilm, box 5, 231v: "Por aca hai mucha agua, que no nos dá lugar á disponer la tierra para hacer una razonable siembra" (first quotation), and "Los soldados que V.S. despachó, y acá llegaron perdieron en el camino sus bestias por lo riguroso del tiempo, solo Juan de Mora llego con numero completo, Arambula llegó tres, y los otros qual llegó dos, y qual uno" (second quotation; both author's translation). On the Spanish troubles at San Antonio, see de la Teja, *San Antonio de Béxar*.

2   The Sabine River was much smaller in the eighteenth century. In the 1960s, the US Army Corp of Engineers flooded the area in constructing the Toledo Bend Reservoir. The lower Red River was log-jammed by the mid-nineteenth century, slowing traffic flow downriver.

3   Cynthia Radding, *Wandering Peoples: Colonialism, Ethnic Spaces, and Ecological Frontiers in Northwestern Mexico, 1700–1850* (Durham, NC: Duke University Press, 1997), xviii, explains that ecological frontiers "refer to the landscape produced by human occupation and to the values that different sets of social actors ascribe to the land." For comparison with Central and South America, see Guy and Sheridan, *Contested Ground*, 4–5; Shawn Miller, *An Environmental History of Latin America* (New York: Cambridge University Press, 2007); and Matthew Restall, "Crossing to Safety? Frontier Flight in Eighteenth-Century Belize and Yucatan," *Hispanic American Historical Review* 94, no. 3 (August 2014). See also John R. McNeill, "The Ecological Atlantic," in *The Oxford Handbook of the Atlantic World, 1450–1850*, ed. Nicholas Canny and Philip Morgan (Oxford: Oxford University Press, 2011).

4   María Elena Santoscoy, Laura Gutiérrez, Martha Rodríguez, and Francisco Cepeda, eds., *Breve historia de Coahuila* (Mexico City: Fondo de Cultura Económica, 2000), 12–13, 17.

5   Miller, *Environmental History*.

6   Susan Midgen Socolow, "Introduction to the Rural Past," in *The Countryside in Colonial Latin America*, ed. Louisa Schell Hoberman and Susan Midgen Socolow (Albuquerque: University of New Mexico Press, 1996), 3, 5, 7–8.

7   Santoscoy, Gutiérrez, Rodríguez, and Cepeda, *Breve historia de Coahuila*, 83–85.

8   Smith, *Caddo Indians*.

9   De la Teja, *San Antonio de Béxar*, 5–6; Donald E. Chipman, *Spanish Texas, 1519–1821* (Austin: University of Texas Press, 1992), 70–85. See also Robert S. Weddle, *The French Thorn: Rival Explorers in the Spanish Sea, 1682–1762*

(College Station: Texas A&M University Press, 1991). Meanwhile, the search for La Salle's colony by Spanish ships along the coastline also led to discovery of the strategic importance of Pensacola as the route of galleons into the Gulf of Mexico. If the French took possession of West Florida, the Spanish believed that France could use it as a base for launching attacks on Mexico; see Marcel Giraud, *A History of French Louisiana*, vol. 1, *The Reign of Louis XIV, 1698–1715* (Baton Rouge: Louisiana State University Press, 1974), 25. For detailed discussion of De León's expedition to find La Salle, see Lola Orellano Norris, *General Alonso de León's Expeditions into Texas, 1686–1690* (College Station: Texas A&M University Press, 2017).

10 Folmer, *Franco-Spanish Rivalry*, 14, 134.

11 Orders for New Discoveries (1573), summarized in Weber, *Spanish Frontier*, 78.

12 Chipman, *Spanish Texas*, 93–100; Elizabeth A. H. John, *Storms Brewed in Other Men's Worlds: The Confrontation of Indians, Spanish, and French in the Southwest, 1540–1795* (Lincoln: University of Nebraska Press, 1975), 165. See also Juliana Barr, "A Diplomacy of Gender: Rituals of First Contact in the 'Land of the Tejas,'" *William and Mary Quarterly* 61 (July 2004): 428, which mentions the rape of Hasinai women by Spanish soldiers that went unpunished and exacerbated hostilities.

13 Chipman, *Spanish Texas*, 102–4. For a biography of St. Denis, see Ross Phares, *Cavalier in the Wilderness: The Story of the Explorer and Trader Louis Juchereau de St. Denis* (Baton Rouge: Louisiana State University Press, 1952).

14 Folmer, *Franco-Spanish Rivalry*, 228–29, 242.

15 For background on this rather complicated relationship, see Patricia R. Lemée, "Manuela Sánchez Navarro," *The Natchitoches Genealogist* 20 (October 1995); 18. Diego Ramón was actually Manuela Sanchez Navarro's step-grandfather.

16 Chipman, *Spanish Texas*, 104–5, 110–14; Folmer, *Franco-Spanish Rivalry*, 238. See also Joan Cain, *The Historical Journal of the Establishment of the French in Louisiana, by Jean-Baptiste Bénard de la Harpe*, ed. Glenn R. Conrad, trans. Virginia Koenig (Lafayette: University of Southern Louisiana Press, 1971), 99; Weddle, *San Juan Bautista*. See also Emily Hyatt and Jonathan Gerland, "Finding Angelina: The Search for East Texas' Little Angel," *Pine Bough* 17 (December 2012): 12–21.

17 For discussion of the Indian fur trade, see Pekka Hämäläinen, *Comanche Empire*; and Hämäläinen, "The Rise and Fall of Plains Indian Horse Cultures," *Journal of American History* 90 (December 2003): 833–62. See also David La Vere, *The Caddo Chiefdoms: Caddo Economics and Politics, 700–1835* (Lincoln: University of Nebraska Press, 1998).

18 Juan Domingo Arricivita, *Apostolic Chronicle of Juan Domingo Arricivita: The Franciscan Mission Frontier in the Eighteenth Century in Arizona, Texas, and*

the Californias, ed. Vivian C. Fisher and W. Michael Mathes, trans. George P. Hammond and Agapito Rey, 2 vols. (Berkeley, CA: Academy of American Franciscan History, 1996), 139–40, 289.

19 Gary B. Mills, "The Chauvin Brothers: Early Colonists of Louisiana," *Louisiana History* 15 (Winter 1974): 121–23. The overtures with Mexico sometimes followed attempts to trade with Cuba. For example, the French in Louisiana failed in their bid to import cattle from Havana in 1717, creating more demand for beef from northern Mexico; see Marcel Giraud, *A History of French Louisiana*, vol. 2, *Years of Transition, 1715–1717* (Baton Rouge: Louisiana State University Press, 1993), 173.

20 Quotation from Charmion Clair Shelby, "St. Denis's Second Expedition from Louisiana to the Rio Grande, 1716–1719, with Illustrative Documents, Translated and Edited" (MA thesis, University of Texas at Austin, 1927), 18–24, 27–28, 33, 41–42; Shelby, "St. Denis's Declaration concerning Texas in 1717," *Southwestern Historical Quarterly* 26 (January 1923): 174; Fray Juan Agustín Morfi, *History of Texas, 1673–1779*, vol. 1, ed. and trans. Carlos E. Castañeda (Albuquerque: Quivira Society, 1935), 187–88; Folmer, *Franco-Spanish Rivalry*, 243.

21 Shelby, "St. Denis's Second Expedition," 36–38, 41–42. French officials in Louisiana began realizing the futility of trying to open legal trade with Mexico, especially after St. Denis's sojourn, and increasingly turned to clandestine trade. Such illicit trading had occurred in Havana, Cuba, where an agent of Crozat secretly sold three thousand deerskins in exchange for specie (currency) and tobacco before departing the port; see Giraud, *History of French Louisiana*, 2:145. Already by this time, the missions of East Texas were reestablished in 1716, followed by the mission and presidio of San Antonio de Béxar in 1718; see letters of the *fiscal*, don Juan de Olivan Rebolledo, recommending establishment of presidios, settlements, and missions to check French encroachment, *Béxar Archives* (hereafter *BA*), microfilm, roll 8, frame nos. 0001–0016. An *oidor* was a judge who served as a member of the royal *audiencia*, or court, which advised the viceroy and whose main responsibility was administration of residencias, or review of an official's conduct in office. A *fiscal* was normally an attorney for the state. See Thomas C. Barnes, Thomas H. Naylor, and Charles W. Polzer, eds., *Northern New Spain: A Research Guide* (Tucson: University of Arizona Press, 1981), 135–36.

22 Charmion Clair Shelby, ed. and trans., "Projected French Attacks upon the Northeastern Frontier of New Spain, 1719–1721," *Hispanic American Historical Review* 13 (November 1933): 472. French occupation of the Mississippi River to block the English threat had attained new importance following the Treaty of Ryswick (1695) ending King Philip's War. Some French officials deemed colonization of its vast territory as necessary to cut off access into

the vulnerable lower valley of the Ohio to Pennsylvania (British) colonists; see Giraud, *History of French Louisiana*, 1:14–16. By the time of St. Denis's second expedition to the Rio Grande in 1716–17, Crozat and other French officials in Louisiana still feared Britain more than Spain; see Giraud, *History of French Louisiana*, 2:39–41.

23 Weber, *Spanish Frontier*, 166–67; Folmer, *Franco-Spanish Rivalry*, 254. See also de la Teja, *San Antonio de Béxar*.

24 George Colpitts, "'Animated like Us by Commercial Interests': Commercial Ethnology and Fur Trade Descriptions in New France, 1660–1760," *Canadian Historical Review* 83 (September 2002): 313–15.

25 Patricia R. Lemée, "Tios and Tantes: Familial and Political Relationships of Natchitoches and the Spanish Colonial Frontier," *Southwestern Historical Quarterly* 101 (January 1998): 342.

26 Francis X. Galán, "Lost in Translation: Tejano Roots on the Louisiana-Texas Borderlands, 1716–1821," in *Recovering the Hispanic History of Texas*, ed. Monica Perales and Raúl A. Ramos (Houston: Arte Público Press, 2010), 6–7, also discusses the assistance Saint Denis and the Spanish reoccupation of Texas received from a Caddo Indian woman named Angelina, who studied at Mission San Juan Bautista on the Rio Grande. For discussion of families and trade ties in the greater American west at a later time, see Hyde, *Empires, Nations, and Families*.

27 Shelby, "Projected French Attacks," 460, 470–72; Henry Folmer, "Report on Louis de Saint Denis' Intended Raid on San Antonio in 1721," *Southwestern Historical Quarterly* 52 (July 1948): 84. See also Ralph A. Smith, trans., "Account of the Journey of Bénard de la Harpe: Discovery Made by Him of Several Nations Situated in the West," *Southwestern Historical Quarterly* 62 (July 1958): 536, 539–40, which also mentions a letter, dated December 12, 1719, from Commandant Blondel of Natchitoches to the friar from mission Los Adaes explaining that the French seized items from that place after its abandonment in 1719 out of fear that these "might be profaned and pillaged by the idolatrous" Indians, meant to deflect the Spanish belief that the French wanted them to leave.

28 Smith, "Account," 539–41.

29 Richard G. Santos, *Aguayo Expedition into Texas, 1721: An Annotated Translation of the Five Versions of the Diary Kept by Br. Juan Antonio de la Pena* (Austin: Jenkins, 1981), 19.

30 For background on the economy of late colonial Mexico and ranching, see Van Young, *Hacienda and Market*. On the Spanish moving settled Indians to other parts of New Spain, see Altman, *War for Mexico's West*. For discussion of Tlascalans in particular, see Porter, *Their Lives*. Sacramental records of San Fernando Church at San Antonio de Béxar reveal that some of the residents

who came from Los Adaes were Indians, including the Musquíz family from Coahuila.

31 Eleanor Claire Buckley, "The Aguayo Expedition into Texas and Louisiana, 1719–1722," *Southwestern Historical Quarterly* 15 (July 1911): 25, 27, 29–30. The ethnic background of the 117 men from Celaya were recorded as follows: 44 Spaniards, 31 *mulattos*, 17 *mestizos*, 21 *coyotes*, 2 *castizos*, 1 free *negro*, 1 Indian, and 1 *lobo*.

32 Santos, *Aguayo Expedition*, 23; Buckley, "Aguayo Expedition," 30. For discussion of symbolic representations of the Virgin Mary and the presence of women on Spanish-Indian relations, see Barr, "Diplomacy of Gender," 393–437.

33 Buckley, "Aguayo Expedition," 30–32, 35, 41–50. Three of the missions—San Francisco de los Tejas, La Purísima Concepción, and San José de los Nazonis—belonged to the Queretaran College, under the protection of Presidio Nuestra Señora de los Dolores. The other three, which were Zacatecan missions—Nuestra Senora de Guadalupe de Nacogdoches, Nuestra Señora de los Ais (near present San Augustine, Texas), and San Miguel de los Adaes (near present Robeline, Louisiana)—were soon to be protected by a newly built presidio at Los Adaes.

34 Santos, *Aguayo Expedition*, 67–69. One league is the equivalent of 2.59 miles according to Barnes, Naylor, and Polzer, "Weights and Measures," in *Northern New Spain*, 68.

35 Quotations from Santos, *Aguayo Expedition*, 68.

36 Meacham, "Population," 353, table A1.1a, "Reported Population for Texas Indian Tribes—East Texas." Quotation from Santos, *Aguayo Expedition*, 70, 72; Fred B. Kniffen, Hiram F. Gregory, and George A. Stokes, *The Historic Indian Tribes of Louisiana: From 1542 to the Present* (Baton Rouge: Louisiana State University Press, 1987), 33, 47; John, *Storms Brewed*, 165–66. The Caddo Indians traded with Southern Plains Indians, who in turn obtained horses from Spaniards in New Mexico for salt, skins, wood bows, and captives; see Dayna Bowker Lee, "Indian Slavery in Lower Louisiana during the Colonial Period, 1699–1803" (MA thesis, Northwestern State University, Natchitoches, 1989). See also Pekka Hämäläinen, "The Western Comanche Trade Center: Rethinking the Plains Indian Trade System," *Western Historical Quarterly* 29 (Winter 1998): 485–513; and David La Vere, *The Texas Indians* (College Station: Texas A&M University Press, 2004).

37 Santos, *Aguayo Expedition*, 68–69.

38 Ibid., 70. The De la Peña diary contradicts the view in La Harpe's account, which portrays the French soldiers as protectors of things sacred at the Mission San Miguel de los Adaes and omitting any references to possible enslavement of the nearby Indian inhabitants. More clear is that the Natchitoches Indians had traded with the French since at least 1700 and had become

allies, especially after St. Denis's arrival; see Elizabeth H. West, ed. and trans., "Bonilla's Brief Compendium of the History of Texas, 1772," *Southwestern Historical Quarterly* 8 (July 1904): 23.

39 Santos, *Aguayo Expedition*, 70.

40 Ibid., 69–70, 83, and 92; see also Jones, *Los Paisanos*.

41 Weber, *Spanish Frontier*, 172–73, adds that Saltillo was the surest source of reasonably priced Spanish goods.

42 "Informe del Gobernador Almazán al Virey sobre el proyecto que tiene de pedir géneros al apoderado de los presidios," October 24, 1724, Real Presidio de San Antonio de Béxar, *Archivo San Francisco el Grande* (hereafter *ASFG*), box 2Q 251, vol. 10, 143, photostat.

43 Letter, Governor Almazán to Viceroy Marqués de Casafuerte, July 1726, Bancroft Library (hereafter *BL*), box 33, folder 532, 2–3, transcription: "Que calmen algo las lluvias, y los Rios dan lugar a Transittarse, cuyo víaje me será penosísimo por el Quebranto de mi salud y ser el tíempo de Rigurosos Calores" (author's translation).

44 *Autos sobre mudar el Presido de los Adais, Provincia de Texas*, September 29, 1730, to December 14, 1733, Mexico City, *AGN—Provincias Internas, MDHMC*, vol. 163, exp. 6, 7, 11, photostat: "Y para que los ganados, y Cavallada beban, se alejan alguna distancia y como es corta la que ay al Parage de Natchitoches donde todo abunda, por estar aquella Población en medio del Rio de los Caudachos; se encuentran facil, los bastimentos que les faltan á nuestros Presidiales" (author's translation).

45 Santos, *Aguayo Expedition*, 71; Weddle, *San Juan Bautista*, 163.

46 Carlos E. Castañeda, *Our Catholic Heritage in Texas, 1519–1936*, vol. 3 (Austin: Von Boeckmann-Jones, 1938), 75; Weber, "Conflicts and Accommodations," 16.

47 Morfi, *History of Texas*, 2:243.

48 Weber, *Bárbaros*.

49 Smith, *Caddo Indians*, 9, 12–15; John, *Storms Brewed*, 165–66. See also Kathleen DuVal, *Native Ground*; and Richard White, *Roots of Dependency*.

50 *Informe* of the College to the King requesting he order the military to help with conversions, August 25, 1728, Colegio de la Santísima Cruz de Milagros de la Ciudad de Santiago de Querétaro, transcription, Bolton Papers, Bancroft Library (hereafter *BP—BL*), University of California–Berkeley, box 33, folder 531, 21, photocopy at Mission Dolores Visitor and Research Center, San Augustine, Texas, transcription: "No se ha podido conseguir el que se junten â Pueblo los Yndios, que derramados viven en aquellos montes, ni ha avido hasta oy quien solicite . . . â parage mas apto para lo necesario â la vida, para assi cathequizar les ê instruirles en los misterios de la fe" (author's translation).

51 Thomas H. Naylor and Charles W. Polzer, eds., *Pedro de Rivera and the Military Regulations for Northern New Spain, 1724–1729: A Documentary*

History of His Frontier Inspection and the Reglamento de 1729 (Tucson: University of Arizona Press, 1988), 83, 158.

52 Naylor and Polzer, *Pedro de Rivera*, 157.

53 Charles Wilson Hackett, ed. and trans., *Pichardo's Treatise*, vol. 4 (Austin: University of Texas Press, 1946), 94.

54 Folmer, *Franco-Spanish Rivalry*, 292; see also Mapp, *Elusive West*, 22, 270–72.

55 Weber, *Spanish Frontier*, 184.

56 See Daniel H. Usner Jr., *Indians, Settlers, and Slaves in a Frontier Exchange Economy: The Lower Mississippi Valley before 1783* (Chapel Hill: University of North Carolina Press, 1992), 6–8, who explains that the "frontier exchange economy" meant the interplay of intercultural strategies with survival amid "substantial interregional connections" and "plenty of common ground"; declaration, don Pedro de Sierra, January 26, 1761, Royal Presidio of Nuestra Señora de los Adaes, *BA*, microfilm, 9:951, for the investigation of censorship against don Jacinto de Barrios y Jáuregui; *Consulta, Bolton Manuscripts* (Bolton MSS), *Bolton Papers*, 1–2, 10; *autos* (judicial writ) of inquiry, *BA*, microfilm, 9:228–29.

57 On Indian, French, and Spanish partnerships, see David La Vere, "Between Kinship and Capitalism: French and Spanish Rivalry in the Colonial Louisiana-Texas Indian Trade," *Journal of Southern History* 64 (May 1998): 198, 211.

58 Baptism, Jeanne de Aramboule, daughter of Spaniard from the post of Los Adays, April 4, 1734, Natchitoches, in Elizabeth Shown Mills, *Natchitoches: Abstracts of the Catholic Church Registers of the French and Spanish Post of St. Jean Baptiste des Natchitoches in Louisiana: 1729–1803* (New Orleans: Polyanthos, 1977), 3, entry no. 2 (hereafter *NACCR*).

59 Hackett, *Pichardo's Treatise*, 3:494–95; Hebert Eugene Bolton, *Texas in the Middle Eighteenth Century* (Austin: University of Texas Press, 1915), 33–34; Burton, "Family and Economy in Frontier Louisiana: Colonial Natchitoches, 1714–1803" (PhD diss., Texas Christian University, 2002), 32; Phares, *Cavalier*, 217–19.

60 Moorhead, *Presidio*, 4, 25–26. After several decades of unsuccessful military campaigns against nomadic Indians in the Chichimeco War, following expansion into silver mining districts north of Mexico City, Spanish officials in the 1580s began a peace policy of purchase and persuasion rather than the sword, offering Indian warriors inducements of food, clothing, land, agricultural tools, religious instruction, and government protection; see Moorhead, *Presidio*, 10, 12–13. See also Weber, *Spanish Frontier*.

61 William S. Kiser, *The Borderlands of Slavery: The Struggle over Captivity and Peonage in the American Southwest* (Philadelphia: University of Pennsylvania Press, 2017), preface.

62 Norwood Andrews, "Muros del presidio y trabajo de los convictos: El examen de los orígenes de los trabajos forzados en la frontera de Nueva España,"

in Porfirio Sanz Camañes and David Rex Galindo, coords., *La frontera en el mundo hispánico* (Quito, Ecuador: Abya-Yala, 2014), 326–27.

63 Moorhead, *Presidio*, 27, 34–35.

64 Naylor and Polzer, *Pedro de Rivera*, 85, 120.

65 Ibid., 157–58.

66 On the assessment of Rivera's inspection, see Jack Jackson and William C. Foster, *Imaginary Kingdom: Texas as Seen by the Rivera and Rubí Military Expeditions, 1727 and 1767* (Austin: Texas State Historical Association, 1995), 61–64.

67 Weber, *Spanish Frontier*, 92 (first quotation); Galindo, "Propaganda Fide," 11 (second quotation).

CHAPTER 2

1 Katherine Bridges and Winston De Ville, trans. and eds., "Natchitoches and the Trail to the Rio Grande: Two Early Eighteenth Century Accounts, by the Sieur Derbanne," *Louisiana History* 8 (Summer 1967): 256.

2 *Informe*, Gov. don Fernando Perez de Almazán, March 24, 1724, San Antonio de Béxar, *ASFG*, Center for American History, University of Texas (UT) at Austin, box 2Q251, vol. 10, 111, photostat: "los Religiosos han ocurrido á administrarles los Santtos Sacramenttos, y decir les misa algunas días festivas, cuio consuelo han apreciado mucho los Franceses por no tener Ministtro Eclesiasttia" (author's translation).

3 François Derbanne, "Report of the Post of Natchitoches," in Katerine Bridges and Winston De Ville, eds. and trans., "Natchitoches and the Trail to the Rio Grande: Two Early Eighteenth-Century Accounts, by the Sieur Derbanne," *Louisiana History* 8 (Summer 1967): 256.

4 On the reasons behind the Pueblo Revolt and strained relations elsewhere in northern New Spain, see David J. Weber, *What Caused the Pueblo Revolt of 1680?* (Boston: Bedford / St. Martin's, 1999); Ramón A. Gutiérrez, *When Jesus Came, the Corn Mothers Went Away: Marriage, Sexuality, and Power in New Mexico, 1500–1846* (Stanford: Stanford University Press, 1991); Steven W. Hackel, *Children of Coyote, Missionaries of Saint Francis: Indian-Spanish Relations in Colonial California, 1769–1850* (Chapel Hill: University of North Carolina Press, 2005); Barr, *Peace Came*; Lisbeth Haas, *Conquests and Historical Identities in California, 1769–1936* (Berkeley: University of California Press, 1995); Albert L. Hurtado, *Intimate Frontiers: Sex, Gender, and Culture in Old California* (Albuquerque: University of New Mexico Press, 1999); and de la Teja, *San Antonio de Béxar*.

5 Fray Pedro Muñoz, visitador, 29 de octubre de 1727, *Las Misiones de Texas en 1727*, Archivo Histórico, Biblioteca Nacional de Antropología e Historia, Fondo Franciscano, volumen 132, folio 11vB, quoted in Rev. Dr. Francisco Morales, OFM, "De la vida conventual a la vida misionera: Un acercamiento a dos formas de vida franciscana" (paper presented at the Franciscan Presence in the Borderlands symposium, Bishop DeFalco Retreat Center, Amarillo, Texas, September 17, 2004): "Pasando a ver los gentiles de esta misión, ninguno hasta ahora reconoce a campana por hallarse bien allá en sus retiros que distan sus jacales, unos de otros y de este, unas ocho leguas, otros más hasta quince, por cuya causa trabajan sumamente los misioneros para ir a ver alguno o algunos de ellos y es la causa de no poderse perfeccionar en la lengua de su idioma" (first quotation) and "alegando las conveniencias temporales que tienen en sus retiros que no tuvieran juntos en un paraje porque la tierra no les ofrece proporcionadas" (second quotation; both author's translation).

6 Report, signed by seven missionaries outlining problems they faced developing the missions, March 18, 1730, at Mission Los Adaes, *Archivo del Colegio de Zacatecas* (hereafter *ACZ*), Guadalupe, Zacatecas, Mexico, in Old Spanish Missions Research Library (hereafter *OSMRL*), Center for Mexican American Research, Our Lady of the Lake University, microfilm, roll 3, frame 3938.

7 Fray Muñoz, October 27, 1727, *Las Misiones de Texas en 1727*, folio 11rB: "que tiene dos altares, pobre y curiosamente adorada y así mismo, ornamentos de todos colores que ha dado el Rey, nuestro señor, que Dios guarde y la casa que se está haciendo" (author's translation).

8 Ibid., October 29, 1727, folio 11vB: "Es lo menos que responden a las persuasiones de los padres, instando ellos a mantenerse así porque tienen sus ritos y para sus chenecies que son unos viejos embusteros y aun hechiceros que persuaden a los ignorantes que solo los que ellos dicen es lo que deben tener, si bien los mas sospechan que aquello es mentira, pero como son de natural apacible y cobarde no quieren desgraciar a los viejos" (first quotation) and "No cesan de hacer diligencia, esperando que Dios nuestro señor, alumbre a todos estos pobres gentiles que habitan el contorno de este país y son los que esperamos que se junten en esta misión los que tienen en su idioma los nombres de Idays (Adaes) y Pachinais y Catanacha" (second quotation; both author's translation).

9 Letter, Fray Miguel Sevillano de Paredes to the king, August 25, 1728, College of Santa Cruz, Querétaro, Mexico, *Informe del colegio al Rey pidiendo mande a los militares fomentan las conversiones*, BL, carton 33, folder 531, 22–23, transcription: "Por la experiencia nos consta no ser dable el congregarlos â esfuerzos de solo los Misioneros . . . el fin primario, que es la reducción de la Gentilidad" (author's translation).

10 *Bando* (decree), Viceroy Marqués de Casafuerte, February 15, 1734, publishing the royal order of July 31, 1733, *Nacodoches Archives* (hereafter *NA*), box 2Q292, vol. 1, 10–11: "el gravamen que de ella se seguia a mi real Hacienda" (author's translation).

11 *Despacho* (dispatch), Viecroy Marqués de Casafuerte, July 1, 1730, Governor Sandoval's inventory of the archives, Presidio Los Adaes, May 9, 1734, *Archivo General de México—Provincias Internas*, vol. 236, box 53.2, folder B, 113; Governor Winthuysen's remittance of the archives, December 7–9, 1741, Presidio Los Adaes, *BA*, 8:0734–0735.

12 *Interrogatorio* (Interrogatory) of *Testigo* (Witness), *Mateo Antonio de Ybarbo, español casado con Juana Lugarda Hernández, Soldado del presidio de los adays*, May 31, 1738, Residencia Proceedings of Governor Sandoval, Presidio Los Adaes, *AGM—Historia*, vol. 524, part 1, Catholic Archives of Texas (hereafter *CAT*), box 38, folder 4c, 140–41, transcription. Response to question 4: "Si algunos se Juian a los montes los hacia traer a las Misiones amonestandoles que alli era donde debían estar y que nunca les permitio el uso de sus Barbajes mitotes ni Juntas desordenadas" (author's translation). Mateo Ybarbo was married to Juana Lugarda Hernández, and they were the parents of Antonio Gil Ybarbo, who later founded present Nacogdoches in deep East Texas during the year 1779.

13 De la Teja, *San Antonio de Béxar*.

14 Book of baptisms, Mission San Antonio de Valero, entry no. 230, Juana Antonia Ybarbo, July 6, 1728, Daughters of the Republic of Texas Research Library at the Alamo (hereafter *DRT Library*), translations by John Ogden Leal, 39.

15 Ibid., entry no. 248, Juana Rosa, September 15, 1728, *DRT Library*, 41.

16 *CAT*, Austin. These records include similar baptisms of Karankawa children, presumably taken captive, at La Bahía.

17 Brian DeLay, "Blood Talk: Violence and Belonging in the Navajo–New Mexican Borderland," in *Contested Spaces*, 247.

18 Report, signed by seven missionaries outlining problems they faced developing the missions, March 18, 1730, Mission Los Adaes, *ACZ*, microfilm, roll 3, frame nos. 3938, 3940. The names of the other Indian nations that appeared on this report were the following: Ahugama, Sata, Sicasse, Juugumi, Thauassa, Parache, Faensa, Vilassi, Pascoguta, Sitimassa, Guassaz, Seg[?]sa, Lapissa, Guma, Maguguta, Yassa, Sacsima, Agute, Nadossa, Cubocace, Yssace, Thanacassa, achinais, Yojuanes, Dadoises, Mitoes, Sores, Cadocdacchos, Neicha, Nabidacho, Sanas, Mayeyes, Nacones, Cujanes, Theracaguases, Copanes, Pantias, Thiopanes, Thacamas, Pampopas, Pa[?], Ortenos, Pellaques, Pota[?], Payayas, and Pitayas; see also *Memoriales* (Petitions) and Letters of Fray Sevillano de Paredes, April 5, 1730, *BL*, carton 33, folder 31, 14–16.

19 Burton and Smith, *Colonial Natchitoches*, 11–12.

20 Report of the Missionaries, *ACZ*, ibid.; *Memoriales* and Letters, *BL*, ibid.

21 *Memoriales* (petitions) and letters of Fray Sevillano de Paredes, April 5, 1730, *BL*, carton 33, folder 31, 14–16: "Passandome a la Miss.n de Nacodoches, en ella no halle persona alg.a y Prosegui a la de los Aez. La que halle con las puertas de las Zeldas hechas pedazos; y la de la Ygl.a arrancada de sus quicios, toda robada p.or sus Yndios" (author's translation).

22 Father Muñoz, Inspection of Mission San Francisco [de Neycha], November 14, 1727, in Rev. Dr. Morales, "De la vida conventual a la vida misionera," 5, transcription: "solo vienen los indios cuando saben que se les han de dar pólvora, velas, ropa, etc." (author's translation).

23 After its transfer to San Antonio from East Texas, Mission San José was renamed San Juan Capistrano to avoid confusion with the larger mission already named San José.

24 Report, Governor Winthuysen on condition of presidios and missions in Texas, August 19, 1744, Presidio Los Adaes, *BA*, microfilm, 8:0796: "[The Bidais, Yadoces, and Texas Indians] Los que son muy diestros en el manejo de la flecha, y major del fusil del qual, y de sus adherents se proven estos en la colonia francesa" (first quotation) and "muy expertos en la caza del osso, y del venado, haziendo de este la gamuza, y sacando de aquel la manteca, con cuyos generos mantienen el comercio con franceses, a algo con los Españes" (second quotation; both author's translation).

25 Ibid.: "De estas tres naciones, los mas aplicados son los texas, pues estos hazen se labor, y siembran sus verduras, y las guarden, pero irreducibles todos a vida política, y â sugetarse â mission aviendose frustrado quantas dilixencias, a este fin" (author's translation).

26 Gary ClaytonAnderson, *The Indian Southwest, 1580–1830: Ethnogenesis and Reinvention* (Norman: University of Oklahoma Press, 1999), 71.

27 Friar Muñoz, Inspection of Mission Los Adaes, October 29, 1727, in Rev. Dr. Morales, "De la vida conventual a la vida misionera," 2, transcription: "Tiene esta dicha misión de San Miguel de los Adáis los aperos proporcionados de hachas, azadones, etc., para lo que tiene de labor que continuamente siembra tres almudes de maíz, unas veces coge la semilla y otras no. Tiene ganado mayor, veinte seis reses chico y grande que está al cuidado de los soldados, más tiene algunas cabalgaduras en que suelen ir los padres a visitar los indios en sus rancherías y transitar de una misión a otra. Más tiene una recua en que condicen las limosnas y está al cuidado del hermano procurador" (author's translation).

28 Anderson, *Indian Southwest*, 71.

29 Félix D. Almaráz Jr., *The San Antonio Missions and Their System of Land Tenure* (Austin: University of Texas Press, 1989), 2.

30 Friar Muñoz, Inspection of Mission Los Adaes, 8.

31 Ibid., 7: "Las naciones que están en el distrito de estas seis misiones que se llaman Asinay, vulgarmente Texas, se componen cada una como de doscientas personas, al parecer, porque ciertamente no se pueden numerar por estar tan esparcidos de manera que así a bulto habrá en las seis, mil y trescientas o cuatrocientos personas, poco más o menos. Estos siembran allá en sus ranchos sus milpitas, maíz, frijol y calabaza, de que de medio mantienen que lo más del tiempo andan a la caza y a la guerra a que son muy dados, sino todos los más de ellos" (author's translation).

32 Smith, "Account," November 6, 1719, visit among the Adaes Indians, 539.

33 Father Ildefonso Joseph Marmolejo, Certification of Baptismal Records and Report on Mission Dolores de los Ais, July 12, 1740, *ACZ*, roll 1, frame no. 2145: "que por el año de veinte y ocho ussando los Yndios de su livertad apetecida, aun esta Rancheria despoblado, hasta que el año de treinta y dos la solicitud y trabajo del onelo[?] Apostolico reduxo no solo estas sino nueve ô dies rancherias que oy se mantienen las mas de ellas en la distancia de legua y media . . . mantenien dose los pobres sin algun granero, atenidos solo â la solicitud de la caza" (author's translation).

34 Friar Muñoz, Inspection of Mission Los Adaes, October 29, 1727, in Rev. Dr. Morales, "De la vida conventual a la vida misionera," 1, 3–6.

35 Letter, Father Paredes to the king, College of Santa Cruz of Miracles of the City of Santiago, Querétaro, Mexico, August 25, 1728, *BP—BL*, carton 33, folder 531, 21–22, transcription.

36 Castañeda, *Our Catholic Heritage*, 3:125–26.

37 John L. Kessell, *Friars, Soldiers, and Reformers: Hispanic Arizona and the Sonora Mission Frontier, 1767–1856* (Tucson: University of Arizona Press, 1976), 7, 102–4, 107.

38 *Libro I, 1726–1731, en que assientan los Bautismos de los Indios de estas Misiones de San Antonio de Valero y de San José de Aguayo, CAT*, box 114, folder 3, entry nos. 168, 169, 170.

39 Book 2 of baptisms, 1807–24, *CAT*, box 113, folder 10, entry nos. 1–23.

40 The lack of complete integration of Caddos through baptism and other sacramental rites did not exclude Indians generally from incorporation into Spanish society at Presidio Los Adaes, since there were other Indians among the mostly *mestizo* (ethnically mixed Spanish and Indian) population at the fort.

41 The introduction of Spanish ranching to the Louisiana-Texas frontier contrasted the gradual transition from hunting-gathering to agriculture centuries before among indigenous societies. Anthropologists Douglas Price and Anne Gebauer argue that farming required "a totally new relationship with the environment," especially since it was "very labor intensive and much more time consuming"; quoted in Price and Gebauer, eds., *Last Hunters-First Farmers:*

New Perspectives on the Prehistoric Transition to Agriculture (Santa Fe, NM: School of American Research Press, 1995), 3–4, 8, who also argue that the last hunters *were* the first farmers, local peoples adopting the "ideas and products of cultivation and herding."

42 Ibid., 85; Burton, "Family and Economy," 55, 115, 137; Derbanne, "Report of the Post of Natchitoches," in Bridges and De Ville, "Natchitoches and the Trail," 256.

43 Burton, "Family and Economy," 293.

44 De la Teja, *San Antonio de Béxar*, 18.

45 Smith, *Caddo Indians*, 7–10; Meacham, "Population," 353 (table A1.1a: "Reported Population for Texas Indian Tribes—East Texas").

46 John, *Storms Brewed*, 165–66; Meacham, "Population," 353.

47 *Informe del gobernador Almazan al virey sobre el proyecto que tiene de pedir géneros al apoderado de los presidios*, October 24, 1724, Presidio San Antonio de Béxar, *ASFG*, UT-Austin, box 2Q251, vol. 10, 139, 141–42, transcription.

48 *Informe del gobernadorde San Antonio de Valero sobre comunicaciones con los franceses y la ayuda que suminstró a ese presidio de los Adaes*, March 24, 1724, Presidio San Antonio de Béxar, *ASFG*, box 2Q251, vol. 10, 113–14.

49 Letter, Gov. Fernando Pérez de Almazán to Viceroy Marqués de Casfuerte, July 11, 1726, Presidio San Antonio de Béxar, *BL*, *MDHMC*, carton 33, folder 532, 1–2.

50 *Informe del gobernador de San Antonio de Valero sobre comunicaciones con los franceses. . .* , March 24, 1724, Presidio de San Antonio de Béxar, *ASFG*, box 2Q251, vol. 10, 111, transcription: "de no haverse podído poner en corriente basttanttes siembras, y cosechas para manttener aquel Presidio por la enfermedad comun que se há padecido los dos veranos que han pasado desde su fundación, y por la insuperables dificultades que se ofrecen para conducír basttimen.s en la distancia de 400 leguas, y con tanttas rios, y arroyos tan inttransittables en sus crecienttes, que el año pasado impudieron el paso siete meses á cien cargas de arína y una partida de vacas, que por la grande detención seme perdío la mayor partte de ello, siendo an que tengo puesttas canoas en los Rios caudalosos, con que por tener algun recurso de basttimientos hastta que aquel Presidio logre cosecha para mantnerse me havia parecido convenientte no cerrar de todo puntto la comunicación con el de Nachitos, y tambíen por que los Religiosos han ocurrido á administtrarles los Santtos Sacramenttos, y decir les misa algunos días festivos, cuio consuelo han apreciado mucho los Franceses por no tener Minísttro Eclesiasttia" (author's translation).

51 Ibid., 111–13. The captain of Presidio Los Adaes, don Joseph Benito de Arroyo, fell gravely ill, which convinced the governor to grant him a passport to leave Los Adaes before winter arrived, an indication of the dire straits of the fort.

52 Different circumstances at polar opposites of the Texas province offer interesting comparisons with historian Brian DeLay's reference to "blood talk" on the Navajo–New Mexican borderlands in that the absence of such dialogue did not bode well for peace; see DeLay, "Blood Talk," 230, who defines "blood talk" as "dialogues about belonging performed not only through words but also through acts of violence and their attendant, urgent statements about who belongs to whom." However, DeLay states that the durability of Navajo–New Mexican relationships depended on a number of factors: (1) the absence of imperial rivals, (2) New Mexico's relatively isolated small colonial population, and (3) the absence of precious metals and unsuitability of most of the land for agriculture.

53 For initial settlement on the land in San Antonio, see Almaráz Jr., *San Antonio Missions*, 1012; de la Teja, *San Antonio de Béxar*.

54 Porter, *Their Lives*, 105.

55 Usner, *Indians, Settlers, and Slaves*, 6; Porter, *Their Lives*, 105, 109.

56 Socolow, "Introduction," 4–5.

57 Porter, *Their Lives*, 108. For background on women and Spanish law, see Jean A. Stuntz, *Hers, His, and Thiers: Community Property Law in Spain and Early Texas* (Lubbock: Texas Tech University Press, 2005).

58 For comparisons with French Natchitoches, see Burton, "Family and Economy," 25, 55; and with San Antonio, see de la Teja, *San Antonio de Béxar*, 122–23.

59 List of soldiers and inventory, Governor Bustillo y Zevallos, April 30, 1731, Presidio Los Adaes, *Archivo General de México—Provincias Internas*, in *CAT*, box 53, folder 2a, 29–31, transcription.

60 Letter, Gov. don Juan Antonio de Bustillo y Cevallos to Brigadier don Pedro de Rivera, May 24, 1731, Presidio Los Adaes, *AGM—Provincias Internas*, *CAT*, box 53, folder 2a, 18–20. The governor had waited until winter had passed before leaving La Bahía for deep East Texas on the eighth day of March because of the rigorous rains and the snow. The account book Governor Bustillo examined with his predecessor also revealed soldiers indebted to the governor for the sum of 6,853 pesos, while the inventory showed no gunpowder whatsoever available for the artillery.

61 Governor Bustillo y Zevallos, *AGM—Provincias Internas*, ibid. The word *truequen* was frequently used in Spanish archival documents.

62 *Bando*, Viceroy Marqués de Casafuerte, December 13, 1733, Mexico City, *NA*, UT-Austin, box 2Q292, vol. 1, 9, transcription.

63 Jackson and Foster, *Imaginary Kingdom*, 38nn72–73.

64 Timothy K. Perttula, *"The Caddo Nation": Archaeological and Ethnohistoric Perspectives* (Austin: University of Texas Press, 1992), 207–8.

65 Folmer, *Franco-Spanish Rivalry*, 291.

66 For comparison to frontier trading in British North America, see Daniel B. Thorp, "Doing Business in the Backcountry: Retail Trade in Colonial Rowan County, North Carolina," *William and Mary Quarterly* 48 (July 1991): 391–92.

67 Smith, "Account," 86.

68 Report, Fray Pedro Muñoz, *visitador*, December 1, 1727, *"Las Misiones de Texas en 1727,"* in Rev. Dr. Morales, "De la vida conventual a la vida misionera," 7.

CHAPTER 3

1 *NACCR*, 4, entry no. 8.

2 Letter, Lt. Joseph Gonzales to Gov. don Manuel de Sandoval, August 29, 1736, Presidio Los Adaes, *AGN—Historia*, in *MDHMC*, San Augustine, Texas, vol. 395, microfilm, box 5, 236v, 238, 238v, photostat; see also Hackett, *Pichardo's Treatise*, 3:488–91.

3 Marriage, April 8, 1736, Natchitoches, "after publication of bans," Jean Baptiste D'Herbanne of this parish, aged twenty-five, son of deceased Francois D'Herbanne and of Jeanne de la Grande Terre, habitants of this parish, and Victoire Marguerite Gonzales of the Spanish post of Adays, fifteen years, daughter of Messire Joseph Gonzales, general of the post, and Dame Marie Gertrude de la Cerda, Witnesses: Pierre Marets de la Tour and Jacques de la Chiase, *NACCR*, 4–5, entry no. 13. For a brief personal background of Lt. Joseph Gonzales, see Patricia R. Lemée, "Manuela Sanchez Navarro," *Natchitoches Genealogist* 20 (October 1995): 20.

4 Moorhead, *Presidio*, 44.

5 *Confesión* (confession in a legal proceeding), Lt. Gen. don Fermín de Ybiricu, June 6, 1737, Presidio Los Adaes, during *residencia* proceeding against former Governor Sandoval and appearing before Gov. Franquis de Lugo, residencia judge, *Archivo General de México—Historia*, vol. 524, *CAT*, Chancery of Austin, box 39, folder 2c, 551–54, and 574, transcription.

6 The regular clergy included the priests and friars who were members of the religious orders, most predominantly the Franciscan, Dominican, and Jesuit, while the secular clergy were the normal parish priests assigned to a cathedral or presidio chapel and subject to the direct authority of a bishop; see John F. Schwaller, "The Clergy," in *The Countryside in Colonial Latin America*, ed. Louisa Schell Hoberman and Susan Migden Socolow (Albuquerque: University of New Mexico Press, 1996): 123, 142.

7 Jay T. Harrison, "Franciscan Missionary Theory and Practice in Eighteenth-Century New Spain: The Propaganda Fide Friars in the Texas Missions, 1690–1821" (PhD diss., Catholic University of America, 2012), 3, 10; Harrison,

"Negociando la supervivencia en la frontera de Texas: Grupos indígenas en las misiones Franciscanas," in Camañes and Rex Galindo, *La frontera en el mundo hispánico*, 483–502; José Gabriel Martínez Serna, "Vineyards in the Desert: The Jesuits and the Rise and Decline of an Indian Town in New Spain's Northeastern Borderlands" (PhD diss., Southern Methodist University, 2009); Galindo, "Propaganda Fide"; and Erick Langer, "Missions and the Frontier Economy: The Case of the Franciscan Missions among the Chiriguanos, 1845–1930," in *The New Latin American Mission History*, ed. Erick Langer and Robert H. Jackson (Lincoln: University of Nebraska Press, 1995), 51.

8 Ann Twinam, "Honor, Sexuality, and Illegitimacy in Colonial Spanish America," in *Sexuality and Marriage in Colonial Latin America*, ed. Asunción Lavrin (Lincoln: University of Nebraska Press, 1989), 123. For an exhaustive discussion of purity of blood and the transfer of the Spanish inquisition from Spain to Mexico, see María Elena Martínez, *Genealogical Fictions: Limpieza de Sangre, Religion, and Gender in Colonial Mexico* (Stanford: Stanford University Press, 2008).

9 Historian Amy (Meschke) Porter did not come across wills for Spanish women native to Los Adaes. Many years after this fort's abandonment in 1773, a few wills appear for Adaeseñas when they resided at San Antonio de Béxar; see Amy Meschke, "Women's Lives through Women's Wills in the Spanish and Mexican Borderlands, 1750–1846" (PhD diss., Southern Methodist University, 2005). See also Porter, *Their Lives*.

10 Charles Edwards O'Neill, *Church and State in French Colonial Louisiana: Policy and Politics to 1732* (New Haven, CT: Yale University Press, 1966), 240.

11 Letter, Lt. Joseph Gonzales to Governor Sandoval, Presidio Los Adaes, *AGN—Historia*, vol. 395, microfilm, box 5, 236v, 238, 238v, photostat. "el dia ocho del mes de Abril quisieron apurar mu paciencia tres franceses acaudillado de Baptista Berban, quines con toda osadia se llevaron á mi hija Victoria â quien solicitara por muger en lexitimo matrimonio el referido Berban" (first quotation); "baliéndose del Reverendo Jesuita, autor y movil detodos inquietudes quien interponiendo la autoridad del Reverendo Padre Presidente quiso que este me la pidiese para dicho Berban" (second quotation); "tanto por la desigualdad entre los desposados" (third quotation; all author's translations).

12 Lt. Joseph Gonzales, ibid., *AGN—Historia*. "pues no digo el que es notoria su hidalguia, sino aunque fuese el mas noble frances resesaría[?] el que mi sangre se mesclase con la suya" (author's translation). See also the full text of Lieutenant Gonzales's letter translated in Hackett, *Pichardo's Treatise*, 3:488–91; see also Father Francisco Vallejo's similar version of the events in his own letter to the governor dated that same day of August 29 in ibid., 3:84–85. The controversy surrounding the D'Herbanne-Gonzales wedding also appears in

Phares, *Cavalier*, 224–25, which states that the soldiers Lieutenant Gonzales dispatched toward Natchitoches "found no trace of the eloping couple."

13 Seed, *To Love, Honor, and Obey in Colonial Mexico: Conflicts over Marriage Choice, 1574–1821* (Stanford: Stanford University Press, 1988), 5–6, 12, 17, 156, also says that wealth, privilege, and improvement of social status were the roots of the demand for equality of marriage partners. See also Porter, *Their Lives*, 109. For concern over equality of marriage partners in late eighteenth-century Spanish Texas, see Jesús F. de la Teja, "Why Urbano and María Trinidad Can't Get Married: Social Relations in Late Colonial San Antonio," *Southwestern Historical Quarterly* 112 (October 2008): 120–46.

14 Seed, *To Love, Honor, and Obey*, 2–3, draws comparisons between Romeo and Juliet's tragedy and the marriage of Gerónimo Valverde and Juana Herrera in Mexico City. Seed notes that while the Mexico City stories she describes and Shakespeare's play both occurred at the close of the sixteenth century, the dramas unfolded in vastly different cultures. The Catholic Church in colonial Mexico played a much stronger role in seeing that young couples got married, while Friar Laurence's part in England was not as a church official who could use the full weight of the institution to protect the children from their parents' opposition or prevent Juliet's father from forcing her to marry another person.

15 Marriage, July 17, 1736, Natchitoches, after publication of bans, Francois LeMoine, soldier, *dit* La Vidette, age forty, son of Francois LeMoine and Marguerite Gentin of the town of Amboise, diocese of Tours, and Jeanne Victoria Garcie, previously of the Spanish post of Adays, living two years in this parish, aged thirteen, daughter of Pierre Garcie, soldier, and of Marie Joseph Condee, Witness: Pierre Marets de la Tour, officer of Mr. Tourangeau, Claud Bertrand *dit* (alias) Dauphine, and Pierre Alorges, both sergeants, *NACCR*, 4, entry no. 8. On the background of the LeMoyne brothers, see Folmer, *Franco-Spanish Rivalry*, 216–17; and Folmer, "Report," 86n10.

16 Louis R. Nardini, *My Historic Natchitoches, Louisiana and Its Environment: A History of Natchitoches, Louisiana and the Neutral Strip Area of the State of Louisiana and Its Inhabitants* (Natchitoches, LA: Nardini, 1963), 61, 68, makes the claim, if Nardini is to be believed, that the couple eloped and the procession made from Natchitoches to Mission Los Adaes occurred sometime in July. Nardini mentioned the year 1735, but the marriage actually occurred in 1736. Also, Nardini claims that despite any misgivings, Lieutenant Gonzales might have had, he profited from his own daughter's marriage to Jean Baptiste D'Herbanne, having presented his son-in-law sometime in 1740 or 1741 with a sack of gold coins with instructions that these were for her daughter's dowry. Lieutenant Gonzales, Nardini said, arrived in Natchitoches for the baptism of his third grandchild.

17 For comparisons, see Andrew Sluyter, *Black Ranching Frontiers: African Cattle Herders of the Atlantic World, 1500–1900* (New Haven, CT: Yale University Press, 2012).

18 Nardini, *My Historic Natchitoches*, 61.

19 James L. McCorkle Jr., "Los Adaes and the Borderlands Origins of East Texas," *East Texas Historical Journal* 22, no. 2 (1984): 9.

20 Marriage, July 27, 1737, Natchitoches, after publication of three bans in this parish and in the parish of Adayes, marriage of Francois de Torres, soldier of the post of Adayes, twenty-five years old, son of Marc de Torres and Luice Garcia of the kingdom of Leon, and . . . Xaviere Dominique Flores, widow of Joseph De Al Barado, seventeen years old, actually living in this parish, daughter of Christophe Flores and Nicole de Boustamante of St. Louis du Potosi, who has for godfather Pedro de Sierra, corporal of the garrison of Adayes, and for godmother Nicole Cordoba, *NACCR*, 20–21, entry no. 158.

21 Marriage, September 22, 1738, Natchitoches, after publication of bans at Natchitoches and at the mission of St. Michel des Adayes, Antoine Rodrigue *dit* Pagnau, a Spanish *mulâtre* . . . and . . . Marie Marcelle, Indian slave of Signora Doña Lucretia, Witnesses: de la Chaise, de la Tour, D'erbanne, and Pedro Reinevint[?], *NACCR*, 22, entry no. 167.

22 Marriage, July 6, 1733, Natchitoches, *NACCR*, 18–19, entry no. 144.

23 Seed, *To Love, Honor, and Obey*, 24–25. For categories of racial difference, see Magnus Mörner, *Race Mixture in the History of Latin America* (Boston: Little, Brown, 1967), 13, who emphasizes that even Spain itself "was anything but ethnically homogeneous" from the ancient Greeks, Phoenicians, Celts, Carthaginians, Romans, Visigoths, Jews, Arabs, Berbers, Gypsies, and medieval slaves of different origins. See also Carla Mendiola, "El mestizaje en la frontera de Texas durante el siglo XVIII," in *La frontera en el mundo hispánico*, coord. Porfirio Sanz Camañes and David Rex Galindo (Quito, Ecuador: Abya Yala, 2014), 292. For discussion of "triracial communities" and ethnic mixing in North America (which also apply to French Natchitoches and Spanish Los Adaes), see Nash, "Hidden History," 948.

24 Seed, *To Love, Honor, and Obey*, 29, 155; Cheryl English Martin, *Governance and Society in Colonial Mexico: Chihuahua in the Eighteenth Century* (Stanford: Stanford University Press, 1996), 15, 125 (quotation), 126–28. For the complicated racial terminology used in colonial Mexico's northern frontier, see Barnes, Naylor, and Polzer, *Northern New Spain*, 90–93.

25 For discussion of middle groups generally in rural societies, see Lowell Gudmundson, "Middle Groups," in *The Countryside in Colonial Latin America*, ed. Louisa Schell Hoberman and Susan Migden Socolow (Albuquerque: University of New Mexico Press, 1996), 147–48, 162–64.

26 See de la Teja, *San Antonio de Béxar*, 24–25, who argues that the few Europeans in Spanish Texas "do not appear to have enjoyed higher status than those individuals in the predominantly creole population." In "Béxareño" society, according to de la Teja, the designation "Indian" included both Texas natives and Hispanicized Indians from other provinces in New Spain. Béxareños also applied terms such as *gentiles*, *enemigos*, and *bárbaros*, as well as tribal names to the surrounding unacculturated Indian populations. The term *negro* appears infrequently in San Antonio de Béxar and is usually associated with slavery. *Mestizo* (technically the offspring of Spanish-Indian unions), *mulatto* (Spanish-black mixtures), and *coyote* (Indian-mestizo unions) were often used interchangeably. The term *lobo* (supposedly Indian-African unions) appeared more frequently in the late eighteenth century. Factors on the frontier restricted the effects of the caste system. De la Teja argues that Indian hostilities and physical isolation drew communities together, while the scarcity of potential mates within one's own caste also weakened ethnic barriers. In addition, there was little consistency from cleric to cleric, or even a single priest, designating ethnicity in birth, marriage, and burial records.

27 For discussion of occupations among castas, see Seed, *To Love, Honor, and Obey*, 24–25, 146, 151, 156, who also discusses that in the sixteenth and seventeenth centuries, the casta labels were synonymous with illegitimacy. By the eighteenth century, many families that became socially mobile were castas, and the Spanish aristocracy began demanding equality of marriage partners in their backgrounds and prospects. See also Martin, *Governance and Society*, 145.

28 See La Vere, "Between Kinship and Capitalism," 205–6, which specifically mentions the lack of Spanish kinship relations with the Caddos and the Wichitas.

29 Barr, "Diplomacy of Gender," 429–30, 432–33; Barr, "From Captives to Slaves," 30. For comparison with intermarriage of Plains Indians, which not only created a "middle ground" but also solidified elite families' privileged access to markets and prestige goods, see Hämäläinen, "Rise and Fall," 849.

30 O'Neill, *Church and State*, 247, 254, 288.

31 See Burton, "Family and Economy," 59, which downplays Franco-Spanish intermarriage as insignificant based on their small number and ignores political, economic, and social links between French Natchitoches and Spanish Los Adaes through baptism and church celebrations. See also Lemee, "Tios and Tantes," 342, 350–51, which gives more weight to intermarriage of the French with the Spaniards and Caddos based on frontier trade; and Burton and Smith, *Colonial Natchitoches*, 20.

32 Marriage, June 2, 1754, Natchitoches, after publication of two bans and dispensation of the third, Manuel Antoine Bermudes, a native of St. Jean [San Juan] Dorron, archbishopric of St. Jacques [Santiago] de Gritierce, Kingdom

of Spain, legitimate son of Dominique Bermudes and of Marie Joseph de Soto, and Marie des Neges de St. Denis, native of this parish, legitimate daughter of the deceased Louis Jucherot de St. Denis, chevalier and commandant of this post during his life, and Dame Manuel Sanchez Navarre, widow of the deceased St. Denis; consent given by the Spanish missionary, Father Pierre [Pedro], who was sick and could not participate in the ceremony; Father Eustache, officiating, also signed: Friar Pedro Ramirez, no other witnesses named, *NACCR*, 90, entry no. 731.

33 Petition, Manuel Antonio de Soto Bermúdez, May 20, 1754, Natchitoches, before Commandant César de Blanc to marry Maria de Nieves des St. Denis, *BA*, 9:0497–0498, which the French commandant granted; "Timeline: Life of Manuel Antonio de Soto y Bermúdez (January 11, 1720–September 1799)," copy in author's possession provided by Troy de Soto, descendant, April 2003, Baton Rouge, Louisiana.

34 Letter, Marqués de Aranda, *fiscal*, to don Domingo Valcarel, *auditor de la Guerra*, January 20, 1756, Mexico City; *decreto*, Conde de Revilla Gigedo, viceroy, February 19, 1756, Mexico City; *concuerda*, signed by Joseph de Gorraez, February 21, 1756, Mexico City, in proceedings relative to desertion of Chirinos, Losoya, Esparza, and de Soto, *BA*, microfilm, 9:0643–0646.

35 Letter, Marqués de Amarillas, viceroy, to Governor Barrios Jáuregui, February 23, 1756, Mexico City, *BA*, microfilm, 9:0673: "para la captura, y remision âesta carzel del citado Soto, y amoneste conla severidad que combiene â Chirinos, y esparza, se abstengan de causar inquietudes entre los vezinos . . . previniendo alos vezinos nosedejen contanta facilidad inducir aque hagan los ocursos sinqueprimero, se inteligencien" (author's translation).

36 Petition, Manuel Antonio de Soto Bermúdez, March 21, 1763, Presidio Los Adaes, *BA*, microfilm, 10:0160: "en lo que mi ignorancia haviere delinquido, mi restitucion aeste Reino. Nuestra Señor guarde la importante vida de vss.a en la maior felicidad dilatados años. Real Pres.o delos Adaes y Marzo 21, de 1763. Manuel de Soto" (author's translation).

37 Governor Martos Navarrete's response to de Soto's petition, March 21, 1763, Presido Los Adaes, *BA*, microfilm, 10:0160–0161: "no me es facultativo el resolver sobre este assumpto (no obstante el Real Yndulto por mi publicado) por tener esta parte Jurado domicilio en Reyno estraño y ademas tener caussa pendiente en este Archivo por mi antescesor don Jacinto de Barrios y Jáuregui" (author's translation).

38 Testimony, *Marcos Losoia, vecino actual de este Presidio* [Los Adaes], twenty-one years old more or less, he did not sign his own name because he said he did not know how, Governor Martos Navarrete signed for him in the presence of the *testigos de mi asistencia, Fran.co Ant.o Solis*, April 6, 1763, Presidio Los Adaes, *BA*, microfilm, 10:0164–0165: "que dhos Vezinos movidos deque

dho Señor d.n Jacinto [Barrios Jáuregui] les havia impedido el paso de comersiar con los Yndios por querer abarcar solo su merced cueros y demas cambalache de Yndios, le presentaron un escripto, sinque para el los induciera dho don Manuel, q.e ratificacion no seleha leido ninguno asta haora que la oyo" (author's translation).

39 *Decreto*, Fiscal, June 17, 1763, Mexico City; *Decreto*, Auditor de Guerra, July 11, 1763, Mexico City; *Concuerda*, Joseph de Gorraez, July 13, 1763, Mexico City; *concuerda*, Governor Martos Navarrete, January 16, 1764, Presidio Los Adaes, *BA*, microfilm, 10:0197–0198.

40 Marriage, April 7, 1755, Natchitoches, after three bans, marriage of Manuel Y Varvo [Barbo], a native of the Adayes, legitimate son of Mathieu [Mateo] Y Barbo, a native of Mexique, and of Jeanne Hernández, a native of Adaye . . . and . . . Manuella Seyena, a native of Adays, legitimate daughter of deceased Joseph Seyena, a native of Mexicque, and of Jeanne de dieu Rodrigue, Witness: Manuel Soto; *NACCR*, 91, entry no. 733.

41 Marriage, June 9, 1750, Natchitoches, *NACCR*, 46, entry no. 355.

42 Phares, *Cavalier*, 232–33. Lieutenant Gonzales did not mention Lieutenant General Ybricu's activities in his letters to Governor Sandoval in 1735–36, nor did the Franciscan missionaries who also wrote the governor during this time. Lieutenant Gonzales just told the governor to hurry back to Presidio Los Adaes as quickly as possible.

43 Asunción Lavrin, "Sexuality in Colonial Mexico: A Church Dilemma," in *Sexuality and Marriage*, 79; and Lavrin, *Sexuality and Marriage*, 3.

44 Seed, *To Love, Honor, and Obey*, 118–19, 123, 126–27.

45 Ibid., 69, 127–28. For Seed's discussion of the shift from honor as virtue to honor as status, see especially pages 91, 96, 98–99, 101–2, and 106–7.

46 Declaration, Lt. Joseph Gonzales, February 17, 1753, Presidio Los Adaes, Spanish War Council and Estates' investigation of French advance into Texas, *BA*, Center for American History, University of Texas at Austin, box 2S27, 7v; also appears in Hackett, *Pichardo's Treatise*, 4:42–43.

47 Meeting, War Council and Estates, January 22, 1754, Mexico City, *BA*, microfilm, 9:0472.

48 Baptism, Louise Lage, J___ 30, 1730, Natchitoches, born the twenty-ninth of same month, "Perre Campo" missionary from the Adailles [Adaes] officiating, in *NACCR*, 64, entry no. 522.

49 Baptism, Marie Louise Manne, September 29, 1737, Natchitoches, legitimate daughter of Francois Manne and Jeanne D'Herbanne, godparents: Jean Baptiste D'Herbanne and Victoria Marguerite Gonzales, *NACCR*, 12, entry no. 83. Victoria did not know how to sign her own name and instead marked an *x* by her name; baptism, Louis Francois, *négrillon* [black child], June 15, 1744, Natchitoches, born on June 13 and son of Nanette, slave of widow St. Denis,

godparents: Louis Marion and Victoire Marguerite Gonzales, *NACCR*, 31, entry no. 245.

50 Baptism, Louis La Malathi, December 21, 1739, Natchitoches, born on December 20 and legitimate son of Louis de la Malathi, native of St. Poirier, diocese of Montauban, habitant of this post, and of Jeanne Victorie Garcia, a Spaniard, godparents: Henry Trichle and Therese Clare [Clairmont], *NACCR*, 23, entry no. 177; Henry Trichle's son was baptized on May 6, 1737, in Natchitoches, *NACCR*, 11, entry no. 72; baptism, Marie Francoise Malathi, November 29, 1741, Natchitoches, legitimate daughter of Louis Jobard *dit* (nickname in place of surname) Malathi, native of St. Porier near Montauban, and Jeanne Victorie, Spanish, godparents: Guillaume Chever and Marie Francoise Le Vasseur, *NACCR*, 26, entry no. 203; baptism, Therese Malatie, June 19, 1744, Natchitoches, legitimate daughter of Louis Malatie and Jeanne Victoire [Garcia], godparents: Jacques Le Vasseur and Therese Barbier, *NACCR*, 31, entry no. 245.

51 Baptism, Louis Pierre, May 15, 1729, Natchitoches, *négrillon*, property of Monsieur de St. Denis and son of Caton and Manon, negroes, godparents: Mr. Pierre Coutoleau Duplessis and Jeanne D'arbanne, *bourgeois*, *NACCR*, 63, entry no. 516; baptism, Marie, July 28, 1729, Natchitoches, born on July 26, property of Mr. de St. Denis and the daughter of César and Marie, negroes, godparents: Henry Le Bel, *bourgeois* of Natchitoches, and Marianne Marchand also of the same place, *NACCR*, 64, entry no. 521; baptism, Marguerite, born May 14, 1729, property of Sieur Duplessis and Tourangeau, *bourgeois* of Natchitoches, legitimate daughter of Janot and Fanchon, negroes, godparents: Pierre Fosse and Louise Marguerite de Juchereaux de St. Denis, *NACCR*, 64, entry no. 519. On the background of Jean Baptiste Derbanne's family, see Lemee, "Tios and Tantes," 350–51n40.

52 Baptism, Pierre, May 15, 1729, *négrillon*, born on April 8, son of Ane?, *négre*, and of Fanilian, *négresse*, belonging to Sieur derbanne, godparents: Pierre Coutaulas Duplessis and Jeanne Darbanne, *NACCR*, 63, entry no. 513; baptism, Louise, May 15, 1729, daughter of Jasmin and Marie, negroes belonging to Mr. Darbanne, godparents: Mr. Derbanne and Mlle. Louise Marguerite de Juchereau [de St. Denis], *NACCR*, 63, entry no. 514.

53 Baptism, Marie Louise, May 20, 1729, Natchitoches, Osage Indian, about twenty years, property of Francois Virad, *bourgeois* at Natchitoches, godparents: Pierre Fossé and Louise Marguerite de Juchero, wife of said Duplessis, *bourgeois* of the same place, *NACCR*, 64, entry no. 520; baptism, Margueritte, August 6, 1735, age four, Indian female of Messire Louis de St. Denys, commandant, and *endoyée* at three months of age, godparents: Pierre de la Tour, officer, and Dame Emmanuele Sanches de Navarre, *NACCR*, 6, entry no. 27.

54 Baptism, Marie Therese, September 11, 1740, an Indian of the Cannecy nation, aged seven or eight years, property of Mr. de St. Denis, godparents: Jean Flores (x) of the parish of the Adaies and Marie Therese Fleur (x), *NACCR*, 24, entry no. 187. *Canneci* was the French-Caddo name for Lipan Apache slaves.

55 Hans W. Baade, "The Law of Slavery in Spanish Louisiana, 1769–1803," in *Louisiana's Legal Heritage*, ed. Edward F. Haas (Pensacola: Perdido Bay Press, 1983), 48–49, 54.

56 Porter, *Their Lives*; Martina Will de Chaparro, *Death and Dying in New Mexico* (Albuquerque: University of New Mexico Press, 2007), 70–72.

57 Burial, Xavier Cortinas, August 26, 1737, Natchitoches, *NACCR*, 18, entry no. 135. See also *AGM—Historia*, vol. 524, *CAT*, box 38, folder 4c, which lists Francisco Xavier Cortinas, son of Juan and a native of the Villa de Saltillo, twenty-three years old, recruited from Coahuila as a soldier and entered Presidio Los Adaes in July 1736. Cortinas quite possibly became a deserter shortly thereafter.

58 Burial, Louis Jucherot de St. Denis, June 12, 1744, Natchitoches, aged seventy years, Chevalier of St. Louis, commandant of the Fort of Jean Baptiste, who died on the eleventh of the same month, witnesses: Juero Bonet [Justo Boneo y Morales, governor of Texas], Father Francisco Vallejo, and Verchus de Terrepuy, *NACCR*, 48, entry no. 369. See also Bolton, *Texas*, 41; and Lemée, "Tios and Tantes: Familial and Political Relationships at Natchitoches and the Spanish Colonial Frontier," 354.

59 Barr, "Diplomacy of Gender" 408–10, 430; Juliana Barr, "The 'Seductions' of Texas: The Political Language of Gender in the Conquests of Texas, 1690–1803" (PhD diss., University of Wisconsin–Madison, 1999), 51–52, 55, 57–58; Santos, *Aguayo Expedition*, 71, 81. For background on Our Lady of Pilar, see Juan Gasca Saló, *Libro del Pilar* (Zaragosa, Spain: Imprímase con licencia eclesiástica, séptima edición, 2001), 12–13; Wifredo Rincón Garcia, *El Pilar de Zaragoza* (León, Spain: Editorial Everest); and Tomás Parra Sánchez, *Diccionario de los Santos: Historia, Atributos y Devoción Popular* (Mexico City: San Pablo, 1997), 102.

60 Barr, "Diplomacy of Gender," 412.

61 Charlene Villaseñor Black, "St. Anne Imagery and Maternal Archetypes in Spain and Mexico," in Allan Greer and Jodi Bilinkoff, eds., *Colonial Saints: Discovering the Holy in the Americas* (New York: Routledge, 2003), 13–14, 17.

62 Letter, Joseph Eugenio Goyeneche to Governor of Texas, December 15, 1756, Madrid, *BA*, microfilm, roll 9, frame no. 0004.

63 One archival source mentions Domingo and Manuel Chirinos, recruited in 1737 (*AGN—Historia, CAT*, box 38, folder 4c, 176–80), but this same document later indicates they entered their plaza at Presidio Los Adaes in December

1735 (*AGN—Historia, CAT*, box 39, folder 2c, 596). Domingo and Manuel were listed in the Spanish archives as "sons of Lazaro" from Saltillo.

64 For discussion of mestizaje, social status, and the phenomenon of "passing" or "whitening," see Weber, *Spanish Frontier*, 328; Chipman, *Spanish Texas*, 189; de la Teja, *San Antonio de Béxar*, 26–27; Martin, *Governance and Society*, 125; and Seed, *To Love, Honor, and Obey*, 25.

65 *Lista, y relacion jurada que yoDn. Juan Anttonio de Bustillo y Zevallos, Governador de esta Provincia de Thexas hago de los Oficiales, y soldados de este Presidio de Nta. Sra. Del Pilar de los Adais para remitir a el Exmo. Señor Virrey de esta Nueba España en cumplim.to de la Ordenanza Veintte y quatro del Reglamentto en la forma siguiente, AGM—Provincias Internas,* vol. 236, *CAT*, box 53, folder 2a, 32–34, transcription.

66 *Lista y relacion,* ibid., *AGM—Provincias Internas.* A *coyote* was someone believed to be a mixture between an Indian and a mestizo or from Indian and mulatto ancestry. A *lobo* was a person supposedly of black and Indian ancestry, while *indio* (Indian) referred to anyone from an Indian nation in New Spain but likely acculturated. During the eighteenth century, the term *nation* was synonymous with ethnicity, and the casta system of labels was applied broadly to people of low status in Spanish colonial society.

67 Letter, Governor don Juan Antonio de Bustillo y Zevallos to Brigadier General don Pedro de Rivera, May 25, 1731, Presidio Los Adaes, *AGI—Provincias Internas, CAT*, box 53, folder 2a, 21–22, transcription.

68 H. F. Gregory, George Avery, Aubra L. Lee, and Jay C. Blaine, "Presidio Los Adaes: Spanish, French, and Caddoan Interaction on the Northern Frontier," *Historical Archaeology* 38 (2004): 65, 69–70. See also Diana DiPaolo Loren, "Colonial Dress at the Spanish Presidio of Los Adaes," *Southern Studies: An Interdisciplinary Journal of the South* 7 (Spring 1996): 55, 59, who argues that the type of clothing at Los Adaes reflected a new identity and style that "was uniquely Adaeseño—not quite Spanish, French, Native American, but a true mixture that bespoke of social and political relationships in that particular context."

69 Gregory, Avery, Lee, and Blaine, "Presidio Los Adaes," 65, 69–70. See also George Avery, "Economic Relations among the Spanish, French, and Caddoan Peoples at Los Adaes, an Eighteenth Century Capital of Texas," paper presented at the 1997 Society for Historical Archaeology Annual Meeting, Corpus Christi, Texas, January 8–12, 1997, cited in Avery, *Los Adaes Station Archaeology Program, 1997 Archaeology Annual Report* (Natchitoches: Department of Social Sciences, Northwestern State University of Louisiana, June 1997), 212–17.

70 Diana DiPaolo Loren, "The Intersections of Colonial Policy and Colonial Practice: Creolization on the Eighteenth-Century Louisiana/Texas Frontier,"

Historical Archeology 34, no. 3 (2000): 85–98; Mendiola, "El mestizaje en la frontera," 301.

71 Richard W. Slatta, "Spanish Colonial Military Strategy and Ideology," in Guy and Sheridan, *Contested Ground*, 95.

CHAPTER 4

1 Letter, Lt. Joseph Gonzalez to Governor don Manuel de Sandoval of Texas, August 29, 1736, Presidio Los Adaes, *AGN—Historia*, vol. 395, microfilm, box 5, 240: "la fatiga que yo tube en vencer, y combenser á toda esta compañía para que diesen dhos poderes . . . estavan resueltos á no dar sus poderes hasta que V.S. les ajustase sus quentas, y les satisfasiese lo que podia deberles" (author's translation).

2 Letter, Fray Father Francisco Vallejo to Governor Manuel de Sandoval, March 9, 1735, Mission San Miguel de los Adaes, *AGN—Historia*, in *MDHMC*, vol. 395, microfilm, box 5, 211v.

3 Letter, Pedro de Rivera to Viceroy Juan de Acuña, July 21, 1731, Mexico City, *AGM—Provincias Internas*, *CAT*, box 53, folder 2a, 24–25, transcription.

4 Susan M. Deeds, *Defiance and Deference in Mexico's Colonial North: Indians under Spanish Rule in Nueva Vizcaya* (Austin: University of Texas Press, 2003), 56.

5 Letter, Rivera to Viceroy Acuña, July 21, 1731, Mexico City, *AGM—Provincias Internas*, 26–27, transcription: "exterminar el abusso introducido de adelantarles por años los suplimentos á todos los soldados" (author's translation).

6 Kiser, *Borderlands of Slavery*, 1–14, contains a splendid discussion about the rise of peonage in New Spain.

7 Letter, Lt. José Gonzalez to Governor Sandoval, April 14, 1735, Presidio Los Adaes, *AGN—Historia*, *MDHMC*, vol. 395, microfilm, box 5, 230v–231v; letter, Lieutenant Gonzalez to Governor Sandoval, November 12, 1735, Presidio Los Adaes, *AGN—Historia*, *MDHMC*, 232v–234v; letter, Fray Father Ignacio Antonio Ciprian to Governor Sandoval, December 4, 1735, Mission Nuestra Señora de los Dolores de los Ais, *AGN—Historia*, *MDHMC*, 225.

8 Letter, Lieutenant Gonzalez to Governor Sandoval, April 29, 1736, Presidio Los Adaes, *AGN—Historia*, *MDHMC*, vol. 395, microfilm, box 5, 240v–243: "tengo prevenido â V.S. del devito que se ha contraido con los franceses por los bastimientos necesarios . . . procure V.S. benir bien ajornado para satisfacer â los acreedores, â quienes se debe la cantidad de casi quatrocientos pesos" (author's translation).

9 Dispatch, don Juan Antonio Visaron y Eguiarreta, Archbishop of México City and of the Viceroy's Council, January 24, 1736, Mexico City, *BA*, microfilm, 8:0395–0396.

10 Letter, Lieutenant Gonzalez to Governor Sandoval, August 29, 1736, Presidio Los Adaes, *AGN—Historia*, *MDHMC*, 243–44: "me ha sido preciso prestarseles â algunos soldados para que medio taparan su desnudez" (author's translation).

11 Letter, Fray Father Ciprian to Governor Sandoval, November 15, 1735, Mission Los Ais, *AGN—Historia*, *MDHMC*, vol. 395, microfilm, box 5, 223v; letter, Fray Father Ciprian to Governor Sandoval, March 14, 1736, Mission Los Ais, *AGN—Historia*, 226v; letter, Lieutenant Gonzalez to Governor Sandoval, August 29, 1736, Presidio Los Adaes, *AGN—Historia*, 241–41v, 243–44.

12 Petition, *el teniente de la compania del Real presidio de Nuestra Señora del Pilar de los Adaes* [Joseph Cayetano de Vergara], *el cabo de escuadra Phelipe Bermudes y los soldados Juan de Mora, Salvador de Esparza, Francisco de la Serda, Andres Sanches*, appeared before don Antonio Francisco de Jáuregui Urrutia, interim governor of Texas, October 5, 1737, Royal Presidio of San Antonio de Bejar, *BA*, microfilm, roll 8, frame nos. 0479–0480.

13 Petition, ibid., *BA*, 8:0480–0481: "dijo que no obstante de no tener mas quelo que nezesita para su compañía, les dara todo lo que pudiere como lo ahecho antes de haora por orn. Verbal de . . . Dn. Carlos de Franquis mediante a no haver tenido abio ninguno que darles" (author's translation).

14 When a new governor assumed command in either San Antonio de Béxar or Presidio Los Adaes, he normally reviewed the account books with his predecessor. The books were then sent to Mexico City. Generally, the transfer of power between governors was peaceful, with the exception of Gov. don Carlos Franquis de Lugo, who had former Gov. don Manuel de Sandoval punished and imprisoned at Presidio Los Adaes in 1737.

15 Gov. don Juan Antonio de Bustillo y Zevallos, "Relación de las quentas que los oficiales y soldados de dho. Presidio [Los Adaes] han tenido hasta el ultimo dia del mes de Abril de este Pres.te año [1731] con D.n Melchor de Mediavilla y Ascona, Gov.or y Capittan Gral que fue de dha Provincia con su assistenz.a y la de dhos. soldados, y a sacar estracto relacion de ellas para remittirla al exmo. Señor Virrey," May 2, 1731, Presidio Los Adaes, *AGN—Provincias Internas*, *BP—BL*, carton 33, folder 532, 6–11, photocopy, *MDHMC*, San Augustine, Texas. Governor Bustillo y Cevallos made this list with the assistance of former governor Mediavilla Ascona.

16 Moorhead, *Presidio*, 204–5.

17 *Libro de cuentas*, February 17–March 6, 1739, Presidio Los Adaes, *AGN—Provincias Internas*, *MDHMC*, microfilm, box 7, vol. 182, 9 (Alférez Joseph Gonzalez), 18 (Matheo Ybarbo), 20 (Phelipe Bermudes), 44 (Pedro de Sierra), 56

(Cristóbal de Santiago), 96 (Domingo Chirino), 103 (Manuel Chirino), and 107 (Juan de Mora); *Excesos en las cuentas de Angel Martos y Navarrete*, January 1, 1759–August 23, 1767, Presidio Los Adaes, *AGI—Guadalajara* 511, Old Spanish Missions Research Library (OSMRL), Our Lady of the Lake University, microfilm, reel 4, doc. 112, 1–19. These excesses show the type of goods and the costs that Governor Martos Navarrete charged annually, not for each individual soldier as in the other documents; *Libro de cuentas de los soldados del Real Presidio de Nra. S.ora de los Adaes desttacados en este* [Presidio] *de San Antonio de Béxar*, January 1, 1771–December 31, 1771, San Antonio de Béxar, *BA*, UT-Austin, box 2S31, 48 (Antonio Gonzalez), 138 (Sgt. Domingo Chirinos), 149 (Francisco de la Zerda), 151 (Agustín Murillo), 154 (Vicente Gonzales), 178 (Joachin Ruiz), 219 (Juan Chirinos), 242 (Pedro Gonzales), and 251 (Lt. Joseph Gonzalez).

18 Power of attorney from the officers and soldiers for collection of annual salaries done before Lieutenant Bergara of Presidio Los Adaes on January 24, 1738, and given to Governor Orobio y Bazterra, March 8, 1738, Presidio San Antonio de Béxar, *BA*, microfilm, roll 8, frame nos. 0488–0489, full text: "en visto de los poderes q. otorgaron los o[?] veinte y quarto dias deel mes de Henero del corriente año [1738] ântte D.n Joseph Cayetano de Bergara, Then.te deel R. Presidio de Nra. S.a deel Pilar delos Adais actuando ânttessea[?] por rectoria los oficiales y Soldados de el [Presidio Los Adaes], en primer lugar â mi favor, y segundo â D.n Domingo de Gomendio Urrutia, Vecino y deel Comercio dela Ziudad de México p.a la âperrep.zn delos Sueldos dedos Tercios Ultima obengados[?] del año proximo pasado de Treinta y Siete me han rremitido orixinales esttos p.a q.sepongan enelprotocolo de Instrumentos publicos deel Archivo de aquel Presidio [Los Adaes] . . . Proveído saque uno, dos, omas testimonios deellos enpublica forma y manera q. Haga see[?] para despacharle almenziona.do D.n Domingo para q. usse deellos y encaso necesario le doy mi poder bastante qual en D.ro. se requiere y es nezesario para q. balgan y baler puedan con todas las clausidas y requisitos en D.ro" (author's translation).

19 Power of attorney by officers and soldiers of Presidio Los Adaes to Governor Sandoval for the collection of their salaries annulled, given in favor to Gov. don Franquis de Lugo and then granted to Governor Orobio y Bazterra, appeared before Lieutenant Vergara, January 24, 1738, Presidio Los Adaes, *BA*, 8:0489–0490.

20 Power of attorney, ibid., *BA*, microfilm, 8:0490–0491. Governor Franquis de Lugo remained in San Antonio de Béxar for nine months before arriving at Presidio Los Adaes by May 1737.

21 Bushnell, *The King's Coffer: Proprietors of the Spanish Florida Treasury, 1565–1702* (Gainesville: University Press of Florida, 1981), 121; Konove, "On the Cheap," 259, 268, and 270.

22 Petition, don Juan Antonio de Bustillo y Cevallos to Gov. don Manuel de Sandoval, June 19, 1734, Presidio Los Adaes, *NA*, UT-Austin, box 2Q292, vol. 1, 13–15, transcription.

23 Account book of war expenses in the Royal Treasury Office for salaries of governors and soldiers from Presidio Los Adaes during the years 1725–38, *AGN—Archivo Histórico de Hacienda, MDHMC*, microfilm, box 1, roll 1, 65–68v, oversize, photostat.

24 Account book, ibid., *AGN—Archivo Histórico de Hacienda*, microfilm, 1:65, 65v, 66, 66v, 67. In 1730, the agent Fernando de Ugarte also had power of attorney to collect salaries for the soldiers at Presidio San Antonio de Béxar.

25 Account book, ibid., *AGN—Archivo Histórico de Hacienda*, microfilm, 1:[?]. The year is not evident from the document, which lists Presidio Los Adaes at 97 pesos; Presidio La Bahía, 90 pesos; Presidio San Antonio de Béxar, 165; Presidio San Saba, 136; Presidio San Juan Bautista del Rio Grande (near present Eagle Pass, Texas), 268; Presidio Santa Fe, New México, 113; Presidio San Francisco, Coahuila, 186; Presidio Janos, Chihuahua, 241; *Punta de Siguenza* (Pensacola), 271; Presidio of Cuba, 138; Presidio of Habana, 148; Presidio of Puerto Rico, 249, and others.

26 *Petición*, Cristóval de Santiago, Felipe de Sierra, y Domingo del Río, soldados de el Real presidio de Nuestra Señora del Pilar de los Adays, y residentes en este [presidio] de San Antt.o, Sierra signed his own name, while Juan Antonio de Luna and Joseph Rivera signed *a ruego de* (at request of; in place of) Domingo del Río and Cristóbal de Santiago, both not knowing how to sign their own names, April 28, 1738, Royal Presidio of San Antonio, and Proveído y Manda (Decision and Order), don Juan Joseph Briseño y Zúñiga, residency judge, April 28, 1738, Royal Presidio of San Antonio, Declaración, escrivano (notary) estando en la Cassa de la morada del Cap.n [and Gov.] D.n Manuel de Sandoval, April 28, 1738, Royal Presidio of San Antonio *AGM—Historia, CAT*, vol. 524, part 1, box 38, folder 4a, 28–30, transcription. Ybiricu was previously the captain of Presidio Texas near Nacogdoches, and arrived at Los Adaes after the former presidio was abandoned in 1730 along with three of the six East Texas missions.

27 *Conocimiento* (understanding), Domingo Chirinos, *soldado contenido en la lista presentada*, he did not know how to sign his own name, May [?], 1738, Royal Presidio of San Antonio de Béxar; *conocimiento*, Salvador de Esparza, *soldado de la Compañía de los Adais*, he did not know how to sign his own name, May 5, 1738, Royal Presidio of San Antonio de Béxar; *conocimiento*, don Joseph Gonzalez, *Alferes del Presidio de los Adais*, he signed his own name, May 7, 1738, Royal Presidio of San Antonio de Béxar; complaint, *los soldados todos juntos de Nuestra Señora del Pilar de los Adais*, all appearing before the residency judge, May [?], 1738, Royal Presidio of San Antonio de Béxar,

AGM—Historia, CAT, vol. 524, part 1, box 38, folder 4b, 45–46, 62–63, and 80–81, transcription: "seria castigado con sepo o baqueteado" (author's translation).

28 Plea, Juan de Tovar, *soldado de este Real Presidio de Nuestra Señora del Pilar de los Adaes,* May [?], 1738, [Presidio San Antonio?], ibid., *AGM—Historia, CAT,* transcription: "una llegua y un caballo que me quito de poder absoluto y yó temiendo no se me vitraxara mi persona aun que soy un pobre con familia hube de cayarme la boca y dexarlo perder" (first quotation) and "era de los criollos" (second quotation); plea, Agustín Morillo, *vecino de este Real Presidio de Nuestra Señora del Pilar de los Adais,* he signed his own name, May [?], 1738, [Presidio San Antonio?], transcription: "dejo dies caballos mansos de rienda, una chupa de gamusa negra abotonada de botones de plata, un capote nuevo, dos pares de medias de seda" (third quotation; all author's translations); plea, Juan Francisco, *vecino de este Real Presidio de Nuestra Señora del Pilar de los Adaes,* he signed his own name May [?], 1738, [Presidio San Antonio?], transcription.

29 Plea, Fernando Santiago de la Serda, May [?], 1738, [Presidio San Antonio?], 86–89, 91; plea, Juana del Toro, *biuda de Pascual de Lunybe* [Luna? or Leyva?] *de este Real Presidio de Nra. Señora del Pilar de los Adaes,* she signed her own name, May [?], 1738, [Presidio San Antonio?], ibid., *AGM—Historia, CAT,* 92, transcription: "ser yo pobre biexa cargada de años sin mas amparo que Dios y averse llevado su divina Mag.d a mi marido," and "sirviendo su plaza" (author's translation).

30 Petition, former Gov. Manuel de Sandoval, May 26, 1738, Royal Presidio of San Antonio de Béxar; order, don Juan Joseph Briseño y Zuñiga, residency judge, May 26, 1738, Royal Presidio of San Antonio de Béxar, ibid., *AGM—Historia, CAT,* vol. 524, box 38, folder 4b, 96–101, transcription.

31 Request, soldiers of Presidio Los Adaes for assistance from Gov. Franquis de Lugo to have former governor Sandoval pay their salaries, May 14, 1737, Presidio Los Adaes, *AGM—Historia, CAT,* vol. 524, part 2, box 39, folder 2a, 342–43, transcription: "con dos mil biolencias q. esperimenttamos de aja-mienttos, como amenanzas y ttropelias q. dho ttenientte G.ral [Ybiricu], uso con cada uno de nosotros" (first quotation); "(Ignacio) le borraron la plaza" (second quotation; all author's translations).

32 Request, ibid. (Ignacio) "por quittarnos nuestra Sangre que es nuesttro Sueldo que nos da nuesttro Rey y S.or, con que manttenemos nuesttras mujeres y yjos, tteniendonos dho D.n Manuel de Sandoval ttodo el ttiempo de su gobi-erno desnudos ttapando nuesttras carnes con una Gamuza y manteniendo a nuesttras mujeres en cueros bibos . . . Pues solo nos a dado Caballos a cincuenta pesos por decir son de su silla los piloncillos a cuattro rr.s cada uno la libra de Azucar a seis rr., obligándonos a rrecebir arina Podrida que apestaba de de corrompida que esttava suspendiendonos la rracion de Maiz

para que la recibiésemos que no aziamos mas que ttomarla Por obedezer y derramarla en el canpo; llegando la iniquidad de dho Dn. Manuel de Sandoval a ttal ttirania que dio la orden a D.n Joseph Gonzalez que hera su ttenientte G.ral, y quien le manexava la ttienda de nuesttro abio; nos Suspendiese de darnos el Javon, el Piloncillo, y el maiz, y q. Solo se nos diese Cualquiera de esttos Jeneros por Caballos con el fin de que lo compraramos a ttruegue de nuesttros mismos Cavallos que tteniamos para azer el Serbizio lo que con efectto consiguio Por que nezesittando del maiz Para nuesttro alimentto del Javon para q. nuesttras Mujeres labasen y en ttrapo y del Piloncillo por que el unico Chocolate que podiamos sacar para siquiera en su lugar beber un poco de attole y bamos con nuesttros cavallos y los dabamos por ttres Almues de Maiz cada cavallo y por dos o ttres p.s, de Javon o piloncillos nos recivian ottro caballo, abiendosenos dado por diez y seis pesos y luego que de la manera que ttenemos espresado a VS.a, lo bendiamos, a dho D.n Joseph Gonzalez quien nos lo compraba luego nos lo volvían a dar por dhos diez y seis, ttreintta, y cncuentta p.s" (author's translation).

33 Request of soldiers for payment of their salaries, May 14, 1737, Presidio Los Adaes, ibid., *AGM—Historia, CAT*, 444, 346, transcription: "y porque bolbemos a pedir lo mismo que en el R.l Presidio de S.n An.tto; pidieron a VS.a, nuesttros compañeros en el escritto . . . de concedernos licencia para ponernos a los pies de la Superior Grandez del Ex.mo, SS.or; Virrey y como Juez Superior Antte cuio ttribunal pediremos justticia de ttantto agrabio" (author's translation).

34 Declaration, Lt. Joseph Gonzalez, May 16, 1737, Presidio Los Adaes, *AGM— Historia, CAT*, vol. 524, part 2, box 39, folder 2a, 359–60, 364, transcription: "Y aunque le Repugnava al que declara executtar ttales tiranias, la fuerza de obedecer las ordenes de el dho. Capittan D.n Manuel de Sandoval, como q. Era su Gov.or le obligava ciegamentte a darles cumplim.tto" (first quotation) and "ya tan despechados que ynttenttaron los mas de la Compania pasarse a la francia, y dejar, estte Presidio [Los Adaes] Abandonado" (second quotation; both author's translation).

35 Declaration, don Manuel Ramírez de la Piscina, *criado de Dn. Manuel de Sandoval . . . y ser su Amanuense*, twenty-eight years old and he signed his own name, May 24, 1737, Presidio Los Adaes, appearing before Gov. don Carlos Franquis de Lugo, *AGM—Historia, CAT*, vol. 524, part 2, box 39, folder 2b, 471–74, transcription.

36 Declaration, Joseph Antonio Rodríguez, *vecino de Real Presidio de San Antonio y recidente en estte* [Los Adaes], May 26, 1737, Presidio Los Adaes, appearing before Gov. Franquis de Lugo, *AGM—Historia, CAT*, vol. 524, part 2, box 39, folder 2b, 478–79, transcription: "con el mottibo de andar buscando su vida, para manttener su Muger, e hijos se condujo a estte Pres.o [Los Adaes] con algunas chucherias hechas de su Muger, las que rreparttio en dibersos

soldados de estta Compañia, y q. Luego que vio esttavan en el ajustte de sus
Quentas D.n Man.l de Sandoval, y D.n Fermin de Ybiricu" (first quotation); "en
mulas, caballos, y gamuzas" (second quotation); and "era el medio q. ttenia
[Rodríguez] para rrecoger su Pobreza, p.r no aver querido dn Manuel de Sandoval, pagarle dicha cantidad, ni hallando Justticia en el dho. Dn. Fermin"
(third quotation; all author's translations).

37 *Obligación*, Juan [Sánchez] de Továr, *vecino de dho presidio* [Los Adaes], for
payment of 105 pesos in mules or deerskins to Joseph Antonio Rodríguez,
March 30, 1737, Presidio Los Adaes, appearing before Lt. don Fermín de Ybiricu,
AGM—Historia, CAT, vol. 524, part 2, box 39, folder 2b, 482, transcription.

38 Petition, Company of Presidio Los Adaes, "seeking justice to satisfy us for
having received insults, injuries, and abuse by Ybricu and Sandoval," [?] 1737,
Presidio Los Adaes, pleading before Gov. Franquis de Lugo, *AGM—Historia,
CAT*, vol. 524, part 2, box 39, folder 2c, 533–34, transcription: "de esta manera
nos destruimos, y los que alcanzabamos mil pesos no llegamos a sacar de
su tienda quatrocientos, con ttanta maldad dho. D.n Manuel de Sandoval . . .
y quedarse entteram.tte con el todo de nros. Sueldos, pusso en poder de Dn.
Fermin de Ybiricu cantidad de p.os y permittiendo hubiesse unos grandes
en este Presidio [Los Adaes] nos reparttia por medio de dho. D.n Fermin los
pesos q. le pediamos en esta manera, por cada cinco p.s que en platta recibi-
amos nos cargaban a nras cuenttas veinte y cinco p.s y por cada diez p.s nos
cargaban cinquentta, y esto con tantto desorden, y publicidad que motibo a
los R.s P.s de esta misión reprehenderlo en el pulpito" (author's translation).

39 Bushnell, *King's Coffer*, 103.

40 Obligación, *AGM—Historia*, 535–36, transcription: "todo el tiempo de su Gov
.no no nos a dado un grano de polbora por cuenta de las seis libras q. el Rey
nos tiene señaladas" (author's translation).

41 Declaration, Lt. Joseph Cayetano y Vergara of Presidio Los Adaes, June 1,
1737, Presidio Los Adaes, appearing before Gov. Franquis de Lugo, *AGM—
Historia*, 541–42, transcription: "que es verdad hubo muchas rifas con los
soldados de estta compania [Los Adaes], y q. el ymbenttor de ellas fue Bacilio Ximenez, soldado de el Pres.o de S.n Antt.o q. se hallava rrecidentte en
estte [Los Adaes]" (first quotation) and "en quantto a los juegos, tambien le
constta los hubo con el mismo exceso de Dados, y naipes" (second quotation;
all author's translations).

42 Confession, Lt. Gen. don Fermín de Ybiricu, June 6, 1737, Presidio Los Adaes,
appearing before Gov. Franquis de Lugo, *AGM—Historia*, 551–54, transcription: "pero q. aunq. rrecivio de dho. D.n Manuel de Sandoval, cinquentta pesos
en platta fue para ponerlos en poder de D.a Manuela, mujer del Comand.tte
D.n Luis de S.n denis" (author's translation).

43 Confession, Lieutenant General Ybiricu, ibid., *AGM—Historia*.

44 Testimony, Mathias de Montes de Oca, *español soltero originario de la Ciudad de Mexico Soldado que fue del Presidio de los Adais y al presente Vecino de este de San Antonio*, twenty-three years old, he signed his own name, May 29, 1738, Presidio San Antonio de Béxar, *AGM—Historia*, vol. 524, part 1, box 38, folder 4c, 127, 129–30, transcription: [Response to question 7] "los soldados de aquel Presidio nunca andaban mal tratados y los oficiales mejor y siempre unos y otros gastaban sus sueldos en estar bien munisionados de Armas y Cavallos y sus familias asistidas de un todo por que nada se les negaba en la tienda del Gobernador [Sandoval] y todo lo que se les dava era el presio del Arancel . . . y tenia amenazado al que gastara mal gastado su sueldo con lo que lo havia de castigar" (first quotation), and [Response to question 8] "save muy bien que no se jugaba a nada con ningun pretesto ni aun una rifa se echaba por que lo tenia prohibido el Gobernador [Sandoval] y lo mismo ha oydo decir delos otros presidios" (second quotation; all author's translations). The interrogatory began on May 27, 1738, in Presidio San Antonio de Béxar, and there were twelve questions total, which was longer than all the residencia proceedings of the other governors of Spanish Texas.

45 Testimony, Mateo Antonio de Ybarbo, *español casado con Juana lugarda* [de la Garza?] *Hernández soldado del presidio de los Hadáis y estando presente*, thirty-six years old, and he signed his own name, May 31, 1738, Presidio San Antonio de Béxar, *AGM—Historia*, 139, 141–43, transcription: [Response to question 7] "por que decia que sino era assi mal pudieran hazer el servicio y que para esso les pagaba el Rey tan puntualmente y no les negaba cossa alguna delas que le pedian en quenta de sus sueldos" (author's translation).

46 Testimony, Montes de Oca, *AGM—Historia*, 129; and testimony, Mateo Ybarbo, *AGM—Historia*, 141: [Response to question 5] "nunca disimulo ni permitio comersio con los estrangeros sobre lo qual dava muy apretados Ordenes alos oficiales y una de ellas era que quando vinieron los franceses a vender legumbres miniestras camotes o otras cossas delas Permitidas no se les consintiera entrar en Casas sino que vendieran en la plaza de Armas publicam.te y assi se observaba y que en una ocasión se cojio a un soldado llamado Pedro Bezerra con una piesa de lienzo blanco que trahia de la francia y se le quito y públicamente la vido[?] este soldado quemar en la Plaza y que coopero en ello como cavo que es de aquella Compañía y al agresor se le apersibio que si otra ves lo hacia seria castigado severamente" (author's translation).

47 Testimony, Montes de Oca, *AGM—Historia*, 130; and testimony, Mateo Ybarbo, *AGM—Historia*, 142–43: [Response to question 10] "siempre que en el tiempo de su govierno [Sandoval] passaba dho governador al presidio de los Adays lo visitaban los oficiales de los franceses y un padre dela Compañía que les Administra y como lo era presiso el ir a cumplimentarles y corresponderles sus visitas lo festejaban con comida y fiestas pero sin salir de los limites de la

modestia y assi este testigo como que era el que passaba con dho Gobernador nunca vido[vio?] desorden alguna ni en Saraos ni en demasiadas Veuidas" (author's translation).

48 Proceedings concerning dispatch of don Juan Antonio Vizarrón de Eguiarreta, Archbishop of Mexico City and of the viceroy's council, to Governor Orobio y Bazterra for the immediate release of Sandoval, who is to withdraw to San Antonio de Béxar until his residencia has ended, December 2, 1737–March 28, 1738, Mexico City, *BA*, 8:0484–0487; *auto*, Gov. Franquis de Lugo, June 8, 1737, Presidio Los Adaes, *AGM—Historia, CAT*, box 39, folder 2c, 592, transcription; *autos sobre la residencia que se tomó al capitán don Manuel de Sandoval del gobierno de Texas*, May 2, 1744, Mexico City, *ASFG*, box 2Q252, vol. 13, 181–82.

49 Report, Gov. don Melchor de Mediavilla y Ascona to the viceroy, April 5, 1730, Presidio Los Adaes, *BP—BL, MDHMC*, carton 33, folder 531, 18, photocopy of transcription.

50 Residencia proceedings of Bustillo y Zevallos, July 8, 1733, to September 30, 1734, San Antonio de Béxar [and Presidio Los Adaes?], *BA*, UT-Austin, box 2S25, 22v–23, 27–28, 31, 34v, 37v, 41, 44v, 46v, 49v, 53, 56.

51 Testimony, Phelipe Muñoz de Mora, resident of Presidio Los Adaes, fifty-eight years old, he signed his own name, January 8, 1745, Presidio Los Adaes, residencia proceeding of former governor, don Felipe de Winthuysen, by Gov. don Justo Boneo y Morales, *BA*, microfilm, 8:0747.

52 Company archives, January 20, 1744, Presidio Los Adaes, residencia of Governor Winthuysen, *BA*, microfilm, 8:0762–0763.

53 Bushnell, *King's Coffer*, 103–5, 107, 120–21. One Treasury official in Spanish Florida even used false scales to cheat the king's soldiers in the distribution of goods.

54 *Testim.o de un Parecer dado en los Autos heachs en Virtud de Real Decula en q.e S.M. se le informa sobre siertos abusos comtetidos en la Provincia de Texas en el tiempo que se expresa, y Tambien de un Parrapho de ottro Parecer dado en los propios Autos, uno y ottro del S.or Auditor Gral de la Guerra*, S.rio Dn. Jph. De Gorraez, March 6, 1744, Mexico City, *NA*, box 2Q292, vol. 1, 28–29, transcription: "viben siempre adeudados, y muchas veces sin armas Caballos y demas apresttos para las funciones hechos puros criados de los commandantes" (author's translation).

55 *Parecer* (opinion), Viceroy Marqués de Altamira, March 6, 1744, Mexico City, *NA*, UT-Austin, box 2Q292, vol. 1, 28, transcription: "aunque por dicho Nuevo Reglamento [of 1729] estan Arancelados los precios de los generos en que les pagan los Gobernadores y Capittanes sacan esttos, y sus corresponsales (que les remiten las factturas de México) crecidas ganancias que reporttan los soldados" (author's translation).

56 *Consulta de el Presidio de Nrâ Señora deel Pilar de los Hadáis, en la Provincia de nuevas Filipinas, vulgarmente a los Texas*, signed by Friar Joseph Ortes de Velasco, February 26, 1726, Apostolic College of San Fernando, Mexico City, *ACZ*, OLLU, microfilm, roll 23, frame 8303: "han practicado sembrar de Compania algun mais, y lo mismo executa el presente son esta forma: el Gov.r apera a los sold.s, dándoles bueyes, semillas, Rexa, Azadones, Mulas, Costales para su acarreto, demas aperos necesarios, y los sold.s concurren con su travajo personal, para Arar, Sembrar, cultivar, guarder, y coger, hasta ponerlo en cassa deel Gov.r El fructo, que produce la siembra pertenece la mitad al Gov.r, y la otra mitad se regaba repartiéndose entre los Yndividuos de la Comp.a y porq. noseles puede fiar la mitad deel fruto, q les toca, por causa de su grande desperdicio, y profusión, se los abona el S. Gov.r en sus quentas a los 5 p.s fanega, que estava tassado en el reglam.to" (first quotation) and "se les permite acada uno que siembra aparte, uno, dos, tres, ô mas . . . cuio fructo, logra cada uno y solo el se aprovecha" (second quotation; all author's translations).

57 Father Velasco, *ACZ*, ibid., 23:8305: "los pobres sldados son pressa de los Governadores en aquel Paramo de Texas" (first quotation), and "pero no ordena, que en los fructos, y esquilmos dela tierra, cultivada por los soldad.s, entren en parte los Gov.s como soberandos aq.nes deban tributar los colonos, como practicado la Francia vieja con los havitantes dela nueva, y recien luciana" (second quotation; all author's translations).

58 Father Velasco, *ACZ*, ibid., 23:8306: "injusticia tiránica, grave detrim.to y daño delos sold.s por.q los privadelo q pudiessen permutar, y comutar con dhos Indios . . . en gamuzas, pieles de Cibolo, manteca de osso, q son las cosas q mas usualm.te comutan dhos Yndios, y las q tienen mas estimación nosolo en el Presidio, mas tambien en toda tierra afuera" (first quotation) and "devia mirar como a hijos, para sus adelantam.tos" (second quotation; all author's translations).

59 Bushnell, *King's Coffer*, 41.

60 Friar Joseph Ortes de Velasco, *Consulta de el Presidio de Nra. Señora deel Pilar de los Adays, en la Provincia de nuevas Filipinas, vulgarmente a los Texas*, February 12, 1746, Apostolic College of San Fernando, México City, *ACZ*, OLLU, microfilm, roll 23, frame 8286, 8289, full text: "se les defraudaba alos sold.s los sueldos, por mal administrados, y atitulo de quites, seles desfalcaba cerca de dies y ocho por ciento" (first quotation) and "de tan avarienta administración, gravissisimo detrim.to alos sold.s; y tanto, q. los mas andaban, descalzos, de pie, y pierna, mal vestidos, mal alimentados, y equipados, siendo su quotidiano sustento tortilla a secas; porq., aun el Chile seles escaciaba, y passando con tanta miseria, siempre se hallaban alcanzados en las quentas, q. las formaban, y ajustaban los Gefes, al tiempo de firmarla asu satisficacion, q. se practica remitir alas Caxas, de estar completas las plazas, bien pagados, y

equipados los Individuos" (second quotation; both author's translation). See also Moorhead, *Presidio*, 34.

61 Friar Joseph Ortes de Velasco, *Consulta de el Presidio de Nra. Señora deel Pilar de los Adays, en la Provincia de nuevas Filipinas, vulgarmente a los Texas*, February 12, 1746, Apostolic College of San Fernando, México City, *ACZ*, microfilm, 23:8289: "dela avaricia delos Govern.es q. no atendían aotra Ley ni regla, q. las q. les sugeria . . . de enrriquescer, y el Hipo de engrassar sus caudales" (author's translation).

62 Moorhead, *Presidio*, 31; see also Jackson and Foster, *Imaginary Kingdom*, 38n72–73, who note the illegal assignments, particularly farming, that soldiers from Presidio Texas were expected to perform at Mission Ais as well, which took them away from their primary duty. The soldiers were also charged overpriced goods.

63 *Consulta*, February 12, 1746, México City, *ACZ*, microfilm, 23:8295, 8306, and 8313: "el monopolio semejante aloq. acontece en esta Corte, quando algunos mercaderes esparcen la vos de q. Se perdieron las Naves, quelaa apresso el Yngles, q. No traen tales, y tales generos, para de este modo vender los suios mas caros, sin repararlos los infelices, q. esta es una de las formas, q. constituyen cierta especia de Monopolio" (author's translation).

64 Father Velasco, consulta, February 12, 1746, Mexico City, ibid., *ACZ*, microfilm, 23:8319.

65 Viceroy don Juan Francisco de Güemes y Horcasitas mentions list of charges (nine total) against Gov. don Francisco Garcia Larios of Texas, January 18, 1747, Mexico City, *BA*, microfilm, 8:0948–0953.

66 Viceroy Güemes y Horcasitas, ibid., *BA*, microfilm, 8:0954–0960: "ala dificultad, y casi impocivilidad dela forma de averiguacion de dhos capitulos" (first quotation) and "por haver venido sin Licencia deel, desamparando el Precidio y la caballada" (second quotation; all author's translations).

67 Viceroy Güemes y Horcasitas, ibid., *BA*, microfilm, 8:0969–0971: "alas vecinos colonias Franseses (Louisiana), y alas barriaras haciendas de aquellos Indios pacificados . . . es dudable la gravedad del punto [?] deesta cargo" (author's translation).

68 Viceroy Güemes y Horcasitas, ibid., *BA*, microfilm, 8:0972–0974: "pero por el governador se rresponde quees vien notorio haversubido desde dho Arancel del año de veinte y nueve los precios un ciento por ciento en los generos de algodón, y lana de la tierra, y china que son alli los mas gastables, y no se quejan los Precidiales de que exceda el gobernador los precios Arancelados a dhos generos" (author's translation).

69 Viceroy Güemes y Horcasitas, Ibid., *BA*, microfilm, 8:0977–0981; appearance of soldiers before Governor Garcia Larios, May 22, 1747, Presidio Los Adaes, *BA*, microfilm, 8:0982.

70 *Relacion y Extracto de los soldados que han deserttado . . . de la Compania de estte R.l Presidio de Nra. S.a de el Pilar delos Adais.* In the year 1734, sdocument included in Residencia of former governor Sandoval conducted by Gov. Franquis de Lugo mentions that Juan Paulino's desertion had occurred on July 15, 1734 (*AGM—Historia, CAT*, box 38, folder 4c, 176, transcription). See also the certification by Francisco Joseph de Arocha, public notary, of three powers of attorney given by Gov. Franquis de Lugo in front of missionaries and officers, June 12, 1737, at Presidio Los Adaes, where reference to Paulino's desertion was also mentioned during the residency of former governor Sandoval, but it was said the desertion happened on July 12, 1734; *AGM—Historia, CAT*, box 39, folder 2c, 595–96, transcription.

71 *Relacion y Extracto de los soldados que han desertado . . . de la Compania de estte R.l Presidio de Nra. S.a de el Pilar delos Adais.* Juan de Villarreal deserted on September 30, 1735; *AGM—Historia*, 176.

72 An early case of banishment occurred under Sandoval's predecessor, Governor Bustillo y Cevallos, who noted in the company archives that there was testimony regarding the exile of Phelipe de Avila ordered by the viceroy on May 18, 1731. Avila was sentenced to Presidio San Juan Bautista on the lower Rio Grande; company archive, May 24, 1734, Presidio Los Adaes, submitted by former Governor Bustillo y Cevallos, during his residency proceeding conducted by Governor Sandoval, *AGM—Provincias Internas, CAT*, box 53, folder 2b, 113–14, transcription.

73 Certification, Arocha, public notary, three powers of attorney given by Gov. Franquis de Lugo, June 12, 1737, Presidio Los Adaes, during residency of former governor Sandoval, *AGM—Historia, CAT*, box 39, folder 2c, 595–96, transcription: [original text:] "les vorraron sus Plazas el dia Nueve de Diziembre [1735]" (author's translation).

74 Testimony, Alférez Gonzalez, June 12, 1737, Presido Los Adaes, appeared before residency judge, Gov. Franquis de Lugo, *AGM—Historia, CAT*, box 39, folder 2c, 598.

75 Company archives, residency proceeding of former governor Orobio y Bazterra conducted by Governor Winthuysen, August [?], 1741, Presidio Los Adaes, *BA*, UT-Austin, box 2S26, 65: "desertor Phelipe Sanchez amparandose en el Presidio de S.n Juan Baptista de Nachitos Frontera de Januer[?] a Luziana y en su lugar se rreenjofazó[?] a don[?] Rafael de Trejo el dia veintte de diciembre de dho. año [1740] quedando a favor de la R.l Hazienda el tiempo de su vacante" (author's translation).

76 Company archives, residency of former governor Winthuysen, January 20, 1744, Presidio Los Adaes, *BA*, microfilm, 8:0763: "Juan Antonio de Luna deserto en la Cuida de Monte Rei en quarto de septiembre de milsetesientos quarenta y dos años biniendo con cavallada a este Pres.o escoltando, y en su lugar entro

deservir la plasa Joseph Ant.o de Peña en primero de henero de milsetesientos quarenta y tres años q.e dando su bacante a favor dela R.l hacienda" (author's translation).

77 Proceedings held by Governor Barrios Jáuregui concerning inquiry into subversive activities of Manuel Antonio de Soto Bermudez, October 8, 1754, Presidio Los Adaes, *BA*, microfilm, 9:0558: "Manuel de Soto desertor de este Pressidio y aberigado[?] en el nachitos" (author's translation). Mills, *NACCR*, 90, entry no. 731.

78 Quotation in Russell M. Magnaghi, ed. and trans., "Texas as Seen by Governor Winthuysen, 1741–1744," *Southwestern Historical Quarterly* 88 (October 1984): 176.

79 Certification, Fray Pedro Ramírez de Arellano, October 6, 1751, Mission Los Adaes, investigation of Caddo Indian visit at Mission Nacogdoches and French movements in Louisiana, *BA*, microfilm, 9:0271–0272; quotation also in Hackett, *Pichardo's Treatise*, 4:14–15; report, Gov. don Jacinto de Barrios y Jáuregui to the viceroy, Marqués de Revilla Gigedo, November 8, 1751, Presidio Los Adaes, in ibid., 4:15–17.

80 This method of posting governmental decrees on church doors was done in New Orleans, while Natchitoches did not build a church until the late 1730s. In the absence of French civil structures in the Illinois country, local priests also served as public notaries; see O'Neill, *Church and State*, 239.

81 Dispatch, Viceroy, don Juan Francisco de Güemes y Horcasitas, Conde de Revillagigedo, February 10, 1751, Mexico City, *BA*, microfilm, roll 9, frame nos. 0226–0227. [Full text]: "mantener el honor de las armas a el Rey en sus fronteras, a vista de una nación que pretende ser dominante, y ser orgullosa … y aunque al presente estan nuestras armas en buen correspondencia, los inopinados accidentes de las cortes pueden indisponerlas y tener anticipado esta noticia las armas francesas … pueden aprovecharse … de la ocasión que les proporciona el deplorable estado de un Presidio, que en ocasiones no le quedarán tres hombres, y en el desamparo de mas de docientos leguas, en que no ai poblado ni tropa que les sustenga" (author's translation).

82 Order, Viceroy Güemes, ibid., *BA*, microfilm, 9:226, 228: "por las armas de Francia si llega el caso de rrompimiento, ô por los Indios, que noticiosos de el estado indefenso de el real Presidio de los Adaes, pueden insultarle, perdiéndose en el credito de las armas de el Rey, y por consequencia el mio" (author's translation).

83 *Obedecimiento* (obedience), Gov. Jacinto de Barrios y Jáuregui, June 23, 1751, San Xavier, *BA*, microfilm, 9:231: "en consideracion de la grave necesidad que … ay en aquel Presidio, como cavezera de esta Prov.a y frontera que sirbe de freno y muralla al enemigo para sostener qualquiera hostilidad, que su dominante orgullo intente, que juztamente puede recelarse y temerse, y hoy mas que nunca" (author's translation).

84 Ibid., *BA*, 9:0230–0233; also in *Testimonio de los autos hechos a consulta del comandante de la Ysla de Santa Rosa Punta de Sigüenza* [Pensacola, Florida], *BP—BL*, *MDHMC*, carton 5, folder 376, 6–8, transcription.

85 Investigation, Gov. don Jacinto de Barrios y Jáuregui, regarding French encroachments among the Bidai and Orcoquiza Indians, April 29, 1755, Presidio Los Adaes, *NA*, UT-Austin, box 2Q292, vol. 4, 1–2, transcription.

86 Investigation, ibid., Witness, Sgt. Domingo del Río, April 29, 1755, Presidio Los Adaes, *NA*, 3–4, transcription: "para obsequio de los Indios Vidasi [Bidais] una patente, decgad. Para el Yndio Llamándose, Mateo, con cazaca encarnada, Galonada, dire, sombrero y cual[?], una camisa, y un baston, y para el yndio Tomas, cazaca y sombrero, como la antecedente, y camisa, para obsequio destos y suscongaderos e rrecibido asipropio veinte y sinco Libras de Ruentas[?], asueles[?] y encarnadas, veinte y cuatro tagarratos[?], encarnados, trese arrobas degolbona [de polvora?] catorse de Balas, tres docenas de belduques, sinco y media Libras de Vermillion, veinte y cuatro Max.s de tabaco, veinte y untaparrabo, digo Sacatrapos y veinte y cuatro peines" (author's translation). One *arroba* is a Spanish unit of weight equivalent to about twenty-five pounds; see Barnes, Naylor, and Polzer, *Northern New Spain*, 73.

87 Investigation, ibid., Witness, Sergeant del Río, *de edad de cuarenta años mas o menos y lo firmó* (eighty years old, more or less, and signed), June 3, 1755, Presidio Los Adaes, *NA*, 4–6.

88 Investigation, ibid., Witness, Cristóbal del Río, *vecino de este Real presidio* [Los Adaes], *es de edad de treinta y ocho años mas o menos y no firmó por no saber* (thirty-eight years old, more or less, and did not sign for not knowing how to write it), June 3, 1755, Presidio Los Adaes, *NA*, 7–9.

89 Investigation, ibid., Witness, Pedro de Granados, *soldado de este Presidio* [Los Adaes], *de edad de treinta y seis años poco mas o menos y lo firmó* (thirty-six years old, more or less, and signed), June 6, 1755, Presidio Los Adaes, *NA*, 13–16, transcription: "sentava a mi mesa a los capitanes y a los de mas les dava carne, mais, sal, manteca y frijol en abundancia, y quando se bolvieron a sus rrancherías se les rrepartieron de nuevo pólvora, balas, peines, mermillon, frijol, y el mais que quisieron llevar cargado y que tambien save de publico q. el capitan mateo de la nación Horcoquiza tiene pedido del R.P. Fr. Joseph Calahorra, Ministro de la Misión de Nacogdoches, les baia a poner Misión de nuevo" (author's translation).

90 Power of attorney by officers and soldiers of Presidio Los Adaes to don Diego Antonio Giraud, *vecino y del comercio dela Ziudad de Mex.co pagador nombrado por dhos ofiziales y soldados* (resident of Mexico City and named power of attorney by said officials and soldiers) for the collection of their salaries,

June 10, 1741, Presidio Los Adaes, appearing before Gov. don Thomas Phelipe de Winthuysen, *BA*, microfilm, roll 8, frame nos. 0496–0497.

91 Power of attorney, ibid., January 27, 1742, and December 30, 1742, Presidio Los Adaes, appearing before Gov. Phelipe Winthuysen, *BA*, microfilm, 8:0498–0501; power of attorney given by officers and soldiers of Presidio Los Adaes to Giraud, December 14, 1743, Presidio Los Adaes, appearing before Gov. don Justo Boneo y Morales, *BA*, 8:0502–0503; power of attorney given by officers and soldiers of Presidio Los Adaes to Giraud, March 2, 1745; December 30, 1745; December 31, 1746; and December 31, 1747, Presidio Los Adaes, appearing before Gov. don Carlos Franquis de Lugo, *BA*, 8:0503–0514; power of attorney given by officers and soldiers of Presidio Los Adaes to Gen. don Juan Antonio Bustillo y Zevallos, *vecino de la ciudad de Mexico aviador actual de este Real Presidio* [Los Adaes] (resident of Mexico City living in this royal presidio of Los Adaes) December 24, 1748; December 28, 1749; December 29, 1750, Presidio Los Adaes, appearing before Gov. don Pedro del Barrio y Espriella, *BA*, microfilm, 8:0514–0520.

92 Power of attorney given by officers and soldiers of Presidio Los Adaes to don Diego Antonio Giraud for the collection of their salaries, December 31, 1751, Presidio Los Adaes, appearing before Gov. don Pedro del Barrio y Espriella, *BA*, microfilm, roll 9, frame nos. 0287–0289; power of attorney given by officers and soldiers of Presidio Los Adaes to Giraud for the collection of their salaries, December 31, 1753, Presidio Los Adaes, appearing before Gov. don Jacinto de Barrio y Jáuregui, *BA*, 9:0454–0458; power of attorney given by officers and soldiers of Presidio Los Adaes to Giraud for the collection of their salaries and gunpowder, December 31, 1759, Presidio Los Adaes, appearing before Lt. Marcos Ruis *por auciencia del Señor Governador* [don Angel de Martos y Navarrete] (in the abcense of Gov. Angel de Martos y Navarrete), *BA*, 9:0871–0873; power of attorney given by officers and soldiers of Presidio Los Adaes to Giraud for the collection of their salaries and gunpowder, December 31, 1760, Presidio Los Adaes, appearing before Gov. don Angel Martos y Navarrete, *BA*, 9:0942–0944; certification of power of attorney granted by the officers and soldiers of Presidio Los Adaes to Giraud for the payment of their salaries, January 2, 1761, Presidio Los Adaes, signed by Gov. don Angel Martos y Navarrete, *BA*, 9:0946; power of attorney given by officers and soldiers of Presidio Los Adaes to don Manuel de Cozuela, *vecino y del comercio de la Ciudad de Mexico* (resident and merchant of Mexico City) for the collection of their salaries, December 31, 1761, Presidio Los Adaes, appearing before Governor Martos Navarrete, *BA*, 9:0994–0996; power of attorney given by officers and soldiers of Presidio Los Adaes to for the collection of their allotment of gunpowder, January 2, 1761, Presidio Los

Adaes, [document executed in the absence of Governor Martos Navarrete], *BA*, 9:0998–0999.

93 Power of attorney given by officers and soldiers of Presidio Los Adaes to Cozuela for the collection of their salaries, December 31, 1762; December 31, 1763; December 31, 1765; December 31; 1766–January 2, 1767, Presidio Los Adaes, appearing before Governor Martos Navarrete, *BA*, microfilm, roll 10, frame nos. 0129–0131, 0182–0184, 0404–0406, and 0457–0459; power of attorney given by officers and soldiers of Presidio Los Adaes to Cozuela for the collection of their salaries, December 31, 1767; December 31, 1768; December 31, 1769, Presidio Los Adaes, appearing before Lt. don Joseph Gonzales, *BA*, 10:0531–0533, 0642–0643, and 0688–0689.

94 Power of attorney granted by officers and soldiers of Presidio San Agustín de Ahumada for the collection of their salaries and gunpowder, December 31, 1759, and December 31, 1760, Presidio San Agustín de Ahumada, appearing before Governor Martos Navarrete, *BA*, microfilm, 9:0874–0876, 0939–0941. Giraud's surname adorns a popular private establishment in modern downtown San Antonio called Club Giraud, where local businessmen, politicians, and professionals gather for dining and where social events such as weddings are also held.

95 Power of attorney, April 20, 1739; June 10, 1741; December 30, 1742; March 2, 1745; December 30, 1745; December 31, 1746; December 31, 1747; December 24, 1748; December 28, 1749; December 29, 1750, *BA*, microfilm, 8:0494, 0497, 0500, 0504, 0507, 0509, 0512, 0515–0516, 0518; December 31, 1751; December 31, 1753; December 31, 1759, *BA*, microfilm, 9:0288, 0455, 0872; 12/31/1762; December 31, 1763; December 31, 1765; December 31, 1768; December 31, 1769, *BA*, microfilm, 10:0129, 0158, 0183, 0404, 0407, 0643, 0689. All given by officers and soldiers at Presidio Los Adaes.

96 Certification of power of attorney dated December 31, 1760, and granted by the officers and soldiers of Presidio Los Adaes to don Diego Antonio Giraud, January 2, 1761, Presidio Los Adaes, signed by Governor Martos Navarrete, *BA*, microfilm, 9:0946: "han servido sus plazas y estan exsistentes exerzitados en el Real Zervicio sinfaltar asu obligazion" (author's translation).

97 Certification, ibid., January 2, 1762, *BA*, microfilm, 9:1004; certification of power of attorney, January 2, 1763, January 2, 1764, January 2, 1766, *BA*, microfilm, 10:0157, 0185, 0411. All signed by Governor Martos Navarrete at Presidio Los Adaes.

98 Certification of power of attorney to don Manuel de Cozuela, including report on gunpowder used at Presidio Los Adaes and Orcoquiza during 1763, "y ademas la que tengo regalado a los Yndios Taguacanas, Yscanis, Texas, Vidays, Adaes, Aix, Nacogdoches," since 1761, *BA*, microfilm, 10:0186. For differences between Tejas or Hasinai and the Tehuacana and Yscanis, see La Vere, *Texas Indians*, 123, 129. The Tehuacana might be the Tawakonis who were Wichita.

99 Carlos E. Castañeda, "The Mission Era: The Passing of the Missions. 1762–1782," in *Our Catholic Heritage in Texas, 1519–1936*, vol. 4 (Austin: Von Boeckmann-Jones, 1939), 37 (re: Presidio Los Adaes).

CHAPTER 5

1 Letter, Juan Bautista "el Gruesso" [Legros] to Gov. Carlos Franquis, May 2, 1737, Natchitoches, Louisiana, in Residencia Proceeding of former Gov. don Manuel de Sandoval, 1737–38, *AGM—Historia*, vol. 524, *CAT*, Austin, box 38, folder 9, 281–82, Spanish transcription; order, Governor Franquis, May 2, 1737, Presidio Los Adaes, *AGM—Historia*, 282–83; letter, St. Denis to Governor Franquis, April 15, 1737, Natchitoches, *AGM—Historia*, 287, Spanish transcription translated from Latin; license, Lt. Gen. don Fermín de Ybiricu to Juan Bautista, resident of the French nation [Louisiana], February 3, 1737, Presidio Los Adaes, *AGM—Historia*, 286. See also Bolton, *Texas*, 37. On the list of goods, see memorial, merchandise confiscated from Juan Bautista [Legros] *El Gordo*, at Presidio Los Adaes, by order of Lt. Gen. don Fermín [de Ybiricu], April 17, 1737, *AGM—Historia*, vol. 524, *CAT*, Austin, box 38, folder 9, 285, transcription. One *arroba* is twenty-five pounds.

2 Memoria de las mercancías vendidas al Señor don Fermín de Ybericu, thnte. gral. de los adayes, por el nombrado Juan Bautista Dhesbanne, francés del Puesto de los natchitoos, [June 2, 1737, Natchitoches], *AGM—Historia*, 577, Spanish transcription; Memorial de las mercancías vendidas al Señor don Fermín de Ybiricu, thnte. gral. de los adayes, por el nombrado hendrique, francés del Puesto de los natchitoos, June 2, 1737, Natchitoches, *AGM—Historia*, 578–79, Spanish transcription. See also request for payment, Delachaise, appearing before Gov. Franquis de Lugo, [June 6, 1737, Presidio Los Adaes?], *AGM—Historia*, 580, Spanish transcription, in which instance De la Chaise requested payment for thirty pounds of gunpowder at three reales per pound and another twenty-five pounds of ammunition at two reales per pound that Ybiricu had "taken" from him.

3 Bolton, *Texas*, 38.

4 Stanley J. Stein and Barbara H. Stein, *The Colonial Heritage of Latin America: Essay on Economic Dependence in Perspective* (New York: Oxford University Press, 1970), 89–90, 95–98, 100–101. The ultimate goal of imperial France was to turn "Spain and its colonies into effective allies in the development of the French economy and in the conflict with England." For discussion on the British occupation of Havana, Cuba, in 1762, see Elena A. Schneider, *The Occpuation of Havana: War, Trade, and Slavery in the Atlantic World* (Chapel

Hill: University of North Carolina Press, 2018); see also Jesse Cromwell, *The Smugglers' World: Illicit Trade and Atlantic Communities in Eighteenth-Century Venezuela* (Chapel Hill: University of North Carolina Press, 2018).

5   Marcy Norton, *Sacred Gifts, Profane Pleasures: A History of Tobacco and Chocolate in the Atlantic World* (Ithaca, NY: Cornell University Press, 2009), 219–20, 226–27.

6   David J. Weber, *The Taos Trappers: The Fur Trade in the Far Southwest, 1540–1846* (Norman: University of Oklahoma Press, 1971), 18. Weber's work remains a classic on the early fur trade in the Spanish Borderlands.

7   Carl J. Ekberg, *French Roots in the Illinois Country: The Mississippi Frontier in Colonial Times* (Urbana: University of Illinois Press, 1998), 160; Rhys Isaac, *The Transformation of Virginia, 1740–1790* (Chapel Hill: University of North Carolina Press, 1982), 24.

8   Norton, *Sacred Gifts, Profane Pleasures*, 11.

9   H. Sophie Burton, "Vagabonds along the Spanish Louisiana-Texas Frontier, 1769–1803: 'Men Who Are Evil, Lazy, Gluttonous, Drunken, Libertinous, Dishonest, Mutinous, etc., etc., etc.—and Those Are Their Virtues,'" *Southwestern Historical Quarterly* 113 (April 2010): 438–67; Burton and Smith, *Colonial Natchitoches*, 14.

10 On Caddo contraband trade, see Perttula, *Caddo Nation*, 207.

11 Folmer, *Franco-Spanish Rivalry*, 15, 246, 293.

12 Henri Folmer, "Contraband Trade between Louisiana and New Mexico in the Eighteenth Century," *New Mexico Historical Review* 16 (July 1941): 264; Daniel H. Usner Jr., *Indians, Settlers, and Slaves in a Frontier Exchange Economy* (Chapel Hill: University of North Carolina Press, 1992), 6.

13 Friar Joseph Ortes de Velasco, *Consulta*, report concerning Presidio Los Adaes and the resolution of problems there, February 12, 1746, *ACZ*, roll 23, frame nos. 8313, 8321: "quitando la livertad, q. Por dro. natural tiene cada uno de comprar y vender aq.n quissiere" (first quotation); "Ympide tambien el q. Los Yndios infieles con qnes es el maior trato de gamussas y pieles de Cibolo baian acariciándose ê intimándose con los españoles, y Gente de razon, deel Presidio, como de otras partes deel Reyno de Leon, y Coaguila [Coahuila], y es ocac.on de displicentarse dhos Yndios, y de occurrir ala Colonia, vecina estrangera" (second quotation); "[los Indios] hazen concepto de q. todos los Españoles son tan codiciosos, y avarientos como los Gov.es por q. estos son los q. con ancia abarcan todas sus Gamuzas, y pieles, por el crecido interes q. logran" (third quotation; all author's translations).

14 Father Velasco, ibid., *ACZ*, roll 23, frame no. 8307: "Si lo es licito ganar en cada cuera 16 p.s y r.s tambien le sera licito ganar en las gamuzas" (author's translation).

15 Father Velasco, ibid., *ACZ*, 23:8307–8, 8311: "Y sele agreguen con rigor todo los costos hasta los Hadáis" (first quotation); "A comprar as Gamussas precissam. te al Gov.r, los priva dela livertad, que en corriente theologia, y jurisprudencia solo ello, anula todo contrato, lo haze illicito, y pecaminoso" (second quotation; all author's translations). Father Velasco recognized that some interest was allowed for the governor, but these were in excessive amounts.

16 Letter, Gov. don Jacinto de Barrios y Jáuregui to the Viceroy, Count of Revilla Gigedo, April 17, 1753, Presidio Los Adaes, quotation translated in Charles W. Hackett, ed., *Pichardo's Treatise on the Limits of Louisiana and Texas*, vol. 4 (Austin: University of Texas Press, 1946), 64.

17 Governor Barrios Jáuregui, ibid., 66–67.

18 Bolton, *Texas*, 65–66.

19 Folmer, *Franco-Spanish Rivalry*, 296.

20 Clyde A. Milner II, "Indulgent Friends and Important Allies: Political Process on the Cis-Mississippi Frontier and Its Aftermath," in *The Frontier in History: North America and Southern Africa Compared*, ed. Howard Lamar and Leonard Thompson (New Haven, CT: Yale University Press, 1981), 137–38.

21 Certified copy of proceedings concerning decision of the Junta de Guerra y Hacienda for investigation of French advance into Spanish territory, September 25, 1752–March 4, 1753, Mexico City and Los Adaes, *BA*, box 2S27, 4, 4v, 5: "para que teniendose pres.te de ebite el peligro de contravenir aqualesqui.a tratado que pueda aver avido entre las dos coronas" (author's translation).

22 *Decreto*, His Excellency señor don Juan Francisco de Güemes y Horcasitas, Conde de Revillagigedo, Viceroy, September 26, 1752, Mexico City, *BA*, box 2S27, 6–6v; *Obecim.to*, don Jacinto de Barrios y Jáuregui, governor of Texas, February 17, 1753, Presidio Los Adaes, *BA*, box 2S27, 6v.

23 Investigation, *Declaración 1.o* [primero], don Juan Antonio Amorín, *then.te reformado*, sixty-eight years old more or less, and he signed his own name in front of Governor Barrios Jáuregui, February 17, 1753, Presidio Los Adaes, ibid., *BA*, box 2S27, 4–4a: "usurpado sera como un tiro de piedra" (author's translation).

24 Investigation, Declaration no. 2, don Joseph Gonzales, reformed lieutenant, fifty-three years old more or less, and he signed his own name, February 17, 1753, Presidio Los Adaes, ibid., *BA*, 4a–5: "ya much antes de lo subcedido se avian pasado algunos vecinos, como permanecido de esta parte del rio tres casitas, que en el mismo lugar se encontraron ala entrada de dho S.r Marq.s" (first quotation) and "como un tiro de escopeta" (second quotation; both author's translation); declaration no. 9, Joseph Antonio Rosales, resident of Presidio Los Adaes, fifty-five years old, February 20, 1753, Presidio Los Adaes, 11.

25 Investigation, ibid., *BA*. The other nine witnesses who testified in the Spanish royal investigation of French encroachment into Spanish Texas were as follows: no. 3, don Felipe Muñoz de Mora, *Alferez reformado*, sixty-six years old and signed his own name, February 17, 1753; no. 4, don Manuel Antonio Losoia, *actual then.te* of the company of Los Adaes, fifty-three years old, and he signed his own name, February 19, 1753; no. 5, don Pedro de Sierra, alférez of the company of Los Adaes, fifty-one years old, and he signed his own name, February 19, 1753; no. 6, Marcos Ruíz, fifty-two years old; no. 7, Phelipe de Sierra, *cavo de esquadra*, fifty-three years old, February 19, 1753; no. 8, Lazaro Ybañez, resident of Presidio Los Adaes, fifty-two years old, February 19, 1753; no. 10, Caietano Gomes, resident of Presidio Los Adaes, fifty-three years old, February 20, 1753; no. 11, Cristóbal de Santiago, *de la dotacion* of Presidio Los Adaes, fifty-three years old, and he did not know how to sign his name, February 20, 1753; and no. 12, Manuel Salbador de Pozos, *de la dotacion* of Presidio Los Adaes, sixty years old, and he did not know how to sign his own name, February 20, 1753.

26 Investigation, Summary of Testimony, Gov. don Jacinto de Barrios y Jáuregui, February 28, 1753, Presidio Los Adaes, *BA*, box 2S27, 15v–16.

27 Certified copy of proceedings of the *Junta de Guerra y Hacienda* concerning the French moving the Natchitoches post across the Louisiana-Texas boundary and encroaching farther into Spanish Texas, January 22, 1754, Mexico City, *BA*, microfilm, roll 9, frame nos. 0463, 0466–0467: "no lo hubiera consequido respecto a sus pocas fuerzas y a las muchas que tiene el frances con la union de los Indios" (first quotation) and "como son fuziles, Polvora, valas, bayetas, bermillion, y otras cosas, apeteciables alos Yndios entre quienes los distribuye" (second quotation; all author's translations).

28 Proceedings, Council of War and Estates, ibid., *BA*, microfilm, 9:0473: "que los franceses tratan, y contratan con los Yndios Texas, Nacogdoches, Nazones, y Nadotes comprehendidos enla Prov.a de Texas, y que aestos los proveen de Camisas, frezadas, taparabos, fuziles, Polvera, balas, quentas, bermellon, y otros efectos apreciables" (author's translation).

29 Proceedings, Council of War and Estates, *Decreto*, January 30, 1754, Mexico City, *BA*, microfilm, 9:0481; *concuerda*, February 1, 1754, Mexico City, ibid., *BA*, 9:0481. Several years later, while France was consumed with the French and Indian War, Governor Barrios Jáuregui held proceedings to determine the sovereignty of land where St. Denis (the younger) constructed a house on a ranch for large livestock at a site called "el arroyo de la Cascara," November 5, 1757, Presidio Los Adaes, *BA*, microfilm, 9:0780. But Spanish royal officials never resolved the boundary issue between Louisiana and Texas, which became a point of conflict years later with the United States' purchase of Louisiana in 1803.

30 Residencia of Governor Orobio y Bazterra, *Declaración No. 1*, Phelippe Muñoz de Mora, resident of Presidio Los Adaes, fifty-five years old, July 18, 1741, [Presidio Los Adaes?], *BA*, box 2S26, 15–15v. "que se haia tenido tratto ni contrato alguno en dhas fronteras [Nachitos]" (author's translation).

31 Residencia of Governor Garcia, *Testimonio No. 7, Domingo Del Rio*, Sergeant of the Company at Los Adaes, thirty-eight years old, July 17, 1748, Presidio Los Adaes, *NA*, box 2Q292, vol. 3, transcription: "algunas camisas y botellas de Ag.te y alguna Polbora, pero q. Habiéndose experimentado q.e ni eso disimulaba y lo mandaba quemar y derramar" (author's translation).

32 Residencia, Governor Garcia, ibid., *Testimonio No. 2*, Thomas de Ojeda, soldier of Presidio Los Adaes, *español natural del Pueblo de Guichapa* [México], thirty-six years old, and he signed his own name, July 16, 1748, Presidio Los Adaes, ibid., *NA*, box 2Q292, 29, transcription: "una Franzesa q.e con titulo de venir a vender Camotes y Duraznos traia Polbora en en el Canasta y no fijandose el dho gral. Del Rexistro De la Guardia se la habia encontrado y que luego habia mandado quemarla, y amonestado a la Franzesa que si otra Vez le sucedía la Castigaria" (author's translation).

33 *Dictamen* (pronouncement), Gov. don Phelipe de Winthuysen, reporting upon the condition of presidios and missions in Spanish Texas and his recommendation that its capital be removed from Presidio Los Adaes to San Antonio de Béxar, August 19, 1744, Mexico City, *BA*, microfilm, 8:0797–0798.

34 Letter, Count of Revilla Gigedo, viceroy, to don Jacinto de Barrios y Jáuregui, February 10, 1751, México City, *BA*, microfilm, 9:0229: "aprovecharse de sus ricos minerales, e introducir su ilicito comercio" (first quotation); "[Captain Mederos] expresando haverse desparramado secretamente que el Governador que acaba D. Pedro del Barrio comerciaba en la colonia franceza, metiendo Generos en su tienda por manos de" (second quotation); "proceda â hazer averiguacion de los culpados en dicho ilicito comersio, ya aprehender alos que resultaren reos deel, y a embargarles todos sus Bienes" (third quotation). Translated in Hackett, *Pichardo's Treatise*, 4:4–5. See also *Archivo General de Indias* (hereafter *AGI*)—*Guadalajara*, legajo 104-2-11, photocopy, box 5.4a, 6–11, *CAT*, Austin, Texas. A transcription is also available in *BP—BL*, MSS, carton 5, folder 376, 1–11, photocopy, *MDHMC*, Mission Dolores Visitors Center, San Augustine, Texas. All of these sources discuss the parallel concerns of Spanish royal officials in Mexico City over contraband trade between the Spaniards at Pensacola and French Louisiana. For a brief discussion of the Spanish West Florida military settlements, whose settlers also came from Mexico, see K. C. Smith, "Colonizing Western Florida," *American Archaeology*, Spring 2005, 26–32.

35 Declaration no. 1, don Phelipe Muñoz de Mora, Second Lieutenant of this company [Los Adaes], sixty-six years old, and he signed his own name, July 20,

1751, Presidio Los Adaes, *BA*, microfilm, 9:0233: "no save, ni menos oio decir" (author's translation).

36 Ibid., *BA*, microfilm, 9:0233–0245. The other Adaeseños who testified in the investigation of former governor Pedro del Barrio y Espriella's alleged smuggling with the French were as follows: [Declaration no. 2] Lt. don Pedro de Sierra de Hernandez, fifty-three years old, and he signed his own name, July 20, 1751, Presidio Los Adaes; [no. 3] Lt. don Juan Antonio de Morin, sixty years old, and he signed his own name, July 21, 1751, Presidio Los Adaes; [no. 4] 2nd Lt. Domingo del Río, forty years old, and he signed his own name, July 21, 1751, Presidio Los Adaes; [no. 5] don Juan de Mora, twenty-eight years old, and he did not know to sign his own name, July 21, 1751, Presidio Los Adaes; [no. 6] *el cabo* Antonio Gregorio Cordobes, *español*, forty-five years old, and he signed his own name, July 22, 1751, Presido Los Adaes; [no. 7] *el cavo* Juan Joseph de Santa Cruz, *español*, forty-seven years old, and he signed his own name, July 22, 1751, Presidio Los Adaes; [no. 8] *cavo* Francisco de la Zerda, *español*, born in Nuevo León, forty-eight years old, and he did not know how to sign his own name, July 22, 1751, Presidio Los Adaes; [no. 9] Joseph de Castro, soldier *antiguo de la dotacion de este presidio* [Los Adaes], thirty-eight years old, and he signed his own name, July [?], 1751, Presidio Los Adaes; [no. 10] Domingo Chirinos, *soldado antiguo de la dotacion de este presidio* [Los Adaes], thirty-seven years old, and he did not know how to sign his own name, July [?], 1751, Presidio Los Adaes; [no. 11] Juan de Lara, *soldado antiguo de este presidio* [Los Adaes], twenty-seven years old, and he signed his own name, July 24, 1751, Presidio Los Adaes; and [no. 12] Cristóbal de Cordoba, *de los de la dotacion de este presidio* [Los Adaes], twenty-seven years old, and he signed his own name, July 24, 1751, Presidio Los Adaes.

37 *Consulta*, ibid., *AGI—Guadalajara*, 1–2; autos de Pesquisa, ibid., *BA*, 9:228–29: "el ingreso anual que tienen los franceses por la parte de los Adais internando sus Ropas a cambio de Carnes, platas, y otros cosas que les conviene, y los Soldados de los Presidios, Españoles, como también los Paisanos mutuamente conducen en balzas de todos estos efectos, con mas las sillas de sus Caballos, que por tierra traen hasta la nueba Orleans para a su regreso levar las ropas y restituirse a los Parajes Españoles de donde son" (author's translation).

38 *Consulta*, Viceroy Conde de Revilla de Gigedo, December 20, 1751, Mexico City, *AGI—Guadalajara*, box 5, folder 4b, 58, transcript photocopy.

39 Royal investigation into French movement of Natchitoches post into Texas and advance farther into interior, January 22, 1754, Council of War and Estates, Mexico City, *BA*, microfilm, 9:0469: "comerciar, o comprar con los franceses de Nachitoos, hasta seis arrobas de Aquardiente, y diez y ocho varriles de vino, respeto aser inexcusable que los soldados, no lo executen permutando los caballos, y sillas por el vino se hizo" (author's translation).

40 Jack Jackson, *Los Mesteños: Spanish Ranching in Texas, 1721–1821* (College Station: Texas A&M University Press, 1986), 118; see also Perttula, *Caddo Nation*, 207–8.

41 Hackett, *Pichardo's Treatise*, 4:6.

42 The information about Manuel de Soto's desertion came later from the testimony of Father Vallejo, March 26, 1761, Mission Los Adaes, *BA*, microfilm, roll 9, frame nos. 0982–0983, during the Spanish royal government's criminal investigation case against de Soto. Father Vallejo added that de Soto initially marched toward Mexico City, but the roads impeded his travel, so he went to French Natchitoches, and it was the second time he had tried to leave.

43 *Testigo* (witness) no. 1, Phelipe Muñoz de Mora, *vecino* (resident) of Presidio Los Adaes, eighty-one years old, and "no lo firmo por temblarle la mano por su abanzada hedad e hizelo yo [Governor Martos Navarrete] dicho Juez de residencia" (second quotation), January 26, 1760, Presidio Los Adaes, *BA*, microfilm, 9:0728–0729: "que de la colonia franzesa no se yntrometan Jeneros de calidad alg.a azepzion de mayz p.a el mantenimiento de esta Compania y Vecindario, y demas bastimientos permitidos, y que quando salen los comboys ha mandado personas de sus satisfaz.n arrejistrarlos (first quotation)" (author's translation).

44 Residencia, Barrios Jáuregui, ibid., *BA*, 9:0735–0736, Witness no. 6, Domingo Chirinos, *cavo de este R.l Presidio* [Los Adaes], forty-five years old, and he did not know how to sign his own name, January 27, 1760, Presidio Los Adaes.

45 Residencia, Barrios Jáuregui, ibid., *BA*, 9:0729–0761, January 26 to February 1, 1760, Presidio Los Adaes. The other witnesses in the residencia proceeding of former governor Barrios Jáuregui were as follows: Witness no. 2, Gil Flores de Abrego, *español*, resident of Presidio Los Adaes, forty-three years old, and he did not know how to sign his own name; no. 3, Lazaro y Bañes, resident of Presidio Los Adaes, sixty years old, and he did not know how to sign his own name; no. 4, Juan Francisco, resident of Presidio Los Adaes, sixty years old, and he did not know how to sign his own name; no. 5, Antonio Cadena, soldier of Presidio Los Adaes, twenty-eight years old, and he did not know how to sign his own name; no. 7, Pedro Pozs, soldier of Presidio Los Adaes, thirty years old, and he signed his own name; no. 8, Simon de los Santos, soldier of Presidio Los Adaes, forty-five years old, and he did not know how to sign his own name; no. 9, Joseph Domingo Carmona, resident of Presidio Los Adaes, twenty-three years old, and he did not know to sign his own name; no. 10, Cristóbal de Santiago, *mulatto*, resident of Presidio Los Adaes and soldier who arrived with Marqués de Aguayo's original expedition in 1721, sixty years old, and he did not know how to sign his own name; no. 11, Marcos Martin, *español*, resident of Presidio Los Adaes, fifty-five years old, and he did not know to sign his own name; no. 12, Manuel de Mora, *español*,

resident of Presidio Los Adaes, twenty-three years old, and he signed his own name; no. 13, Sebastian Camacho, soldier of this Company [Presidio Los Adaes], forty years old, and he did not know how to sign his own name; no. 14, Joseph de Castro, *cavo de esquadra* of the Company of this Royal Presidio [Los Adaes], forty-five years old, and he signed his own name; no. 15, Miguel Losoya, soldier of Presidio Los Adaes, twenty-three years old, and he did not know how to sign his own name; no. 16, Joseph Maria Rodriguez, soldier of Presidio Los Adaes, twenty-five years old, and he did not know how to sign his own name; no. 17, Francisco de Torres, soldier of Presidio Los Adaes, forty-six years old, and he did not know how to sign his own name; no. 18, Tadeo Ramos, soldier of Presidio Los Adaes, thirty years old, and he did not know how to sign his own name; no. 19, Agustin Sanchez, resident of Presidio Los Adaes, forty-five years old, and he did not know how to sign his own name; no. 20, Francisco Villlarreal, resident of Presidio Los Adaes, forty years old, and he did not know how to sign his own name; no. 21, Cayetano Gamez, resident of Presidio Los Adaes, ninety years old, and he signed his own name; no. 22, Gaspar Ruiz, soldier of Presidio Los Adaes, twenty-six years old, and he did not know how to sign his own name; no. 23, Joaquin Mansolo, soldier of Presidio Los Adaes, twenty-four years old, and he did not know how to sign his own name; and no. 24, Antonio Barreda, resident of Presidio Los Adaes, fifty years old, and he did not know how to sign his own name.

46 Letter, don Angel de Martos y Navarrete, governor of Texas, to the viceroy, September 14, 1761, Presidio Los Adaes, *ASFG*, box 2Q252, vol. 13, 18–20, transcript.

47 Letter, don Domingo Valcarzel, *auditor*, to the viceroy, March 2, 1762, Mexico City, *BA*, microfilm, 9:1005–6, where the auditor refers to Governor Martos Navarrete's letter: "sobre el comercio ilicito, que tubo durante su Govierno con los Yndios Barbaros, d.n. Jacinto de Barrios [y Jáuregui]" (author's translation).

48 Declaration, Juan Antonio Maldonado, *arriero cargador de don Jacinto de Barrios*, January 31, 1761, Presidio Los Adaes, before Governor Martos Navarrete, *BA*, microfilm, 9:0952–0953: "q.e desde el primer año q.e entro dho S.r D.n Jas.to mantubo comersio conlos Vidais, tejas, Nabidachos, S.n Pedro, Tancaques, y llojuanes" (author's translation).

49 Declaration, ibid., *BA*, Maldonado: "y q.e otras muchas veces trajo el declarante polbora balas y fusiles y demas trafigues de Nachitos para que llebaran los ya arriba expresados" (first quotation); "q.e trajo las dos veces q.e fue cueros gamuzas sibolas, y caballos q.e estos y las gamuzas se rrepartian a la comp.a, y que no tiene presente el numero de lo que era cada especie y que los demas mencionados traian lo mismo" (second quotation); "q.e fueron bastantes veces de Nachitos" (third quotation; all author's translations). Maldonado was sixty

years old at the time of his declaration, and he did not sign his own name afterward because he said he did not know how.

50 Declaration, Lt. Joseph Gonzales, February 10, 1761, Presidio Los Adaes, before Governor Martos Navarrete, *BA*, 9:0961–0962: "que unas veces llebaban â mill y quinientos, otras mill y otras ocho sientos" (author's translation). Lieutenant Gonzales was sixty years old at the time of his declaration, and he signed his own name.

51 Declaration, Lieutenant Gonzales, ibid., *BA*: "porque no le hisiesen daño a los q.e dho S.or mantenia" (author's translation).

52 Appearance of Caddo and Orcoquiza captains, February 19, 1761, Presidio Los Adaes, before Governor Martos Navarrete for his investigation of Barrios Jáuregui's illicit trade with the Indians, *BA*, 9:0970. [Governor Martos Navarrete:] "que su sustencia pendia de la caza pues con ella, comian y bestian, y que para esta les era preciso el canbalache de fusiles polbora y otros menestres, y que vino franquearselos, los franceses le brindaban con ello, que diese providencias para su consuelo pues delo contrario ocurririan a nachitos" (author's translation).

53 Investigation, ibid., *BA*. [Governor Martos Navarrete:] "de no poder por otro medio sujetar tan bastas nasiones di licencia a Joseph de Acosta, y Antonio Morales, ves.os de esta Jurisdicc.on para que pasasen a dho trafique con los enunciados Indios . . . paraque con canbalache superabundante fuesen a ellas paratenerlas anuestra devocion" (first quotation); "regalando a los capp.es tamas e yndios le se quito para tranquilisanles y arraigarles en la obedencia" (second quotation; all author's translations).

54 The expression "handcuffed colonists" comes from Miller, *Environmental History*, which discusses the stifling of trade under Spanish and Portuguese mercantilism.

55 Weber, *Taos Trappers*, 19. In 1723, shortly after Presidio Los Adaes was founded, Almazán had assigned some land, *Rancho Baño*, for the support of Mission Los Adaes; see Louis R. Nardini, *My Historic Natchitoches*, 41. Ranches like this were well positioned for contraband trade with the French and Indians in addition to other mission lands in East Texas.

56 Folmer, *Franco-Spanish Rivalry*, 245.

57 Declaration, Juan Antonio Maldonado, *arriero y cargador* of former governor Jacinto de Barrios y Jáuregui, sixty years old, and he did not know how to sign his own name, January 31, 1761, Presidio Los Adaes, Investigation into contraband trade, *BA*, microfilm, 9:0951–0953: "los RRPP.es [missionaries] de las Mision de Nacogdoches, y aix, quando no tenian manteca mandaban â Nachitos algunos cueros p.a comprar la, y p.r algunos efec.tos gastables entre los Yndios y ademas como quatro ô seis l.s de polvora y ocho ô doze de balas p.a rrepartirlas entre los Yndios de sus Ymediatas missiones paraque

estos le diesen en cambio la mant.ca de oso p.a su anual manutencion, todo lo qual era en tmpô de el S.r D.n Jas.to debarrios" (author's translation).

58 Declaration, Pedro de Sierra, alférez from Los Adaes, January 26, 1761, Presidio Los Adaes, Investigation, ibid., *BA*, 9:951; Jesús F. de la Teja, "The Saltillo Fair and Its San Antonio Connections," in *Faces of Béxar: Early San Antonio and Texas* (College Station: Texas A&M University Press, 2016), 82.

59 See Jesús F. de la Teja, "St. James at the Fair: Religious Ceremony, Civic Boosterism, and Commercial Development on the Colonial Mexican Frontier," *The Americas* 57, no. 3 (January 2001), 395–97, which mentions the medieval origins of these fairs that also had religious functions.

60 Testimony, Sergeant Domingo Chirino, fifty-two years old, and he did not know how to sign his own name, December 1, 1766, Presidio Los Adaes, *Diligencias Practicadas por el Governador de Texas* [Martos Navarrete] *sobre la aprehension de los generos de contrabando que en ellas se expresan*, *BA*, microfilm, 10:0444–0466. See also the document copy from *Archivo de la Secretaria de Gobierno, Saltillo, Coahuila, México* (hereafter *ASG*), microfilm, roll 1, frame nos. 561–80, in the Old Spanish Missions Records Library, Our Lady of the Lake University, San Antonio, Texas.

61 Testimony, Joseph Vicente de Anda, twenty-five years old, and he did not know how to sign his own name, December 3, 1766, Presidio Los Adaes, Diligencias, ibid., *BA*, 10:0448–0449. Agustín Rodríguez was from Los Adaes, and he appeared later as one of the leaders from East Texas who sought land in San Antonio for himself and other Adaeseños following its abandonment in 1772.

62 Certification, Fray Bernardo de Silva and Fray Ignacio Laba of Friar Concepcion, December 3, 1766, Mission Los Adaes, Investigation, ibid., *BA*, 10:0451; testimony, Friar Francisco Xavier de la Concepcion, December 4, 1766, Presidio Los Adaes, *BA*, 10:0452. See also *ASG*, 1:579: "a los indios de la Mission dela Bajia del Espiritu Santo, a causa de q.e estos como su mnrô melotiene muchas vezes significado apostatan de su mission porla falta, q.e de esta especie experimentan por ser el tabaco francés p.a ellos el mas apetecible, en atención a q.e dho tabaco es unicam.te p.a el fin de rrecoger adhos yndios como lo demuestran las adjuntas certificaciones, se ha de servir Vs. mandar, ô q.e dho tabaco seme devuelva, ô q.e rrespecto a q.e es el fin expressado disponga a del lo q.e mas conveniente pareciere" (author's translation).

63 Valuation of the Goods and Bill of Sale, Governor Martos Navarrete, December 3, 1766, Presidio Los Adaes, Investigation, ibid., *BA*, 10:0449–0450.

64 Order, Governor Martos Navarrete, to sell the French tobacco seized from Friar Zedano, December 2, 1766, Presidio Los Adaes, *ASG*, 1:576.

65 Letter, Diego Gonzalez[?], royal advisor for Viceroy Marqués de Croix, to Governor Martos Navarrete, July 9, 1767, Mexico City, *Saltillo Archives*, Center for American History, UT-Austin, box 2Q313, 31–33, which included a copy of

Governor Martos Navarrete's letter to the viceroy dated December 30, 1766, written from Presidio Los Adaes. Interestingly, Father Zedano had mentioned that the *tercio pelo galón* (suede/braid) was for an ornament at Mission La Bahía, which suggests that missionaries in East Texas used the French and Indian trade to relieve their Franciscan brethren from scarcity of supplies elsewhere in Texas.

66 Folmer, "Contraband Trade," 264.

67 De la Teja, "Saltillo Fair," 86.

68 Perttula, *Caddo Nation*, 149–50, 169, 171, 208; quotation from Hackett, *Pichardo's Treatise*, 3:417. For comparison with the deerskin trade among Choctaws and Europeans in the Southeast, see White, *Roots of Dependency*, 43, 47.

69 Perttula, *Caddo Nation*, 200–201.

70 Robert C. Vogel, "Paul Boüet Laffitte: A Borderlands Life," *East Texas Historical Journal* 41 (Spring 2003): 17. For a more detailed geographic description of the area, see Vogel, "The Bayou Pierre Settlements," *North Louisiana Historical Association Journal* 7 (Spring 1976): 110.

71 On French contraband activity in New Mexico, see Folmer, *Franco-Spanish Rivalry*, 298–303; Folmer, "Contraband Trade," 259–62; and Weber, *Taos Trappers*, 32–37. The first successful journey overland from Louisiana to New Mexico was made in 1739 by the Mallet brothers, French traders who endured treatment similar to Juan Bautista Legros at Los Adaes a couple years earlier. Other French merchants followed, but the short-lived Santa Fe trail to Louisiana virtually halted with Louisiana's transfer to Spain in 1762.

72 Letter, Viceroy Conde de Revilla Gigedo to the Marqués de la Enseñada, June 29, 1753, Mexico City, *AGI—Guadalajara, BL*, MSS box 5, folder 377, 2–5, 8–10, in *MDHMC*, San Augustine, Texas, transcription; letter, Viceroy Conde de Revilla Gigedo to the Marqués de la Enseñada, September 17, 1754, Mexico City, *AGI— Guadalajara*, BL MSS box 5, folder 378, 1–2, in *MDHMC*, transcription.

73 Letter, Gov. don Jacinto de Barrios y Jáuregui to the viceroy, Count of Revilla Gigedo, November 8, 1751, Presidio Los Adaes, in Hackett, *Pichardo's Treatise*, 4:16–17. The Spanish governor had also mentioned the French intermarrying with the Indians.

74 Letter, Governor Barrios Jáuregui to the viceroy, October 30, 1752, Presidio Los Adaes, in Hackett, *Pichardo's Treatise*, 4:54–55. Antonio Barrera might have been a fellow Adaesaño resident from Los Adaes. He might have been from the same family as a Spanish woman named Josepha Barrera who resided at Nacogdoches years later in 1792 and was two years old when Presidio Los Adaes was abandoned in 1773.

75 Opinion of the auditor, don Domingo Valcárcel, Council of War and Estates, September 25, 1753, Mexico City; quotation from Hackett, *Pichardo's Treatise*, 4:98–99.

76 Weber, *Spanish Frontier*, 230.

77 Report, don Manuel Antonio de Soto Bermúdez, February 16, 1753, Presidio Los Adaes, in Hackett, *Pichardo's Treatise*, 4:56. De Soto Bermúdez visited the Nacogdoches Indians on November 12, 1752, and gave similar accounts of other Caddo nations in East Texas that same month.

78 Meeting, Council of War and Estates, January 21–22, 1754, México City, in Hackett, *Pichardo's Treatise*, 4:104.

79 Bolton provides a good overview of Spanish colonization attempts on the Lower Trinity River between 1746 and 1771 in chapter 4 of his book *Texas in the Middle Eighteenth Century*, 325–74.

80 Order, Governor Barrios Jáuregui, Investigation of French activity and settlement on the Lower Trinity River, September 20, 1754, Presidio Los Adaes, *BA*, microfilm, 9:0509–0511; record, Governor Barrios Jáuregui, Return of soldiers with letter and inventory from Lieutenant Ruíz, October 22, 1754, Presidio Los Adaes, *BA*, 9:0511–0512, 0515.

81 *Memoria de los viveres* (list of provisions) from the French among the Orcoquiza Indians on the Lower Trinity River. Inventory made in October 1754 by Lt. Marcos Ruíz, also signed by *testigos* (witnesses) who were all soldiers from Los Adaes: Sgt. Domingo del Río, Christoval de Cordova, Bernando Cerbantes, Juachin Mansolo, Visente Trejo, Juan Joseph de Losoya, and Joaquín del Río, in *BA*, microfilm, roll 9, frame no. 0515, author's translation.

82 *Parecer* (opinion), don Antonio Gallardo, *auditor*, concerning establishment of four Frenchmen with arms and ammunition at the mouth of the Trinity River, February 11, 1755, Mexico City, *ASFG*, Center for American History, University of Texas at Austin, box 2Q249, vol. 6, 19–20, photostat: "el Governador [Barrios Jáuregui] haverse enttregado en el Presidio de San Xavier de Gigedo, p.ra remitirlos á estta capital, se les tomarron ttodas las municiones, mercaderias, y drogas que constuan por inventario, y sesuqione[?] haverse repartido alos auxiliares afecttissimos alpillage" (author's translation).

83 Opinion, Gallardo, ibid., *ASFG*, 22–23: "en sostener el honor del esttado, mantteniendo aquel descubrimiento ocupado por nuesttras armas, y Nacion, y mas brindando la fecundidad del terreno para una hermosa, y bien guarncida Poblazon, quando en ello . . . sino quese evita el gravisismo inconveniente de que la Nacion fran.sa entienda sus Colonias en perjuicio de las nuestras" (author's translation).

84 Opinion, don Domingo Valcarcel, October 11, 1755, Mexico City, *ASFG*, box 2Q249, 48, 55–56, photostat: "manttenerles [los Yndios] en una firme amistad, y buena correspondencia, y vajo de ella ir poco a poco introduciéndoles la luz del Evangelio, inflamar sus corazones del amor á el verdadero Dios, mediante el conocimientto de nuesttra Religión" (first quotation); "para cuio efecto propone se podrían sacar veintte ó mas familias de dho Presidio delos Adays, avilittandolas por una vez con Bueyes, arados, y lo demas q.e es costumbre dar anuestro Pobladores" (second quotation; all author's translations).

85 Interrogatory, Joseph Blancpain, taken by don Domingo Valcarcel, auditor, through the interpreter don Joseph de Cuenca, February 19, 1755, Mexico City, *BA*, microfilm, roll 9, frame nos. 0573–0574.

86 Interrogatory, Blancpain, February 19, 1755, Royal Prison of the Court and Hall of Confessions, Mexico City, *BA*, microfilm, roll 9, frame nos. 0576–0577.

87 Interrogatory, Blancpain, ibid., *BA*, 9:0574–0577: "que altiempo de mi prission le quitaron, que havia cambalachado, algunos generos, por pieles de

benado, que llegaria en balor âtrescientos, ô quatrocientos pessos" (author's translation).

88 Ibid., *BA*, 9:0758: "que solo havia comersiado con la nasion delos Atacapas, con quienes hizo las cambalaches, que ha expresado, y atratado, y comerciado, veinte y sinco años, con lizensia" [longer version] (author's translation).

89 Ibid., *BA*, 9:0578–0580: "que los Yndios Atacapas ban tambien â la Nueba Orleáns a comerciar, y lleven caballos, pieles, y aseite de Osso y que ha treinta y dos años que los Franzes tienen comersio con dicha Nasion que es muy numerosa, tiene muchas rancherias, y se estiende desde el Rio de la Trinidad hasta laguna Lecheti[?], que dista cinco leguas del Rio Missisipi" (first quotation); "que expresó â los Horquissas hiva â decir al Gov.r español [Governor Barrios Jáuregui] para saber si hera justoel embargo, y les dixo, que se sosegasen, que el Gobernador Franzes, y el español heran una misma cosa" (second quotation; all author's translations).

90 Notification, Spanish official, Juaquin de Balbuena, to Joseph Blancpain, October 21, 1755, Mexico City, *ASFG*, box 2A249, 65.

91 *Memoria* [List of Goods], Blancpain, October 25, 1755, Mexico City, *BA*, microfilm, 9:0581–0588.

92 *Razon de la Rutta que yo, d.n. Jph Blancpain, tuve en mi viage, desde la nueva orleans hastta los Atacapas, â donde* [los españoles] *me aprehendieron . . .* (Account of the route that I, Joseph Blancpain, had on my travel from New Orleans up to the Atacapas where [the Spaniards] arrested me . . .), October 25, 1755, Mexico City, *ASFG*, box 2Q249, vol. 6, 66–67, photostat: "De Plaquemina caminamos cinco leguas para baxar al lago nombrado Chettinacha, en cuia frontera estta la nación Atacapas" (first quotation); "hicimos veinte y cinco leguas p.ra llegar a la Bahía de los Atacapas, la que tendrá como quince leguas de fondo y forma dos brazos el uno á el oestte, y el ottro al Estte que es el mismo en donde nos aprehendieron" (second quotation; all author's translations).

93 Bolton, *Texas*, 337–39; Folmer, *Franco-Spanish Rivalry*, 304. Although Blancpain described in his diary that his two white companions were also servants like his two black ones, Bolton only said the former were Blancpain's two French companions and that they were with two blacks.

94 Folmer, *Franco-Spanish Rivalry*, 304–5.

95 Morfi, *History of Texas*, 373.

96 Ibid.

97 Letter, Father Abad Didier to the viceroy, Marqués de Amarillas, July 19, 1756, Adaes, *AGI—Guadalajara* 401, in *OSMRL*, Our Lady of the Lake University, microfilm, reel 3, doc. 23, 1–2, photostat.

98 Letter, Father Didier, ibid., *AGI—Guadalajara*, 2–4: "son una semilla" (first quotation); and "M. Massè conoce el fondo y la devilidad de las naciones

del Norte como los tabayages, Letas, y Patoca, Ycarra, y Paris, por haver estado entre ellos" (second quotation; all author's translations).

99   Letter, Governor Barrios Jáuregui to Viceroy Marqués de Amarillas, July 22, 1756, Adaes, ibid., *AGI—Guadalajara*, 1–3.

100   Bolton, *Texas*, 327–28.

101   Letter, Kerlérec to [Rouille], October 1, 1753, M. de Villiers, ed., "Un mémoire politique du xviiie siècle relatif au Texas," *Journal de la Société des Américanistes de Paris* 3 (1906): 68, quotation in Folmer, *Franco-Spanish Rivalry*, 303–4.

102   Certification, Father Fray Joseph Calahorra, investigation of outcome of don Manuel Antonio de Soto Bermudez's visit with the Hasinai Caddo Indians, February 23, 1753, Mission Los Adaes; quotation in Hackett, *Pichardo's Treatise*, 4:61.

103   Certification, ibid., *Pichardo's Treatise*, 4:61–62.

104   Letter, Governor Kerlérec to Governor Martos Navarrete, New Orleáns, March 13, 1760, *BA*, microfilm, roll 9, frame nos. 0883–0884, original French language translated into *Castellano* (Castillian Spanish): "Estoi tan sorprendido, è indignago dela conducta, que se acumula al Señor San Denis" (first quotation); "San Denis Alférez de las tropas, destacado â los Natchitoches V.S. me dice: que se le imputó haver despachado un salvage de la nacion de los Ados, para empeñar â los Gefes de Orkokisas (con quienes se halla V.S. domiciliado) que fuesen â encontrarle, â fin de recivir una dadiba de polvora, balas, fusiles, tabaco, bermellon, y otror efectos, con la condicion de que matasen vuestro soldados, y destruiesen vuestro Fuerte, y con la promesa de que si executaban estas horribles proposiciones, que no se acordaria mas de lo que acaecio con Blancpain" (second quotation; all author's translations).

105   Letter, Governor Kerlérec, ibid., *BA*, 9:0884: "pues no se tendra la temeridad de exponerlo, a una residencia" (author's translation).

106   Ibid., *BA*, 9:0884–0885: "entonces no ignorará V.S. que el Señor Dn. Jacinto de Barrios, su predecesor, ha vendido toda especie de efectos, durante su gobierno, â los Tankaoneys, y otros Barbaros, que no huvieran llegado â ser sus enemigos, si no huviese tenido negocios interesantes" (first quotation); "reconocer igualm. te que sus Misiones de los Ayches, de los Nakodoses, y de los Orkokisas sacan diariamente de los Nattchitoches â precio de dinero, los efectos, cuia distribución parece ser, que V.S. no aprueba entre sus vecinos. V.S. sabe finalmente, que ellos hacen una negociacion publica y verificada con los Assinayes, Nadacotes, Nacodosses" (second quotation; all author's translations). On the background of the Tawakonis and their relations with the Spanish, see Todd F. Smith, *The Wichita Indians: Traders of Texas and the Southern Plains, 1540–1845* (College Station: Texas A&M University Press, 2000), 28–30, 35–36; and La Vere, *Texas Indians*, 145.

107 Interestingly, later that year in fall 1760, Governor Martos Navarrete authorized limited trade between Béxareños (Spanish soldier-settlers at San Antonio de Béxar) and Indians in consideration of the "poor residents" of San
Antonio as long as there was no "disturbance" among the Indians and that
such commerce with them would not involve "horses, gunpowder, guns, and
ammunition." Letter, Gov. don Angel de Martos y Navarrete to Señor Justicia
Myor Alcaldes y Regimento de la Villa de San Fernando, October 20, 1760, *BA*,
microfilm, 9:0933 (author's translation).

108 Ibid., *BA*, 9:0885. [Full text:] "no debo omitar hazer presente â V.S. que los
Pueblos, que se le han sublevado, comunican tambien en el Nortte con los
<u>Oragos</u>, <u>Arcansas</u>, <u>Ylinoeses</u>, <u>Peanguichias</u>, <u>Viatones</u>, <u>choanones</u>, <u>Miamises</u>,
<u>Potuamises</u>, <u>Misuries</u>, <u>Kanses</u>, <u>Naytanes</u>, <u>Picaras</u>, <u>Panises</u>, <u>Negros</u>, y <u>Blancos</u>,
y una infinidad de otros sus Aliados, y los de S.M. Christianissima, que en
las turbelencias presentes, en que nos veemos empeñados con los Yngleses,
prodigan su sangre, su vida, y su libertad por nosotros, â quienes despues de
tiempo immemorial, les franqueamos los socorros de que V.S. se quexa, que
son mui importantes â fin de impedirles, que vayan â sacarlos de nuestros
enemigos, los quales especialmente en actuales circunstancias, no dexarian
de aplaudirlo, y vanagloriare de su necesidad, para disponer, que esta cediese
en nuestro perjuicio" (author's translation); the underlined names appear in
the original text.

109 Ibid.

110 Certification, don Phelipe Cleere, translation of Governor Kerlérec's letter to
Governor Martos Navarrete, August 19, 1760, Mexico City, *BA*, 9:0886.

111 *Respuesta fiscal* (fiscal's response), Marqués de Aranda, to the correspondence
between Governor Kerlérec and Governor Martos Navarrete, August 26, 1760,
Mexico City, *BA*, 9:0886–0887: "procure, que los mencionados Yndios Orcoquisas, y demas de aquellas fronteras, no se convengan en manera alguna con
dichos franceses en los referidos pactos, ni en otros algunos, que puedan ser
perjudiciales â la quietud publica" (author's translation).

112 Ibid., *BA*, 9:9:0888–0889: "los missioneros de los Yndios Ayches, de los Naco-
doses, y de los Orcoquisas, sacan diariamente de los Yndios Natchitoches,
â precio de dinero los efectos . . . convengan â evitar, que los referidos missioneros tengan los expresados tratos, y contratos con los expresados Yndios"
(first quotation); "se debera valer de algun soldado, ô vezino, de ella, que
entienda el tal Ydioma, y haga, que forme traducción de ellas, para poder
con este medio, instruirse, y contestarlas, segun convenga, y corresponda"
(second quotation; all author's translations); *decreto* (order) by the fiscal,
Marqués de Aranda, sent to the *auditor*, don Domingo Valcarcel, August 27,
1760, Mexico City. The auditor then wrote his *Dictamen* (pronouncement) in
agreement and established a four-question investigation based on the fiscal's

response, September 1, 1760, Mexico City, *BA*, 9:0889–0890. The viceroy then issued his own order in agreement with the fiscal and auditor, September 5, 1760, Mexico City, *BA*, 9:0890–0891.

113 Declaration, Captain Calzones of the Orcoquiza Nation, before don Domingo del Rio and don Juan Prieto, March 28, 1761, Presidio San Agustín de Ahumada, *BA*, microfilm, 9:0972: "no era verdad por que dho S.or Sn Dioni no les avia dho tal cosa, que ellos lo dijeron por ver si que riamos a los Españoles" (author's translation). Captain Calzones gave his declaration in his own language, and it was signed by del Río and Prieto, but apparently Calzones himself did not sign; declaration, Captain Gordo of the Orcoquiza Nation, April 2, 1761, *BA*, 9:0972–0973, "jugando" (playing or joking).

114 Declaration, Famages (Orcoquiza?), April 4, 1761; declaration, Captain Boca-flores of the Orcoquiza Nation, April 6, 1761; Captain Thomas of the Bidais Nation, April 11, 1761; and Captain Antonio of the Bidais Nation, April 16, 1761. All appeared before del Río and Prieto at San Agustín de Ahumada, *BA*, 9:0973–0974.

115 *Dictamen*, don Domingo Valcarcel, auditor, September 1, 1762, Mexico City, *ASFG*, box 2Q249, vol. 6, 127–33, photostat.

116 Report, Julian de Arriaga, December 16, 1762, Madrid, first report on the cession of Louisiana to Spain by France, Williams Research Center—Historic New Orleans Collection, 24–33, Spanish transcription (author's translation).

117 Letter, Commandant McCarty to Governor Martos Navarrete, November 17, 1763, Natchitoches, *Nacogdoches Archives* (hereafter *NA*), Center for American History, University of Texas at Austin, box 2Q292, vol. 5, p. 16, Spanish transcription (author's translation). McCarty also informed Martos Navarrete about the history of French and Spanish claims to the country west of the Mississippi ever since La Salle's exploration and fiasco in Texas. McCarty believed Spanish mission Nacogdoches was located near French posts in Illinois Country.

118 Ibid., 1–15.

119 Report, Lt. Joseph Gonzales, August 13, 1766, Presidio Los Adaes, *AGI—Cuba* 149A, microfilm, reel 13, doc. 33, 1, in Old Spanish Mission Records, Our Lady of the Lake University, San Antonio, Texas: "como alas óraciones de la noche llego ála casa de morada Francisco Ramírez, alias el Badeño, vecino de este R.l Presidio, dandome noticia de la que como alponerse el sol, cerca del Rancho que llaman de Bermudez, Jurisdicc.on de este Presidio havia visto como diez Franceses que marchavan con caballos cargados con polvora, balas, fusiles, y otros efectos á comerciar entre nrâs. Naciones de Indios Gentiles" (author's translation). Acting as Lieutenant Gonzales's *testigos de asistencia* (witnesses) were don Antonio Gallardo and don Bernardo de Miranda. The viceroy, Marqués de Cruillas, originally ordered O'Conor to conduct the

investigation against Governor Martos Navarrete in August 1765. See John, *Storms Brewed*, 374.

120 Report, Lieutenant Gonzales, ibid., *AGI—Cuba* 149A, 13:1–2: "por cuia causa seacen mas ósados, y atrebidos y suceden en esta Prov.a tantos robos y muertes" (author's translation); report, Lt. Joseph Gonzales, August 14, 1766, Presidio Los Adaes, *AGI—Cuba* 149A, 13:2–3.

121 *Incontinenti* (in continuance), Lt. Joseph Gonzales, August 14, 1766, Presidio Los Adaes, *AGI—Cuba* 149A, 13:3. [Duzan Lodre:] "todos los efectos eran suios y que quatro delos Franceses eran sus sirvientes y los llevava asalariados para que le ayudasen á comerciar entre las Naciones de Indios los efectos que llevaban, que los ótros Franceses yvan con Pasaporte de d.n Luis dela Periere állevar una canoa que cerca de Bermudez havian ocultado en un arroyo de los que desaguan enla Laguna de este Presidio la que se forma del Rio de Narchitos" (author's translation). Lodre did not sign his testimony because he said he did not know how to sign his own name.

122 Declaration, Duzan Lodre, a French trader, appearing before Lt. Joseph Gonzales in the Spanish investigation of French contraband trade, August 14, 1766, Presidio Los Adaes, *AGN—Cuba* 149A, microfilm, reel 13, doc. 33, 3–4, Old Spanish Mission Records, Our Lady of the Lake University, San Antonio, Texas.

123 *Auto* (judicial writ), Lt. Joseph Gonzales, granting liberty to two French traders and holding the remaining five in custody under company guard, August 14, 1766, Presidio Los Adaes, *AGI—Cuba* 149A, 13:4; submission of autos, Lieutenant Gonzales to Governor O'Conor, August 23, 1766, Presidio Los Adaes, *AGI—Cuba* 149A, 13:4. Lieutenant Gonzales did not state the names of the Frenchmen he freed, but one was quite possibly Duzan Lodre.

124 John, *Storms Brewed*, 374. See also David M. Vigness, "Don Hugo Oconor and New Spain's Northeastern Frontier, 1764–1776," *Journal of the West* 6 (January 1967): 29–30.

125 Letter, Gov. don Hugo O'Conor to the viceroy, Marqués de Croix, December 23, 1767, San Antonio de Béxar, *AGI—Cuba* 149A, 13:5–6: "por hallarse los caballos de la tropa imposibilitados de poder proseguir" (first quotation); "Ataqué a los enemigos, con bastante brio. La funcion duró desde las tres de la tarde, hasta las cinco y media, since que en este tpô hayan podido los enemigos ganan ventaxa alguna, mas que de haber herido dos soldados, y seis caballos que en la funcion murieron" (second quotation; all author's translations).

126 Quotation in Vigness, "Don Hugo Oconor," 32. For a general discussion of Governor O'Conor's handling of French contraband trade and Indian hostilities, see John, *Storms Brewed*, 378–82.

127 Letter, Governor O'Conor to Viceroy Marqués de Croix, *AGI—Cuba* 149A, 13:6–7: "el Presidio de los Adaes, ámas de ser inútil al Rey, y que jamas severificará

en el, Poblzon alguna; estoi muy seguro de que los enemigos lo ofendan por el comercio que con ellos han tenido, algunos sujetos como percibirá V.E. por la representacion del cavildo" (author's translation).

128 Letter, Viceroy Marqués de Croix to Governor O'Conor, January 18, 1768, Mexico City, *AGI—Cuba* 149A, 13:8–9: "y haciendolo de Armas, y municiones, á los indios que estan en guerra cogiendolos con ellas seles impondrá lapena del ultimo suplicio" (first quotation); "en las Fronteras esta resolucion, y pasarle con un oficio al Governador de Nachitos para que disponga se haga lo mismo en su partido a fin de que llegue a noticia de todos, y no aleguen ignorancia" (second quotation; all author's translations).

129 Letter, Viceroy Marqués de Croix to Sir don Antonio de Ulloa, governor of Louisiana, January 18, 1768, Mexico City, *AGI—Cuba* 149A, microfilm, doc. 32, reel 13, 1–4: "el gran perjuicio que estos hacen y especialmente en proveheer de Armas, y Municiones de Guerra álos Yndios Apaches, y Comanches, con lo que executan tantos rovos, y muertes en aquella provincia de Texas" (first quotation); "estando ôy; vajo el dominio de nuestro monarca, considero que alguno de ellos será inútil, y quese puede librar al R.l Herario de sus costtos" (second quotation); "pues siendo competente extinguir alguno de dhos Presidios" (third quotation; all author's translations).

130 Letter, Viceroy Marqués de Croix to Governor Ulloa, *AGI—Cuba* 149A, 13: coversheet. On the background of Governor Ulloa's troubles in New Orleans, see Weber, *Spanish Frontier*, 200–203.

131 Letter, Viceroy Marqués de Croix to Governor O'Conor, September 3, 1768, Mexico City, *BA*, microfilm, roll 10, frame nos. 0634–0635. For more discussion of Spanish concerns about Comanches obtaining guns, see Barr, "From Captives to Slaves," 38–39. By the late 1750s, following their attack on Mission San Sabá in the hill country region of central Texas, the Comanches and their Wichita allies became the most pressing concern of Spanish royal officials.

132 Stein and Stein, *Colonial Heritage*, 99–100.

133 Letter, Viceroy Marqués de Croix, to Governor Martos Navarrete, December 1, 1766, *BA*, 10:0454–0456: "los Barbaros enemigos" (first quotation); "del comercio libre del tabaco" (second quotation; all author's translations).

134 Proclamation, Viceroy de Croix, February 2, 1770, Mexico City, copy sent to the governor of Texas, *BA*, 9:0699.

135 Norton, *Sacred Gifts, Profane Pleasures*, 11, 201.

136 Bushnell, *King's Coffer*, 68, 105–6.

137 Account book for troops from Presidio Los Adaes detached in Béxar, January 1, 1771, to December 31, 1771, San Antonio de Béxar, *BA*, Center for American History, UT-Austin, box 2S31, 178, Joaquín Ruiz, August 1 entry: "pagados a dn. Jph Hidalgo en chocolate" (author's translation).

138 Norton, *Sacred Gifts, Profane Pleasures*, 250, 255.

139 Letter, Commandant Athanase de Mézières to Governor Unzaga Amezaga, March 14, 1771, Natchitoches. Quotations in Herbert Eugene Bolton, trans. and ed., *Athanase de Mézières and the Louisiana-Texas Frontier, 1768–1780* (Cleveland: Arthur H. Clark, 1914), 243.

CHAPTER 6

1 Thomas D. Hall, *Social Change in the Southwest, 1350–1880* (Lawrence, University Press of Kansas, 1989), 24. On periphery versus core, see Immanuel Wallerstein, *The Modern World-System III: The Second Era of Great Expansion of the Capitalist World-Economy, 1730–1840s* (San Diego, CA: Academic Press, 1989). For more discussion of local dynamics on the peripheres and core, see Adelman and Aron, "From Borderlands to Borders," 814–41.

2 Deeds, *Defiance and Deference*, 71. For an overview of Indian slavery in colonial Mexico, see Silvio Zavala, *Los esclavos indios en Nueva España* (Mexico City: El Colegio Nacional, 1967).

3 Chipman, *Spanish Texas*, 49. The encomienda had its roots with the Reconquest of Spain from the Moors by *adelantados* who were given the right to collect tribute from Muslims and other peasants in the areas theys conquered and resettled in the name of Christianity. For more discussion, see Lesley Byrd Simpson, *The Encomienda of New Spain: The Beginnings of Spanish Mexico* (Berkeley: University of California Press, 1950).

4 Weber, *Spanish Frontier*, 112.

5 Royal decree, May 9, 1672, Madrid, in Cavazos Garza, *Breve historia de Nuevo Leon*, 54–56: "no se consienta que los indios puedan hacerse esclavos con pretexto alguno, ni venderse, ni enajenarse . . . [y que] la conversión de los indios se haga en predicaciones congregándolos en pueblos y repartiéndoles tierras" (author's translation); see also Porter, *Their Lives*, 59, which discusses prohibition of Indian slavery under the Recopilación of 1681.

6 Ibid., 56. For discussion of *capitán protector*, see Charles R. Cutter, *The Protector de Indios in Colonial New Mexico, 1659–1821* (Albuquerque: University of New Mexico Press, 1986); David J. Weber, *The Spanish Frontier in North America* (New Haven, CT: Yale University Press, 1992), 128.

7 Barr, *Peace Came*, 170.

8 Barr, "'Seductions' of Texas," 344–45, 403, argues that gender was the main signifier of difference in Spanish Texas before it was supplanted by notions of race with the introduction of African slavery in the early nineteenth century.

9 Inspection, Marques de Rubí, September 23, 1767, Presidio Los Adaes, *AGI—Guadalajara* 511, OLLU, microfilm, reel 4, doc. 111, 2.

10 Deeds, *Defiance and Deference*, 72. She also refers to the labor force evolving haphazardly, or as a "hodgepodge of labor practices" (60, 66).

11 Testimony, witness #6, Mattheo Ybarbo, July 19, 1741, Presidio Los Adaes [?], Residencia proceeding of Gov. Prudencio Orobio y Basterra, *BA*, box 2S26, 28v–29: (question 6) "que solamente en una ocas.n endho. Presidio de Sn. Anttonio yen Guerra hiba a prisiono dho D.n Prudencio diez y seis Yndios Apaches de los que haviendo dado quentta i por superior decretto los remittio la Tierra afuera" (author's translation).

12 Archives of the Residencia proceedings against Gov. Justo Boneo y Morales, desceased, *BA*, microfilm, 8:0836: "Un testimontio de autos echo por dho d.n Prudencio, s.re unos Yndios, e Yndios Apaches que remitó a la carcel publica de México, por ordern de su Ex.a" (author's translation); testimony, 8:0862; 8:0863; and 8:0865 (question 6).

13 See Max L. Moorhead, "Spanish Deportation of Hostile Apaches: The Policy and the Practice," *Arizona and the West*, 206. See also, in general, William E. Dunn, "Apache Relations in Texas, 1718–1750," *Southwestern Historical Quarterly* 14 (January 1911): 199–274. For background on captivity, see Barr, "'Seductions' of Texas," 287–301.

14 During the period that Presidio Los Adaes served as the capital of Spanish Texas (1729–73), there were residencia proceedings held to review the conduct of seven different governors, some of whom were good administrators and commandants, while others were notoriously bad. Most governors were also career military officers, having served in Spain before coming to Mexico. A *pesquisa secreto* (secret investigation) usually included a lengthy introduction of the examiner, who was often the incoming governor; an eight- to twelve-question interrogatory; and the testimony of (eight to twenty-four) witnesses, their declarations, *autos* (judicial writs), decrees, and an inventory of the presidios' books, archives, and occurrences during the governors' adminis-tration. When the governor's conduct was good or his service brief, then the proceedings ranged from one hundred to two hundred pages long. The longest investigation concerned Governor Sandoval's administration (more than six hundred pages long), which included a *demanda* (lawsuit) against him by soldiers of Presidio Los Adaes for back pay and abuse by his first lieutenant, Fermín Ybiricu, discussed in chapter 5. No other governor, besides Sandoval, was found negligent of his duties while in office, but even Sandoval was exonerated years later for having resided in San Antonio de Béxar to closely monitor Spanish-Apache troubles instead of being at Presidio Los Adaes to guard against French encroachment.

15 Question 6 of interrogatory, residencia proceedings of Gov. don Francisco Gar-cia Larios, July 15, 1748, Presidio Los Adaes, *NA*, box 2Q292, vol. 3, pp. 19–20,

transcription: "Si ha condenado algunos Yndios a servicio personal temporal o perpetuo" (author's translation).

16 Ibid., 35, transcription: "q.e no sabe, ni oyo dezir q.e durante el Gov.or del gral. Dn. Fran.co Garcia Larios huviese su Señoria condenado a Indio alguno a ninguna pena antes si tratadolos con todo amor y obsequiándolos De su Bolsillo" (author's translation).

17 Ibid., testimony, witness no. 7, Domingo del Río, July [?], 1748, Presidio Los Adaes, Residencia proceedings of Governor Sandoval, 46, transcription (question 4): "con los Yndios de esta inmediación que con todo Cariño los Rezibia y Regalaba lo q. le pedian como era tabaco y algunas vezes Maiz y esto sin interes" (author's translation).

18 Barr, *Peace Came*, 174.

19 Interrogatory, January 26, 1760, Presidio Los Adaes, residencia proceedings against Lt. Col. don Jacinto de Barrios y Jáuregui of his time as governor of Texas, *BA*, microfilm, 9:0726–0727 (question 5): "si saben â y an bendido algunos yndios de los Barbaros sacandolos de sus rancherias, osian dexado de castigar a los que an cometido este eszeso[?]" (author's translation).

20 Ibid., testimony, witness #1, Phelipe Muñoz de Mora, *vecino* [of Presidio Los Adaes], *ser de edad de ochenta y un años, y que no le tocan las generales de la Ley*, January 26, 1760, residencia proceedings of Governor Barrios Jáuregui, 9:0728–0729 (question 5): "que no ha tenido motibo de bender ningún Yndio Barbaro, ni menos permitido que ninguno se aya propasado a estraerlo de sus Rancherias" (author's translation).

21 Ibid., testimony, witness #10, Cristóbal de Santiago, *mulatto y Vecino ara de dho Presidio el que fue soldado desde que entro el Marques de San Mig.l deaguayo*, sixty years old, January 28, 1760, Presidio Los Adaes, residencia proceeding of Govenor Barrios Jáuregui, 9:0741–0742 (question 5): "que no sabe ni ha oydo decir . . ." (author's translation).

22 Hiram F. Gregory, "Eighteenth Century Caddoan Archaeology: A Study in Models and Interpretations" (PhD diss., Southern Methodist University, 1973), 262; Pekka Hämäläinen, "The Comanche Empire: A Study of Indigenous Power, 1700–1875" (PhD diss., University of Helsinki, Finland, 2001), 165; Barr, "'Seductions' of Texas," 299. See also Barr, "From Captives to Slaves," 20; and Brooks, *Captives and Cousins*, 33, who adds that Indian captives and horses were commodities for sale that ended up as far away as Mexico City, California, Louisiana, Cuba, and New England.

23 The impossibility of quantifying Indian captives has also been said about the Comanche-Wichita-French slave traffic. See Hämäläinen, "Comanche Empire," 164.

24 Gregory, "Eighteenth Century Caddoan Archaeology," 262, 287, mentions the sale of Apache slaves at Los Adaes, who were also baptized and assigned

godparents, and that the primary markets for such sales were French Natchitoches and Spanish Los Adaes; see also Lee, "Indian Slavery," 68–69, who specifically mentions Lipan Apache captives. According to my own estimation, based on the practice elsewhere in French North America, the number of Apache captives on the Spanish-Franco-Caddo frontier probably numbered in the hundreds. This figure is comparable to the number of Fox Indian captives, mostly women and children, taken during a similar time period (1716–44) by Illinois and Ottawa allies and sold into slavery at Montreal, New France, where they were baptized and given French godparents, who were also their masters. See Brett Rushforth, "Slavery, the Fox Wars, and the Failures of the Middle Ground," paper presented at the Omohundro Institute of Early American History and Culture, College of William and Mary, October 26, 2004, 21, 25–29.

25 Barr, *Peace Came*, 165, 324n20.

26 For further discussion, see Hämäläinen, "Comanche Empire," 165, which describes the height of the Apache wars during the mid-eighteenth century as a "boon for slaving" for the Comanche, for whom captives became a "by-product of their incessant livestock raids and Indian wars"; Smith, "Account," 529–30. For comparison, see John L. Kessell, *Kiva, Cross, and Crown: The Pecos Indians and New Mexico, 1540–1840* (Albuquerque: University of New Mexico Press, 1987), 136–37.

27 The *genízaros* of New Mexico were detribalized, acculturated Indians and former captives. For discussion of genízaros, see Hämäläinen, "Comanche Empire," 166; Weber, *Spanish Frontier*, 308; and Kessell, *Kiva, Cross, and Crown*, 366.

28 Letter, Governor Martos Navarrete to Viceroy Marqués de Cruillas, September 14, 1761, Presidio Los Adaes, *ASFG*, box 2Q 252, vol. 13, 18–19, photostat: "Cauptibadas con otras muchas, por los Alitanes, ó Apaches Pelones, en el Rancho de Santa feê" (author's translation).

29 Letter, don Domingo Valcarzel, *auditor*, to Viceroy Marqués de Cruillas, March 2, 1762, Mexico City, *BA*, microfilm, 9:1006.

30 Letter, Viceroy Marqués de Cruillas to Governor Martos Navarrete, March 5, 1762, Mexico City, *BA*, microfilm, 9:1007.

31 For background on the Spanish policy of ransoming captives from Indians, see Oakah L. Jones Jr., "Rescue and Ransom of Spanish Captives from the *indios bárbaros* on the Northern Frontier of New Spain," *Colonial Latin American Historical Review* 4 (Spring 1995): 129–48.

32 Letter, Comandant McCarty to Governor Martos Navarrete, September 10, 1763, Natchitoches, Louisiana, *NA*, vol. 5, box 2Q292, 3–4, transcription in Spanish [Full Quotation]: "(mas bien lo save Vs.a q.e ninguno) de el paso abierto que incesantemente por los españoles se franquea a nuestros yndios de adentro

pa. q.e vaian a guerear con el perjuicio de visible redunda en la nación de los Apaches . . . abiendo sido de los indibiduos de dha. villa [San Antonio de Vejar] hospedados y atendidos, no se restituyeron a su Pueblo donde llebaron Captivos algunos niños, con yntenzion de venderles, la que a poco tmpo. lograron con ciertos vezinos de los Adaes siendo así los q.e fomentan por medio de el trafique la avaricia, y sangrientos hechos de los propios naturales de su reino" (author's translation).

33 See Barr, "'Seductions' of Texas," 344, who argues that captive taking and exchange among Spaniards and Indians was a "system not of slave trade and labor, but . . . fully within the politics of diplomacy and post-fight reparations." However, captives were also a source of labor for Indians and Spaniards; see Hämäläinen, "Comanche Empire," 164, who mentions that by the late 1740s, Comanches sold Apache captives to the Wichitas, who utilized these slaves "as extra labor on their own cornfields" or sometimes resold them to French merchants. Israel Cavazos Garza, *Breve historia de Nuevo León* (Mexico City: Fondo de Cultura Económica, 1994), 49–51, discusses Spaniards in the seventeenth century capturing Indians from their rancherías and transporting them to *haciendas* ("large landed estates") in northeastern New Spain, where they became laborers. The sale or transfer of land also included the Indian rancherías. David Frye, "The Native Peoples of Northeastern Mexico," in *The Cambridge History of the Native Peoples of the Americas*, vol. 2, *Mesoamerica*, ed. Richard E. W. Adams and Murdo J. MacLeod (Cambridge: Cambridge University Press, 2000), 110, states that Indians and mulattoes from farther south in Mexico provided the labor for the ranching economy in northeastern New Spain. See also James F. Brooks, *Captives and Cousins: Slavery, Kinship, and Community in the Southwest Borderlands* (Chapel Hill: University of North Carolina Press, 2002), 31, who argues that indigenous and Spanish slave sales in the Southwest borderlands together formed a "slave system" whereby "victims symbolized social wealth, performed services for their masters, and produced material goods under the threat of violence."

34 For comparison elsewhere on the far northern frontier of New Spain, see Hämäläinen, "Comanche Empire," 164, who says Indian slaves among New Mexico Hispanos were valued domestic servants as well as important symbols of status and wealth; and de la Teja, *San Antonio de Béxar*, 123, who argues that slavery in San Antonio was "more a matter of status than of economics."

35 This argument derives from reading Brett Rushforth on alliance and slavery in New France. Russforth explains that some of the Algonquian Indian nations, particularly the Ottawas, Illinois, Ojibwas, and Hurons, had their own concerns about preventing French imperial expansion westward and became upset when the French negotiated a separate peace with their Fox

enemies, which resulted in the series of Fox Wars from 1712 to 1744 in New France. This warfare fulfilled the plans of most Algonquians by embroiling the French in a quagmire and frustrating French commercial and territorial ambitions. Rushforth, "Slavery," 31–32.

36 Letter, Commandant McCarty to Governor Martos Navarrete, November 17, 1763, Natchitoches, *NA*, box 2Q292, vol. 5, 1, 14, transcription in Spanish: "que en controverzias vayamos perdiendo un tiempo, que seria mas vien dedicado a el gusto y alegria conque devieramos Zelebrar el pacto de familia que tan estrechamente vincula ambas naciones" (author's translation); Letter, Commandant McCarty to Governor Martos Navarrete, September 10, 1763, Natchitoches, *NA*, box 2Q292, 4, transcription in Spanish. For more discussion of rescue and ransom in northern New Spain, see Porter, *Their Lives*, 59.

37 Ibid., 8–9, transcription in Spanish: "Posible es que con tan poca atencion seais mirando los usos, ynclinaziones, y leyes de tan distintos pueblos? el modo con que componen sus cavellos? pintan sus rostros, y cuerpos? tienen asiento o son vagamondos? hazen sembraduras o se contentan de las silvestres frutas? comen unos queman los muertos, s otros les dan sepultura: y la mayor parte les dexa en campo razo, sin apurarse de que sirben de pasto a las auras, y vorazes animales?" (author's translation). McCarty added, "respondeme señor es acazo tan notable diversidad de costumbres, seña de la armonia que entre si profesan los indibiduos de un mismo estado, tal qual la vemos establecida en las demas partes del mundo y tal qual en tpo. De la española conquista se mantenia en las naciones de este nuevo orbe, que avasalladas tenian los mexicanos, y Peruvianos?"

38 Ibid., 9–10, transcription in Spanish: "vienen los Bidays, Acinais, Nacogdoches, Nazones y Aizes hazernos la suplica de que cuidemos (para usar yo de sus terminos) qe. los caminos que limpio dho Don Luis de San Dioniz, no vayan ccriando nuevas espinas y que en el cielo que visito de azul no se amontonen nubes, sinistros y espantosos presagios de las tempestades que les han acometido" (author's translation).

39 Declaration, *Juan Pheliciano Cassanova*, January 16, 1773, San Antonio de Béxar, *BA*, microfilm, 11:0309–0310: "Fue uno de los q.e componian dho. Destacam.to a ultimo del verano antesed.te q.e los treze o catorce dias de camino en la arrinconada, entre la costa y este lado de Rio G.de, coxieron diez y nueve almas Gentiles entre Hombres, Mugeres, y niños, haviéndose escondido la mayor parte de la rancheria en la espesura del monte, q.e ni aun a pie podia penetrarse" (author's translation).

40 Ibid., 11:0308.

41 Letter, Viceroy Antonio Bucarely y Ursua to Governor Ripperdá, November 16, 1772, México City, *BA*, microfilm, 11:0285: "sobre los excesos que cometen los vecinos de la Colonia de Nuevo Santander quitan de los hixos â los Gentiles

amigos para venderlos por esclavos en perjuicio de su reducion, en oposicion de la humanidad anque debe tratarseles para unirlos al gremio de Nuestra s.ta fee y lo que es mas encontravencion de las practisas intencionesde S.M." (author's translation).

42 Letter, Governor Martos Navarrete to Father Calahorra, March 21, 1765, Presidio Los Adaes, in proceedings concerning the return of Antonio Treviño by the Taovaya Indians, *BA*, microfilm, 10:0375: "no se dude de la amistad q.e esa nacion no profesa, y del deseo que tienen de mantener con nosotros la paz" (author's translation). The captivity of Antonio Treviño is a story that most scholars discuss; see John, *Storms Brewed*, 370–74; Barr, "'Seductions' of Texas," 175–79; Barr, *Peace Came*, 197–203; and Smith, *Wichita Indians*, 39–41.

43 Ibid., *BA*, microfilm, 10:0375: "Pues de lo contrario no podremos ser sus amigos, por sernos yndispensable defender â aquellos quando los hostilizen" (author's translation).

44 Letter, Friar Calahorra to Governor Martos Navarrete, Mission Guadalupe de Nacogdoches, July 30, 1765, in proceedings regarding the return of Antonio Treviño by the Taovaya Indians, *BA*, microfilm, 10:0376; Barr, *Peace Came*, 197.

45 Barr, *Peace Came*, 330n3. For more discussion, see Jones Jr., "Rescue and Ransom," 129–48.

46 Letter, Friar Calahorra to Governor Martos Navarrete, Mission Guadalupe de Nacogdoches, July 30, 1765, *BA*, microfilm, 10:0376–377: "en un parage no muy distante de San Saba por averse defendido con valor de quarenta y siete yndios de su [Eiasiquiche's] nación que le combatieron, mientras que el con quarto quedaron siguió los que a dho treviño acompañaban: que siendo quatro, quedaron muertos los tres que alcancio, que fueron dos hombres y una mujer . . . al qual gravamente herido de quarto valazos y dos glpes de chuzo que recibio" (first quotation); "en las campañas que se le ofreciera contra sus enemigos los Yndios Guasas [Osage], fue generalmente de todos chicos y grandes bien recivido, cuidado, y atendido; y con mas esmero desde que este [Treviño] dio a entender al expresado Capitan [Eiasiquiche], quando sobre ello fue por el preguntado en presencia de los mas del Pueblo que el era de donde avia salido [from Presidio Los Adaes]" (second quotation); "de traerlo en persona â esta Mision sin embargo de lo mucho que todos lo amaban, y querian con extremo, para que por este hecho acabaran de convencerse los Españoles de esta parte de la benevolencia que les profesan, y de el deseo que tenian de mantener con ellos la paz" (third quotation; all author's translations).

47 Ibid., 10:0377: "respondio por la voz de ellos que con los [Spaniards] de San Saba no podian observar la paz que protejian y defendían â los Apaches â quienes escolataban quando salian â carnear sabiendo que estos eran sus mortales enemigos, y tan ladrones que no solo atrevian âir â sus pueblos â

ofenderlos sino tambien â robarlos la caballada q.e tenian como assi acaba de suceder en el tehuacanas, en donde entraron, mataron y apresaron, yndios, y se llevaron todos los caballos que encontraron" (author's translation).

48 Barr, *Peace Came*, 199.

49 John, *Storms Brewed*, 370.

50 Certification, *Alferez de este Presidio don Pedro de Sierra . . . de edad de setenta años poco mas o menos*, August 9, 1765, Presidio Los Adaes, and Certification, *Antonio treviño, recidente en este sobre dho presidio . . . de edad de treinta y quarto años poco mas o mensos*, August 9, 1765, Presidio Los Adaes, proceedings concerning captivity and return of Antonio Treviño, *BA*, microfilm, 10:0377–0378.

51 Declaration, Antonio Treviño, August 13, 1765, Presidio Los Adaes, *BA*, microfilm, 10:0378: "Que han puesto los indios apartadas unas de otras para servirse por entre ellos de lo fuciles que son las armas que usan, las que le consta al declarante [Treviño] por averlo visto en los seis meses que alli vivio adquieren como la polbora, valas, paño, camisas, y todo lo demas que usan en sus vestuarios de los franceses, quienes les entran toda lo referido, y se lo dan en cambio de pieles de cibola, de venado, de apachitos, y Apaches que apresan en la guerra, de caballos, de mulas, y de todo lo demas que roban â los españoles" (author's translation).

52 Ibid., *BA*, 10:0379: "al norte viven los comanches con quienes tienen alianza; cuia nacion que no tiene morada fixa en parte alguna es numerosa, y comienza a usar fuciiles los quales adquieran de los franceses quienes los conducen allá, y los dan en cambio de todo lo demas que arriba queda expresado" (first quotation) and "vio en las muchas ocasiones que salio con ello â carnear, abunda con exceso en aquellos paises, que son llanos y pingues de pastos por las muchas aguas que los bañan, y de mais frijol y calabazas, que cojen en abundancia, cuias sementeras mantienen en las cercanias del pueblo" (second quotation; all author's translations).

53 Ibid., *BA*: "tirados por tierra en dos casas contiguo del fuerte . . . quienes dijeron al declarante se lo avian enseñado un frances" (author's translation).

54 Governor Martos Navarrete, August 16, 1765, Presidio Los Adaes, *BA*, microfilm, 10:0379.

55 John, *Storms Brewed*, 374; letter, Viceroy Cruillas to Governor Martos Navarrete concerning reinforcements to protect Béxar from threatened Indian attack, January 16, 1764, Mexico City, *BA*, 10:0189. The letter refers specifically to "varios Ynsultos" against the Villa de San Fernando by the "Naciones del Norte" (Nations of the North) that were expected to continue through March 1764.

56 The French from Natchitoches had to go around Presidio Los Adaes to communicate with its fort among the Cadodachos and to trade with New Mexico; see Hackett, *Pichardo's Treatise*, 3:410.

57 Restall, "Crossing to Safety," 389.

58 Konove, "On the Cheap," 250, 257–58. Konove carries discussion of the Baratillo from late colonial Mexico into the twentieth century with his book *Black Market Capital: Urban Politics and the Shadow Economy in Mexico City* (Oakland: University of California Press, 2018).

59 Ibid., 258, 268–70. Konove notes that the merchant guild of Mexico City was the sole legal importer of overseas goods into Mexico form its incorporation in 1592 until 1778.

60 Smith, *Wichita Indians*, 36.

61 Burton, "Family and Economy," 64, mentions that "an influx of Africans in the 1730s resulted in a majority slave population in Natchitoches by 1737, keeping the wary French population on guard." In 1737, the Natchitoches free population was 112 persons (48.1 percent of the total population), while the combined Indian and African slave population was 121 persons (51.9 percent of the total population), or 14 Indian slaves (6.0 percent) and 107 African slaves (45.9 percent); ibid., 46 (table 2.1), 115 (table 4.2), and 137 (table 5.1). James T. McGowan, "Creation of a Slave Society: Louisiana Plantations in the Eighteenth Century" (PhD diss., University of Rochester, New York, 1976), 24, 26–27, states that the Louisiana Colony's first two decades (1699–1719) were outside the mainstream of French slave trade and migratory patterns, dependent on Indians, convicts, and soldiers as laborers or colonists. See also Berlin, *Many Thousands Gone*, 8, who defines "slave societies" as those where "slavery stood at the center of economic production, and the master-slave relationship provided the model for all social relations," while "societies with slaves" had multiple forms of labor available besides slaves, who were "marginal to the central productive processes." For comparison to the development of a "slave system" in the American Southwest, see Brooks, *Captives and Cousins*, 31.

62 On the notion of slaveholders anxious over the enslaved population and a precipitating cause of revolution, see Woody Holton, *Forced Founders: Indians, Debtors, Slaves, and the Making of the American Revolution in Virginia* (Chapel Hill: University of North Carolina Press, 1999).

63 On the background of English and French rivalry in North America, see Milner, "Indulgent Friends," 123–48; Ekberg, *French Roots*; and Rushforth, "Slavery." See also Eric Hinderaker and Peter C. Mancall, *At the Edge of Empire: The Backcountry in British North America* (Baltimore: Johns Hopkins University Press, 2003).

64 De la Teja, *San Antonio de Béxar*, 122.

65 Jones, *Los Paisanos*, 28.

66 For background on government and law on the northern frontier of New Spain, see Charles R. Cutter, *The Legal Culture of Northern New Spain* (Albuquerque: University of New Mexico Press, 1995).

67 Bill of sale, September 6, 1748, Presidio Los Adaes, *BA*, microfilm, 8:1056–57: "que vende en venta Rl, desde oy en Adelante y para siempre un Negro esclavo llamado Luis de Urrutia Cofre de Pazas" (first quotation) and "y sele vende por esclavo captivo sujeto â servidumbre y por Livre de empeño Ypoteca, ni otra enagenacón, y sin Asegurárselo de enfermedad, thacha, ni otro Defecto Publico ni secreto" (second quotation; both author's translations).

68 Letter, don Francisco García Larios to *Justicia y Rejim.to de la Villa de Sn. Fernando* (Justice and Town Council of San Fernando [San Antonio de Béxar]), November 11, 1744, Mexico City, *BA*, microfilm, 8:0835, announcing the viceroy's appointment of him as temporary governor replacing Lt. Col. don Justo Boneo, who died and was governor of Texas.

69 Bill of sale, September 7, 1748, Presidio Los Adaes, *BA*, microfilm, 8:1058.

70 On the beginning of African slavery in Mexico City, see Lourdes Mondragón Barrios, *Esclavos africanos en la Ciudad de México: El servicio doméstico durante el siglo XVI* (Mexico City: Ediciones Euroamericanos, 1999).

71 On African slavery in southern Mexico, see Patrick J. Carroll, *Blacks in Colonial Veracruz: Race, Ethnicity, and Regional Development* (Austin: University of Texas Press, 1991); and María Luisa Herrera Casasús, *Presencia y Esclavitud del Negro en La Huasteca* (Mexico City: Miguel Angel Porrúa, 1989). On the slave trade and origins of African slaves in colonial Mexico, see Gonzalo Aguirre Beltrán, "The Slave Trade in Mexico," *Hispanic American Historical Review* 24 (August 1944): 412–31; Aguirre Beltrán, "Tribal Origins of Slaves in Mexico," *Journal of Negro History*, July 1946, 269–352. On black and mulatto slaves in Northern New Spain, see Carlos Manuel Valdés and Ildefonso Dávila, *Esclavos Negros en Saltillo* (Saltillo, Mexico: Universidad Autónoma de Coahuila, 1989); Robert C. West, *The Mining Community in Northern New Spain: The Parral Mining District* (Berkeley: University of California Press, 1949), 53–56; and Martin, *Governance and Society*, 2, 59, 66. See also Berlin, *Many Thousands Gone*, 12, who distinguishes "plantation generations" of African slaves as the children or grandchildren of the "charter generations," or first arrivals, and the subsequent "revolutionary generations." Using this analogy, Luís and Antonio might fall under the "plantation generation."

72 Baptism, Manuel Marianne, November 11, 1754, *négritte*, daughter of Nanette and Pierrot, negroes belonging to Madame de St. Denis, godparents: Manuel de choto vermudes, Spaniard [Manuel de Soto y Bermudez] and Madame de Blanc, *NACCR*, 71, entry no. 579; baptism, Louise Cirena, February 8, 1757, *mulâttresse* belonging to Monsieur de Blanc, godparents: Emmanuel Soto and Marie Soto *ditte* St. Denis, *NACCR*, 78–79, entry no. 646.

73 Baade, "Law of Slavery," 48–49, 54.

74 Baptism, Marie Emmanuel de Soto, May 27, 1756, Natchitoches, born May 11, legitimate daughter of Emmanuel Antonio Soto Bermúdez and Marie des Neges de St. Denis, godparents: Pierre de la Ronde, officer and Marie Emmanuela Sanchez Navarro de St. Denis, *NACCR*, 71, entry no. 579; baptism, Marie Josephe Damasene de Soto Bermudez, February 6, 1760, Natchitoches, legitimate daughter of don Emmanuel de Soto and Marie des Neges de St. Denis, godparents: Pierre Antoine de St. Denis, ensign, and Marie de Soto, Friar Valentin, witness, Friar Franciscus Caldes of Los Adaes, *NACCR*, 51, entry no. 406; baptism, Louis Joseph Firmin de Soto, October 23, 1761, Natchitoches, legitimate son of don Manuel Soto and Dame Marie des Neges de St. Denis, godparents: Louis Antoine de St. Denis, ensign, and Marie Soto, Friar Valentin, witness, R. Joseph Diaz Infante [from Los Adaes], officiating, *NACCR*, 58, entry no. 464; baptism, Joseph Francois de Soto, September 19, 1763, Natchitoches, legitimate son of don Manuel de Soto and Maria da Nieba de San Denis, godparents: Juan Prieto and Fca. Le bru, *NACCR*, 60, entry no. 485; baptism, Eulalie Marie Anne de Soto, December 22, 1763, Natchitoches, legitimate daughter of Manuel de Soto and Maria de Niebas [Marie des Nieges de St. Denis], godparents: Gov. Angel de Marthos y Navarreti and Madama Borme, *NACCR*, 61, entry no. 490; baptism, Severine Antoine Gertrude de Soto, [mo./ day?], 1766, Natchitoches, born the eleventh of same month, legitimate son of don Manuel de Soto, Spaniard, absent from this place, and Marie de Nieges de St. Denis, godparents: Antoine Solis, secretary of Mr. [?] at Adailles [Los Adaes], and Gertrude [?], *NACCR*, 105, entry no. 860.

75 Baptism, Louis Antoine, May 20, 1752, Natchitoches, legitimate son of Joseph Antoine and Julienne, Spaniards, godparents: Pierre Antoine de St. Denis and Madame de Blanc, *NACCR*, 65, entry no. 533; baptism, Jeanne Coulas de Sta. Theresia, October 2, 1752, Natchitoches, legitimate daughter of Coulas de Sta. Theresia and Anne de Deos, Spaniards, godparents: Messr. De St. Denis, officer (Louis de St. Denis) and Dame Doloritte de Blanc (Marie de Blanc), *NACCR*, 67, entry no. 545; baptism, Marie Antoinette Pagnot, December 18, 1753, Natchitoches, born on December 14, legitimate daughter of Antonne Pagnot and Marie Hynes, Spaniards, godparents: Antoine de St. Denis (Chevalier de St. Denis) and Marie de Neges de St. Denis, *NACCR*, 70, entry no. 572; baptism, Margueritte, August 25, 1758, daughter of Antoine [?] and Jeanne Antoine, Spaniards, godparents: Guillaume Chever and Margueritte Prudhomme, *NACCR*, 83, entry no. 688.

76 Baptism, Perrine Isabelle Langlois, August 31, 1759, Natchitoches, daughter of Francois Langlois *dit* Sans Regret and Marie Gregorie de Sta. Crux, godparents: Francois Ruiz and Barbara Victoria Ruiz, *NACCR*, 86, entry no. 712.

77 Elizabeth Shown Mills, *Natchitoches Colonials: Censuses, Military Rolls, and Tax Lists, 1722–1803* (Chicago: Adams Press, 1981), 11–12.

78 "Timeline: Life of Manuel Antonio de Soto y Bermúdez (January 11, 1720–September 1799)," copy in author's possession provided by Troy de Soto, descendant, April 2003, Baton Rouge, Louisiana; *NACCR*, 71, entry nos. 579, 581; *NACCR*, 72, entry no. 592; *NACCR*, 74, entry no. 602; *NACCR*, 77, entry no. 637; *NACCR*, 78, entry no. 638; *NACCR*, 78–79, entry no. 646; *NACCR*, 98, entry no. 784; *NACCR*, 101, entry no. 823; *NACCR*, 104, entry no. 852; *NACCR*, 105–6, entry no. 862; *NACCR*, 112, entry no. 919, all in Natchitoches.

79 Armando C. Alonzo, *Tejano Legacy: Rancheros and Settlers in South Texas, 1734–1900* (Albuquerque: University of New Mexico Press, 1998), 38.

80 Margaret Kenney Kress, trans., "Diary of a Visit of Inspection of the Texas Missions Made by Fray Gaspar José de Solís in the Year 1767–68," *SWHQ* 35 (July 1931): 65–66.

81 See David J. Weber, "The Spanish Borderlands of North America: A Historiography," in the OAH *Magazine of History* 14 (Summer 2000): 7, who states that "although blacks and mulattos could be found throughout the borderlands, African American history has more relevance to the Southeast than the Southwest" and was "tied to slave societies of the Atlantic and Caribbean."

82 Letter, Commandant McCarty to Governor Martos Navarrete, September 10, 1763, Natchitoches, *NA*, box 2Q292, 1–2, transcription in Spanish: "los disparates el que todos quantos indibiduos de ambos sexos assi negros como de otro color, se aplican en las regions de el nuevo mundo a las labores de sus manufacturas, quedasen esclabos sino muy poco tiempo: pues no pudiendo mantener, sino con la condicion de q.e, enseñados en la doctrina; se entreguen a la sagrada fuente de el Baptismo luego quedarian libres de el serbizios de sus amos, assi que conseguirian el bien de la regeneración? no o cierto: pero este les suelta de el tremendo captiverio de el Demonio, estrechándole la ley se serbir con mayores anhelos a sus patrones y vien echores[?]" (author's translation).

83 This form of corporal punishment was not unique to French masters; see Robert L. Paquette, *Sugar Is Made with Blood: The Conspiracy of La Escalera in Cuba and the Conflict between Empires over Slavery* (Middletown, CT: Wesleyan University Press, 1988). "La Escalera" meant the ladder, atop which slaves in Cuba were brutally whipped.

84 Letter, Gov. don Jacinto de Barrios y Jáuregui to the Count of Revilla Gigedo, April 17, 1753, Presidio Los Adaes. Quotations in Charles W. Hackett, ed., *Pichardo's Treatise*, vol. 4 (Austin: University of Texas Press, 1946), 65–66.

85 Restall, "Crossing to Safety," 382.

86 Jane Landers, *Black Society in Spanish Florida* (Urbana: University of Illinois Press, 1999), 26–27. See also Restall, "Crossing to Safety," 383, who notes that

the governor of Yucatan still asked his superiors in Mexico City for clarification of the law of religious refuge in 1801 after Spain went to war against Britain. Other regions between Catholic rivals where the law of refuge could have been tested were the frontiers or borders between Haiti and the Dominican Republic in the Caribbean, where French-owned sugar plantations on the western side of Hispaniola abutted the Spanish ranching society on the eastern side of the island, or between Brazil and Río de la Plata (Argentina), where the Portuguese discovered gold in the interior of southwestern Brazil during the early eighteenth century and relied on African labor.

87 Restall, "Crossing to Safety," 385.

88 Charles F. Nunn, *Foreign Immigrants in Early Bourbon Mexico, 1700–1760* (London: Cambridge University Press, 1979), 41.

89 Letter, Dr. Andreu, *fiscal*, to don Domingo Valcárcel, *auditor*, July 28, 1753, Mexico City; letter, don Domingo Valcárcel to Dr. Andreu, September 25, 1753, Mexico City. Quotation in Hackett, *Pichardo's Treatise*, 4:80, 97–98. For background of Britain's occupation of Havana, see Elena A. Schneider, *The Occpuation of Havana: War, Trade, and Slavery in the Atlantic World* (Chapel Hill: University of North Carolina Press, 2018), who says the English goal was to sever Spain from the "global circulation in American silver and valuable Asian trade goods." Britain also sought to absorb Havana into "markets for their goods and stepping-stones for trade" (6).

90 Meeting, *Junta de guerra y hacienda*, January 21–22, 1754, Mexico City; viceroy's confirmation of the Royal Council's decision, January 30, 1754, Mexico City, quoted in Hackett, *Pichardo's Treatise*, 4:113, 115; Nunn, *Foreign Immigrants*, 41.

91 Letter, Marqués de Aranda to the fiscal, April 5, 1758, México City, *BA*, microfilm, 9:0795–0797: "gozar de la immunidad local" (author's translation); and in *AGM—Historia*, vol. 91, *CAT* 32.5a, 136–39, transcription.

92 Letter, Marqués de Amarillas to Governor Barrios Jáuregui of Texas, April 22, 1758, San Angel, Mexico, *BA*, 9:0809–0810; and in *AGM—Historia*, vol. 91, *CAT* 32.5a, 140, transcription. Amarillas succeeded the Marqués de Aranda as viceroy in 1758.

93 Letter, Marqués de Aranda to Viceroy Marqués de Cruillas[?], June 7, 1758, Mexico City, *BA*, microfilm, 9:0813.

94 Letter, Marqués de Amarillas to Governor Barrios Jáuregui of Texas, June 17, 1758, San Angel, Mexico, *BA*, microfilm, 9:0817–0818: "en que me da cuenta de haver entregado â los Franceses de Nuevo Orleáns el Negro esclavo que se hallava refugiado de la immunidad del sagrado en esa Provincia" (first quotation); "he venido en disimilar por ahora la entrega del citado esclavo sin esperar mi resoluccion en este negocio" (second quotation; all author's translations).

95 Letter, Gov. don Hugo Oconor to Viceroy Marqués de Amarillas, July 7, 1768, Presidio Los Adaes, *AGM—Historia*, vol. 91, *CAT* 32.5a, 135, transcription.

96 Letter, Viceroy Marqués de Croix to Governor Oconor of Texas, September 24, 1768, Mexico City, *BA*, microfilm, 10:0639: "quedo enterado de la duda que a vm se le ofrecio, para no entregar el esclavo que le pedia el comandante de la Nueva Luisiana, y respecto la diferencia que ay de aquel tpo. al presente, si el tal esclavo no ha cometido delito por que se le quiera castigar lo podrá vm mandar entregar prontam.te para que sirva asu dueño; pero si el haverse retraido â la Mision huirse solo por delito, podrá havisar vm al Comandante Frances haga la caucion Juratoriaa favor de la immunidad, y hecha esta sele entregará, y lo mismo podrá vm practicar en lo subcesivo" (author's translation).

97 See also Douglas W. Richmond, "Africa's Initial Encounter with Texas: The Significance of Afro-Tejanos in Colonial Tejas, 1528–1821," *Bulletin of Latin American Research* 26, no. 2 (2007): 205, who argues that *cimarrones* (runaway slaves) "became a constant feature of resistance to Spanish rule," especially in East Texas on the eve of Mexico's independence struggle from Spain. While there might have been more fugitive slaves in the eighteenth century, the likelihood of greater numbers of fugitive slaves increased after the Louisiana Purchase of 1803.

98 See Baade, "Law of Slavery," 43–86; and Zavala, *Esclavos indios*, 249.

99 For discussion of slavery in Louisiana under Spain, see Din, *Spaniards, Planters, and Slaves*.

100 Interrogation, Etienne, July 13, 1757, Natchitoches, Louisiana, *Natchitoches Parish Legal Records* (hereafter *NPLR*), vol. 1, trans. Elizabeth A. Rubino (Natchitoches, LA: Natchitoches Genealogical and Historical Association, 2003), 68–69. In her own interrogation, Marion claimed she did not know that the goods had been stolen in the first place; ibid., 73–74.

101 Interrogation, Christophe Haische, ibid., September 20, 1762, Natchitoches, *NPLR*, 125. According to historians H. Sophie Burton and F. Todd Smith, *piaster* was the French term for one Spanish peso and the equivalent of an American dollar during most of the eighteenth century; Burton and Smith, *Colonial Natchitoches*, 172–73n14. I would like to thank Dr. George Avery, archaeologist and program coordinator with the Center for Regional Heritage at Stephen F. Austin State University in Nacogdoches, Texas, for bringing the NPLR to my attention in March 2006.

102 Restall, "Crossing to Safety," 389.

103 Francis X. Galán, "Between Imperial Warfare: Crossing of the Smuggling Frontier and Transatlantic Commerce on the Louisiana-Texas Borderlands, 1754–1785," in *Texans and War: New Interpretations of the State's Military*

History, ed. Alexander Mendoza and Charles David Grear (College Station: Texas A&M University Press, 2012), 157–77.

CHAPTER 7

1 Letter, Antonio Gil Ybarbo to O'Conor, January 8, 1774, [San Antoino de Béxar], *AGM—Historia*, vol. 51, *CAT*, box 29, folder 3, 261-261-268, transcription; letter, O'Conor to Governor Ripperdá, February 17, 1774, Chihuahua, *AGM— Historia*, vol. 51, *CAT*, box 29, folder 2, 246, 251–53, transcription; *escrito* (petition), Ybarbo and Gil Flores to Governor Ripperdá, February 28, 1774, Mexico City, *AGM—Historia*, vol. 84, *CAT*, box 31, folder 3, 323, transcription; Bolton, *Texas*, 391–92.
2 Walter L. Dorn, *Competition for Empire, 1740–1763* (New York: Harper and Row, 1940), 122, 124–25, 129. The rise of Prussia on the European continent in the mid-eighteenth century presents tantalizing comparisons with the rise of the Comanche on the North American continent.
3 DuVal, *Native Ground*. On the Caddos, see La Vere, *Caddo Chiefdoms*; and Smith, *Caddo Indians*.
4 Quotation in Stanley J. Stein and Barbara H. Stein, *Apogee of Empire: Spain and New Spain in the Age of Charles III, 1759–1789* (Baltimore: Johns Hopkins University Press, 2003), 359n27, author's translation; Fred Anderson, *Crucible of War: The Seven Years' War and the Fate of Empire in British North America, 1754–1766* (New York: Random House, 2000), 348–62; Robert S. Weddle, *After the Massacre: The Violent Legacy of the San Sabá Mission* (Lubbock: Texas Tech University Press, 2007), 1–13.
5 Stein and Stein, *Apogee of Empire*, 11–13, 315–16. English woolens were already less costly as French woolens to Spain and its colonies peaked during the 1750s. By the 1770s, English woolens comprised 50 percent of total sales to Spanish markets; see also Elliott, *Empires*, 293. Britain pre-emptively declared war on Spain in January 1762. On the secret transfer of Louisiana from France to Spain, see Arthur S. Aiton, "The Diplomacy of the Louisiana Cession," in *The Louisiana Purchase Bicentennial Series in Louisiana History*, vol. 2, *The Spanish Presence in Louisiana, 1763–1803*, ed. Gilbert C. Din (Lafayette: University of Southwestern Louisiana, 1996), 13, 22. In the subsequent Treaty of Paris, Spain gave up Florida to Britain for the return of Havana, Cuba, which the English had captured in 1762. Spanish officials considered Florida as less harmful than English acquisition of Louisiana with the resulting danger of smuggling into Mexico and their advance into the silver mines.

6　Daniel K. Richter, *Facing East from Indian Country: A Native History of Early America* (Cambridge: Harvard University Press, 2001), 151.

7　Weber, *Spanish Frontier*, 176.

8　Stein and Stein, *Apogee of Empire*, 4–5. Stein and Stein explain that institutionalization of smuggling in Spain occurred at five levels by the 1730s: large landlords, merchant bankers in foreign ports, the church, underpaid petty officials, and powerless bureaucrats; see also Francis X. Galán, "The Chirino Boys: Spanish Soldier-Pioneers from Los Adaes on the Louisiana-Texas Borderlands, 1735–1792," *East Texas Historical Journal* 46, no. 2 (Fall 2008): 43–44.

9　Weber, *Spanish Frontier*, 173, 176; Burton and Smith, *Colonial Natchitoches*, 110; Stein and Stein, *Apogee of Empire*, 6; Weber, *Bárbaros*, 173. For discussion of barter exchange on the frontier, see Usner, *Indians, Settlers, and Slaves*.

10　Jorge Canizares-Esguerra, *Nature, Empire, and Nation: Explorations of the History of Science in the Iberian World* (Stanford: Stanford University Press, 2006), 104; Stein and Stein, *Apogee of Empire*, 59, 319, 352; Paul Mapp, "British Culture and the Changing Character of the Mid-Eighteenth Century British Empire," in *Cultures in Conflict: The Seven Years' War in North America*, ed. Warren R. Hofstra (Lanham, MD: Rowman & Littlefield, 2007), 49.

11　Canizares-Esguerra, *Nature, Empire, and Nation*, 100–102; Anthony Pagden, *Lords of All the World: Ideologies of Empire in Spain, Britain and France, c. 1500–c. 1800* (New Haven, CT: Yale University Press, 1995), 118, 123. The War for Spanish Succession ended in 1713 with the ascension of King Louis XIV's grandson upon the Spanish throne.

12　Weber, *Spanish Frontier*, 214.

13　Instructions, Marqués de Rubí to O'Conor, interim governor of Texas, September 12, 1767, Presidio Los Adaes, *BA*, 10:0511–0513. [Full text:] "*el Lunes 14 del conferentte[?] â cuio fin se servirá Vm mandar, que anttes de salir el sol, se halle aquella formada â Caballo en la Plaza de Aramas de estte Presidio* [Los Adaes], *ttrayendo todos sus efecttos de Armamento, Montura, y Vestuario, paraque â un mismo tpo reconozca yo su consisttencia en Hombres, Caballos, y Menages respecttivos*" (author's translation).

14　Instructions, Rubí to O'Conor, ibid., *BA*, 10:0513: "de la Equidad con que haya sido trattado el soldado, enel cargo de algunos xros. de ynferior Calidad â los señalados enel Reglamentto, las Facturas, ô Conozim.tos delas Memorias ttraydas, para la satisfazion en xros. del haver de esta tropa . . ." (author's translation). Along with this request, O'Conor was to hand over whatever papers were stored in the archives at Presidio Los Adaes and any goods the former governor had seized. In his fifth demand, Rubí wanted the commissions of those officers and subalterns at Presidio Los Adaes to recognize their service, other requisites for their respective qualification, and a copy of the new viceroy's latest order for the separation and surrender of command, and the proprietary government.

15 Instructions, Rubí to O'Conor, ibid., *BA*, 10:0513–0515: "*âsu sittuazion, venttajas, consequentte utilidad al R.l Servicio*" (first quotation); "del Zelo, yntelligencia, y experiencia Militar de Vm" (second quotation; all author's translations).

16 *Exttracto de la Revista de Ynspeccion executtada de orden del Rey, por mi el Mariscal de Campo de sus Reales Exersitos, Marques de Rubi, â la expresada Compania* [Presidio Los Adaes], April 3, 1768, Tacubaya, *AGI— Guadalajara* 511, in Old Spanish Mission Records, OLLU, microfilm, reel 4, Document 114, 1–3. [Rubí's remarks about Sgt. Domingo Chirino:] *"es natural de la Villa del Saltillo Gobernación dela N.a Vizcaya de edad de 54 años, mediana disposicion, y Ynteligencia del servicio, y sin circunsttancias para ser asiendido*[?] *â oficial"* (author's translation). Rubí's inspection of Presidio Los Adaes began on September 14, 1767, and continued for several weeks.

17 Ibid., *AGI—Guadalajara*, 1–5. Rubí wrote that the firearms consisted of two carbines in good working order, but the rest unserviceable due to these being broken or missing parts. There were only six cueras, two unfinished coats of cotton, and twenty-three other cueras in poor condition. This left nine of the thirty-eight soldiers without any armor and only two serviceable *adargas* (leather shields).

18 Rubí, *Revista de Ynspeccion* [Presidio Los Adaes], ibid., *AGI—Guadalajara* 511, microfilm, 4:3–5.

19 Estracto de la Revista de Inspeccion, September 14, 1767, Presidio Los Adaes, Rubí's Report, April 3, 1768, Tacubaya, *AGI—Guadalajara* 511, OLLU, reel 4, doc. 114, 1–5: "como puede reconocerse por los repretidos y exscedenttes cargos de las quenttas liquidadas" (first quotation) and "de Arina dela Colonia, Cafee, Piloncillo, Tabaco, y Livranzas â favor del cagero Francisco Antonio que deven suponerse de peor naturaleza" (second quotation; all author's translations).

20 Moorhead, *Presidio*, 57. For discussion about Rubí's inspections of presidios at San Antonio de Béxar, San Sabá (near present Menard in the hill country region of central Texas), San Agustín (El Orcoquisac), and La Bahía, see Chipman, *Spanish Texas*, 173–80. Rubí found Presidio San Agustín as bad as Presidio Los Adaes. While Rubí held great contempt also for Presidio San Sabá, he considered the ones at San Antonio de Béxar and La Bahía in more favorable conditions.

21 Marqués de Rubí, *Revista de Ynspeccion* [Presidio Los Adaes], April 4, 1768, Tacubaya, *AGI—Guadalajara* 511, in Old Spanish Mission Records, OLLU, microfilm, reel 4, Document 111, 1–6, 8. This part of the inspection was made at Presidio Los Adaes on September 23, 1767.

22 Letter, Marqués de Rubí to don Hugo O'Conor, September 23, 1767, Presidio Los Adaes, *BA*, 10:0516–0518, and 0520: "la mala calidad" (first quotation); "para que se entretenga con la Linpieza devida" (second quotation); "notorio el deplorable estado . . . y en fatal decadencia" (third quotation; all author's translations). Rubí suggested O'Conor place the account books of Presidio Los Adaes and Presidio San Agustín in safe custody, or deposited in his power at all times.

23 Letter, Rubí to O'Conor, ibid., *BA*, 10:0518: "podra Vmb. permitir, que para la festividad de la Ptrona de esta Comp.a y alguna o la de especial recomendación" (first quotation); "en la fiesta de Yglesia" (author's translation); *concuerda* (agreement) with Rubí's recommendations, don Hugo O'Conor, interim governor of Texas, with don Bernardo de Miranda, don Joseph Gonzales, and don Francisco Maldonado, witnesses, October 14, 1767, Presidio Los Adaes, *BA*, microfilm, 10:0520.

24 Report on Inspection of Presidio Los Adaes made on September 14, 1767, Marqués de Rubí, April 3, 1768, Tacubaya, *AGI—Guadalajara* 511, reel 4, doc. 114, 3: "siendo su Tropa dela Ynferior Talla, que es demuestra al margen, y compuestta de gente collectticia, fugitiva de ottras Provincias, y Perseguida por la Justicia, con Cattorse Reclutas alistados enel año de 1767, dela peor Calidad, y Disposicion, en lugar de ottros tantos Vetteranos, que usaron de Lizensia, ô Deserttaros, exasperados del mal ttratto del Govern.or D.n Angel de Martos" (author's translation).

25 After Rubí completed his last inspections, he returned to Mexico City by February 1768 and took another six weeks to prepare his assessment of military defenses along northern New Spain. His report enumerated thirty articles, the first three were general theories, followed by seventeen specific proposals, then six general reflections, and the last four were his conclusions.

26 Instructions, Viceroy Marqués de Croix to don Hugo O'Conor, April 14, 1768, Mexico City, *BA*, microfilm, 10:0561–0562; warning, Viceroy de Croix to Captain of Presidio Los Adaes by way of O'Conor, April 14, 1768, Mexico City, *BA*, microfilm, 10:0560.

27 Letter, O'Conor to Viceroy de Croix, August 28, 1768, San Antonio de Béxar[?], *AGM—Historia*, vol. 91, *CAT*, box 32, folder 5a, 158–59, 163, transcription.

28 Letter, Viceroy de Croix to Captain of Presidio Los Adaes [Lt. Joseph Gonzales], June 12, 1771, Mexico City, *BA*, 11:0015–0016; letter, Viceroy Bucarley y Ursua to Captain of Presidio Los Adaes [Lt. Joseph Gonzales], November 8, 1772, Mexico City, *BA*, 11:0272–0274.

29 Bolton, *Texas*, 379–80.

30 Letter, O'Conor to Viceroy de Croix, September 1, 1769, San Antonio de Béxar[?], *AGM—Historia*, vol. 91, *CAT*, box 32, folder 5b, 196–202, transcription.

31 *Ripperda a Arriaga sobre presidios y misiones en Texas*, June 26, 1769, Mexico City, *AGI—Guadalajara* 302, in Old Spanish Mission Records, OLLU, microfilm, reel 2, Document 110, 1–2: "la infeliz situaz.n en que se hallan constituidas las pocas, y deviles Poblaz.s de la Provincia de Texas (â que estóy destinado)" (author's translation); announcement, Ripperdá to the Justice and Regiment of San Fernando [San Antonio de Béxar], his appointment as governor of Texas, October 12, 1769, Mexico City, *BA*, 10:0685.

32 Letter, Viceroy de Croix to Señor Barón de Ripperdá, July 24, 1770, Mexico City, *BA*, 10:0739–0741; letter, Viceroy de Croix to Captain of Los Adaes [Lt. Joseph Gonzales], July 24, 1770, *BA*, 10:0736–0737.

33 Letter, Viceroy de Croix to Texas governor Ripperdá, July 24, 1770, Mexico City, *BA*, 10:0742. Viceroy de Croix also instructed Governor Ripperdá to discontinue the practice of demanding accounts from the captains at Presidio San Antonio de Béxar and Presidio La Bahía because it was deemed unnecessary, in Letter, de Croix to Ripperdá, July 24, 1770, Mexico City, *BA*, 10:0743.

34 Letter, Viceroy de Croix to Texas governor Ripperdá, July 13, 1771, Mexico City, *BA*, microfilm, roll 11, frame nos. 0023–0024. Spanish royal officials in Madrid simultaneously corresponded with Governor Ripperdá about a decree backing the proposal by the Archbishop in Mexico City "of the goal in pursuing the banishment of different languages used in those dominions [the Indies and Philippines] and only allowing Castilian to be spoken." Governor Ripperdá responded that he publicized this royal dispatch at the presidio of San Antonio de Béxar and the Villa de San Fernando, as well as the other presidios in the Texas province, in Royal Dispatch, Thomas del Mello to Texas governor Ripperdá, August 20, 1770, Madrid, *BA*, 10:0759; letter, Governor Ripperdá to Thomas del Mello, June 16, 1771, San Antonio de Béxar, *BA*, 10:0759.

35 Moorhead, *Presidio*, 64–68. For more detailed discussion of the New Regulations of 1772, which replaced the Regulations of 1729, see Weber, *Spanish Frontier*, 215–20.

36 Letter, Viceroy Bucareli y Ursua to governor of Texas [Juan María Barón de Ripperdá], December 15, 1772, Mexico City, *BA*, microfilm, 11:0297 (author's translation).

37 Power of attorney, Lt. don Joseph Gonzalez, *vecino de este real presidio* [Los Adaes], to Thomás de Ojeda, *soldado de este presidio* [Los Adaes], for purchase of mules [three hundred pesos] from don Asencio Rasso in Villa de San Fernando and Royal Presidio of San Antonio de Béxar, January 19, 1749, Presidio Los Adaes, appearing before Gov. don Pedro del Barrio Junco y Espriella, *BA*, microfilm, 8:1059–60.

38 Certified copy of petition, Juan Manuel de Bustamante, *residente en la actualidad en este Real Presidio* [Los Adaes], July 5, 1766, Presidio Los Adaes, appearing before Governor Martos Navarrete, *BA*, microfilm, 10:0431–0432.

39 *Cargos, que en Visita de las Declaraciones Juradas, resividas à la Compañía*
    del Presidio de los Adaes de Nros de Filaciones, y Caxa, y demás Docum.tos
    presentados en la Revista de Ynspección executtada dha. Comp.a, resul-
    tan contra el Govern.or de esta Prov.a de los Texas D.n Angel de Martos y
    Navarrete, à quien or su ausencia, y defectto de Apoderado, no se han podido
    comunicar para que dé à ellos la sattisfazion que sele ofreciere, September 23,
    1767, Tacubaya, *AGI—Guadalajara* 511, reel 4, doc. 111, 1–2: "trueque con los
    Indios" (first quotation) and "los espresados, sin mas Mozo, ni arriero, que
    los mismos soldados, quines le prestaban el Serivico" (second quotation; all
    author's translations).

40 Rubí, Report on Inspection of Presidio Los Adaes, ibid., 2: "siendo aun mucho
    mas frequenttes los Viages, que hazian con la propia requa en calidad
    de Mozos siempre y en la de Encomenderos del Govern.or â las Misiones, â
    las rancherías de los Yndios Texas, que están â 50, y 60 Leguas de este Presidio,
    para adquirir las Gamuzas Manteca de Oso, y otros efectos que trafican, y casi
    Diarios los que hazian al Presidio de Nachittoche de la Ynmediata Colonia
    Francesa, de donde se traian todos los efectos necesarios para el enttrettenim
    .to de esta Compañía, para la que no se ha conducido Abio alguno de zinco
    a. â estta parte" (author's translation).

41 Rubí's military inspection, ibid., 5. For more discussion of the Marqués de Rubí
    military inspection of northern New Spain, see Weber, *Spanish Frontier*, 204–12.

42 For comparisons elsewhere, see Weber, *Spanish Frontier*, 125–26, who men-
    tions that in New Mexico the encomenderos formed the local aristocracy
    before the Pueblo Revolt of 1680, after which Spanish officials discontin-
    ued the encomienda system, while it "never took root in southeastern North
    America." On the cabildo of San Antonio, see de la Teja, *San Antonio de Bexár*,
    32, 35–36.

43 Letter, Texas governor O'Conor to Viceroy Marqués de Croix, March 11, 1768,
    San Antonio de Béxar, *Archivo General de México—Historia*, vol. 91, in the
    Spanish and Mexican Collection, *CAT*, Austin, Texas, box 32, folder 5a, 132–
    33, transcription. Spanish royal officials used the term *embriaquez* in the
    archives to refer to drunkenness or intoxication, while *barbaros* (savages)
    frequently referred to nonmission Indians, which in the case of Los Adaes
    meant the Caddos. Governor O'Connor had recommended that Lieutenant
    Sierra be allowed to retire in the status as first settler from Los Adaes, which
    the viceroy approved. For the Spanish view of "savage" Indians during this
    period of military reform in the 1760s, see Weber, *Bárbaros*.

44 On the general outline of the Marqués de Rubí's military inspection, his rec-
    ommendations, and the New Regulations of 1772, see Bolton, *Texas*, 377–86;
    see also Weber, *Spanish Frontier*, ch. 8.

45 Letter, Viceroy Marques de Croix to Hugo O'Conór, interim governor of Texas, February 7, 1769, Mexico City, *BA*, microfilm, roll 10, frame no. 646: "Su avansada hedad y achaques que le imposivilitan del servicio ... podrá concederle el retíro, dejándole en la classe de Poblador" (author's translation). On Pedro de Sierra's background, see "Vita, et moribus de los actuales oficiales, que sirven en los presidios de Nueva España, según las Libretas, que originales paran en la Secretaria del Virreynato, México, 10 de Abril de 1766," *AGI—Guadalajara* 514, *OSMRL*, Our Lady of the Lake University, San Antonio, Texas, microfilm, reel 7, 2. Sierra apparently had been feeling ill for several years.

46 Letter, Viceroy Bucarely y Ursua, to Governor Ripperdá, November 18, 1772, Mexico City, *BA*, 11:0288–0289: "ni menos continuar el comercio con el Presidio de Natchitoches, por ser ilicito, pribado, y contra las Leyes establecidas en estos Dominios" (author's translation).

47 Letter, Viceroy Bucarely y Ursua to Governor Ripperdá, December 9, 1772, Mexico City, *BA*, 11:0290–0291: "el comercio que solicita con la Colonia de la Luisiana absolutamente prohibido" (first quotation); "encargo a v.s. haciendole responsables de qualquiera infraccion que se experimente por falta del devido celo, y cuidado" (second quotation; all author's translations).

48 Letter, Viceroy Bucarely y Ursua to Governor Ripperdá, December 9, 1772, Mexico City, concerning Indian relations and repeating the ban on trade with Natchitoches, *BA*, 11:0294–0296: "¿Que seguridades han dado a V.S. los Indios del Norte para mantener la Paz haviendola quebrantado tantas vezes com la han ofrecido?" (first quotation); "Que confianza podra tener V.S. de que sus variables ideas, no las conviertan con el auxilio de las Armas que se les faciliten en destruir essa Provincia, introduciéndose acaso hasta la Villa del Saltillo, y aun hasta S.n Luis Potosí?" (second quotation); "Que puede esperarse de unas Naciones que desde la conquista no han dado señales de reducirse al gremio de nuestra Religion santa, pues manteniendo S.M. desde la erección del Presidio de los Adaes quatro Misiones no se ha logrado convertir V.S. que àora se consiga franqueando: Fuciles, Polvora, y Valas, cuio medio le considero el mas eficaz para impedir la conversion tan encargada por las Leyes?" (third quotation; all author's translations).

49 Testimony of witness #1, *don Manuel Anttonio Losoya, teniente de la compañía de este Real Presidio* [Los Adaes], fifty-one years old, he signed his own name, August 1, 1751, Presidio Los Adaes, response to question 4; testimony of witness #2, *don Pedro de Sierra, Alférez de esta Compañía* [Los Adaes], fifty-three years old, August 2, 1751, Presidio Los Adaes, response to question 4; testimony of witness #3, *don Domingo del Rio, Sargento de esta Compañía* [Los Adaes], forty years old more or less, August 2, 1751, Presidio Los Adaes, response to Qustion #4; testimony of witness #6, *don Antonio*

Gregorio Cordoves, cavo actual de esta Compañía [Los Adaes], forty-five years old, he signed his own name, August 3, 1751, Presidio Los Adaes, reeponse to question 4; testimony of witness #15, *Joseph de Castro, soldado de este Real Presidio* [Los Adaes] *que dijo ser de doce años a esta parte*, thirty-eight years old, he signed his own name, August 8, 1751, Presidio Los Adaes, response to question 4, *NA*, UT-Austin, box 2Q292, vol. 4, transcription. 27–28, 32–33, 36–37, 48, and 72.

50 Ibid., testimony, Lieutenant Sierra, *NA*, vol. 4 (question 4) *"se desveló dicho Señor en la solicitud del mayor cumplido Alivio de los soldados"* (author's translation).

51 For the most complete work on ranching in Spanish Texas, see Jackson, *Los Mesteños*.

52 Letter, Viecroy Marqués de Amarillas to Gov. Barrios Jáuregui of Texas, June 30, 1757, Mexico City, *BA*, microfilm, 9:0709, 0711–0712: "significandome la nezezidad en que se halla aquella colona [Louisiana] por falta de carnes, y que no ha tenido efecto el ocurso q.e hizieron a V.S. a esto intento, pidiéndome almismo tiempo que siendo esa Provincia mui abundante de bestias" (first quotation) and "mas prompto posible socorro" (second quotation; all author's translations).

53 Viceroy Amarillas reiterated to Gov. Barrios Jáuregui that cattle be sent to Louisiana "which is necessary for their maintenance . . . and at moderate prices for the portion of livestock that the said [commissary] solicits." Dispatch, Viceroy Marqués de Amarillas to Texas Officials concerning cooperation with agent appointed to secure stock for the French, July 1, 1757, Mexico City, *BA*, 9:0713–0714: "aprecios moderazos la porsion de Ganados, que solisitare dicho comisario" (author's translation).; letter, Governor Martos Navarrete to Viceroy Amarillas, December 16, 1759, Presidio San Agustín de Ahumada, *BA*, microfilm, 9:0868–0869.

54 Testimony, *Luis Menard, Negociante deel real presidio de San Juan Baptista de Nachitos Jurisdicion de la Nueva Luciana*, appeared before Governor Martos Navarrete, February 20, 1767, Presidio Los Adaes, *Diligencias practicadas por el Governador de Texas â pedimento de D.n Luis de Menard sobre lo que en ellas se contiene, Año de 1767, BA*, microfilm, 10:0466–0467.

55 Ibid., testimony, *Marcos Hernandez*, resident of Presidio Los Adaes, thirty-seven years old, he did not know how to sign his own name, February 20, 1767, Presidio Los Adaes, *BA*, microfilm, 10:0467–0468: "lo acomodó por quince pesos cada mes para Maiordomo de la Vaquería que tiene establecida en el sitio que se llaman el petit écor, con el fin de que le juntar los ganados que alli auice introducido, para conducirlos â la buelta de su viage del rapi â la Puente Cupi . . . y que teniendo ya recojidos y juntas sesenta reses grandes veinte y una bestias mulares y veinte y nueve caballos y lleguas se vio obligado â abandonar con sugente dha Vaquería por averle ordenado el Señor de la Perier

Comandante del Real Presidio de Nachitos se devolviese a este de los Adaes" (author's translation).

56 Ibid., testimony, *Joseph Luis Hernandez*, resident of Presidio Los Adaes, twenty-two years old, he did not know to sign his own name, February 20, 1767, Presidio Los Adaes, *BA*, microfilm, 10:0468.

57 Ibid., testimony, *Phelipe de la Garza*, resident of Presidio Los Adaes, twenty-four years old, he did not know how to sign his own name, February 20, 1767, Presidio Los Adaes; testimony, *Joseph Salazar*, resident of Presidio Los Adaes, sixty-one years old, he did not know how to sign his own name, February 21, 1767, Presidio Los Adaes; *Joseph de Torres*, resident of Presidio Los Adaes, twenty-four years old, he did not know how to sign his own name, February 21, 1767, Presidio Los Adaes; testimony, *Salvador Esparza*, resident of Presidio Los Adaes, sixty-one years old, he did not know how to sign his own name, February 21, 1767, Presidio Los Adaes; testimony, *Dimas Moya*, resident of Presidio Los Adaes, forty-nine years old, he did not know how to sign his own name, February 21, 1767, Presidio Los Adaes; testimony, *Andres Esparza*, resident of Presidio Los Adaes, twenty-six years old, he did not know how to sign his own name, February 21, 1767, Presidio Los Adaes; and Testimony, *Phelipe Sanchez*, resident of Presidio Los Adaes, fifty-seven years old, he did not know how to sign his own name, February 21, 1767, Presidio Los Adaes, *BA*, microfilm, 10:0468–471. The Menard case remained pending as Governor Martos Navarrete placed the record in the company archives; ibid., *BA*, microfilm, 10:0471. A note in French at the bottom of the document refers to the actions of the commandant at Natchitoches.

58 *Proveido del Gobernador de Texas* [Barrios Jáuregui] *para que declare el périto lo necesario para saca de aqua de Santa Rosa de Alcazar*, August 19, 1757, Presidio Los Adaes, *ASFG*, box 2Q250, vol. 7, 1–2, photostatic copy: "declare la Herramienta precisa inescusable que se necesitta para poner en efecto las sacas de aqua ya citadas, y con su respuestta, mandar q.e el Herr.o de estte Presidio [Los Adaes] fabrique la que supiere, y pudiere, y en caso de no poder por insuficiencia dar la providencia de comprar la que se puede en el puesto de Nachitos" (first quotation); *Declaraciones de Francisco Xavier Hernández sobre lo necesario para la saca de aqua*, [1757?], Presidio Los Adaes, *ASFG*, box 2Q250, 2, photostatic copy: "palas de fresno, achas, azadones, y varras" (second quotation; all author's translations).

59 Official investigation conducted at Presidio Los Adaes, Presidio San Agustin de Ahumada, and Santa Rosa del Alcazár to ascertain the best site for a Spanish presidio, missions, and settlement on the Trinity River, October 25, 1756, Presidio Los Adaes, *NA*, UT-Austin, box 2Q292, vol. 4, 42, transcription.

60 Investigation, ibid., *NA*, IV, 4.

61 The intermittent clashes between Adaeseños and the governor's rule also occurred at Presidio San Agustín on the lower Trinity River in 1764 where desertions were commonplace. During an investigation into charges of cruelty against its captain, don Raphael Pacheco, Governor Martos Navarrete sent Sgt. Domingo Chirino and four other soldiers from Los Adaes—Joseph Valentin, Domingo Diego, Santos de la Garza, and Melchor Benites—in pursuit of deserters from Presidio San Agustín, headed east across the Sabine River into Louisiana. The governor wrote that Chirino returned "at four in the afternoon . . . but did not find any of the deserters they pursued in all the lands that pertain to this Presidio, and instead saw [the deserters] headed for Natchitoches at an accelerated pace." Proceedings held against Captain Pacheco for cruelty against soldiers at Presidio San Agustín, August 16, 1764, Presidio Los Adaes, *BA*, UT-Austin, box 2S30, 2a: "no avian encontrado ni visto en todas los terminos que pertenecen â este Presidio â ninguno de los desertores que avian seguido, y si reconocido por el rastro que atrás dejaban, iban con pasa acelerado para el de Nachitos" (author's translation). *Handbook of Texas Online*, Robert Wooster, "San Agustin de Ahumada Presidio," accessed June 3, 2019, http://www.tshaonline.org/handbook/online/articles/uqs01.

62 Letter, Gov. Antonio de Ulloa to Governor Martos Navarrete, May 18, 1767, Isla de San Carlos, *BA*, microfilm, 10:0474–0475: "practicando robos de consideración" (first quotation) and "que persona alguna Española, Francesa, ô de otra Nación passe de ésta Colonia â esse territorio; y haya arrestar â quantos lo hizeron, y los remita en derechura â la Capital" (second quotation; all author's translations). For background on Gov. Ulloa's troubles in New Orleans, see Weber, *The Spanish Frontier*, 200–201.

63 Letter, Governor Martos Navarrete to Commandant LaPerrier of Natchitoches, June 6, 1767, *BA*, 10:0476–0477: "siete Desertores Marineros españoles de los que se conboyaban para los Ylinois al cargo de un Cap.n de esta nacion" (author's translation). Six of these Spanish maritime deserters were mentioned by name, including *Diego Basques, Xptobal Boeta, Diego Moreno, Juan Morin, Juan de Acosta, y Antonio Dias.*

64 Letter, ibid., *BA*, 10:0477. [Governor Martos Navarrete:] "adquieran con su [seven Spanish maritime deseters] trabaxo en los contornos de este Pres.o [Los Adaes] con que mantenerse, bien entendido que an de residir ellos hasta en tanto que su Exa. Me ordena lo que dexa executar sobre ello, y que si alguno intentarse ô verificarse ausentarse sera severamente castigado; como el que lo abilitare de los vecinos que tienen sus ranchos en estas immediaciones ô vien los soldados misioneros de las tres Misiones Adaes, Aix, ô Nacodoches, quienes si así lo hisieren, sufriran ademas de las penas que estos huvieren incurrido, las en que por inovedientes â los superiores ordenes . . . los vesinos

de todos sus viesses, y para q.e llegue a notisia de todos y que ninguno alegue ignorancia devia mandar y mando que en el dia de mañana domingo despues de Misa se haga notorio, y fixe este mi auto en el cuerpo de guardia de este Pres.o [Los Adaes]" (author's translation).

65 *Diligencias* (investigation), Gov. Hugo O'Conor, July 20, 1768, Presidio Los Adaes, against Patricio Padilla, resident from Los Adaes, *AGM—Historia*, vol. 91, *CAT*, box 32, folder 5a, 143, 155, transcription.

66 Investigation, ibid., *AGM—Historia*, 143, transcription: "las que se concluieron esta Mañana dejando los Indios, todos los señales de su amistad" (author's translation).

67 Investigation, witness, Joseph Hidalgo, alférez, forty-two years old and signed his own name, July 20, 1768, Presidio Los Adaes, appeared before Governor O'Conor, ibid., *AGM—Historia*, 146–48: "al sitado Pedro Simon quien tenia la cavesa mala, que todo estaba Bueno, y que ellos mantendrian siempre la paz con los españoles" (first quotation); the expression "á bailarle al Señor Governador" was used to refer to French demonstration of peace with the Spaniards; "dejarle la Pluma en señal de Amistad" (second quotation; all author's translations).

68 Investigation, Witness, Joseph Antonio Cruz, soldier from Los Adaes, twenty-eight years old and he did not know how to sign his own name, July 20, 1768, Presidio Los Adaes, ibid., *AGM—Historia*, 149–50, transcription: "Padilla les dijo que el tenia entre los españoles tres hermanos y tres hermanas, y que asi le avisasen cuando querian venir a cavar estas Misiones, y presidio para poder el retirar sus hermanos y hermanas, y que después vendría el y sus hermanos con los referidos Yndios á avisarles a matar a todos los españoles" (full text; author's translation). Ildefonso Garces, another soldier from Presidio Los Adaes, and two additional witnesses testified similarly as Hidalgo and Cruz.

69 Investigation, ibid., Witnesses Ildefonso Garces (25 years old), Juan Remigio de Thorres (26 years old), and Margil Cadena (29 years old), all soldiers from Presidio Los Adaes and did not know how to sign their names, July 20, 1768, Presidio Los Adaes, *AGM—Historia*, 150–55, transcription.

70 Interestingly, Patricio Padilla had signed a petition in 1773 with other Adaesaños for permission to leave San Antonio de Béxar and resettle at the site of former Mission Ais in East Texas, see *AGM—Historia*, vol. 84, *CAT*, box 31, folder 3, 315–17, transcription. He was also among soldiers at San Antonio de Béxar in 1780, who were owed part of their salaries, see *BA*, microfilm, roll 14, frame nos. 0704–0705.

71 Letter, Viceroy Marqués de Croix to Governor Ulloa of Louisiana, April 5, 1769, *BA*, microfilm, 10:0665–0666: "el escandoloso suceso acaecido en el R.l Presidio de S.n Aug.n de Ahumada" (first quotation), "diez y siete soldados

[from Presidio San Agustín] que salieron fugitivos de él y se acoxieron âl de Nachitos" (second quotation), and "q.e d.n Manuel Soto Bermúdez fue el que ocasionó el Yncendio y extragos que se hicieron en el referido Presid.o [San Agustín] sin embargo de haberse comprendido este en la substancion dela causa en rebeldía como alos demas Revs. ausentes; respecto â constar hallarse en el R.l Presidio de Nachitos . . . dee la orden correspondiente al Comandante del Presidio de Nachitos para que solicite el arresto del enunciado Soto Bermúdez, y consiguiéndolo, lo remita al Govern.or interino de texas para q.e este, con el seguro conveniente, lo pase â esta Cui.d que en hazerlo assi administrará V.S. Justicia" (third quotation; all author's translations).

72 For background on French rebellion in New Orleans against Spanish Gov. Ulloa (1766–69) until Gov. O'Reilly assumed command, see Weber, *Spanish Frontier*, 200–203.

73 Letter, Lt. Joseph González to governor [Oconor] of Texas, December 7, 1769, Presidio Los Adaes, *BA*, microfilm, 10:0686–0687.

74 Letter, Viceroy de Croix to governor [Oconor] of Texas, January 29, 1770, Mexico City, *BA*, microfilm, 10:0694: "q.e haviendose arrestado al Persona de D.n Manuel de Soto Bermudez, en conformidad de la Requisitoria passada al Governador de la Luisiana, lo remita contoda seguridad por cordillera â esta corte como previene aquel" (author's translation).

75 Letter, Viceroy de Croix to Gov. don Juan María Barón de Ripperdá of Texas, July 24, 1770, Mexico City, *BA*, microfilm, 10:0744.

76 Letter, Viceroy de Croix to Governor Ripperdá, August 5, 1770, Mexico City, *BA*, microfilm, 10:0747: "por que siendo como es correo con d.n Angel Martos, no puede evacuarse la causa de estte sin la asistencia del sobre dicho p.a substanciarla con los dos[?]" (author's translation).

77 Burton and Smith, *Colonial Natchitoches*, 109. The record trails off as to whether de Soto was punished, but evidently his family continued to live in Louisiana as his direct descendants are still there. Electronic correspondence, de Soto to Francis Galán; report, Cristóbal Ylario de Cordobes to Gov. Hugo Oconór, January 3, 1768, Orcoquiza, *BA*, microfilm, roll 10, frame no. 0534. Adaeseño troops at the presidios of San Xavier, on the San Marcos River, and San Sabá, northwest of present Austin near Menard, had similar internal problems but greater Indian troubles. For events at the San Xavier presidio and missions in Central Texas, see Donald E. Chipman and Harriett Denise Joseph, *Spanish Texas, 1519–1821* (Austin: University of Texas Press, 1992), 156–60.

78 Petition, Andrés Chirino, resident, before Gov. don Hugo O'Connor, May 17, 1768, Presidio Los Adaes, *BA*, microfilm, roll 9, frame no. 0626: "ocupando una Esquadra de soldados como lo era la q.e comandava el Sarxento Domingo del Rio viviendose por temporadas de pie entre las barbaras naciones afin de

consequir las crecidas cantidades de pieles, q.e nezesitaba para sus grandes correspondencias" (author's translation).

79 Complaint, don Juan Antonio Amorín, May 6, 1755, Presidio Los Adaes, before Gov. don Jacinto de Barrios y Jáuregui, *BA*, microfilm, roll 9, frame nos. 0591–92; declaration, Amorín, May 8, 1755, Presidio Los Adaes, before Gov. Barrios Jáuregui, *BA*, 9:0597, [Amorín's cow] "esta en el Rancho de los padres" (author's translation); petition, Andrés Chirino, May 17, 1768, Presidio Los Adaes, before don Hugo O'Conor, interim governor of Texas, *BA*, 9:0625–27. The complainant, Amorín, had arrived with Gov. Aguayo's original expedition that founded Presidio Los Adaes in 1721 and became a lieutenant. On his background, see Testimony #17, don Juan Antonio de Amorín, July 27, 1748, Presidio Los Adaes, in the Residencia of Gov. don Francisco Garcia Larios, *NA*, vol. 3, box 2Q292, 69, 71: "Then.te que ha sido de este Compania y primer poblador español y vecino actualmente de este Presidio [Los Adaes]" (author's translation). Amorín was around sixty-seven years old when he lodged his complaint against Andrés Chirino in 1755, and had higher status as a "first Spanish settler" from Los Adaes than Chirino, who arrived there in 1741 from Saltillo, Mexico.

80 Petition, Chirino, May 17, 1768, Presidio Los Adaes, before Governor O'Conor, *BA*, 9:0626: "siendo el principal motivo de su rincore se proceden contra mi persona el heconomico agrabio q.e lo le hazia con mi solicitud en adquirir pieles de Venado los mismos, q.e por varios modos adquiria el referido S.r Gover.or para las correspondienzias de sus tratos con los franceses en Nachitos sin hazerse el cargo dho S.r, q.e esta mi solicitud solo se dirixia amantener mi familia, y no ha enriquezer coneste trato pues, aunq.e quisiera no lo permitia mi pobreza" (author's translation).

81 *Revista de Inspección*, Marqués de Rubí, Presidio Los Adaes, September 23, 1767, Tacubaya, *AGI—Guadalajara* 511, Old Spanish Mission Records, OLLU, San Antonio, Texas, microfilm, reel 4, doc. 111, 5, 7: "vecino puestto de los Franzeses" (first quotation); "Las libranzas dadas para sattifazer al cagero, â algunos comerziantes Franceses, y ottros Yndividuos, con quienes havian conttraydo los soldados alguna lexittima dependenzia, cargadas ttres tanttos mas de su Ymportte, ô por lo menos al doble y esttto en canttidades considerables, y con mui frequente repettizion; cargándose ttambien â la quentta del soldado, los gasttos de la saca de sittuado, los de la polbora, y sus fletes, y ottras libranzas" (second quotation; all author's translations).

82 Order, King Carlos III, to his viceroy, governor, and captain general of the provinces of New Spain, and president of his royal *audiencia* in Mexico City, April 21, 1768, Aranjuez, in Hackett, eds., *Pichardo's Treatise*, 4:240–42.

83 Petition, Andrés Chirino, May 17, 1768, Presidio Los Adaes, before Governor O'Connor, *BA*, microfilm, 9:0626, 0630.

84 Petition, Andrés Chirino, *BA*, 9:0627. [Lieutenant Prieto about Chirino:] "era un hombre pobre" (first quotation), "una mala obra" (second quotation); [Chirino:] "me mando poner el Cabeza en el zepo con un par de grillos" (third quotation); "a esto le dixe q.e no me coxia de susto; pues lo propio me avia ofrecido d.n Manuel el dia antes en Nachitos" (fourth quotation; all author's translations).

85 Petition, Andrés Chirino, ibid., *BA*: "omnes ad unum, q.e mi continuo proceder asido perjudical en la Republica asi por mi altivez, y soberbia, como por uinar en mi todos los vizios siendo el mas continuo, y excesivo el de la embriaguez con el, a falto del respecto a todo el Mundo" (author's translation).

86 Petition, Andrés Chirino, ibid., *BA*, 9:0630–0631: "a el mismo tiempo me mandava ami preso, y desterrado a el Castillo de Morro" (author's translation). Andrés Chirinos's signature was made by Alexandro Repisso since he apparently was illiterate.

87 Order, Gov. O'Conor, May 17, 1768, transmitting testimony in Andrés Chirino's case to the viceroy, *BA*, 9:0637.

88 Testimony, don Juan Antonio Amorín, May 6, 1755, Presidio Los Adaes, before Gov. Barrios Jáuregui, *BA*, microfilm, roll 9, frame nos. 0591, 0594: "por allarse en los aix, Juana Maria Berban, con quien el dicho Chirino tubo amista ylicito, escalando la casa de su suegra, y dando otro escandalos" (author's translation). See also Donald E. Chipman and Harriett Denise Joseph, *Explorers and Settlers of Spanish Texas* (Austin: University of Texas Press, 2001), 236–39.

89 Review of Andrew Chrino's legal troubles, Governor Martos Navarrete, January 20, 1763, Presidio Los Adaes, *BA*, 9:0617; Y'barbo Family Genealogy, *Antonio Gil Y'barbo Collection*, East Texas Research Center, Stephen F. Austin State University, Nacogdoches, Texas, A-175, box 2, folder 2.

90 Testimony, Lt. don Marcos Ruíz, May 6, 1755, Presidio Los Adaes, appeared before Gov. Barrios Jáuregui, *BA*, 9:0595: "le quiso matar" (first quotation); "estaba ôculto en el monte obelinda[?] de esta mission, esperando la noche para el logro de su deseo" (author's translation).

91 Document, Governor Martos Navarrete, December 29, 1765, Presidio Los Adaes, discussing transfer of prisoner Andrés Chirino from El Lobanillo, *BA*, 9:0617–0618; order, Governor Martos Navarrete, July 2, 1766, Presidio Los Adaes, for Chirino to be imprisoned in the Company Guard of this presidio, *BA*, 9:0620; see also Order, Lieutenant Prieto, June 12, 1762, Presidio Los Adaes, that Chirino be kept in prison, *BA*, 9:0616.

92 Petition, don Antonio Gil Ybarvo, July 2, 1766, Presidio Los Adaes, appearing before Governor Martos Navarrete, *BA*, 9:0619–0620: "Ynquietud y discordia con que conttinuamente bibiamos mi muger i yo porcauso de Andres Chirinos residente entonces en este sobre dh.o Presidio se sirvio VS.a desterrarlo . . . ô darme lisensia para retirarme con mi familia de este Presidio no teniendo

lugar esta mí Petición" (first quotation); "por su altibes y acostumbrados esesos" (second quotation; both author's translation); order, Governor Martos Navarrete, July 12, 1761, Presidio Los Adaes, transfer of Andrés Chirino to prison in Havana, Cuba, *BA*, 9:0620. See also Chipman and Joseph, *Explorers and Settlers*, 236–39, about the illicit affair between Andrés Chirino and Maria Padilla.

93 Notice, Governor Martos Navarrete, July 26, 1766, Presidio Los Adaes, from Commandant of Natchitoches regarding Andrés Chirino's escape, *BA*, 9:0621: "aviendo quebrado los grillos con que era remitido . . . y puestose en salvo se hallaba acogido en la habitasion de S.n Luis de Sn. Deni" (first quotation); "respondido dho d.n Luis que desde la mañana del veinte y dos del mencionado sequia desparecido el dho Chirinos" (second quotation; all author's translations).

94 Warning, Governor Martos Navarrete, July 26, 1766, Presidio Los Adaes, threatening banishment for any Adaeseño resident or soldier who helped Andrés Chirino, *BA*, 9:0621: "para siempre desterrado de esta sobre dicha provincia" (author's translation).

95 See La Vere, "Between Kinship and Capitalism," 211–12, who argues that male settlers and soldiers at Presidio Los Adaes often had sexual relations with Caddo women. La Vere based his argument upon the 1793 census record, which lists many Indians and *mestizos*, or Indian-Spanish mixed-bloods, born at Los Adaes.

96 Vigness, "Don Hugo Oconor," 29, 31; see also King's order, April 21, 1768, in Hackett, eds., *Pichardo's Treatise*, 4:241.

97 Matthew Babcock, "Roots of Independence: Transcultural Trade in the Texas-Louisiana Borderlands," *Ethnohistory* 60, no. 2 (Spring 2013): 250–51.

98 Military Inspection Review of Presidio Los Adaes, September 23, 1767, Marqués de Rubí, Tacubaya, *AGI—Guadalajara* 511, in Old Spanish Mission Records, Our Lady of the Lake University, microfilm, reel, 4, document 111, 8, photocopy: "multtidud de Fiesttas de Yglesia" (author's translation).

99 Jesús F. de la Teja, "Introduction," in de la Teja and Frank, eds., *Choice, Persuasion, and Coercion*, xiii.

100 *Petición*, Lt. Joseph Gonzalez, April 26, 1770, Presidio Los Adaes, *AGI—Cuba* 70a, OLLU, microfilm, reel 13, doc. 46, 1: "total miseria en los Viveres Nezezarios, p.ra la manutencion corporal Ocurre a la Justificada prudencia de VSS.a p.ra q.e se le suplan docientas fanegas de Mais en lugar de los del mando de VSS.a y de nó haver Mais sea Arina, ârroz ô semillas semejantes . . . â este puesto" (author's translation).

101 Letter, don Luís de Vergara to *Señor don Atanazio Demezieres*, May 9, 1770, New Orleans, *AGI—Cuba* 110, microfilm, reel 24, doc. 16, 1–2: "Digo quehallandose vm con viveres suficientes para socorer dho Presidio sin que hagan

falta los habitantes de Nathcitoches, puede vm desde luego proveer lo de los q.e necesite dho precidio de Adayes pagándolos con anticipacion alos recios que establece la tarifa formada en virtud de orden del Exmo S.or D.n Alejandro ô Reilly" (author's translation).

102 Letter, Vergara, ibid., *AGI—Cuba* 110, microfilm, 24:16, 3.

103 Letter, Vergara to de Mézières, May 15, 1770, New Orleans, *AGI—Cuba* 110, microfilm, reel 24, doc. 16, 5–6: "[Pedro Primo and Juan LeBlanc] son de las 7 familias acadianos que deven vajar, y establecerse en la costa de Ybervila según que yo he determinado" (first quotation), "[Juan Cruz] por haver cinco años que esta en Natchitoches y es Irlandés, cuya nacion esta con naturalizada con la Española, y no es contra las leyes de estado, su residencia en nuestros Reinos" (second quotation), and "[Guillermo Ovarden and Jamien Peret] buelven a ese Puesto a fenecer sus negocios para despues salir de esta Provincia pues como de Nación Ingleses no pueden ser admisibles en nuestros Dominios" (third quotation; all author's translations).; Nunn, *Foreign Immigrants*, 20.

104 *Declaración del Reo* (defandant), Juan Chirinos, January 16, 1772, Royal Presidio of San Antonio de Béxar, Gov. Juan María Barón de Ripperdá of Texas vs. Juan Chirinos in the murder of Cristóbal Carvajal, *BA*, microfilm, roll 11, frame no. 0121: "tener muchas deudas el Def.to" (author's translation). See also Carmela Leal, trans., Murder of Christoval Carvajal, January 16, 1772, *Béxar Archives Translations* (hereafter *BAT*), vol. 51 (1772), Daughter of the Republic of Texas Research Library, Alamo.

105 Order, Governor Ripperdá, June 22, 1772, Presidio San Antonio de Béxar, ibid., *BA*, microfilm, 11:0153: "dándole por enteram.te, absuelto, y livre" (author's translation). Three of Carvajal's aunts had sought justice in this case, December 17, 1772, San Antonio de Béxar, *BA*, microfilm, 11:0298.

106 Letter, Domingo Valcarcel, auditor, to Governor Ripperdá, April 29, 1772, with approval of decision by Viceroy Bucareli, Mexico City, *BA*, microfilm, 11:0152: "no puede quedar duda en que Chirinos, como que usso de su propria defensa, no cometio delito alguno. Por la Ley 4. tit. 23. Lib. 8 de la Recopilasion de Castilla, se previene: que todo Hombre que matare â otro â sabiendas muera por ello, salbo si matares â su enemigo, ó defendiendose. Y por Doctrinas bien recevidas se assienta: que lícitamente puede uno matar â otro, quando le sigue armado con animo de ofenderle" (author's translation).

107 Order, Governor Ripperdá setting Juan Chirino free to continue royal military service, June 22, 1772, Presidio San Antonio de Béxar, *BA*, microfilm, 11:0153.

108 Letter, Viceroy Bucarely y Ursua to the governor of Texas, Juan María Barón de Ripperdá, February 24, 1773, Mexico City, *BA*, microfilm, 11:0319–0320; letter, Governor Ripperdá to the governor of Louisiana, don Luís de Unzaga y Amezaga, April 17, 1773, San Antonio de Béxar, in Herbert E. Bolton, *Athanase*

de Mézières and the Louisiana-Texas Frontier, 1768–1780, vol. 2 (Cleveland: Arthur H. Clark, 1914), 29–31.

109 Bolton, *Texas*, 388–91. For a brief biography of Antonio Gil Ybarbo, see Donald E. Chipman and Harriett Denise Joseph, *Notable Men and Women of Spanish Texas* (Austin: University of Texas Press, 1999), 192–201.

110 Testimony and petition, Antonio Gil Ybarbo and other Adaesaños, to Governor Ripperdá, San Antonio de Béxar, October 4, 1773, requesting permission to settle in Mission Ais, *AGM—Historia*, vol. 84, *CAT*, box 31, folder 3, 316, transcription. [Full text:] "mas comodas nos parescan para nuestro establecimiento, siembras, crias de Ganados, y demas que proficuo sea a nuestro bien estar, sin que por nosotros Redunde daño o incomunidad, en los Vecinos, y Pobladores, de dicho Precidio, y Villa, por lo que procurando guardar en este caso la mejor armonia, y practicar general atención, Paz, quietud, y sosiego (sino tan solamente con los primeros del Referido Precidio, y Villa, sino hasta con los ultimos de ella)" (author's translation).

111 Testimony and petition, ibid., *AGM—Historia*, transcription: "y hecho a saver, como a las lamentables miserias con que pasamos tan prolongado Camino, experimentado en el sed, mucha seca, falta de cabalgaduras, muerte de algunos hijos y deudos, y principalmente el abandono de la mayor parte de nuestros cortos y bienes . . " (author's translation).

112 Order, Governor Ripperdá, December 7, 1773, San Antonio de Béxar, responding to petition by Ybarbo and the Adaesaños, *CAT*, *AGM—Historia*, vol. 84, box 31, folder 3, 318–19, transcription: "si estos vecinos no hallaran Solares, y tierras que puedan convenirles, en este Precidio, y Villa, en el fuerte de Santa Cruz, del Sibolo, en unas, y otras immediaciones, las de los antiguos Ranchos y otros parages, con la seguridad que permite un Paiz de Guerra . . " (author's translation).

113 *Consulta*, Governor Ripperdá to Viceroy Bucareli, San Antonio de Béxar, December 10, 1773, *CAT*, *AGM—Historia*, vol. 84, box 31, folder 3, 320–22, transcription: "para precentarse a los pies de V. Exa." (first quotation); "de no poder labrar la tierra, hacer saca de Agua, ni tampoco pedir solares para establecerse como la seguridad, y quietud, que les facilitaban las naciones de Yndios circunvecinas . . " (second quotation; all author's translations). For more background on Hugo O'Conor, see Weber, *Spanish Frontier*, 220–26. For discussion about the importance of water in San Antonio, see Charles R. Porter Jr., *Spanish Water, Anglo Water: Early Development in San Antonio* (College Station: Texas A&M University Press, 2009); and Michael C. Meyer, *Water in the Hispanic Southwest: A Social and Legal History, 1550–1850* (Tuscon: University of Arizona Press, 1984).

114 *Consulta*, Governor Ripperdá to Viceroy Bucareli, ibid., *AGM–Historia*.

EPILOGUE

1 *Escrito* (petition), Ybarbo and Flores, February 28, 1774, Mexico City, *AGM— Historia*, vol. 84, *CAT*, box 31, folder 3, 323–25, transcription; *consulta*, Viceroy Bucarely, March 7, 1774, Mexico City, refers Adaesaños' petition to his *Junta de Guerra y Hacienda* ("junta" or council), ibid., *AGM—Historia*, 325–27; *auto*, Viceroy Bucarely, March 7, 1774, Mexico City, for his council to determine what is most convenient, ibid., *AGM—Historia*, 327; junta, March 17, 1774, Mexico City, in agreement with Adaesaños' petition, ibid., *AGM—Historia*, 327–29: "y procure establecer las demas Poblaciones cercas, que aseguren la Paz y sociego de los Yndios, y eviten la comunicacion con los Yngleses, y demas naciones extrangeros" (author's translation); *auto*, Viceroy Bucarely, March 18, 1774, Mexico City, granting Adaesaños' petition, ibid., *AGM—Historia*, 331. Included among the documents were the certification dated December 7, 1773, in San Antonio de Béxar made by *El Bachillar*, don Pedro Fuentes, *cura* (priest), from the Villa de San Fernando, and the Adaesaños' petition.

2 Letter, O'Conor to the fiscal, March 28, 1774, Chihuahua, *AGM—Historia*, vol. 51, *CAT*, box 29, folder 2, 278, transcription: "ilicito, abominable comercio." See also letter, Arriaga, advisor, to Viceroy Bucarely, November 26, 1773, Mexico City, expressing concern over armaments left behind at Los Adaes for lack of mules and oxen.

3 Order, Viceroy Bucarely to Governor Ripperdá, February 9, 1774, Mexico City, *BA*, 11:0386–0387; letter, Bucarely to Governor Ripperdá, September 14, 1774, Mexico City, *BA*, 11: 0453–0454. See also letter, Commandant General de Croix to governor of Texas, May 16, 1778, Chihuahua, ordering payment to Christóbal Vallejo for transporting cannons from Los Adaes to San Antonio de Béxar, *BA*, 12:0285–0286.

4 McCorkle Jr., "Los Adaes," 10; Cutter, *Legal Culture*, 18. For the global economic level, see Alan L. Karras, *Smuggling: Contraband and Corruption in World History* (Lanham, MD: Rowman & Littlefield, 2010), who states, "Several world regions were engaged in intraregional contraband in much the same way that the Caribbean and the Atlantic World were," and he argues that "individuals, whether smugglers or consumers of those smuggled products, have forced the development and coordination of laws and regulations, even as they have found wasy to avoid thse very same policies" (ix). In much the same way, so did Adaeseños and other settlers in northern New Spain with the proverbial adage *obedezco pero no cumplo* (I obey but do not comply), as noted in de la Teja, *San Antonio de Béxar*, 85.

5 Letter, O'Conor to Governor Ripperdá, February 17, 1774, Chihuahua, *AGM— Historia*, vol. 51, 227, 246–47; Weber, *Spanish Frontier*, 222.

6 Quotation from Bolton, *Texas*, 393.

7 Order, Viceroy Bucarely, May 17, 1774, Mexico City, denying the request of citizens of Los Adaes to settle in Natchitoches, *BA*, 11:0411–0412.

8 Letter, Bucarely to Governor Ripperdá, concerning order to report to O'Conor all matters pertaining to the resettlement of people from Los Adaes, February 28, 1775, Mexico City, *BA*, 11:0529–0530: "al contravando que cometen, y pueden hacer allí con gran facilidad" (author's translation).

9 Letter, Captain Ybarbo to Commandant General de Croix, May 13, 1779, Nacogdoches, *AGM—Historia*, vol. 51, 520–23, transcription. For de Croix's background, see Weber, *Spanish Frontier*, 224–25.

10 Letter, Father De la Garza, April 30, 1779, Nacogdoches, *AGM—Historia*, vol. 51, *CAT*, box 29, folder 6a, 524–25, transcription.

11 Letter, Governor Cabello to de Croix, August 20, 1779, San Antonio de Béxar, reporting visit by the Texas Indians, *BA*, 13:0321–0322. [Viceroy to Texas Indian chief:] "dandole un bestido, y un baston de cap.n, siendo esta Yndio mui Ladino, Racional, y Adbentido" (first quotation); "Ydioma texa" (second quotation); [Cabello on Pedro Gonzales' ability to speak the Texas Indian language:] "acciona perfectam.te, y es conocido de todos ellos" (third quotation); [de Mézières allegedly told the friendly Indian nations,] "prebinieran todos, p.a benir à esta Prov. â haser la Grra. â los Apaches" (fourth quotation; all author's translations). Some of the other Indian nations mentioned as allies in a war against the Apaches were the "Taboyas, Aguages, and Tancabos," in addition to the Texas Indians.

12 De la Teja, *San Antonio de Béxar*, 84.

13 *Instancia* (petition), *Expediente promovido por los vecinos del extinguido Presidio de los Adaes*, January 4, 1778, San Antonio de Béxar, *AGI—Guadalajara* 267, in Old Spanish Mission Research Library, OLLU, microfilm, reel 2, doc. 25, 1–6: "como si fueramos de alguno otro Reyno estraño" (first quotation); "como al presente estamos prontos à derramar hasta la ultima gota de sangre por ntro Rey" (second quotation); "imploramos el Paternal amor con que S.M. (Dios le guarde) se digna de amparar à sus vasallos" (third quotation; all author's translations). See also de la Teja, *San Antonio de Béxar*, 84.

14 *Dictamen* (judgment), Commandant General de Croix, January 8, 1778, San Antonio de Béxar, *AGI—Guadalajara* 267, ibid., 6–8.

15 Letter, Peter Galindo Navarro, advisor [to de Croix], regarding the Adeaseños' petition [1778], *ACZ*: "dividirlas igualm.te en suertes, que por sortèo repartira entre los sesenta y tres Vezinos Españoles" (author's translation).

16 *Decreto*, de Croix, June 8, 1779, Chihuahua, ibid., *ACZ*, 13:0691–0692.

17 Certified copy of royal dispatch to officers in America to guard against illegal trade, August 15, 1776, to March 1, 1779, Chihuahua, signed by Antonio Bonilla,

BA, 11:0753–0754; letter, de Croix to Cabello, enclosing copy of royal decree concerning Spain's declaration of war against Great Britain, *BA*, 13:0498.

18 Proceedings concerning de Croix's dispatch transmitting royal decree, February 11, 1780, San Antonio de Béxar, *BA*, microfilm, 13:0909–0910; de Croix to Gov. Domingo Cabello of Texas, February 18, 1780, Arispe, *BA*, microfilm, 13:0922; Governor Cabello to the Cabildo, Justice and Regiment of San Fernando, April 20, 1780, La Bahía, *BA*, microfilm, 13:1076–77.

19 De Croix to Cabello, March 30, 1780, Arispe, *BA*, microfilm, 13:1024–25. For discussion of Spanish concerns in the American Revolution, see Light Townsend Cummins, *Spanish Observers and the American Revolution, 1775–1783* (Baton Rouge: Louisiana State University Press, 1991). On Bernardo de Galvez, see Weber, *Spanish Frontier*, 227.

20 De Croix to Cabello, April 4, 1780, Arispe, *BA*, microfilm, 13:1040–42.

21 Weber, *Spanish Frontier*, 222.

22 Burton, "Family and Economy," 113–14.

23 Weber, *Spanish Frontier*, 230.

24 Certified copy of Father Vallejo's letter to Jose Maria Guadiano, Nacogdoches, February 20, 1797, *BA*, microfilm, 27:0064–0065; letter, Guadiana to Gov. Coronel don Manuel Muñoz, forwarding copies of Father Vallejo's request for definition of border with Louisiana and discussing its importance, *BA*, microfilm, 27:0086–0087.

25 Certified copy of a list of ranches east of the Sabine River that lie within Spanish territory, Jose Maria Guadiano, *BA*, 27:0077: [Francisco Prudome] "en el Pueblo de los Yndios Adaes" and [Manuel Prudome] "en el Arroyo ondo de los Adaes" (third quotation); "Morfil . . . Bouguier en la laguna de los Adaes" (fourth quotation); "don Pablo Lafita en el Arroyo de las Piedras"; and "Samuel el Yngles en el Arroyo de San Juan" (fifth quotation; all author's translations).

26 Capt. Luís Antonio Menchaca, sums due soldiers of abandoned Presidio Los Adaes, November 28, 1780, Presidio San Antonio de Béxar, *BAT* online, 15–24; Captain Menchaca, report, distribution of goods to soldiers of abandoned Presidio Los Adaes, December 11, 1780, Presidio San Antonio de Béxar, *BAT*, 54–57; certified copy of proceedings concerning payment to soldiers of the abandoned presidio of Los Adaes, Gov. Domingo Cabello, March 5, 1782–June 16, 1792, Presidio de Béxar y Villa de San Fernando, *BA*, microfilm, 15:0047–0073; Gov. Rafael Martinez Pacheco, report on delivery made by former Gov. Domingo Cabello of the ornaments used in the chapel of the abandoned presidio of Los Adaes and later in the chapel of Fort Santa Cruz of Cibolo, January 28, 1787, and November 27, 1790, *BAT*, 44–46; reports, individuals from Presidio Los Adaes resident in San Antonio de Béxar regarding payment made to them of their salaries at the time that it was closed and transportation of artillery

and other war equipment from Los Adaes to San Antonio de Béxar, 1792, *BAT*, 156–59.

27 Spanish census records for Nacogdoches during the 1790s have a separate list for foreigners as residents of that town in East Texas; letter, Marqués de Casa Calvo, governor of Louisiana, to don Juan Bautista de Elguezábal, governor of Texas, March 10, 1800, New Orleans, *BA*, microfilm, reel 29, frame nos. 0395–0397; certified copies, Miguel de Musquíz, invoice by Barr and Davenport, merchandise received from Natchitoches, March 5, 1803, in wagons brought by Ruíz and Seguin; and passport, translated from the French language into Castilian, to Juan Bach and Samuel Norris, and to Guillermo Barr with permission to travel to San Antonio de Béxar, April 4, 1803, Nacogdoches, *BA*, 30:0860–0861. Among the goods listed were 3 barrels of wheat, 11 bags of lead weighing 600 pounds, 192 pounds of *balas* (bullets), 400 pounds of *polvora* (gunpowder), nearly 1 barrel of salt, 180 bundles of tobacco, 1 barrel of sugar, 2 barrels of coffee, clothing-related items, and so on. Report, Miguel de Musquíz, Indian expenditures, including certified copies of 28 invoices by Barr and Davenport, December 31, 1802, Nacogdoches, *BA*, 30:1029–45. The expenditures were for the Caddo, Nacogdoches, Tejas, Bidais, *Quichas*, and Ais plus other Indian nations and mentions names of some of their Indian captains.

28 Weber, *Spanish Frontier*, 289; letter, Francisco Requeña to Miguel Cayetano Soler, April 19, 1799, Madrid, *The Historic New Orleans Collection* (hereafter *THNOC*), 2–4 (first quotation); evaluation of Luís Vilemont's report, May 19, 1799, Madrid, *THNOC*, 4–8 (second quotation; all author's translations). For further discussion of US expansionism, see Narrett, "Liberation and Conquest: John Hamilton Robinson and U.S. Adventurism toward Mexico, 1806–1819," *Western Historical Quarterly* 40 (Spring 2009): 23–50.

29 Matthew Babcock, "Roots of Independence: Transcultural Trade in the Texas-Louisiana Borderlands," *Ethnohistory* 60, no. 2 (Spring 2013): 255; Dan Flores, "Bringing Home All the Pretty Horses: The Horse Trade and the Early American West, 1775–1825," *Montana: The Magazine of Western History*, Summer 2008, 21.

30 Letter, Pedro de Nava, commander in chief of the Interior Provinces of New Spain, to the governor of Texas, August 8, 1800, Chihuahua, ordering the arrest of Felipe Nolan, *BA*, 29:0628–0630; letter, José Vidal to commandant of Nacogdoches, October 20, 1800, Concordia, giving personal information about Nolan and Cook, *BA*, 29:0747–0749; letter, Philip Nolan to Amigo Cook, October 21, 1800, Natchez, *BA*, 29:0753–0754; letter, Governor Elguezábal, to the governor of Nuevo Santander, November 30, 1800, San Antonio de Béxar, reporting line of march proposed by Nolan and thirty armed men and the robbery of horses in territories north of Béxar, *BA*, 29:0815; letter, Governor

Elguezábal to don Antonio Cordero, November 30, 1800, San Antonio de Béxar, reporting news received from Nacogdoches about Nolan, an "American of Irish nationality," and his robberies, *BA*, 29:0816. For the best discussion of the Nolan drama, see Chipman and Joseph, *Spanish Texas*, 226–29. Spanish officials continued rooting out Nolan's co-conspirators. See letter, Miguel Francisco Musquíz, military commander, to Governor Elguezábal, May 1, 1801, Nacogdoches, acknowledging receipt of order concerning trial of Spaniards accompanying Nolan, *BA*, 30: 0047; and letter, Musquíz to Governor Elguezábal, May 1, 1801, acknowledging receipt of orders concerning trial of Englishmen accompanying Nolan, *BA*, 30:0048.

31 Babcock, "Roots of Independence," 253–54.

32 Ibid., 245–46, 252.

33 David E. Narrett, "Geopolitics and Intrigue: James Wilkinson, the Spanish Borderlands, and Mexican Independence," *William and Mary Quarterly* 69, no. 1 (January 2012): 108; Dan L. Flores, *Southern Counterpoint to Lewis & Clark: The Freeman & Custis Expedition of 1806* (Norman: University of Oklahoma Press, 1806), 86, 286 (first quotation); Weber, *Spanish Frontier*, 295 (second quotation).

34 Petition, April 17, 1801, Chihuahua, *BA*, 30:0021; order, April 20, 1803, Chihuahua, *BA*, 30:0022–23; letter, July (?), 1804, Nacogdoches, *BA*, 33:0067; Weber, *Spanish Frontier*, 296; Lance R. Blyth, "Fugitives from Servitude: American Deserters and Runaway Slaves in Spanish Nacogdoches, 1803–1808," *East Texas Historical Association* 38 (Fall 2000): 3–14.

35 Bradley Folsom, "Trinidad de Salcedo: A Forgotten Villa in Colonial Texas, 1806–1813," *East Texas Historical Journal* 52, no. 2 (Fall 2014): 49; Weber, *Spanish Frontier*, 296.

36 De la Teja, *San Antonio de Béxar*, 86.

37 *Expediente instruido sobre el reparto de las tierras de San Antonio Valero a los vecinos del Presidio de los Adaes* (Partition of the Suertes of Mission San Antonio de Valero to Adaeseños), don Manuel Muñoz, judge and governor of the Province of Texas, Year 1793, Béxar County Archives, Spanish deeds, book 3, 311.

38 De la Teja, *San Antonio de Béxar*, 85.

39 Petition, Jose Cristobal de los Santos and Maria Mendez, San Antonio de Béxar, 1772–73, in Marriage Petitions and Permissions of San Fernando Church in San Antonio, Texas, trans. John Ogden Leal, Daughters of the Republic of Texas Library at the Alamo (hereafter *DRT Archives*), 12; petition, Aniceto Camaño and Juana Bercuda Saucedo, San Antoino de Béxar, 1772, *DRT Archives*, 8. See also petition, Pedro Joseph Texeda and Francisca Perez, San Antonio de Béxar, 1773, *DRT Archives*, 24.

40 Lemée, "Tios and Tantes," 351n40.

41 De la Teja, *San Antonio de Béxar*, 89.

42 Porter Jr., *Spanish Water*, ix, 27.

43 Information about Juan Chirino obtained from "Ojos de Servicio" in the Siman-
    cas Archives, microfilm, and Spanish census data for La Bahía in the year 1811
    from the Béxar Archives. See also petition, Juan Chirino and Xaviera Flores,
    San Antonio de Béxar, 1779–80, *DRT Archives*, 121.

44 De la Teja, *San Antonio de Béxar*, 26; see also de la Teja, "Urbano and María
    Trinidad," 121–46.

45 Antonio Bonilla, copy, "Estado en que se patentiza el numero de Indios
    de ambos sexos de que se compone cada una de la veinte y una Naciones
    del Norte, Amigas de la Provincia de los Texas y las cantidades de Generos y
    efectos que se necesitan para hacerles el regalo annual que se ha establecido
    repartirles para obsequiarlas," June 26, 1790, Mexico City, *Archivo General
    de Simancas*, Spain, in *OSMRL*, Our Lady of the Lake University, microfilm,
    roll 1, C. M. leg. 7019, no. 37, oversize page. Gov. Domingo Cabello distributed
    the gifts on October 25, 1785, from San Antonio de Béxar.

46 Bonilla, copy, "Estado que manifiesta los efectos que se han regalados á los
    Capitanes é Indios de las 21 Naciones de el Norte, Amigas de la Provincia de
    los Texas en meses de Junio, Julio, y Agosto de el año 1785 de los Generos
    venidos á este fin de la Nueva Orleáns por disposición del señor comandante
    general de las Provincias Internas del Reyno de Nueva España," *AGS—Spain*,
    ibid., no. 35, oversize page. Governor Cabello distributed these gifts Octo-
    ber 25, 1785.

47 F. Todd Smith, "Dehahuit: An Indian Diplomat on the Louisiana-Texas Frontier,"
    in Smith and Hilton, eds., *Nexus of Empire*, 140–41.

48 Census report, Jose Maria Guadiana, Nacogdoches, May 31, 1809, *BA*, micro-
    film, 41:0544–0599. English translation also available: *BAT*, DeGolyer Library,
    Southern Methodist University, microfilm, reel 2, 286–300. The remaining
    occupations after farmer, officially listed, were blacksmith, hatter, shoe-
    maker, trader, silversmith, carpenter, muleteer, servant, field worker, and
    notary.

49 From records found in Mills, *NACCR*, vol. 1; and John and Betty Oglesbee,
    *Reminiscing the Road: El Camino Real de los Tejas National Historic Trail
    from Los Adaes to the Trinity River* (Nacogdoches: East Texas Historical
    Association, 2007), 28. See also J. Edward Townes, "The Nature of Loyalty:
    Antonio Gil Ibarvo and the East Texas Frontier," in *Nexus of Empire: Negoti-
    tating Loyalty and Identity in the Revolutionary Borderlands, 1760s–1820s*,
    ed. Gene Allen Smith and Sylvia L. Hilton (Gainesville: University Press of
    Florida, 2010), 163–82.

50 Aileen Curl Metteauer, "A Brief History about Chireno," in *Memories of Chireno*
    (Chireno, TX: Chireno Historical Society, 1994), 42–43.

51 Census report, Nacogdoches, *BA*, microfilm, 41:0544–0559; see also Jackson, *Los Mesteños*, 491–93.

52 Weber, *Spanish Frontier*, 299. On the Battle of Medina and its aftermath, see Bradley Folsom, *Arredondo: Last Spanish Ruler of Texas and Northeastern New Spain* (Norman: University of Oklahoma Press, 2017).

53 Mary B. Van Rheenen, "Can You Tell Me Who My People Are? Ethnic Identity among the Hispanic-Indian People of Sabine Parish, Louisiana" (MA thesis, Louisiana State University, 1987), 12. Interestingly, a former chief, Tommy Bolton of the Choctaw-Apache Tribe of Ebarb, corresponded by stating that "thirteen of our families are associated with Los Adaes: Sanchez, Ramirez (Remedies), Padilla (Paddie), Del Rio (Rivers), Ybarbo (Ebarb), Procella (Procell), Cordova, Cartinez[?], De Los Santos Coy (Santos), Garcia (Garcie), Mora, Martinez, and Torres," in letter, Tommy Bolton to Francis X. Galán, December 28, 2005, Zwolle, Louisiana, 3 (in author's possession).

54 Reséndez, *Changing National Identities*; Richard Hurzeler, "People of Faith: The Old Spanish of East Texas" (MA thesis, Stephen F. Austin State University, 1989), 1; Gilberto M. Hinojosa, "The Enduring Faith Communities: A Historiography of the Spanish and Mexican Texas Catholic Church," *Journal of Texas Catholic History and Culture*, March 1990, 21–40; Robert E. Wright, "Local Church Emergence and Mission Decline: The Historiography of the Catholic Church in the Southwest during the Spanish and Mexican Period," *U.S. Catholic Historian* 9 (Winter/Spring 1990): 27–48. For comparison, see Mills, *Forgotten People*.

55 Oral History Project, interviews conducted with twenty-four respondents, mostly residents from nearby Robeline, Louisiana, January–April, 1999, George Avery, interviewer, *Los Adaes Station Archaeology Program, 1999 Annual Report* (Natchitoches: Northwestern State University of Louisiana), 33–76.

56 Raymond Berthelot, "Los Adaes State Historical Site: Bringing Texas and Louisiana Spanish Colonial Heritage to Life," *El Campanario: Texas Old Missions and Forts Restoration Association* 35 (December 2004): 2–6.

57 Letter, Mary Lucille Rivers (affectionately known as "Betty") to family and friends, December 14, 2016, Zwolle, Louisiana.

58 Weber, "Conflicts and Accommodations," 15.

59 For comparison, see Omar S. Valerio-Jiménez, *River of Hope: Forging Identity and Nation in the Rio Grande Borderlands* (Durham, NC: Duke University Press, 2013).

60 Lyman L. Johnson, *Workshop of Revolution: Plebeian Buenos Aires and the Atlantic World, 1776–1810* (Durham, NC: Duke University Press, 2011); John Lynch, *The Spanish American Revolutions, 1808–1826* (New York: W. W. Norton, 1973).

Bibliography

ARCHIVAL SOURCES

Archivo de la Secretaria de Gobierno. Microfilm. Saltillo, Mexico. Old Spanish Missions Research Library. Center for Mexican American Studies and Research, Our Lady of the Lake University, San Antonio, TX.

Archivo del Colegio Querétaro. Microfilm. Convento de Santa Cruz, Convento de San Francisco. Celaya, Mexico. Old Spanish Missions Research Library. Center for Mexican American Studies and Research, Our Lady of the Lake University, San Antonio, TX.

Archivo del Colegio de Zacatecas. Microfilm. Convento de Guadalupe. Zacatecas, Mexico. Old Spanish Missions Research Library. Center for Mexican American Studies and Research, Our Lady of the Lake University, San Antonio, TX.

Archivo Franciscano de Zapopán. Microfilm. Jalisco, Mexico. Old Spanish Missions Research Library. Center for Mexican American Studies and Research, Our Lady of the Lake University, San Antonio, TX.

Archivo General de Indias. Transcripts. Spanish and Mexican Manuscript Collection. Catholic Archives of Texas, Archdiocesan Office, Austin, TX.

Archivo General de Indias—Cuba. Microfilm. Old Spanish Missions Research Library. Center for Mexican American Studies and Research, Our Lady of the Lake University, San Antonio, TX.

Archivo General de la Nación—Historia. Mission Dolores Historical Materials Collection, Mission Dolores Research Center, San Augustine, TX.

Archivo General de México. Transcripts. Spanish and Mexican Manuscript Collection. Catholic Archives of Texas, Archdiocesan Office, Austin, TX.

Archivo General de Simancas. Spain. Special Collections, John Peace Library. University of Texas at San Antonio.

Archivo San Francisco el Grande. Photostatic copy. The Dolph Briscoe Center for American History, University of Texas at Austin.

Bexar Archives. Manuscripts. Microfilm. The Dolph Briscoe Center for American History, University of Texas at Austin. Special Collections, John Peace Library. University of Texas at San Antonio.

Biblioteca Nacional de México. Microfilm. Mexico City. Old Spanish Missions Research Library. Center for Mexican American Studies and Research, Our Lady of the Lake University, San Antonio, TX.

Herbert E. Bolton Papers. Transcript photocopies. University of California at Berkeley. Mission Dolores Historical Materials Collections. Mission Dolores Visitor and Research Center, San Augustine, TX.

Nacogdoches Archives. Photostatic copy. The Dolph Briscoe Center for American History, University of Texas at Austin.

Saltillo Archives. Photostatic copy. The Dolph Briscoe Center for American History, University of Texas at Austin.

PRINTED PRIMARY SOURCES

Avery, George. *Los Adaes Station Archaeology Program: 1997 Archaeology Annual Report*. Natchitoches: Department of Social Sciences, Northwestern State University of Louisiana, June 1997.

———. *Description of Documents Related to Presidio Nuestra Señora del Pilar de los Adaes, Misión San Miguel de Cuellar de los Adaes, Adaes Indians, Natchitoches, Adaesaños, and Pueblo of Bucareli*. San Antonio, TX: Old Spanish Missions Historical Research Library, Our Lady of the Lake University, n.d.

Benavides, Adán, Jr. *A Catalog of Documents and Maps of the Mission Dolores de los Ais Historical Materials Collection, San Augustine, Texas*. Austin: Texas Department of Transportation, Archaeological Studies Program, August 1998.

Bolton, Hebert E., trans. *Athanase de Mézières and the Louisiana-Texas Frontier, 1768–1780*. 2 vols. Cleveland: Arthur H. Clark, 1914.

Bridges, Katherine, and Winston De Ville, eds. and trans. "Natchitoches and the Trail to the Rio Grande: Two Early Eighteenth Century Accounts, by the Sieur Derbanne." *Louisiana History* 8 (Summer 1767): 239–59.

Byrd Simpson, Lesley. *The Encomienda of New Spain: The Beginnings of Spanish Mexico*. Berkeley: University of California Press, 1950.

Cunningham, Debbie S. "The Domingo Ramón Diary of the 1716 Expedition into the Province of the Tejas Indians: An Annotated Translation." *Southwestern Historical Quarterly* 110, no. 1 (July 2006): 38–67.

———. "Friar Simón del Hierro's Diary of the Preliminary Colonization of Nuevo Santander, 1749: An Annotated Translation." *Catholic Southwest: A Journal of History and Culture* 23 (2012): 36–55.

Guajardo, Dahlia Rose, Dahlia Palacios, Eusebio Benavidez, Tony Vincent Garcia, and Crispin Rendon, trans. *Slaves of Monterrey, Nuevo Leon, Mexico:*

Hundreds of Notary Documents. San Antonio: Los Bexareños Genealogical Society, 2010.

Hackett, Charles Wilson, ed. and trans. *Pichardo's Treatise on the Limits of Louisiana and Texas.* 4 vols. Austin: University of Texas Press, 1946.

Hatcher, Mattie Austin, ed. "Diary of a Visit of Inspection of the Texas Missions Made by Fray Gaspar José de Solis in the Year 1767–68." Translated by Margaret Keney Kress. *Southwestern Historical Quarterly* 35 (July 1931): 28–76.

Jackson, Jack, and William C. Foster. *Imaginary Kingdom: Texas as Seen by the Rivera and Rubí Military Expeditions, 1727 and 1767.* Austin: Texas State Historical Association, 1995.

Kinnaird, Lawrence. *The Frontiers of New Spain: Nicolas LaFora's Description, 1766–1768.* Berkeley: Quivira Society, 1958.

Magnaghi, Russell M., ed. and trans. "Texas as Seen by Governor Winthuysen, 1741–1744." *Southwestern Historical Quarterly* 88 (October 1984): 167–80.

McDonald, Dedra S., comp. *Guide to the Spanish and Mexican Manuscript Collection.* Edited by Kinga Perzynska. Austin: Catholic Archives of Texas, 1994.

Mills, Elizabeth Shown. *Natchitoches, 1729–1803: Abstracts of the Catholic Church Registers of the French and Spanish Post of St. Jean Baptiste des Natchitoches in Louisiana.* 2 vols. New Orleans: Polyanthos, 1977.

———. *Natchitoches Colonials: Censuses, Military Rolls, and Tax Lists, 1722–1803.* Chicago: Adams Press, 1981.

Morfi, Juan Agustín. *History of Texas, 1673–1779.* Edited and translated by Carlos Eduardo Castañeda. 2 vols. Albuquerque: Quivira Society, 1935.

Nathan, Paul, trans. *The San Sabá Papers: A Documentary Account of the Founding and Destruction of San Sabá Mission.* Edited by Lesley Byrd Simpson. San Francisco: John Howell-Books, 1959.

Naylor, Thomas H., and Charles W. Polzer, eds. *Pedro de Rivera and the Military Regulations for Northern New Spain, 1724–1729.* Tucson: University of Arizona Press, 1988.

Santos, Richard G. *Aguayo Expedition into Texas, 1721: An Annotated Translation of the Five Versions of the Diary Kept by Br. Juan Antoino de la Peña.* Austin: Jenkins, 1981.

Sibley, Marilyn McAdams, ed. "Across Texas in 1767: The Travels of Captain Pagès." *Southwestern Historical Quarterly* 70 (April 1967): 593–622.

Smith, Ralph A., trans. "Account of the Journey of Bénard de la Harpe: Discovery Made by Him of Several Nations Situated in the West." *Southwestern Historical Quarterly* 62 (July 1958): 75–86, 246–59, 371–85, 525–41.

West, Elizabeth H., ed. and trans. "Bonilla's Brief Compendium of the History of Texas, 1772." *Southwestern Historical Quarterly* 8 (July 1904): 3–78.

Adelman, Jeremy, and Stephen Aron. "From Borderlands to Borders: Empires, Nation-States, and the Peoples in between in North American History." *American Historical Review* 104 (June 1999): 814–41.

Aiton, Arthur S. "The Diplomacy of the Louisiana Cession." In *The Louisiana Purchase Bicentennial Series in Louisiana History*, vol. 2, *The Spanish Presence in Louisiana, 1763–1803*, edited by Gilbert C. Din, 11–27. Lafayette: University of Southwestern Louisiana, 1996.

Almaráz, Félix D., Jr. *The San Antonio Missions and Their System of Land Tenure.* Austin: University of Texas Press, 1989.

———. *Tragic Cavalier: Governor Manuel Salcedo of Texas, 1808–1813.* College Station: Texas A&M University Press, 1971.

Anderson, Fred. *Crucible of War: The Seven Years' War and the Fate of Empire in British North America.* New York: Random House, 2000.

Anderson, Gary Clayton. *The Indian Southwest, 1580–1830: Ethnogenesis and Reinvention.* Norman: University of Oklahoma Press, 1999.

Aron, Stephen. *American Confluence: The Missouri Frontier from Borderland to Border State.* Bloomington: Indiana University Press, 2006.

Baade, Hans W. "The Law of Slavery in Spanish Louisiana, 1769–1803." In *Louisiana's Legal Heritage*, edited by Edward F. Haas, 43–56. Pensacola: Perdido Bay Press, 1983.

Babcock, Matthew. *Apache Adaptation to Hispanic Rule.* New York: Cambridge University Press, 2016.

———. "Roots of Independence: Transcultural Trade in the Texas-Louisiana Borderlands." *Ethnohistory* 60 (Spring 2013): 245–68.

Barr, Juliana. "A Diplomacy of Gender: Rituals of First Contact in the 'Land of the Tejas.'" *William and Mary Quarterly* 61 (July 2004): 393–437.

———. "From Captives to Slaves: Commodifying Indian Women in the Borderlands." *Journal of American History* 92 (June 2005): 19–46.

———. "Geographies of Power: Mapping Indian Borders in the 'Borderlands' of the Early Southwest." *William and Mary Quarterly* 68, no. 1 (January 2011): 5–46.

———. *Peace Came in the Form of a Woman: Indians and Spaniards in the Texas Borderlands.* Chapel Hill: University of North Carolina Press, 2007.

———. "There's No Such Thing as 'Prehistory': What the Longue Durée of Caddo and Pueblo History Tells Us about Colonial America." *William and Mary Quarterly* 74, no. 2 (April 2017): 203–40.

Barr, Juliana, and Edward Countryman, eds. *Contested Spaces of Early America.* Philadelphia: University of Pennsylvania Press, 2014.

Barth, Fredrik. *Ethnic Groups and Boundaries: The Social Organization of Culture Difference*. Prospect Heights: Waveland Press, 1998.

Beltrán, Gonzalo Aguirre. "The Slave Trade in Mexico." *Hispanic American Historical Review* 24 (August 1944): 412–31.

———. "Tribal Origins of Slaves in Mexico." *Journal of Negro History*, July 1946, 269–352.

Berlin, Ira. *Many Thousands Gone: The First Two Centuries of Slavery in North America*. Cambridge: Harvard University Press, 1998.

Berthelot, Raymond. "Los Adaes State Historical Site: Bringing Texas and Louisiana Spanish Colonial Heritage to Life." *El Campanario: Texas Old Missions and Forts Restoration Association* 35 (December 2004): 2–6.

Blackhawk, Ned. *Violence over the Land: Indians and Empires in the Early American West*. Cambridge: Harvard University Press, 2006.

Blyth, Lance R. *Chiricahua and Janoes: Communities of Violence in the Southwestern Borderlands, 1680–1880*. Lincoln: University of Nebraska Press, 2012.

———. "Fugitives from Servitude: American Deserters and Runaway Slaves in Spanish Nacogdoches, 1803–1808." *East Texas Historical Association* 38 (Fall 2000): 3–14.

Bolton, Herbert E. *Texas in the Middle Eighteenth Century*. Reprint. Austin: University of Texas Press, 1970.

Bradley, Jared W. "W. C. C. Claiborne and Spain: Foreign Affairs under Jefferson and Madison, 1801–1811." In *The Louisiana Purchase Bicentennial Series in Louisiana History*, vol. 3, *The Louisiana Purchase and Its Aftermath, 1800–1830*, edited by Dolores Egger Labbe, 110–37. Lafayette: University of Southwestern Louisiana, 1998.

Brooks, James F. *Captives and Cousins: Slavery, Kinship, and Community in the Southwest Borderlands*. Chapel Hill: University of North Carolina Press, 2002.

Bryan, Jimmy L., Jr. "The Enduring People: Tejano Exclusion and Perseverance in the Republic of Texas, 1836–1845." *Journal of the West* 47, no. 3 (Summer 2008): 40–47.

Buckley, Eleanor Claire. "The Aguayo Expedition into Texas and Louisiana, 1719–1722." *Southwestern Historical Quarterly* 15 (July 1911): 1–65.

Burton, H. Sophie. "'To Establish a Stock Farm for the Raising of Mules, Horses, Horned Cattle, Sheep, and Hogs': The Role of Spanish Bourbon Louisiana in the Establishment of Vacheries along the Louisiana-Texas Borderland, 1766–1803." *Southwestern Historical Quarterly* 104 (July 2005): 98–132.

———. "Vagabonds along the Spanish Louisiana-Texas Frontier, 1769–1803: 'Men Who Are Evil, Lazy, Gluttonous, Drunken, Libertinous, Dishonest, Mutinous, etc., etc., etc—and Those Are Their Virtues.'" *Southwestern Historical Quarterly* 113 (April 2010): 438–67.

Burton, H. Sophie, and F. Todd Smith. *Colonial Natchitoches: A Creole Community on the Louisiana-Texas Frontier*. College Station: Texas A&M University Press, 2008.

Bushnell, Amy. *The King's Coffer: Proprietors of the Spanish Florida Treasury, 1565–1702*. Gainesville: University Press of Florida, 1981.

Cain, Joan. *The Historical Journal of the Establishment of the French in Louisiana, by Jean-Baptiste Bénard de la Harpe*. Edited by Glenn R. Conrad. Translated by Virginia Koenig. Lafayette: University of Southern Louisiana Press, 1971.

Camañes, Porfirio Sanz, and David Rex Galindo, coords. *La frontera en el mundo hispánico*. Quito, Ecuador: Abya-Yala, 2014.

Cañizares-Esguerra, Jorge. *Nature, Empire, and Nation: Explorations of the History of Science in the Iberian World*. Stanford: Stanford University Press, 2006.

Carey, Elaine, and Andrae M. Marak, eds. *Smugglers, Brothels, and Twine: Historical Perspectives on Contraband and Vice in North America's Borderlands*. Tucson: University of Arizona Press, 2011.

Carroll, Patrick J. *Blacks in Colonial Veracruz: Race, Ethnicity, and Regional Development*. Austin: University of Texas Press, 1991.

Castañeda, Carlos E. *Our Catholic Heritage in Texas, 1519–1936*. Reprint. 7 vols. New York: Arno Press, 1976.

Cavazos Garza, Israel. *Breve historia de Nuevo León*. Mexico City: Fondo de Cultura Económica, 1994.

Chipman, Donald E. *Spanish Texas, 1519–1821*. Austin: University of Texas Press, 1992.

Chipman, Donald E., and Harriett Denise Joseph. *Notable Men and Women of Spanish Texas*. Austin: University of Texas Press, 1999.

Cole, John W., and Eric R. Wolf. *The Hidden Frontier: Ecology and Ethnicity in an Alpine Valley*. New York: Academic Press, 1974.

Colpitts, George. "'Animated like Us by Commercial Interests': Commercial Ethnology and Fur Trade Descriptions in New France, 1660–1760." *Canadian Historical Review* 83, no. 3 (September 2002): 305–37.

Cromwell, Jesse. *The Smugglers' World: Illicit Trade and Atlantic Communities in Eighteenth-Century Venezuela*. Chapel Hill: University of North Carolina Press, 2018.

Cruz, Gilbert R. *Let There Be Towns: Spanish Municipal Origins in the American Southwest, 1610–1810*. College Station: Texas A&M University Press, 1988.

Cummins, Light Townsend. *To the Vast and Beautiful Land: Anglo Migration into Spanish Louisiana and Texas, 1760s–1820s*. College Station: Texas A&M University Press, 2019.

Cutter, Charles R. *The Legal Culture of Northern New Spain*. Albuquerque: University of New Mexico Press, 1995.

Deeds, Susan M. *Defiance and Deference in Mexico's Colonial North: Indians under Spanish Rule in Nueva Vizcaya*. Austin: University of Texas Press, 1995.

de la Teja, Jesús F. *Faces of Béxar: Early San Antonio and Texas*. College Station: Texas A&M University Press, 2017.

———. *San Antonio de Béxar: A Community on New Spain's Northern Frontier*. Albuquerque: University of New Mexico Press, 1995.

———. "St. James at the Fair: Religious Ceremony, Civic Boosterism, and Commercial Development on the Colonial Mexican Frontier." *Americas* 57, no. 3 (January 2001): 395–416.

———. "Why Urbano and María Trinidad Can't Get Married: Social Relations in Late Colonial San Antonio." *Southwestern Historical Quarterly* 112, no. 2 (October 2008): 121–46.

de la Teja, Jesús F., and Ross Frank, eds. *Choice, Persuasion, and Coercion: Social Control on Spain's North American Frontier*. Albuquerque: University of New Mexico Press, 2005.

Díaz, George T. *Border Contraband: A History of Smuggling across the Rio Grande*. Austin: University of Texas Press, 2015.

Din, Gilbert C. *Spaniards, Planters, and Slaves: The Spanish Regulation of Slavery in Louisiana, 1763–1803*. College Station: Texas A&M University Press, 1999.

Dorn, Walter L. *Competition for Empire, 1740–1763*. New York: Harper Torchbooks, 1963.

Du Val, Kathleen. *The Native Ground: Indians and Colonists in the Heart of the Continent*. Philadelphia: University of Pennsylvania Press, 2006.

Ekberg, Carl J. *French Roots in the Illinois Country: The Mississippi Frontier in Colonial Times*. Urbana: University of Illinois Press, 1998.

Elliott, J. H. *Empires of the Atlantic World: Britain and Spain in America, 1492–1830*. New Haven, CT: Yale University Press, 2006.

Fernández-Armesto, Felipe. *Our America: A Hispanic History of the United States*. New York: W. W. Norton, 2014.

Fisher, Vivian C., and W. Michael Mathes, eds. *Apostolic Chronicle of Juan Domingo Arricivita: The Franciscan Mission Frontier in the Eighteenth Century in Arizona, Texas, and California*. Translated by George P. Hammond and Agapito Rey. 2 vols. Berkeley, CA: Academy of American Franciscan History, 1996.

Flores, Dan L. "Bringing Home All the Pretty Horses: The Horse Trade and the Early American West, 1775–1825." *Montana: The Magazine of Western History*, Summer 2008, 3–21.

———. *Southern Counterpoint to Lewis and Clark: The Freeman and Custis Expedition of 1806*. Norman: University of Oklahoma Press, 1984.

Folmer, Henry. "Contraband Trade between Louisiana and New Mexico in the Eighteenth Century." *New Mexico Historical Review* 16 (July 1941): 249–74.

———. *Franco-Spanish Rivalry in North America, 1524–1763*. Glendale, CA: Arthur H. Clark, 1953.

Folsom, Bradley. "Trinidad de Salcedo: A Forgotten Villa in Colonial Texas, 1806–1813." *East Texas Historical Journal* 52, no. 2 (Fall 2014): 49–78.

Frank, Ross. *From Settler to Citizen: New Mexican Economic Development and the Creation of Vecino Society, 1750–1820.* Berkeley: University of California Press, 2000.

Frye, David. "The Native Peoples of Northeastern Mexico." In *The Cambridge History of Native Peoples of the Americas,* vol. 2, *Mesoamerica,* edited by Richard E. W. Adams and Murdo J. MacLeod, 89–135. Cambridge: Cambridge University Press, 2000.

Galán, Francis X. "Between Esteban and Joshua Houston: Women, Children and Slavery in the Texas Borderlands." *Journal of South Texas* 27 (Fall 2014): 22–36.

———. "Between Imperial Warfare: Crossing of the Smuggling Frontier and Transatlantic Commerce on the Louisiana-Texas Borderlands, 1754–1785." In *Texans and War: New Interpretations of the State's Military History,* edited by Alexander Mendoza and Charles David Grear, 157–77. College Station: Texas A&M University Press, 2012.

———. "Presidio Los Adaes: Worship, Kinship, and Commerce with French Natchitoches on the Spanish-Franco-Caddo Borderlands, 1721–1773." *Louisiana History* 49, no. 2 (Spring 2008): 191–208.

Gerhard, Peter. *The North Frontier of New Spain.* Princeton, NJ: Princeton University Press, 1982.

Giraud, Marcel. *A History of French Louisiana.* Vol. 1, *The Reign of Louis XIV, 1698–1715.* Baton Rouge: Louisiana State University Press, 1974.

———. *A History of French Louisiana.* Vol. 2, *Years of Transition, 1715–1717.* Baton Rouge: Louisiana State University Press, 1993.

Greer, Allan, and Jodi Bilinkoff, eds. *Colonial Saints: Discovering the Holy in the Americas.* New York: Routledge, 2003.

Gregory, H. F., George Avery, Aubra L. Lee, and Jay C. Blaine. "Presidio Los Adaes: Spanish, French, and Caddoan Interaction on the Northern Frontier." *Historical Archaeology* 38 (2004).

Gutiérrez, Ramón A. *When Jesus Came, the Corn Mothers Went Away: Marriage, Sexuality, and Power in New Mexico, 1500–1846.* Stanford: Stanford University Press, 1991.

Guy, Donna, and Thomas E. Sheridan, eds. *Contested Ground: Comparative Frontiers on the Northern and Southern Edges of the Spanish Empire.* Tucson: University of Arizona Press, 1998.

Haas, Lisbeth. *Conquests and Historical Identities in California, 1769–1936.* Berkeley: University of California Press, 1995.

Hackel, Steven W. *Children of Coyote, Missionaries of Saint Francis: Indian-Spanish Relations in Colonial California, 1769–1850.* Chapel Hill: University of North Carolina Press, 2005.

Hall, Gwendolyn Midlo. *Africans in Colonial Louisiana: The Development of Afro-Creole Culture in the Eighteenth Century*. Baton Rouge: Louisiana State University Press, 1992.

Hall, Thomas D. *Social Change in the Southwest, 1350–1880*. Lawrence: University Press of Kansas, 1989.

Hämäläinen, Pekka. *The Comanche Empire*. New Haven, CT: Yale University Press, 2008.

———. "The Western Comanche Trade Center: Rethinking the Plains Indian Trade System." *Western Historical Quarterly* 29 (Winter 1998): 485–513.

Hämäläinen, Pekka, and Samuel Truett. "On Borderlands." *Journal of American History* 98, no. 2 (September 2011): 338–61.

Herrera Casasús, María Luisa. *Presencia y esclavitud del negro en la Huasteca*. Mexico City: Miguel Angel Porrúa, 1989.

Herzog, Tamar. *Frontiers of Possession: Spain and Portugal in Europe and the Americas*. Cambridge: Harvard University Press, 2015.

Hinderaker, Eric. *Elusive Empires: Constructing Colonialism in the Ohio Valley, 1673–1800*. New York: Cambridge University Press, 1997.

Hinderaker, Eric, and Peter C. Mancall. *At the Edge of Empire: The Backcountry in British North America*. Baltimore: Johns Hopkins University Press, 2003.

Hinojosa, Gilberto M. "The Enduring Faith Communities: A Historiography of the Spanish and Mexican Texas Catholic Church." *Journal of Texas Catholic History and Culture* 1 (March 1990): 21–40.

Hoberman, Louisa Schell, and Susan Migden Socolow, eds. *The Countryside in Colonial Latin America*. Albuquerque: University of New Mexico Press, 1996.

Hofstra, Warren R. *Cultures in Conflict: The Seven Years' War in North America*. Lanham, MD: Rowman & Littlefield, 2007.

Hurt, R. Douglas. *The Ohio Frontier: Crucible of the Old Northwest, 1720–1830*. Bloomington: Indiana University Press, 1996.

Hurtado, Albert L. *Intimate Frontiers: Sex, Gender, and Culture in Old California*. Albuquerque: University of New Mexico Press, 1999.

Hyatt, Emily, and Jonathan Gerland. "Finding Angelina: The Search for East Texas' Little Angel." *Pine Bough* 17 (December 2012): 12–21.

Hyde, Anne F. *Empires, Nations, and Families: A New History of the North American West, 1800–1860*. New York: HarperCollins, 2011.

Isaac, Rhys. *The Transformation of Virginia, 1740–1790*. Chapel Hill: University of North Carolina Press, 1982.

Jackson, Jack. *Los Mesteños: Spanish Ranching in Texas, 1721–1821*. College Station: Texas A&M University Press, 1986.

John, Elizabeth A. H. *Storms Brewed in Other Men's Worlds: The Confrontation of Indians, Spanish, and French in the Southwest, 1540–1795*. Lincoln: University of Nebraska Press, 1975.

Johnson, Lyman L. *Workshop of Revolution: Plebeian Buenos Aires and the Atlantic World, 1776–1810*. Durham, NC: Duke University Press, 2011.

Jones, Oakah L., Jr. *Los Paisanos: Spanish Settlers on the Northern Frontier of New Spain*. Norman: University of Oklahoma Press, 1979.

———. "Rescue and Ransom of Spanish Captives from the *indios bárbaros* on the Northern Frontier of New Spain." *Colonial Latin American Historical Review* 4 (Spring 1995): 129–48.

Karras, Alan L. *Smuggling: Contraband and Corruption in World History*. Lanham, MD: Rowman & Littlefield, 2010.

Kessell, John L. *Friars, Soldiers, and Reformers: Hispanic Arizona and the Sonora Mission Frontier, 1767–1856*. Tucson: University of Arizona Press, 1976.

———. *Kiva, Cross, and Crown: The Pecos Indians and New Mexico, 1540–1840*. Albuquerque: University of New Mexico Press, 1987.

———. *Spain in the Southwest: A Narrative History of Colonial New Mexico, Arizona, Texas, and California*. Norman: University of Oklahoma Press, 2002.

Kiser, William S. *Borderlands of Slavery: The Struggle over Captivity and Peonage in the American Southwest*. Philadelphia: University of Pennsylvania Press, 2017.

Kniffen, Fred B., Hiram F. Gregory, and George A. Stokes. *The Historic Indian Tribes of Louisiana: From 1542 to the Present*. Baton Rouge: Louisiana State University Press, 1987.

Konove, Andrew. "On the Cheap: The Baratillo Marketplace and the Shadow Economy of Eighteenth-Century Mexico City." *Americas*, April 2015, 249–78.

Lamar, Howard, and Leonard Thompson, eds. *The Frontier in History: North America and Southern Africa Compared*. New Haven, CT: Yale University Press, 1981.

Landers, Jane. *Black Society in Spanish Florida*. Urbana: University of Illinois Press, 1999.

Landers, Jane, and Barry M. Robinson, eds. *Slaves, Subjects, and Subversives: Blacks in Colonial Latin America*. Albuquerque: University of New Mexico Press, 2006.

Langer, Erick, and Robert H. Jackson, eds. *The New Latin American Mission History*. Lincoln: University of Nebraska Press, 1995.

La Vere, David. "Between Kinship and Capitalism: French and Spanish Rivalry in the Colonial Louisiana-Texas Indian Trade." *Journal of Southern History* 64 (May 1998): 197–218.

———. *The Caddo Chiefdoms: Caddo Economics and Politics, 700–1835*. Lincoln: University of Nebraska Press, 1998.

———. *The Texas Indians*. College Station: Texas A&M University Press, 2004.

Lavrin, Asunción, ed. *Sexuality and Marriage in Colonial Latin America*. Lincoln: University of Nebraska Press, 1989.

———. "Sexuality in Colonial Mexico: A Church Dilemma." In *Sexuality and Marriage in Colonial Latin America*, 47–95. Lincoln: University of Nebraska Press, 1989.

Lemée, Patricia R. "Tios and Tantes: Familial and Political Relationships of Natchitoches and the Spanish Colonial Frontier." *Southwestern Historical Quarterly* 101, no. 3 (January 1998): 341–58.

Loren, Diana DiPaolo. "Colonial Dress at the Spanish Presidio Los Adaes." *Southern Studies: An Interdisciplinary Journal of the South* 7 (Spring 1996): 45–64.

———. "The Intersections of Colonial Policy and Colonial Practice: Creolization on the Eighteenth-Century Louisiana/Texas Frontier." *Historical Archeology* 34, no. 3 (2000): 85–98.

Lynch, John. *The Spanish American Revolutions, 1808–1826*. New York: W. W. Norton, 1973.

Mancall, Peter C. *At the Edge of Empire: The Backcountry in British North America*. Baltimore: Johns Hopkins University Press, 2003.

Mapp, Paul W. *The Elusive West and the Contest for Empire, 1713–1763*. Chapel Hill: University of North Carolina Press, 2011.

Martin, Cheryl English. *Governance and Society in Colonial Mexico: Chihuahua in the Eighteenth Century*. Stanford: Stanford University Press, 1996.

Martínez, María Elena. *Genealogical Fictions: Limpieza de Sangre, Religion, and Gender in Colonial Mexico*. Stanford: Stanford University Press, 2008.

McCorkle, James L., Jr. "Los Adaes and the Borderlands Origins of East Texas." *East Texas Historical Journal* 22 (1984): 3–12.

Merrell, James H. *Into the American Woods: Negotiators on the Pennsylvania Frontier*. New York: W. W. Norton, 1999.

Merritt, Jane T. *At the Crossroads: Indians and Empires on a Mid-Atlantic Frontier, 1700–1763*. Chapel Hill: University of North Carolina Press, 2003.

Meyer, Michael C. *Water in the Hispanic Southwest: A Social and Legal History, 1550–1850*. Tuscon: University of Arizona Press, 1984.

Miller, Shawn. *An Environmental History of Latin America*. New York: Cambridge University Press, 2007.

Mills, Gary B. "The Chauvin Brothers: Early Colonists of Louisiana." *Louisiana History* 15, no. 2 (Spring 1974): 117–31.

———. *The Forgotten People: Cane River's Creoles of Color*. Baton Rouge: Louisiana State University Press, 1977.

Moorhead, Max L. *The Presidio: Bastion of the Spanish Borderlands*. Norman: University of Oklahoma Press, 1975.

Mörner, Magnus. *Race Mixture in the History of Latin America*. Boston: Little, Brown, 1967.

Nardini, Louis R. *My Historic Natchitoches, Louisiana and Its Environment: A History of Natchitoches, Louisiana and the Neutral Strip Area of the State of Louisiana and Its Inhabitants*. Natchitoches, LA: Nardini, 1963.

Narrett, David E. "Geopolitics and Intrigue: James Wilkinson, the Spanish Borderlands, and Mexican Independence." *William and Mary Quarterly* 69 (January 2012): 101–46.

———. "Liberation and Conquest: John Hamilton Robinson and U.S. Adventurism toward Mexico, 1806–1819." *Western Historical Quarterly* 40 (Spring 2009): 23–50.

Nash, Gary B. "The Hidden History of Mestizo America." *Journal of American History* 82 (December 1995): 941–64.

Norton, Marcy. *Sacred Gifts, Profane Pleasures: A History of Tobacco and Chocolate in the Atlantic World*. Ithaca, NY: Cornell University Press, 2009.

Nugent, Paul. *Smugglers, Secessionists and Loyal Citizens on the Ghana-Togo Frontier*. Athens: Ohio University Press, 2002.

Nunn, Charles F. *Foreign Immigrants in Early Bourbon Mexico, 1700–1760*. London: Cambridge University Press, 1979.

O'Neill, Father Charles Edwards. *Church and State in French Colonial Louisiana: Policy and Politics to 1732*. New Haven, CT: Yale University Press, 1966.

Pagden, Anthony. *Lords of All the World: Ideologies of Empire in Spain, Britain and France, c. 1500–c. 1800*. New Haven, CT: Yale University Press, 1995.

Perttula, Timothy K. *"The Caddo Nation": Archaeological and Ethnohistoric Perspectives*. Austin: University of Texas Press, 1992.

Phares, Ross. *Cavalier in the Wilderness: The Story of the Explorer and Trader Louis Juchereau de St. Denis*. Baton Rouge: Louisiana State University Press, 1952.

Porter, Amy M. *Their Lives, Their Wills: Women in the Borderlands, 1750–1846*. Lubbock: Texas Tech University Press, 2015.

Porter, Charles R., Jr. *Spanish Water, Anglo Water: Early Development in San Antonio*. College Station: Texas A&M University Press, 2009.

Poyo, Gerald E. *Tejano Journey, 1770–1850*. Austin: University of Texas Press, 1996.

Poyo, Gerald E., and Gilberto M. Hinojosa. "Spanish Texas and Borderlands Historiography in Transition: Implications for United States History." *Journal of American History* 75 (September 1988): 393–416.

Radding, Cynthia. *Wandering Peoples: Colonialism, Ethnic Spaces, and Ecological Frontiers in Northwestern Mexico, 1700–1850*. Durham, NC: Duke University Press, 1997.

Reséndez, Andrés. *Changing National Identities at the Frontier: Texas and New Mexico, 1800–1850*. New York: Cambridge University Press, 2005.

———. *The Other Slavery: The Uncovered Story of Indian Enslavement in America*. Boston: Houghton Mifflin Harcourt, 2016.

Restall, Matthew. "Crossing to Safety? Frontier Flight in Eighteenth-Century Belize and Yucatan." *Hispanic American Historical Review* 94, no. 3 (August 2014): 381–419.

Richter, Daniel K. *Facing East from Indian Country: A Native History of Early America*. Cambridge: Harvard University Press, 2001.

Robles, Vito Alessio. *Coahuila y Texas en la época colonial*. Mexico City: Editorial Cultura, 1938.

Rupert, Linda M. *Creolization and Contraband: Curaçao in the Early Modern Atlantic World*. Athens: University of Georgia Press, 2012.

Sahlins, Peter. *Boundaries: The Making of France and Spain in the Pyrenees*. Berkeley: University of California Press, 1989.

Santoscoy, María Elena, Laura Gutiérrez, Martha Rodríguez, and Francisco Cepeda, eds. *Breve historia de Coahuila*. Mexico City: Fondo de Cultura Económica, 2000.

Schneider, Elena A. *The Occupation of Havana: War, Trade, and Slavery in the Atlantic World*. Chapel Hill: University of North Carolina Press, 2018.

Secoy, Frank Raymond. *Changing Military Patterns of the Great Plains Indians*. Lincoln: University of Nebraska Press, 1953.

Seed, Patricia. *To Love, Honor, and Obey in Colonial México: Conflicts over Marriage Choice, 1574–1821*. Stanford: Stanford University Press, 1988.

Shelby, Charmion Clair. "St. Denis's Declaration concerning Texas in 1717." *Southwestern Historical Quarterly* 26 (January 1923): 165–83.

———, ed. and trans. "Projected French Attacks upon the Northeastern Frontier of New Spain, 1719–1721." *Hispanic American Historical Review* 13 (November 1933): 457–72.

Simpson, Lesley Byrd. *The Encomienda in New Spain: The Beginnings of Spanish Mexico*. Berkeley: University of California Press, 1982.

Sluyter, Andrew. *Black Ranching Frontiers: African Cattle Herders of the Atlantic World, 1500–1900*. New Haven, CT: Yale University Press, 2012.

Smith, F. Todd. *The Caddo Indians: Tribes at the Convergence of Empires, 1542–1854*. College Station: Texas A&M University Press, 1995.

———. *From Dominance to Disappearance: The Indians of Texas and the Near Southwest, 1786–1859*. Lincoln: University of Nebraska Press, 2005.

———. *The Wichita Indians: Traders of Texas and the Southern Plains, 1540–1845*. College Station: Texas A&M University Press, 2000.

Smith, Gene Allen, and Sylvia L. Hilton. *Nexus of Empire: Negotiating Loyalty and Identity in the Revolutionary Borderlands, 1760s–1820s*. Gainesville: University Press of Florida, 2010.

Spicer, Edward H. *Cycles of Conquest: The Impact of Spain, Mexico, and the United States on the Indians of the Southwest, 1533–1960*. Tucson: University of Arizona Press, 1962.

Stein, Stanley J., and Barbara H. Stein. *Apogee of Empire: Spain and New Spain in the Age of Charles III, 1759–1789*. Baltimore: Johns Hopkins University Press, 2003.

———. *The Colonial Heritage of Latin America: Essays on Economic Dependence in Perspective*. New York: Oxford University Press, 1970.

St. John, Rachel C. *Line in the Sand: A History of the Western U.S.-Mexico Border*. Princeton, NJ: Princeton University Press, 2011.

Stuntz, Jean A. *Hers, His, and Thiers: Community Property Law in Spain and Early Texas*. Lubbock: Texas Tech University Press, 2005.

Taylor, Alan. *The Divided Ground: Indians, Settlers, and the Northern Borderland of the American Revolution*. New York: Alfred A. Knopf, 2006.

Thonhoff, Robert H. *The Texas Connection with the American Revolution*. Austin: Eakin Press, 2000.

Thorp, Daniel B. "Doing Business in the Backcountry: Retail Trade in Colonial Rowan County, North Carolina." *William and Mary Quarterly* 48 (July 1991): 387–408.

Tjarks, Alicia V. "Comparative Demographic Analysis of Texas, 1777–1793." *Southwestern Historical Quarterly* 77 (January 1974): 291–339.

Torget, Andrew J. Seeds of Empire: Cotton, Slavery, and the Transformation of the Texas Borderlands, 1800–1850. Chapel Hill: University of North Carolina Press, 2015.

Truxes, Thomas M. *Defying Empire: Trading with the Enemy in Colonial New York*. New Haven, CT: Yale University Press, 2008.

Twinam, Ann. "Honor, Sexuality, and Illegitimacy in Colonial Spanish America." In *Sexuality and Marriage in Colonial Latin America*, edited by Asunción Lavrin, 118–155. Lincoln: University of Nebraska Press, 1989.

Usner, Daniel H., Jr. *Indians, Settlers, and Slaves in a Frontier Exchange Economy: The Lower Mississippi Valley before 1783*. Chapel Hill: University of North Carolina Press, 1992.

Valdés, Carlos Manuel, and Ildefonso Dávila. *Esclavos negros en Saltillo*. Saltillo, Mexico: Universidad Autónoma de Coahuila, 1989.

Valerio-Jiménez, Omar S. *River of Hope: Forging Identity and Nation in the Rio Grande Borderlands*. Durham, NC: Duke University Press, 2013.

Van Young, Eric. *Hacienda and Market in Eighteenth-Century Mexico: The Rural Economy of the Guadalajara Region, 1675–1820*. Berkeley: University of California Press, 1981.

Vigness, David M. "Don Hugo O'Conor and New Spain's Northeastern Frontier, 1764–1776." *Journal of the West* 6 (January 1967): 27–40.

Vogel, Robert C. "The Bayou Pierre Settlements." *North Louisiana Historical Association Journal* 7 (Spring 1976): 110–12.

———. "Paul Boüet Laffitte: A Borderlands Life." *East Texas Historical Journal* 41 (Spring 2003): 15–27.

Wallerstein, Immanuel. *The Modern World-System III: The Second Era of Great Expansion of the Capitalist World-Economy, 1730–1840s*. San Diego, CA: Academic Press, 1989.

Weber, David J. *Bárbaros: Spaniards and Their Savages in the Age of Enlightenment*. New Haven, CT: Yale University Press, 2005.

———. "Conflicts and Accommodations: Hispanic and Anglo-American Borders in Historical Perspective, 1670–1853." *Journal of the Southwest* 39 (Spring 1997): 1–28.

———. *Myth and the History of the Hispanic Southwest*. Albuquerque: University of New Mexico Press, 1988.

———. *The Spanish Frontier in North America*. New Haven, CT: Yale University Press, 1992.

———. *The Taos Trappers: The Fur Trade in the Far Southwest, 1540–1846*. Norman: University of Oklahoma Press, 1971.

———. *What Caused the Pueblo Revolt of 1680?* Boston: Bedford / St. Martin's, 1999.

Weddle, Robert S. *After the Massacre: The Violent Legacy of the San Sabá Mission*. Lubbock: Texas Tech University Press, 2007.

———. *The French Thorn: Rival Explorers in the Spanish Sea, 1682–1762*. College Station: Texas A&M University Press, 1991.

———. *San Juan Bautista: Gateway to Spanish Texas*. Austin: University of Texas Press, 1968.

———. *The San Sabá Mission: Spanish Pivot in Texas*. Austin: University of Texas Press, 1964.

———. *Wilderness Manhunt: The Spanish Search for La Salle*. College Station: Texas A&M University Press, 1999.

West, Elliot. *The Contested Plains: Indians, Goldseekers, and the Rush to Colorado*. Lawrence: University Press of Kansas, 1998.

West, Robert C. *The Mining Community in Northern New Spain: The Parral Mining District*. Berkeley: University of California Press, 1949.

White, Richard. *The Middle Ground: Indians, Empires, and Republics in the Great Lakes Region, 1650–1815*. New York: Cambridge University Press, 1991.

———. *The Roots of Dependency: Subsistence, Environment, and Social Change among the Choctaws, Pawnees, and Navajos*. Lincoln: University of Nebraska Press, 1983.

Will de Chaparro, Martina. *Death and Dying in New Mexico*. Albuquerque: University of New Mexico Press, 2007.

Wood, Peter H., Gregory A. Waselkov, and M. Thomas Hatley, eds. *Powhatan's Mantle: Indians in the Colonial Southeast*. Lincoln: University of Nebraska Press, 1989.

Wright, Robert E. "Local Church Emergence and Mission Decline: The Historiography of the Catholic Church in the Southwest during the Spanish and Mexican Period." *U.S. Catholic Historian* 9 (Winter/Spring 1990): 27–48.

Zavala, Silvio. *Los esclavos indios en Nueva España*. Mexico City: El Colegio Nacional, 1967.

THESES AND DISSERTATIONS

Burton, Helen Sophie. "Family and Economy in Frontier Louisiana: Colonial Natchitoches, 1714–1803." PhD dissertation, Texas Christian University, 2002.

Eakin, William L. "The Kingdom of the Tejas: The Hasinai Indians at the Crossroads of Change." PhD dissertation, University of Kansas, 1997.

Gregory, Hiram F. "Eighteenth Century Caddoan Archaeology: A Study in Models and Interpretations." PhD dissertation, Southern Methodist University, 1973.

Hämäläinen, Pekka. "The Comanche Empire: A Study of Indigenous Power, 1700–1875." PhD dissertation, University of Helsinki, Finland, 2001.

Harrison, Jay T. "Franciscan Missionary Theory and Practice in Eighteenth-Century New Spain: The Propaganda Fide Friars in the Texas Missions, 1690–1821." PhD dissertation, Catholic University of America, 2012.

Hurzeler, Richard. "People of Faith: The Old Spanish of East Texas." MA thesis, Stephen F. Austin State University, 1989.

Lee, Dana Bowker. "Indian Slavery in Lower Louisiana during the Colonial Period, 1699–1803." MA thesis, Northwestern State University, Natchitoches, LA, 1989.

Martínez Serna, José Gabriel. "Vineyards in the Desert: The Jesuits and the Rise and Decline of an Indian Town in New Spain's Northeastern Borderlands." PhD dissertation, Southern Methodist University, 2009.

McGowan, James T. "Creation of a Slave Society: Louisiana Plantations in the Eighteenth Century." PhD dissertation, University of Rochester, New York, 1976.

McReynolds, James M. "Family Life in a Borderland Community: Nacogdoches, Texas, 1779–1861." PhD dissertation, Texas Tech University, 1979.

Meacham, Tina Laurel. "The Population of Spanish and Mexican Texas, 1716–1836." PhD dissertation, University of Texas at Austin, 2000.

Meschke, Amy. "Women's Lives through Women's Wills in the Spanish and Mexican Borderlands, 1750–1846." PhD dissertation, Southern Methodist University, 2005.

Rex Galindo, David. "Propaganda Fide: Training Franciscan Missionaries in New Spain." PhD dissertation, Southern Methodist University, 2010.

Shelby, Charmion Clair. "St. Denis's Second Expedition from Louisiana to the Rio Grande, 1716–1719, with Illustrative Documents, Translated and Edited." MA thesis, University of Texas at Austin, 1927.

Van Rheenen, Mary B. "Can You Tell Me Who My People Are? Ethnic Identity among the Hispanic-Indian People of Sabine Parish, Louisiana." MA thesis, Louisiana State University, 1987.

Index

Arredondo, Joseph, 136
Arroyo Hondo, 1, 15, 38, 128, 227
Atacapa Indians, 145, 148
Atlantic economy, 136
Avila, Agustín, 114

baptism, 80–83, 182; captive, 45;
  en articulo mortis, 51, 52, 53; of
  Indians, 52–53, 165, 286n40, 336n24;
  interethnic, 61; of slaves, 181
Barrera, Antonio, 141, 325n74
Barrio, Pedro de, 204
Barrios, Manuela Alcázar, 119
Barrios Jáuregui, Jacinto de, 75, 76–78,
  114, 115–17, 124–25, 127–28, 148–50;
  Indian policy, 117; investigation
  of, 153; residencia of, 131–32, 166,
  321–22n45; on slavery, 183–86; trade
  and, 130, 131–32, 133, 136, 141, 146,
  147, 151, 204, 206
barter, 101–2, 109–10, 123, 124, 135,
  161; religious, 61
Battle of Medina, 235
Battle of Quebec, 192
Bayou Pierre, Louisiana, 1, 122, 140, 235
Becerra, Pedro, 106
Berbán, Manuel, 232
Bergara, Joseph Cayetano de, 87
Bermudes, Felipe, 104
Béxar, Texas. See San Antonio, Texas
Bidai Indians, 117, 125, 134–35, 141,
  142, 145, 154
Bigotes (Tejas chief), 190
Blancpain, Joseph, 142–43, 144–47,
  150–51, 152, 327n93
Bocaflores (Orcoquiza captain), 154
Bonaparte, Napoleon, 1, 227, 237
Boneo Morales, Justo, 180
borderlands, definition of, 5–6
borders, definition of, 5
Bourbon dynasty, 24, 36, 40, 191;
  alliance against England, 37;

French, 2, 26, 27; Spanish, 22,
  121
Bourbon Reforms, 7, 14, 79, 157, 160,
  166, 191–92, 202–3, 214
Brazos River, 47–48
Briseño Zúñiga, Juan Joseph, 99, 105
Bucareli, Texas, 7, 223–24, 226
Bucarely, Antonio, 203–4, 217, 221
burial, 61, 83–84
Bustamante, Juan Manuel de, 201
Bustillo, Juan Antonio, 35, 58, 87, 91,
  101, 107–8, 118

Cabello, Domingo, 224, 225, 226
Cabeza de Vaca, Álvar Núñez, 19
Cadalso, José, 193
Caddo Indians, 2, 4–5, 25, 72, 123,
  126, 149–50, 167–68, 191, 233, 236;
  agriculture and, 48, 53; conflict with
  Apaches, 47; demographics of, 54–55;
  depopulation of, 55; French alliance
  with, 29, 93; French posts among,
  27; fur trade and, 134; kinship and,
  9, 10–11; as nonthreatening, 39,
  56; resistance to conversion, 10,
  21–22, 43, 85; settlement of, 34–35;
  settlements of, 50–51; Spanish peace
  with, 93, 208, 227; trade with French,
  47, 124–25, 139, 172; trade with Los
  Adaes, 93, 109–10, 134, 172; trade
  with Spanish, 48, 77
Cadillac, Antoine de la Mothe, 22, 24, 74
Cadiz, Spain, 191
Cadodacho Indians, 120
Calahorra (Los Adaes friar), 149–50
Calahorra, José de, 117, 171–73
California, 2
Calsones (Orcoquiza captain), 154
Calvillo, Ignacio, 231
Camaño, Aniceto, 232
Camino Real (Royal Road), 4, 7, 13, 19,
  231; extension of, 17–18, 140

61; secular role of, 37, 60, 115, 213–14; as spies, 60; trade and, 60, 135, 136, 138. *See also* missionaries

Francisco, Juan, 100, 101

Franco-Indian alliances, 93, 126, 169–70; Spanish fear of, 45–47, 116, 128

Franquis, Carlos de, 94

free trade, 81, 110, 121, 130, 140, 154, 193, 199

French and Indian War, 125, 126

French Company of the West, 27

frontera, 4, 5–6, 237

frontier: borders and, 14, 26; definition of, 5–6; women and, 11

frontier exchange economy, 36, 50, 57, 94, 122–23, 140

fur trade, 26, 123–24, 126, 133–34, 139, 140, 146, 210, 211

gambling, 103, 104–6, 161

Gándara, Manuel Antonio de, 193

García, Juana Victoria (Jeanne Victoria), 66–67, 81

García, Pedro, 66, 67

García Larios, Francisco, 111–13, 123–24, 166, 180; residencia of, 129

Georgia, 2, 36

Giraud, Diego Antonio, 118

godparents (padrinos), 10, 52–53, 74, 81–82; of Indians, 44, 336n24; of slaves, 181

Gomendio Urrutia, Domingo de, 96, 98, 118

Gomes, Ygnacio, 108

Gonzalez, José Maria, 230

Gonzalez, Joseph, 67, 81, 91–93, 99, 102, 104, 130, 195, 198–200; on border location, 80, 128; correspondence with O'Conor, 209; correspondence with Sandoval, 2–4, 17, 66, 90, 106–7; daughter's

marriage, 4, 11, 61–62, 64, 102, 156, 291n16; death of, 13, 190; and Los Adaes abandonment, 190, 218; on trade, 133–34, 155–57

Gonzalez, Pedro, 224

Gonzalez, Victoria, 64, 66, 81, 232; marriage of, 4, 11, 61–62, 102

Gordo (Orcoquiza captain), 154

governor-commandants, 75, 87, 95, 108, 125; corruption of, 11, 12, 92; indebtedness to, 94

governors, 108, 118, 334–35n14; as authoritarian, 89, 214; corruption of, 110–11, 122, 129, 146, 214–15; salaries of, 97–98; threats against, 207–8; trade and, 124–25, 135, 141; wealth of, 179, 180, 202

Granados, Pedro, 117, 133

Great Britain, 121, 126; colonies of, 2, 7, 36, 116; conflict with, 152, 191, 226, 237, 347–48n5; Indian allies of, 46; smuggling and, 193; as threat to France, 178; as threat to New Spain, 93, 116; trade and, 139, 160, 188–89, 203

Guadalajara region, Mexico, 11

Güemes Horcasitas, Juan Francisco, 111–12

Gulf of Mexico, 21, 22, 115, 188, 228

Gumiel, Juan de, 157

gunpowder, 104, 123–24; given to Indians, 112–13, 118

haciendas, 20, 54, 179

Haische, Christophe, 188

Hapsburg monarchy, 18, 40, 161

Hasinai Confederacy, 6, 21, 27, 29, 34, 55, 139, 169; defense against Natchez, 46; religion and, 85; trade with, 122, 141

Hasinai revolt, 149

Havana, Cuba, 121, 139, 160, 184

trade: as bringing Indians to missions, 48; as cover for smuggling, 59, 131; directions of, 137; as diverting resources, 95; levels of, 12–13, 36, 40; multiethnic, 59; reinforced by marriage, 66–67. *See also* barter; contraband: trade in; fur trade
Treaty of Guadalupe Hidalgo, 5
Treaty of Paris, 192, 347–48n5
Treaty of Tordesillas, 20
Trejo, Joseph, 101
Trejo, Rafael del, 114
Treviño, Antonio, 171–76, 177
Trinidad de Salcedo, Texas, 231
Trinity River, 7–8, 142–43, 144–45, 150, 154; French settlement on, 149
Tunica revolt, 93
Turner, Edward, 230

Ugarte, Fernando de, 98
Ugarte, Francisco de, 98
Ulloa, Antonio de, 159–60, 207
United States, 227, 234; conflict with Spain, 229–30; westward expansion of, 228, 236
Unzaga Amezaga, Luís de, 161–62, 217–18
Urrutia, Joseph, 93–94
Urrutia, Toribio de, 166

Valcárcel, Domingo, 76, 144, 154
Valentín, Joseph, 132
Vallejo, Francisco, 68, 80, 90, 227
Velasco (friar), 109–11
Velasco, Joseph Ortes de, 123–24
Veracruz, New Spain, 22
Vergara, Joseph Cayetano, 93, 100, 104
Vergara, Luís de, 215–16
Vilemont, Luís, 228
Villa de San Fernando, San Antonio, Texas, 44
Villa Franca, Diego, 114

Villanueva, Manuel de, 180
Villarreal, Joseph, 112
Villarreal, Juan, 114
Virgin Mary, 85–86. *See also* Our Lady of the Pillar
Virgin of Guadalupe, 86

warfare, 39, 189; against Indians, 72; intertribal, 35, 170; social status and, 72
War of Austrian Succession, 125
War of the Quadruple Alliance, 36
War of the Spanish Succession, 22, 121
Wichita Indians, 151, 157
Wilkinson, James, 1, 229–30
wills, 57, 62, 63, 83
Winthuysen, Felipe, 47–48, 112, 114, 115, 123, 129; residencia of, 108
women: frontier economy and, 57; marriage and, 60; power of, on borderlands, 11, 64; roles of, 54, 73; as settlers, 28

Ximénez, Bacilio, 103, 104

Yatasi Indians, 122, 140, 142
Ybarbo, Antonio Gil, 7, 77–78, 86, 188, 212, 213, 214, 218–19; Adaeseño resettlement and, 221, 223–24, 226–27; legacy of, 234
Ybarbo, Juana Antonia, 44
Ybarbo, Juana Rosa, 44
Ybarbo, Manuel, 77–78
Ybarbo, Mateo, 44–45, 86, 102, 105–6, 165
Ybarbo family, 67
Ybiricu, Fermín, 62, 78, 99, 100, 101, 102–5, 120
Ygnacio, the Parraleño, 101

Zacatecas, New Spain, 28
Zedano, Francisco, 137–38s

CPSIA information can be obtained
at www.ICGtesting.com
Printed in the USA
LVHW092355160121
676668LV00001B/1